Impact of Market Sentiment on Green Valuations

Truc Thi Nha Phan
Ho Chi Minh City University of Economics and Finance, Vietnam

IGI Global
Scientific Publishing
Publishing Tomorrow's Research Today

Vice President of Editorial	Melissa Wagner
Director of Acquisitions	Mikaela Felty
Director of Book Development	Jocelynn Hessler
Production Manager	Mike Brehm
Cover Design	Jose Rosado

Published in the United States of America by
IGI Global Scientific Publishing
701 East Chocolate Avenue
Hershey, PA, 17033, USA
Tel: 717-533-8845 | Fax: 717-533-7115
Website: https://www.igi-global.com E-mail: cust@igi-global.com

Library of Congress Cataloging-in-Publication Data

LCCN: 2026004822 (CIP Data Pending)
ISBN13: 979-8-3373-8392-7
Isbn13Softcover: 979-8-3373-8393-4
EISBN13: 979-8-3373-8394-1
British Cataloguing in Publication Data
A Cataloguing in Publication record for this book is available from the British Library.

Editorial Advisory Board

Table of Contents

Detailed Table of Contents

for nuanced, contextual adjudication, financial markets can scale their detection capabilities without compromising regulatory integrity.

This chapter analyzes ESG disclosure in sustainability reports of Vietnamese commercial banks using PhoBERT-based text mining. The dataset includes 25 reports from 13 banks listed on the Ho Chi Minh City Stock Exchange. After text preprocessing and Vietnamese word segmentation, PhoBERT embeddings were used to compare report paragraphs with MSCI-based ESG theme representations. The findings show that ESG disclosure is mainly concentrated in the governance pillar, especially corporate governance, reflecting the banking sector's focus on transparency, internal control, compliance, and risk management. The social pillar follows, with human capital as the most visible theme. The study contributes to ESG disclosure research by providing empirical evidence on the thematic structure of ESG reporting in Vietnamese banking and by demonstrating the usefulness of Vietnamese-language NLP for sustainability disclosure analysis.

This study examines the relationship between green credit, Indian bank competitiveness, and bank risk-taking through a systematic literature review of 40 peer-reviewed articles published between 2015 and 2025. Findings showed that green credit initiatives strengthen banks' long-term competitiveness by improving sustainability performance, lowering environmental compliance costs, and enhancing market reputation. Evidence also suggested that while green credit generally reduces credit and operational risks due to better asset quality and government-backed incentives, some banks face short-term risks linked to limited borrower history, high monitoring costs, and evolving regulatory frameworks. The review concludes that integrating green credit is strategically beneficial for Indian banks, promoting both competitiveness and stable risk profiles. Policymakers should expand green-finance

Foreword

Sustainable finance finds itself at a critical juncture in its evolution. What began as a niche of ethical investing has become one of the most powerful forces driving the world's capital markets. Investors, regulators, banks, firms, and policymakers are increasingly required to consider climate risk, environmental responsibility, social impact, governance quality, and long-term sustainability when making financial decisions. Yet valuing green assets remains one of the trickiest and least-resolved problems in modern finance.

This book, Impact of Market Sentiment on Green Valuations, is a current and excellent contribution to this vital issue. It acknowledges that the value of green financial assets is not entirely determined by fundamentals. Cash flows, risk exposure, legislative incentives, ESG ratings and environmental performance remain significant. However, perception, confidence, expectations and mood also play a role in determining the market value of sustainable assets. In other words, green valuation is not just a technical financial exercise but also a process of behaviour and knowledge.

The strength of this volume is its ability to integrate key subjects that are commonly explored individually. It includes sustainable finance, behavioural finance, ESG disclosure, green bonds, fintech, artificial intelligence, climate risk assessment, green credit, renewable energy finance, and greenwashing detection. This multidisciplinary approach is particularly significant because the problems of sustainable finance are multi-disciplinary themselves. Climate change is not simply an environmental problem. It is also a financial risk, a governance issue, a tech opportunity and a behavioural issue.

The chapters in this book indicate that investor mood can significantly shape how ESG information is interpreted and valued. A positive attitude toward green industries, renewable energy, or responsible enterprises can attract capital and generate valuation premiums. At the same time, negative mood, policy uncertainty, insufficient disclosure or suspicion of greenwashing can undermine confidence and cause volatility. This is an essential understanding for academics and practitioners alike. It reminds us that financial markets do not respond only to data, but also to narratives, credibility, trust, and expectations.

Of special welcome in this edition is the emphasis paid to behavioural finance. Optimism, anxiety, moral preferences, herding behaviour, trust, cognitive biases, and social expectations can influence judgements about sustainable investment. These behavioural forces may promote the expansion of green finance by spurring cash to flow into sustainable industries. But they can also lead to mispricing, bubbles, overreaction, and abrupt corrections. To make sustainable finance not just bigger but also more stable, transparent and credible, these behavioural dynamics need to be understood.

The book also provides valuable insights into the role of technology in the future of sustainable finance. Fintech, blockchain, digital payments, artificial intelligence, and machine learning. They can increase transparency, foster financial inclusivity, improve climate-risk assessment, and more readily detect greenwashing. But the book also acknowledges rightly that technology is not a cure-all. If the data on which they are built is weak, AI models can be prejudiced, opaque, and unreliable. Responsible governance, human judgment, ethical safeguards, and regulatory control remain important.

Another major feature is the inclusion of insights from emerging markets. Green finance is developed differently in different countries. The valuation of green assets is determined by market maturity, regulatory frameworks, banking structures, disclosure quality, investor awareness, and institutional capability. Case studies from India, Vietnam and other emerging contexts show that sustainable finance must be understood in the context of local economic and institutional circumstances. This is particularly significant given that many of the world's most pressing climate finance requirements are in emerging and developing economies.

This book provides scholars with a foundation for future study of sentiment-driven green valuation, ESG transparency, sustainable asset pricing, and technology-enabled climate finance. It provides investors and finance professionals with practical insight into the role of sentiment, credibility and information quality in green asset performance. For politicians and regulators, it underscores the importance of clear disclosure rules, improved green taxonomies, greater governance of ESG claims and more robust measures to maintain market trust. It gives students a comprehensive and approachable entrée into one of the most significant fields of contemporary finance.

This volume is published at a propitious period. As the world looks to mobilise finance for climate transition, renewable energy, sustainable infrastructure and ethical corporate practices, it has become crucial to understand the processes that define green valuation. Market mood can either accelerate change by channelling capital into sustainable prospects, or hinder it by feeding speculation, mistrust and instability. The challenge for scholars and practitioners, therefore, is to view emotion not as an ancillary issue but as a key element of sustainable financial markets.

I congratulate the editors and writers of the contributing chapters for assembling such a relevant and diverse collection of works. Impact of Market Sentiment on Green Valuations fills an essential gap in the literature and provides readers with a thoughtful assessment of the interactions among sustainability, behaviour, technology, and finance. This is a valuable contribution to the developing field of sustainable finance and will be of interest to academics, policymakers, investors, financial institutions and anybody interested in the future of green capital markets.

This book is not to be missed. It reminds us that developing sustainable financial systems involves more than cash. It needs credible information, responsible innovation, effective regulation, investor confidence and a deeper knowledge of human behaviour. In this respect, this volume makes a significant contribution to the future of finance.

Xuan Vinh Vo

University of Economics Ho Chi Minh City, Viet Nam

Preface

The global financial system is undergoing a fundamental shift as sustainability, climate responsibility, technological innovation, and investor psychology become ever more central to how markets allocate capital and assess value. The move to green finance is no longer only about ethical investment preferences or voluntary corporate responsibility. It is a structural change that affects asset pricing, banking competitiveness, capital market regulation, renewable energy finance, ESG disclosure, green bonds, fintech innovation, artificial intelligence and behavioural dynamics of investors.

This book, *Impact of Market Sentiment on Green Valuations*, explores how market sentiment affects the valuation of green assets and sustainable financial instruments. It brings together a diverse set of chapters that show that green valuing is not a function of financial factors alone. Instead, it is driven by the confluence of ESG information, investor views, behavioural biases, policy signals, technology development, disclosure credibility and market narratives. In sustainable finance, prices are typically driven not just by verifiable environmental performance, but also by expectations, trust, uncertainty, optimism, fear of greenwashing and confidence in the long-term transition to a low-carbon economy.

The chapters in this volume examine the behavioural foundations of green investment decisions, including investor sentiment, cognitive biases, herding behaviour, moral preferences, trust in ESG information, and psychological motivations for sustainable investing. These contributions explain why investors may attribute a premium to green enterprises, green bonds, renewable-energy projects and ESG-aligned portfolios, and how excess optimism, uncertainty, poor disclosure or greenwashing concerns can generate volatility and mispricing. The book integrates behavioural and sustainable finance to demonstrate the relevance of understanding the way investors interpret ESG signals and how interpretations affect the allocation of capital

A large part of the book is devoted to the value of ESG and market sentiment in green stock and bond markets. The chapters explore the impact of ESG scores, ESG news sentiment, media narratives, market-based sentiment indicators, and machine-learning-based sentiment models on stock returns, Tobin's Q, return on equity, green bond yields, and broader valuation outcomes. These findings suggest that ESG information is only financially significant when it is perceived by investors, institutions, analysts, and regulators within a specific informational and behavioural environment. The book therefore underscores the significance of more transparent, consistent and reliable ESG reporting methods, to minimise uncertainty and promote market efficiency.

The volume also examines the growing significance of fintech and artificial intelligence in sustainable finance. Chapters on fintech explain how digital payments, blockchain, smart contracts, peer-to-peer renewable-energy markets, digital-ledger supply-chain financing, and AI-based credit scoring may increase financial inclusion, transparency, and climate-aligned investment. Other chapters cover AI's role in climate risk assessment, green credit rating, ESG disclosure analysis, and greenwashing detection. These contributions illustrate how technology can enhance sustainable finance through improved data processing, risk modelling, traceability, and decision-making. At the same time, the book highlights critical concerns such as algorithmic bias, data quality, cybersecurity, model transparency, ethical AI governance and the risk of replacing opaque automated systems for human judgment.

Some chapters include sectoral and country-specific viewpoints. The studies on green credit in Indian banking explore the impact of sustainable lending on bank competitiveness, risk-taking behaviour, credit quality and long-term financial resilience. The chapter on Vietnamese commercial banks employs a PhoBERT-based text-mining approach to examine ESG disclosure patterns, showing the need for language-specific artificial intelligence for sustainability research in emerging countries. Other chapters address India's green finance sector, renewable energy investment, pricing regulation, climate-aligned financing methods, and the role of public policy in lowering investment risk and attracting private participation. These contributions enhance the book by illustrating how local institutions, regulatory maturity, financial market depth, and the trustworthiness of sustainability information affect green valuation.

OVERVIEW OF CHAPTERS

Chapter 1: Investor Sentiment in Sustainable Finance: Behavioral Drivers of Green Investment Decisions

Green investment has expanded rapidly as environmental, social, and governance (ESG) considerations reshape financial markets. However, existing research provides limited theoretical insight into how ESG information translates into investor sentiment and influences capital allocation. This chapter addresses this gap by developing a conceptual framework that models investor sentiment as a behavioral transmission mechanism linking ESG information to investment decisions. Drawing on behavioral finance and sustainable investment research, the framework identifies cognitive biases and emotional responses as key mediating processes, while also incorporating the role of moral preferences and sustainability narratives. By integrating behavioral and sustainable finance perspectives, the chapter advances a structured explanation of sentiment formation in ESG contexts and establishes a foundation for future empirical research on sentiment-driven dynamics in sustainable financial markets.

Chapter 2: Behavioural Drivers of Green Valuations-Understanding Investor Sentiment in Sustainable Financial Markets

Green asset valuations now appear to be influenced by various behavioral factors in addition to fundamental factors. This chapter examines the impact of investor sentiment, norms, and cognitive factors on green financial markets. This study uses various research studies on behavioral finance and sustainability to examine the factors that influence green asset valuations. This chapter examines how positive sentiments lead to green asset premiums, reduced required rates of return, and increased flows into green assets, while changes in sentiments may cause increased asset price volatility and mispricing. It will also test the reaction of different types of investors to green asset valuation, such as the way institutional investors, retail investors, and different generations respond to the risks of climate change. The present study synthesizes research studies on green asset valuations that provide insights into the effect of various factors on green asset valuation, such as whether green premiums are caused by long-run risk mitigation or behavioral overreaction

Chapter 3: Measuring Market Sentiment in Green Asset Valuation: A Structured Analytical Review

The growth of environmental, social, and governance (ESG) investing has intensified interest in the role of market sentiment in the valuation of green assets. As sustainability considerations shape capital markets, sentiment-related factors increasingly influence pricing dynamics. This chapter provides a structured analytical review of sentiment indicators used in the valuation of green and ESG-related assets. It classifies existing measures into text-based indicators, market-based proxies, survey and attention measures, and machine-learning-generated composite indices. The review identifies methodological heterogeneity, endogeneity concerns, and limited standardization in sentiment measurement. It also highlights overlap between sentiment proxies and sustainability-related fundamentals. The chapter concludes that developing a unified, transparent measurement framework is essential to improving comparability and strengthening empirical research in green asset valuation.

Chapter 4: Empirical Studies Linking Sentiment, ESG Scores, and Financial Performance

The growing integration of Environmental, Social, and Governance (ESG) considerations into investment decision-making has fundamentally reshaped global capital markets, prompting extensive academic and practitioner interest in understanding how ESG-related information influences asset prices and financial performance. Beyond static ESG scores and disclosures, recent research increasingly emphasises the role of sentiment-driven ESG momentum—the dynamic flow of market perceptions, narratives, and investor attitudes toward ESG factors—in shaping stock returns. Sentiment-driven ESG momentum refers to the cumulative effect of changing investor sentiment, media coverage, analyst opinions, regulatory signals, and stakeholder discourse related to a firm's ESG profile, which together create positive or negative momentum in how ESG characteristics are priced by financial markets. This empirical review synthesises existing literature on the mechanisms, measurement approaches, and financial implications of ESG sentiment momentum, highlighting how sentiment dynamics interact.

Chapter 5: Policy Shocks, Climate Risk, and Sentiment Spillovers Pricing Green Bonds and Carbon Assets Under Uncertainty

Green bonds and carbon assets are linked through regulation, investor mandates, and climate news, responding to policy credibility, macro conditions, and sentiment shifts. Under uncertainty, pricing becomes state dependent: the same policy surprise can compress green-bond yields while raising carbon-price volatility, or trigger joint selloffs when doubt and risk aversion rise together. Policy surprises affect valuation through four channels — cash flows, discount rates, liquidity, and sentiment contagion — with responses shaped by verification quality, issuer type, and market depth. Carbon assets react more to regulatory credibility and energy conditions; green bonds more to investor clienteles, taxonomies, and balance-sheet constraints. Sentiment spillovers amplify both markets most when policy uncertainty is high and news spreads fast. The chapter proposes a state-dependent joint-pricing framework, draws implications for portfolio and issuance strategy, and outlines a research agenda integrating policy uncertainty, climate tail risk, and network effects into asset-pricing models.

Chapter 6: Financial Innovations and Circular Economy: Pathways Toward a Sustainable Future

As the global community faces increasing environmental challenges and resource depletion, the concept of a circular economy (CE) has emerged as a key strategy for achieving sustainable development. The circular economy model, focuses on minimizing waste, maximizing resource efficiency, and encouraging the reuse and recycling of materials, presents significant opportunities for economic, environmental, and social benefits. However, the transition to a circular economy requires robust financial innovations to drive investment, scale circular business models, and align economic activities with sustainability goals. This chapter explores the intersection of financial innovations and the circular economy, investigating how new financial instruments, strategies, and investment vehicles can support the scaling and mainstreaming of circular practices. By examining various financial tools—including green bonds, impact investing, and sustainable business models—this chapter aims to provide insights into how financial markets can support a transition toward a more sustainable, circular economy.

Chapter 7: Artificial Intelligence in Sustainable Finance: ESG-Based Financial Instruments and Decisions

Sustainable finance integrates environmental, social, and governance considerations into financial decision-making to promote long-term value creation and systemic resilience. Recent advances in artificial intelligence have enhanced the assessment, monitoring, and implementation of sustainability criteria across financial markets. This chapter examines how machine learning, natural language processing, predictive analytics, and blockchain-based systems support ESG evaluation, climate risk assessment, and performance measurement. Particular attention is given to green bonds, sustainability-linked loans, carbon credit mechanisms, and trade finance applications. The analysis also addresses governance challenges related to data reliability, transparency, and algorithmic bias. By synthesizing insights from finance and digital innovation research, the chapter outlines how AI-enabled analytics can strengthen sustainable investment practices and improve risk management frameworks.

Chapter 8: Algorithmic Accountability in Greenwashing Detection: Hybrid Governance in ESG Auditing

The rapid growth of ESG investing has intensified corporate greenwashing and overwhelmed traditional human auditing mechanisms. This chapter examines the comparative efficacy of Large Language Models and human analysts in detecting corporate greenwashing. As sustainable finance expands, deceptive environmental reporting exploits the capacity constraints, biases, and structural limitations inherent in manual auditing. To address these vulnerabilities, institutions deploy automated semantic analysis to systematically cross-reference corporate narratives against objective data. However, relying on opaque algorithms introduces novel risks, particularly statistical hallucinations and algorithmic audit washing, wherein flawed environmental claims receive unwarranted mathematical validation. The chapter advances a Human-in-the-Loop governance framework. By utilizing language models strictly for high-volume text processing while retaining human experts for nuanced, contextual adjudication, financial markets can scale their detection capabilities without compromising regulatory integrity.

Chapter 9: Analyzing ESG Disclosure Patterns in Vietnamese Commercial Banks: A Phobert-Based Text Mining Study

This chapter analyzes ESG disclosure in sustainability reports of Vietnamese commercial banks using PhoBERT-based text mining. The dataset includes 25 reports from 13 banks listed on the Ho Chi Minh City Stock Exchange. After text preprocessing and Vietnamese word segmentation, PhoBERT embeddings were used to compare report paragraphs with MSCI-based ESG theme representations. The findings show that ESG disclosure is mainly concentrated in the governance pillar, especially corporate governance, reflecting the banking sector's focus on transparency, internal control, compliance, and risk management. The social pillar follows, with human capital as the most visible theme. The study contributes to ESG disclosure research by providing empirical evidence on the thematic structure of ESG reporting in Vietnamese banking and by demonstrating the usefulness of Vietnamese-language NLP for sustainability disclosure analysis.

Chapter 10: Green Credit - Indian Bank Competitiveness and Bank Risk Taking

This study examines the relationship between green credit, Indian bank competitiveness, and bank risk-taking through a systematic literature review of 40 peer-reviewed articles published between 2015 and 2025. Findings showed that green credit initiatives strengthen banks' long-term competitiveness by improving sustainability performance, lowering environmental compliance costs, and enhancing market reputation. Evidence also suggested that while green credit generally reduces credit and operational risks due to better asset quality and government-backed incentives, some banks face short-term risks linked to limited borrower history, high monitoring costs, and evolving regulatory frameworks. The review concludes that integrating green credit is strategically beneficial for Indian banks, promoting both competitiveness and stable risk profiles. Policymakers should expand green-finance guidelines and incentives, while banks must strengthen risk assessment tools and build sector-specific expertise to scale green lending sustainably.

Chapter 11: Financial Innovation and the Role of Fintech in Sustainable Finance

Fintech has emerged as a powerful engine driving the creation and evolution of sustainable financial ecosystems by reshaping how financial services are designed, delivered, and governed in an increasingly interconnected world. At its core, fintech integrates digital technologies such as artificial intelligence, blockchain, big data analytics, cloud computing, and mobile platforms into financial systems, enabling greater efficiency, transparency, inclusivity, and resilience. These capabilities directly support sustainability by reducing operational costs, lowering environmental footprints through paperless and branch-light models, and expanding access to financial services for underserved populations, including low-income households, small and medium enterprises (SMEs), rural communities, and informal sector participants. Through digital payments, mobile banking, micro-lending platforms, and alternative credit scoring models that rely on non-traditional data, fintech bridges long-standing gaps in financial inclusion.

The book also addresses policy and regulatory issues of green finance. Chapters on price regulation, renewable-energy finance, carbon pricing, green bonds, and climate-aligned investment mechanisms illustrate that regulatory stability, policy credibility, disclosure obligations, the green taxonomy, and public-sector backing heavily influence market attitudes. Good laws may reduce uncertainty, decrease the cost of capital and incentivise long-term investment in renewable energy and sustainable infrastructure. Poor regulation, inconsistent standards, policy reversals and unreliable disclosures, on the other hand, can shake investor confidence and lead to more volatile valuations.

One major theme of this volume is that green valuations are built at the junction of fundamentals and perception. Valuation continues to be driven by ESG performance, carbon intensity, renewable energy possibilities, climate risk exposure and financial strength. But the market impact depends on how investors perceive, interpret and believe such signals. This is particularly true in sustainable finance, where many outcomes are long-term, unclear, and hard to assess in the short term. Sentiment, therefore, may be a source of both danger and opportunity: it can be a trigger for a capital rally into sustainable industries, but it can also generate bubbles, mispricing, and abrupt declines as expectations change.

It is aimed at researchers, graduate students, policymakers, financial analysts, banking professionals, sustainability officers, fintech entrepreneurs, institutional investors and anybody interested in learning more about how sustainable finance is emerging. It includes theoretical insights, empirical perspectives, methodological frameworks, and practical implications for those seeking to understand the behavioural, technological, and institutional drivers of green asset value.

We hope this volume adds to the increasing literature on sustainable finance by showing that the future of green valuation will rely not just on stronger ESG performance, but also on better information, governance, technology and knowledge of investor behaviour. The role of market sentiment will remain crucial as financial markets continue to react to climate change, environmental risk and the search for responsible investment. Understanding this function is critical to establishing financial systems that are profitable and innovative, but also transparent, robust, inclusive and linked with long-term sustainable development.

The editors appreciate the earnest contributions of all authors, reviewers, and publishing professionals who helped develop this book. Their research, perspectives and commitment to promoting sustainable finance make this volume possible.

Acknowledgment

The editors wish to offer their heartfelt appreciation to everybody who helped to make this publication, *Impact of Market Sentiment on Green Valuations,* a success. The significant work, cooperation and intellectual commitment of numerous people have resulted in this volume.

We are especially grateful to the contributing authors for sharing their research, knowledge, and views on sustainable finance, market sentiment, ESG valuation, green bonds, fintech, artificial intelligence, climate risk assessment, green credit, and renewable energy finance. Their contributions have enriched the present volume and fostered a multidisciplinary conversation on one of the most significant areas of current finance.

We also thank the reviewers and academic experts for their helpful comments, critical criticism, and thoughtful recommendations during the review process. Their thorough review and professional views helped to improve the quality, clarity and academic worth of the chapters in this book.

We would also like to extend our sincere gratitude to the IGI Global Scientific Publishing team for their direction, coordination and support during the preparation and production of this volume. Thanks to them for their support during the editorial and production process.

We would also like to recognise the assistance of our colleagues, institutions, and professional networks, whose encouragement and cooperation contributed to the progress of this project. Their scholarly engagement and assistance were invaluable in guiding the evolution of this volume from its inception to its completion.

Finally, we appreciate all readers, academics, practitioners, policymakers and students who will engage with this volume. We believe that this book may contribute to ongoing research, informed debate and practical development in the field of sustainable finance and green asset appraisal.

Chapter 1
Investor Sentiment in Sustainable Finance:
Behavioral Drivers of Green Investment Decisions

Afef Amdouni
http://orcid.org/0000-0001-9625-300X
Taibah University, Saudi Arabia

Chokkamreddy Prakash
http://orcid.org/0000-0002-3832-3740
Guru Nanak Institutions Technical Campus, India

ABSTRACT

Green investment has expanded rapidly as environmental, social, and governance (ESG) considerations reshape financial markets. However, existing research provides limited theoretical insight into how ESG information translates into investor sentiment and influences capital allocation. This chapter addresses this gap by developing a conceptual framework that models investor sentiment as a behavioral transmission mechanism linking ESG information to investment decisions. Drawing on behavioral finance and sustainable investment research, the framework identifies cognitive biases and emotional responses as key mediating processes, while also incorporating the role of moral preferences and sustainability narratives. By integrating behavioral and sustainable finance perspectives, the chapter advances a structured explanation of sentiment formation in ESG contexts and establishes a foundation for future empirical research on sentiment-driven dynamics in sustainable financial markets.

DOI: 10.4018/979-8-3373-8392-7.ch001

1. INTRODUCTION

Sustainable finance has become an increasingly important area of financial research and practice as environmental, social, and governance (ESG) considerations are incorporated into portfolio allocation, risk assessment, and corporate valuation. This development has expanded academic interest in green bonds, ESG-screened equities, climate-aligned portfolios, and other sustainable financial instruments. Much of this literature has examined the relationship between ESG information and financial outcomes, including performance, valuation, disclosure quality, and capital allocation.

Yet green investment decisions are not determined by financial information alone. Unlike conventional investment settings, sustainable finance involves ethical preferences, environmental concerns, climate-related uncertainty, and heterogeneous ESG information. These characteristics create a decision environment in which investors may not evaluate sustainability-related information through purely rational risk–return calculations. Instead, ESG signals may be interpreted through cognitive shortcuts, emotional reactions, moral preferences, and socially transmitted sustainability narratives.

This chapter is motivated by a specific theoretical problem: existing research has not sufficiently explained how ESG-related information is transformed into investor sentiment and how that sentiment subsequently influences green capital allocation. Behavioral finance provides well-established explanations of how investor sentiment, cognitive biases, and emotional responses affect financial markets. Sustainable finance, by contrast, has mainly examined ESG information, disclosure, and market outcomes. However, the connection between these two streams remains underdeveloped. In particular, the behavioral transmission process linking ESG information, psychological interpretation, investor sentiment, and capital allocation has not been clearly specified.

This chapter addresses this gap by developing a conceptual-theoretical framework of investor sentiment formation in sustainable finance. It is not intended as a systematic literature review or as an empirical test of causal relationships. Rather, it offers an integrative theoretical synthesis that explains how ESG information may function as a behavioral stimulus in green investment decisions. The central argument is that investor sentiment operates as a behavioral transmission mechanism through which ESG information affects capital allocation under conditions of sustainability-related uncertainty.

The proposed framework explains how ESG-related information is cognitively and emotionally interpreted, transformed into investor sentiment, and subsequently reflected in sustainable capital allocation decisions. First, ESG information, including disclosures, ratings, policy signals, and sustainability-related narratives, provides the informational input. Second, investors interpret this information through cognitive processes that may involve heuristics, confirmation bias, herding, or overconfidence. Third, emotional responses, including environmental concern, optimism, anxiety, or moral satisfaction, shape the affective dimension of sentiment formation. Fourth, investor sentiment influences capital allocation toward green assets, including green bonds, ESG-oriented equities, and climate-aligned investment portfolios.

The chapter makes three contributions. First, it clarifies the theoretical positioning of investor sentiment in sustainable finance by treating sentiment not merely as a market indicator, but as a behavioral mechanism linking ESG information to investment behavior. Second, it integrates behavioral finance and sustainable finance by explaining how cognitive and emotional processes mediate the interpretation of ESG signals. Third, it distinguishes sentiment-driven dynamics from preference-based explanations of sustainable investing, thereby providing a more precise conceptual basis for future empirical research.

The remainder of the chapter proceeds as follows. Section 2 reviews the relevant literature on investor sentiment, behavioral finance, and sustainable finance, with attention to the limitations of existing research. Section 3 develops the theoretical foundations of the proposed framework. Section 4 presents the behavioral transmission framework linking ESG information, cognitive biases, emotional responses, investor sentiment, and capital allocation. Section 5 formulates the conceptual propositions. Section 6 discusses structural moderators and market dynamics. Section 7 outlines an empirical research agenda. The final sections discuss the theoretical implications, limitations, and future research directions.

2. LITERATURE REVIEW

This section reviews the two principal research streams underlying the present chapter: investor sentiment in behavioral finance and ESG-related decision-making in sustainable finance. Rather than providing a descriptive survey of prior studies, the review focuses on the conceptual limitations of existing research and identifies the missing theoretical link between ESG information, psychological interpretation, investor sentiment, and capital allocation.

2.1 Investor Sentiment in Financial Markets

The behavioral finance literature provides the primary theoretical foundation for understanding how investor sentiment emerges under conditions of uncertainty and imperfect information.

Investor sentiment occupies a central position in behavioral finance research as an explanation for deviations between market prices and underlying fundamentals. Early theoretical contributions challenged the assumption that investors process information in a fully rational manner. De Long et al. (1990) argue that noise traders acting on sentiment rather than fundamentals may generate persistent mispricing and excess volatility. Similarly, Barberis, Shleifer, and Vishny (1998) explain how biased belief formation and heuristic-driven expectations can produce systematic distortions in asset valuation.

Subsequent research extended these arguments by examining the market consequences of sentiment-driven trading behavior. Baker and Wurgler (2007), for example, show that investor sentiment tends to exert stronger effects on securities characterized by valuation uncertainty and limited arbitrage. Shiller (2000) further emphasizes the importance of narratives and collective expectations in shaping market behavior, suggesting that financial markets are influenced not only by information, but also by socially transmitted interpretations of economic events.

Despite these contributions, two limitations remain relevant for the present study. First, much of the literature concentrates on market outcomes such as returns, volatility, or trading activity, while devoting comparatively less attention to the psychological transmission processes through which sentiment is formed. Second, existing sentiment research has largely developed within conventional financial settings and therefore provides limited explanation of how sustainability-related information may alter investor interpretation and behavior.

These limitations become particularly important in sustainable finance contexts, where investors face ambiguous ESG information, heterogeneous disclosure standards, and substantial uncertainty regarding long-term environmental and regulatory outcomes.

While these studies provide important explanations of sentiment formation in conventional financial markets, they offer only limited insight into how sustainability-related information influences investor interpretation and behavior in ESG-oriented investment settings.

2.2 Sustainable Finance and ESG Information

Against this behavioral perspective, the sustainable finance literature examines how sustainability disclosures affect investment decisions, firm valuation, and capital allocation in increasingly sustainability-oriented financial markets.

The sustainable finance literature has expanded rapidly in response to the growing integration of ESG considerations into financial decision-making. Existing research has examined how ESG disclosures, sustainability ratings, and climate-related information influence firm valuation, investment flows, and corporate financial performance (Friede et al., 2015).

Several studies included in this literature suggest that sustainability disclosures affect investor perceptions and market behavior. Su et al. (2024), for instance, examine the relationship between investor sentiment and the green bond market, while Christensen, Hail, and Leuz (2021) discuss the informational role of sustainability reporting frameworks in reducing information asymmetry. Other studies focus on how climate-related attention, media coverage, or ESG disclosures influence investment decisions and market expectations. However, existing findings remain methodologically fragmented, as studies employ different measures of ESG quality, investor sentiment, and sustainability performance, leading to inconsistent interpretations of investor behavior across sustainable finance contexts.

However, this literature also exhibits important conceptual limitations. A substantial portion of sustainable finance research adopts an outcome-oriented perspective by focusing primarily on financial consequences such as returns, cost of capital, or investment performance. As a result, ESG information is frequently treated as an external informational variable rather than as a behavioral stimulus interpreted through cognitive and emotional processes.

In addition, the literature does not provide a sufficiently clear distinction between preference-based sustainable investing and sentiment-driven investment behavior. Some explanations assume that investors allocate capital toward green assets because they derive non-pecuniary utility from sustainability preferences. Other interpretations imply that investment behavior may be influenced by optimism, narratives, or behavioral amplification mechanisms. Yet these perspectives are rarely integrated within a unified analytical structure.

The absence of such integration limits the ability of existing research to explain how ESG information is transformed into investor sentiment and subsequently affects capital allocation decisions.

Consequently, although sustainable finance research recognizes the growing importance of ESG information, it still provides an incomplete explanation of the behavioral mechanisms through which such information influences investor sentiment and investment decisions.

2.3 Integrative Gap: The Missing Behavioral Transmission Mechanism

The limitations identified in the preceding research streams reveal the absence of an integrated framework capable of explaining how ESG information is behaviorally translated into investor sentiment and capital allocation decisions.

The preceding discussion reveals an important conceptual fragmentation between behavioral finance and sustainable finance research. Behavioral finance explains how cognitive biases, heuristic reasoning, and emotional responses shape investor behavior under uncertainty. Sustainable finance research, by contrast, documents the increasing importance of ESG information in investment decision-making and market valuation.

Nevertheless, the interaction between these two domains remains insufficiently theorized. Existing studies frequently examine isolated components of the process, including ESG disclosures, investor sentiment indicators, sustainability preferences, or market outcomes, without specifying the behavioral mechanism linking these elements together.

This limitation is particularly significant in sustainable finance environments characterized by informational complexity, regulatory uncertainty, and strong normative narratives. Under such conditions, investors may rely more heavily on heuristic interpretation, affective reactions, and socially transmitted expectations when evaluating ESG information. Consequently, investor sentiment cannot be understood solely as a market indicator or trading outcome; rather, it must be examined as a behavioral process through which sustainability-related information influences investment decisions.

This chapter addresses this conceptual gap by proposing a behavioral transmission framework that links ESG information, cognitive interpretation, emotional responses, investor sentiment, and capital allocation within a unified analytical structure. The objective is not to empirically validate causal relationships, but to provide a coherent theoretical explanation of sentiment formation in sustainable finance markets.

Accordingly, the literature review suggests that existing research remains theoretically fragmented. Behavioral finance explains how sentiment and cognitive biases influence investor behavior, while sustainable finance research explains the growing importance of ESG information in financial markets. However, the interaction between these dimensions has not been systematically integrated within a unified analytical framework. This gap motivates the theoretical foundations developed in the following section.

3. THEORETICAL FOUNDATIONS

The purpose of this section is not to review behavioral and sustainable finance theories independently, but to establish the analytical foundations of the proposed behavioral transmission framework. The discussion therefore focuses on how different theoretical perspectives collectively explain the transformation of ESG information into investor sentiment and capital allocation decisions under conditions of sustainability-related uncertainty.

3.1 Cognitive Foundations of Investor Behavior

The behavioral interpretation of investor sentiment begins with the cognitive processes through which investors evaluate uncertain and incomplete information.

The behavioral finance literature provides the micro-level foundation for understanding how investors process information under uncertainty. Contrary to the assumptions of classical financial theory, investors do not always form expectations through fully rational Bayesian updating. Instead, decision-making is frequently shaped by cognitive biases and heuristic-based reasoning.

Seminal contributions by Daniel Kahneman and Amos Tversky demonstrate that individuals rely on mental shortcuts when evaluating uncertain outcomes, leading to systematic deviations from rational choice. Prospect Theory, in particular, highlights key behavioral patterns such as loss aversion, reference dependence, and nonlinear probability weighting. These mechanisms imply that investor responses to information are inherently subjective and context-dependent.

In the context of sustainable finance, ESG signals are often complex, multidimensional, and forward-looking. Investors must interpret uncertain signals related to climate risks, technological transitions, and regulatory developments. Under such conditions, reliance on heuristics is likely to increase, making cognitive biases central to the interpretation of ESG information.

These cognitive mechanisms become particularly relevant in sustainable finance contexts, where ESG signals are often ambiguous, difficult to standardize, and strongly influenced by future-oriented expectations regarding climate transition, regulation, and corporate sustainability performance.

3.2 Sentiment Formation and Market Dynamics

While cognitive biases explain how investors interpret information at the individual level, investor sentiment emerges through the aggregation of these individual expectations at the market level.

Beyond individual cognition, investor sentiment emerges as an aggregate market-level phenomenon. The noise trader framework developed by De Long et al. (1990) provides a theoretical basis for understanding how sentiment-driven investors can influence asset prices and market dynamics. In this framework, investors who trade based on beliefs or emotions—rather than fundamentals—can generate persistent mispricing and excess volatility.

These dynamics are particularly relevant in markets characterized by valuation ambiguity. Green assets often lack standardized valuation metrics, and ESG ratings may vary across providers. In such environments, differences in interpretation can lead to sentiment-driven trading behavior, amplifying price fluctuations and capital flows.

Empirical evidence suggests that investor sentiment plays a significant role in shaping green financial markets, affecting both pricing dynamics and investment flows. However, the noise trader framework primarily explains the consequences of sentiment, rather than its underlying formation process.

Accordingly, sentiment formation in sustainable finance markets cannot be reduced to individual psychology alone, but must also account for the market-level amplification of collective expectations under conditions of valuation uncertainty.

3.3 Narrative Amplification in ESG Contexts

Beyond cognitive interpretation and market aggregation, investor sentiment in sustainable finance is also shaped through socially transmitted narratives that influence collective expectations.

Financial markets are influenced not only by quantitative information, but also by narratives that shape collective expectations. Narrative economics emphasizes that widely shared stories—such as technological transitions, environmental crises, or sustainability innovations—can influence investor perceptions and market behavior.

In sustainable finance, narratives related to climate change, renewable energy, and corporate responsibility play a particularly important role. These narratives are disseminated through media, policy discourse, and social platforms, and they can amplify investor reactions to ESG information. As a result, investor sentiment is not solely an individual cognitive construct, but also a socially transmitted phenomenon.

Narrative amplification therefore extends the behavioral transmission process beyond individual cognition by embedding ESG interpretation within broader social and informational environments.

3.4 Preference-Based Equilibrium and Its Limits

Although behavioral finance emphasizes sentiment-driven deviations from fundamental valuation, sustainable finance research also provides an alternative explanation for green asset pricing based on investor preferences. From this perspective, investors may intentionally allocate capital toward environmentally responsible assets because they derive non-financial utility from sustainability objectives, ethical alignment, or climate-related concerns.

For example, investors may accept lower expected returns in exchange for alignment with environmental or ethical objectives. This phenomenon, often referred to as a "green preference" or "green tilt," can influence equilibrium asset prices and lead to systematic differences between green and conventional assets.

However, preference-based explanations do not fully account for short-term market fluctuations, volatility patterns, or sentiment-driven mispricing. In practice, sustainable financial markets may reflect a combination of preference-driven equilibrium forces and behavioral dynamics.

The distinction between preference-based valuation and sentiment-driven pricing dynamics is analytically important because the two mechanisms imply different interpretations of green asset pricing behavior. The former reflects long-term equilibrium preferences, whereas the latter may generate temporary valuation distortions under conditions of uncertainty and behavioral amplification.

3.5 Theoretical Synthesis

The preceding theoretical perspectives explain different but interconnected dimensions of investor behavior in sustainable finance markets. Behavioral finance explains how investors interpret ESG information through heuristic reasoning and cognitive biases in uncertain sustainability environments. Sentiment-based approaches explain how these individual interpretations aggregate into collective market expectations capable of influencing pricing dynamics and capital allocation. Narrative perspectives extend this analysis by explaining how sustainability-related stories, media discourse, and social attention amplify investor reactions and reinforce shared market beliefs. Finally, preference-based approaches explain why some investors may allocate capital toward green assets even in the absence of purely financial incentives.

Considered independently, each perspective captures only a partial dimension of investor behavior in sustainable finance. Behavioral theories explain cognitive and emotional distortions but do not fully explain why sustainability-related information acquires strong social and normative influence. Preference-based models explain long-term allocation toward green assets but provide limited explanation of short-term fluctuations, sentiment persistence, or valuation instability. Similarly, narrative approaches explain social amplification mechanisms without fully specifying how informational signals are translated into investment decisions.

The present chapter integrates these perspectives within a unified analytical structure. Specifically, the proposed framework conceptualizes investor sentiment as a behavioral channel through which ESG information influences capital allocation decisions. Within this mechanism, sustainability-related signals function as the informational input; cognitive biases and emotional responses shape interpretation; narratives amplify collective expectations; and investor sentiment influences investment behavior in sustainable finance markets.

This synthesis provides the theoretical basis for the conceptual framework developed in the following section.

4. CONCEPTUAL FRAMEWORK: BEHAVIORAL TRANSMISSION OF INVESTOR SENTIMENT

The conceptual framework developed in this chapter explains investor sentiment as a transmission process through which ESG information influences capital allocation in sustainable finance markets. The framework is designed to integrate informational, psychological, social, and institutional dimensions within a unified analytical structure. Rather than treating investor sentiment as a residual market outcome, the framework conceptualizes sentiment as an intermediate behavioral process linking ESG-related signals to investment behavior in uncertain sustainability environments.

Investment decisions in sustainable finance markets are shaped within informational environments characterized by uncertainty, heterogeneous disclosures, evolving regulatory conditions, and competing sustainability narratives. Unlike conventional financial settings, sustainability-related signals are frequently multidimensional, forward-looking, and difficult to evaluate using standard valuation models. Under such conditions, investors may rely not only on financial analysis, but also on heuristic interpretation, affective responses, and collective expectations when evaluating green assets.

4.1 Structural Components of the Behavioral Transmission Framework

The proposed framework consists of four interconnected analytical layers through which ESG information is translated into capital allocation decisions.

The first layer concerns informational inputs. ESG disclosures, sustainability ratings, climate-related policy signals, and media narratives provide the informational environment within which investors evaluate green assets. Because ESG information is frequently heterogeneous, forward-looking, and difficult to standardize, investors often face substantial interpretive uncertainty.

The second layer involves cognitive interpretation. Investors process climate-related information through heuristic reasoning and cognitive biases rather than through fully rational evaluation alone. Mechanisms such as confirmation bias, herding behavior, selective attention, and overconfidence influence how sustainability-related signals are interpreted and prioritized.

The third layer concerns emotional and collective sentiment formation. Climate-related information may trigger affective responses associated with environmental concern, optimism regarding green innovation, moral satisfaction, or climate-related anxiety. These emotional responses interact with cognitive interpretation and contribute to the formation of investor sentiment at the aggregate market level.

The fourth layer involves capital allocation outcomes. Investor sentiment influences investment decisions involving green bonds, ESG-oriented equities, sustainable investment funds, and climate-aligned portfolios. Accordingly, investor sentiment operates as the central behavioral transmission mechanism linking sustainability narratives to capital allocation outcomes in sustainable finance markets.

Figure 1. Behavioral Transmission Framework of Investor Sentiment in Sustainable Finance

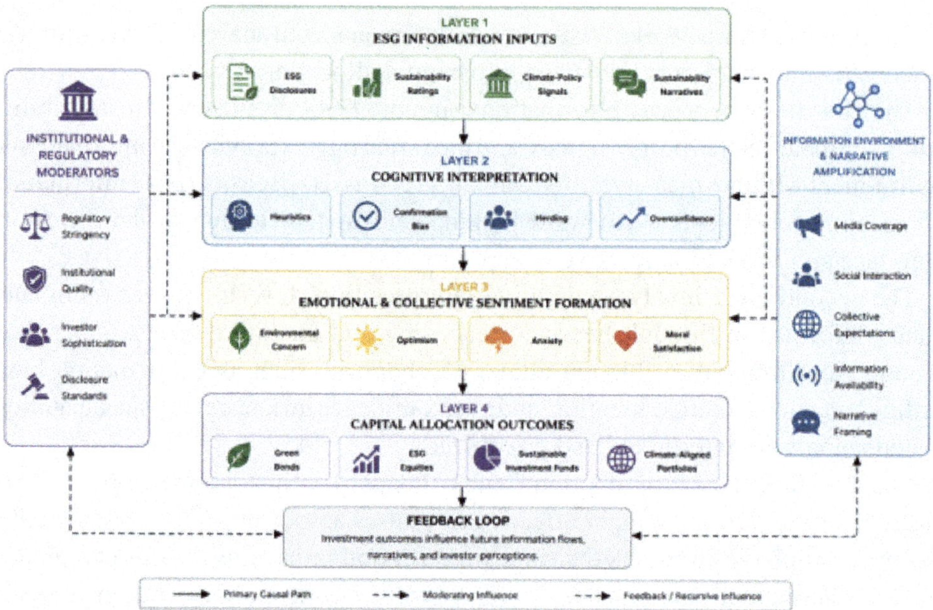

Source: Developed by the authors.

Note: Solid arrows represent the primary behavioral transmission path, whereas dashed arrows indicate moderating and recursive influences within sustainable finance markets.

4.2 Institutional and Regulatory Moderators

The behavioral transmission process does not operate independently of institutional and regulatory conditions. Instead, the strength and direction of the relationships within the framework are conditioned by structural moderators that influence informational credibility, uncertainty, and market interpretation.

Regulatory clarity plays an important role in reducing informational ambiguity in sustainable finance markets. Standardized ESG disclosure frameworks, sustainability taxonomies, and climate-reporting requirements may strengthen the credibility and comparability of ESG information, thereby reducing interpretive uncertainty.

Institutional investor participation constitutes an additional moderating factor. Institutional investors often possess greater analytical capacity, longer investment horizons, and more structured ESG evaluation processes than retail investors. Their participation may therefore stabilize sentiment dynamics and reduce the amplification of short-term behavioral reactions.

The broader information environment also shapes sentiment formation. Media coverage, digital communication platforms, and sustainability-related narratives can amplify investor reactions by accelerating the diffusion of ESG-related interpretations and expectations across financial markets.

4.3 Boundary Conditions of the Framework

The proposed framework is not intended to imply that investor sentiment dominates all sustainable finance markets under all conditions. The relative importance of sentiment transmission pathways may vary depending on market structure, regulatory maturity, and informational efficiency.

In highly regulated environments characterized by standardized ESG disclosure systems and strong institutional monitoring, behavioral distortions may become less pronounced because investors face lower informational ambiguity. Similarly, markets dominated by long-term institutional investors may exhibit greater resistance to short-term sentiment fluctuations than markets characterized by high levels of speculative participation.

The framework is therefore most applicable to sustainable finance contexts in which ESG information remains heterogeneous, future-oriented, and subject to competing interpretations.

4.4 Dynamic Feedback Effects

The framework also incorporates dynamic feedback mechanisms through which investor sentiment may reinforce subsequent market behavior. Positive sentiment toward green assets may increase capital inflows, attract greater media attention, and strengthen sustainability-related narratives, thereby reinforcing optimistic investor expectations. Conversely, negative sentiment may intensify volatility, reduce participation in sustainable investment markets, and amplify pessimistic interpretations of ESG-related risks.

These feedback effects suggest that investor sentiment in sustainable finance markets should be understood as a recursive process rather than as a purely linear sequence of informational reactions.

Taken together, the framework conceptualizes investor sentiment as a multilevel behavioral process shaped by informational inputs, cognitive interpretation, emotional responses, social amplification mechanisms, and institutional conditions. This integrated structure provides the analytical foundation for the conceptual propositions developed in the following section.

5. CONCEPTUAL PROPOSITIONS

Building on the behavioral transmission framework developed in the previous section, the following propositions specify the expected relationships between ESG information, cognitive interpretation, emotional responses, investor sentiment, and capital allocation in sustainable finance markets. The propositions are conceptual rather than empirically validated and are intended to provide a structured foundation for future empirical investigation.

Proposition 1: ESG Information and Investor Sentiment

ESG-related information constitutes the primary informational input within the proposed framework. In sustainable finance markets characterized by informational ambiguity and future-oriented uncertainty, ESG disclosures, sustainability ratings, climate-related news, and policy signals may influence investor expectations beyond traditional financial indicators alone.

P1: ESG-related information is positively associated with investor sentiment toward green assets under conditions of sustainability-related uncertainty.

Proposition 2: Cognitive Interpretation of ESG Information

The impact of ESG information on investor sentiment depends not only on the availability of information, but also on how investors cognitively interpret sustainability-related signals. Amid interpretive complexity, investors may rely on heuristic reasoning and cognitive biases when evaluating ESG information.

P2: Cognitive biases mediate the relationship between ESG-related information and investor sentiment in sustainable finance markets.

Proposition 3: Emotional Responses and Sentiment Formation

ESG-related information frequently carries normative and affective dimensions associated with environmental responsibility, climate risks, and sustainability transitions. These characteristics may trigger emotional responses that shape investor perceptions of green assets.

P3: Emotional responses mediate the relationship between ESG-related information and investor sentiment.

Proposition 4: Investor Sentiment and Capital Allocation

Investor sentiment reflects collective expectations regarding the attractiveness, legitimacy, and future prospects of green assets. Positive sentiment may increase investor willingness to allocate capital toward sustainable investment instruments, whereas negative sentiment may reduce participation in sustainable finance markets.

P4: Positive investor sentiment is positively associated with capital allocation toward green assets.

Proposition 5: Institutional and Regulatory Moderation

The influence of ESG information on investor sentiment is conditioned by institutional and regulatory environments that affect informational credibility and interpretive uncertainty. Standardized disclosure systems and institutional investor participation may strengthen the credibility of ESG-related signals and reduce informational ambiguity.

P5: Regulatory clarity and institutional investor participation strengthen the positive relationship between ESG-related information and investor sentiment.

Proposition 6: Narrative Amplification and Sentiment Dynamics

Sustainability-related narratives disseminated through media, policy discourse, and digital communication channels may amplify collective investor expectations and reinforce sentiment dynamics in sustainable finance markets.

P6: Sustainability-related narratives positively amplify the relationship between ESG-related information and investor sentiment through social diffusion mechanisms.

Proposition 7: Sentiment-Driven Market Dynamics

When investor sentiment becomes strongly amplified amid interpretive complexity, capital allocation in sustainable finance markets may temporarily deviate from underlying financial fundamentals.

P7: Elevated investor sentiment increases the likelihood of temporary valuation distortions in green asset markets.

6. STRUCTURAL MODERATORS AND MARKET DYNAMICS

The behavioral transmission framework developed in this chapter operates within broader institutional, informational, and market environments that shape how ESG-related information is interpreted and translated into investor sentiment and capital allocation decisions. Investor sentiment in sustainable finance markets therefore emerges not only from individual cognitive and emotional responses, but also from structural conditions that influence informational credibility, interpretive uncertainty, and the diffusion of sustainability-related expectations.

Accordingly, the behavioral influence of ESG-related information may vary across sustainable finance environments depending on regulatory maturity, disclosure quality, institutional participation, and the surrounding information ecosystem. These conditions affect both the intensity of sentiment formation and the extent to which sentiment-driven expectations influence market behavior.

6.1 Regulatory and Institutional Moderators

Regulatory and institutional conditions play an important role in shaping the credibility and comparability of ESG-related information. Sustainable finance markets differ substantially in terms of disclosure standardization, reporting requirements, sustainability taxonomies, and regulatory enforcement. In environments characterized by inconsistent reporting standards and fragmented disclosure practices, investors may face elevated interpretive uncertainty when evaluating sustainability-related signals.

By contrast, standardized ESG disclosure frameworks and climate-reporting requirements may improve informational comparability and reduce ambiguity surrounding sustainability performance. Greater regulatory clarity may therefore weaken excessive behavioral reactions by improving the reliability of sustainability-related information available to investors.

Institutional investor participation also influences the operation of sentiment dynamics in sustainable finance markets. Institutional investors generally possess greater analytical resources, more formalized ESG evaluation procedures, and longer investment horizons than retail investors. Their participation may therefore stabilize market expectations by limiting short-term behavioral amplification associated with speculative trading and emotionally driven investment behavior.

At the same time, institutional influence does not necessarily eliminate sentiment-driven dynamics entirely. Even sophisticated investors may respond to sustainability-related narratives, transition uncertainty, or evolving regulatory expectations under conditions of incomplete information.

6.2 Information Environment and Narrative Amplification

Investor sentiment in sustainable finance markets is strongly influenced by the broader information environment through which ESG-related information is communicated and interpreted. Sustainability-related narratives disseminated through media coverage, policy discourse, corporate communication, and digital platforms shape collective expectations regarding green assets and sustainability transitions.

Because sustainable finance is closely associated with long-term environmental uncertainty and normative expectations, narrative processes may exert stronger influence than in conventional financial settings. Positive narratives surrounding climate innovation, renewable energy transitions, or sustainability leadership may reinforce optimistic market expectations, whereas narratives associated with greenwashing, regulatory inconsistency, or transition risks may intensify pessimistic reactions.

Digital communication platforms may further accelerate these dynamics by increasing the speed and scale of information diffusion. Social media interactions, online investment communities, and real-time news circulation may amplify investor attention toward sustainability-related developments and contribute to the persistence of sentiment-driven market reactions.

Narrative amplification therefore extends sentiment formation beyond individual cognitive interpretation by embedding ESG-related expectations within broader social and informational environments.

6.3 Dynamic Feedback Effects

Investor sentiment in sustainable finance markets should not be understood as a static response to isolated informational events. Instead, sentiment formation involves recursive feedback mechanisms through which market behavior, investor expectations, and sustainability-related information continuously interact.

Positive sentiment toward green assets may increase capital inflows into sustainable investment markets, attract additional media attention, and strengthen optimistic sustainability-related narratives. These developments may subsequently reinforce favorable investor expectations and contribute to additional investment activity in green financial instruments.

Conversely, negative sentiment may contribute to capital withdrawals, increased volatility, and broader pessimism regarding sustainability-related investment opportunities. Adverse policy developments, climate-related controversies, or concerns regarding ESG credibility may intensify uncertainty and amplify negative market reactions.

These recursive interactions suggest that sentiment dynamics in sustainable finance markets may exhibit persistence and path dependence, particularly in environments characterized by informational ambiguity and heterogeneous sustainability disclosure practices.

6.4 Sentiment-Driven Dynamics and Valuation Distortions

The framework developed in this chapter distinguishes between preference-based sustainable investing and sentiment-driven market dynamics. Preference-based approaches suggest that investors may rationally allocate capital toward green assets because they derive non-financial utility from sustainability objectives, ethical alignment, or climate-related concerns.

At the same time, some sustainability-related pricing dynamics may also reflect rational expectations regarding regulatory transition, long-term climate risk, and future cash-flow adjustments rather than sentiment-driven distortions alone.

However, behavioral amplification mechanisms may generate temporary valuation dynamics that exceed changes justified by underlying financial fundamentals. Under conditions of strong optimism, sustainability-related narratives, herding behavior, and heightened investor attention may contribute to excessive pricing dynamics in green asset markets. Conversely, negative sustainability-related developments may intensify pessimistic expectations and accelerate capital outflows from sustainable investment vehicles.

Distinguishing between equilibrium adjustments associated with sustainability preferences and temporary sentiment-driven distortions represents an important analytical challenge for future sustainable finance research.

Taken together, these structural and dynamic considerations indicate that investor sentiment in sustainable finance markets is shaped not only by informational inputs and psychological interpretation but also by regulatory conditions, institutional participation, narrative amplification mechanisms, and recursive market interactions.

7. EMPIRICAL RESEARCH AGENDA

The behavioral transmission framework developed in this chapter provides a conceptual basis for future empirical investigation of investor sentiment in sustainable finance markets. Because the framework involves informational, psychological, institutional, and market-level dimensions, empirical analysis requires research designs capable of capturing both direct and indirect relationships among these components.

The empirical agenda proposed here focuses on four main analytical priorities: measurement of ESG-related information, identification of sentiment formation mechanisms, analysis of capital allocation effects, and examination of dynamic market interactions.

7.1 Measurement of Core Constructs

Empirical investigation of the proposed framework requires the operationalization of several interrelated constructs. ESG-related information may be measured using sustainability disclosures, ESG ratings, climate-related announcements, or sustainability reporting indicators. These measures capture the informational environment within which investors evaluate green assets.

Investor sentiment in sustainable finance markets may be proxied using market-based and text-based indicators, including ESG-related news sentiment, social media sentiment measures, trading activity, and fund flows associated with sustainable investment vehicles.

In contrast, cognitive biases and emotional responses are less directly observable. These dimensions may therefore require indirect measurement through experimental methods, survey-based approaches, behavioral proxies, or investor attention indicators.

7.2 Empirical Identification of Behavioral Transmission Mechanisms

The proposed framework implies that ESG-related information influences capital allocation through mediating behavioral processes. Empirical investigation of these mechanisms therefore requires methodologies capable of modeling indirect relationships among variables.

Approaches such as Structural Equation Modeling (SEM) may be useful for examining mediation effects within the proposed framework.

Regression-based approaches may also be used to examine moderation effects associated with institutional and regulatory environments. Interaction terms may help identify whether disclosure quality, regulatory clarity, or institutional investor participation influence the strength of the relationship between ESG information and investor sentiment.

7.3 Capital Allocation and Market-Level Analysis

The relationship between investor sentiment and capital allocation may be examined using panel-data approaches linking sentiment indicators to investments in green bonds, ESG-oriented equities, or sustainable investment funds. Such approaches may help evaluate whether investor sentiment influences sustainable investment flows after controlling for firm-level and macroeconomic conditions.

Event-study methodologies may additionally be used to examine investor reactions to ESG-related announcements, sustainability disclosures, or climate-policy developments. These approaches are particularly useful for evaluating short-term market responses to sustainability-related informational events.

Quasi-experimental designs, including difference-in-differences approaches, may further support analysis of regulatory changes or sustainability-related policy interventions. Such methods may help distinguish between structural market adjustments and temporary sentiment-driven reactions.

7.4 Dynamic and Cross-Market Analysis

The framework also suggests the importance of dynamic interactions between investor sentiment, market volatility, and sustainability-related information environments. Time-series approaches may therefore provide additional insights into the persistence and amplification of sentiment dynamics in sustainable finance markets.

Methods such as vector autoregression (VAR) may be useful for examining feedback relationships between sentiment indicators, capital flows, and asset-price dynamics over time. Cross-country and cross-market comparisons may additionally help identify how institutional environments, regulatory systems, and disclosure quality influence sentiment formation across different sustainable finance settings.

Overall, the proposed empirical agenda is intended to support future investigation of the behavioral mechanisms linking ESG-related information to investor sentiment and capital allocation. The objective is not merely to measure market outcomes, but to examine how sustainability-related information is psychologically and socially translated into investment behavior within sustainable finance markets.

8. DISCUSSION AND CONTRIBUTIONS

The framework developed in this chapter provides a behavioral interpretation of sustainable investment decisions by explaining how ESG-related information is translated into investor sentiment and capital allocation through cognitive and emotional processes. Rather than assuming that investors respond to sustainability-related information through purely rational evaluation, the framework emphasizes that investment behavior in sustainable finance markets is shaped by informational ambiguity, heuristic interpretation, affective reactions, and socially transmitted expectations.

This perspective contributes to behavioral finance by extending investor sentiment theory into sustainable finance contexts characterized by uncertainty, heterogeneous disclosure practices, and normative investment considerations. While traditional sentiment research has primarily focused on conventional financial markets, the present framework highlights how sustainability-related information may function as a behavioral stimulus capable of influencing investor expectations and market behavior.

The chapter also contributes to sustainable finance research by shifting attention from outcome-oriented analysis toward the behavioral mechanisms underlying ESG-related investment decisions. Existing research has frequently examined ESG disclosure effects, financial performance, or capital flows independently. In contrast, the proposed framework integrates informational inputs, cognitive interpretation, emotional responses, investor sentiment, and capital allocation within a unified analytical structure.

A further contribution lies in the distinction between preference-based sustainable investing and sentiment-driven market dynamics. The framework suggests that investment in green assets may reflect both non-financial sustainability preferences and behavioral amplification mechanisms. This distinction is analytically important because the two mechanisms imply different interpretations of pricing dynamics in sustainable finance markets. Preference-based investment behavior may reflect long-term equilibrium adjustment, whereas sentiment-driven dynamics may generate temporary valuation distortions under incomplete sustainability disclosure and narrative amplification.

The framework additionally highlights the importance of institutional and informational environments in shaping investor sentiment. Regulatory clarity, disclosure quality, institutional investor participation, and sustainability-related narratives influence how ESG information is interpreted and transmitted into market behavior. As a result, investor sentiment should be understood not solely as an individual psychological phenomenon, but as a multi-level process shaped by interactions between investors, information systems, and market structures.

Taken together, the chapter contributes to the development of a more integrated behavioral perspective on sustainable finance. By conceptualizing investor sentiment as a behavioral mediation process, the framework provides a structured theoretical foundation for future empirical research examining the interaction between ESG-related information, investor behavior, and capital allocation in sustainable finance markets.

9. IMPLICATIONS, LIMITATIONS, AND CONCLUSION

9.1 Theoretical and Practical Implications

The framework developed in this chapter has several implications for research and practice in sustainable finance. From a theoretical perspective, the analysis suggests that ESG-related investment decisions cannot be fully explained through conventional risk–return models alone. Investor behavior in sustainable finance markets is also shaped by cognitive interpretation, emotional responses, informational ambiguity, and collective expectations.

This perspective implies that future sustainable finance research may benefit from incorporating behavioral variables into models of ESG-related investment behavior. Approaches focusing exclusively on financial fundamentals may overlook important mechanisms through which sustainability-related information influences market outcomes.

The framework also has implications for empirical research design. Because investor sentiment is conceptualized as a behavioral mediation process, future empirical studies should move beyond the isolated examination of ESG disclosures or market outcomes and instead investigate the intermediate psychological and informational processes linking sustainability-related information to capital allocation decisions.

From a practical perspective, the framework highlights the importance of informational credibility and regulatory clarity in sustainable finance markets. Standardized ESG disclosure systems and transparent sustainability-reporting practices may reduce interpretive uncertainty and mitigate excessive sentiment-driven reactions. Institutional investors may additionally play a stabilizing role by anchoring market expectations through longer investment horizons and more structured ESG evaluation processes.

9.2 Limitations

Several limitations of the present chapter should be acknowledged. First, the analysis is conceptual and does not empirically test the proposed relationships. The framework should therefore be interpreted as a theoretical structure intended to guide future empirical investigation rather than as a validated causal model.

Second, the framework simplifies complex psychological and market processes by organizing them into analytical stages. In practice, cognitive interpretation, emotional responses, investor sentiment, and market behavior may interact simultaneously and recursively rather than through strictly sequential relationships.

Third, the framework does not explicitly model heterogeneity across countries, regulatory systems, or investor categories. Differences in institutional quality, sustainability disclosure practices, and market maturity may influence the operation of the behavioral transmission mechanism across sustainable finance environments.

Finally, the framework focuses primarily on investor sentiment in relation to ESG-related information and green asset allocation. Other dimensions of sustainable finance, including corporate governance dynamics, macroeconomic transition risks, and political uncertainty, remain outside the scope of the present analysis.

9.3 Conclusion

This chapter developed a conceptual framework explaining how ESG-related information may influence capital allocation through a behavioral mediation process in sustainable finance markets. The analysis proposed that investor sentiment operates as an intermediate process linking sustainability-related informational signals to investment behavior under incomplete sustainability disclosure.

By integrating insights from behavioral finance and sustainable finance research, the chapter conceptualized investor sentiment as a multi-level phenomenon shaped by cognitive interpretation, emotional responses, narrative amplification, and institutional conditions. The framework additionally distinguished between preference-based sustainable investing and sentiment-driven market dynamics, thereby providing a more differentiated interpretation of pricing behavior in green asset markets.

Overall, the chapter provides a structured behavioral interpretation of how ESG-related information may influence investor sentiment and capital allocation in sustainable finance markets.

REFERENCES

Baker, M., & Wurgler, J. (2007). Investor sentiment in the stock market. *The Journal of Economic Perspectives, 21*(2), 129–152. DOI: 10.1257/jep.21.2.129

Barberis, N., Shleifer, A., & Vishny, R. (1998). A model of investor sentiment. *Journal of Financial Economics, 49*(3), 307–343. DOI: 10.1016/S0304-405X(98)00027-0

Christensen, H. B., Hail, L., & Leuz, C. (2021). Mandatory CSR and sustainability reporting: Economic analysis and literature review. *Review of Accounting Studies, 26*(3), 1176–1248. DOI: 10.1007/s11142-021-09609-5

De Long, J. B., Shleifer, A., Summers, L. H., & Waldmann, R. J. (1990). Noise trader risk in financial markets. *Journal of Political Economy, 98*(4), 703–738. DOI: 10.1086/261703

Friede, G., Busch, T., & Bassen, A. (2015). ESG and financial performance: Aggregated evidence from more than 2,000 empirical studies. *Journal of Sustainable Finance & Investment, 5*(4), 210–233. DOI: 10.1080/20430795.2015.1118917

Kahneman, D., & Tversky, A. (1979). Prospect theory: An analysis of decision under risk. *Econometrica, 47*(2), 263–291. DOI: 10.2307/1914185

Shiller, R. J. (2000). *Irrational exuberance*. Princeton University Press.

Su, C. W., Song, X. Y., Qin, M., Lobon , O. R., & Umar, M. (2024). Optimistic or pessimistic: How do investors impact the green bond market? *The North American Journal of Economics and Finance, 74*, 102248. DOI: 10.1016/j.najef.2024.102248

Chapter 2
Behavioural Drivers of Green Valuations:
Understanding Investor Sentiment in Sustainable Financial Markets

Muhammad Usman Tariq
http://orcid.org/0000-0002-7605-3040
Abu Dhabi University, UAE & University College Cork, Ireland

ABSTRACT

Green asset valuations now appear to be influenced by various behavioral factors in addition to fundamental factors. This chapter examines the impact of investor sentiment, norms, and cognitive factors on green financial markets. This study uses various research studies on behavioral finance and sustainability to examine the factors that influence green asset valuations. This chapter examines how positive sentiments lead to green asset premiums, reduced required rates of return, and increased flows into green assets, while changes in sentiments may cause increased asset price volatility and mispricing. It will also test the reaction of different types of investors to green asset valuation, such as the way institutional investors, retail investors, and different generations respond to the risks of climate change. The present study synthesizes research studies on green asset valuations that provide insights into the effect of various factors on green asset valuation, such as whether green premiums are caused by long-run risk mitigation or behavioral overreaction

INTRODUCTION

The significant increase in the development of green finance over the past two decades has substantially impacted how financial markets channel their resources,

DOI: 10.4018/979-8-3373-8392-7.ch002

measure their risks, and create value. Initially, green finance was a niche topic that primarily focused on ethical investing. However, green finance is now an integral part of the global financial landscape and is being promoted and facilitated by regulators, institutions and investors. The development of green finance is influenced by a combination of environmental objectives, financial decisions and human activities. However, green finance does not entirely rely on rational factors and is influenced by perceptions, beliefs, emotions, and social factors. Hence, the importance of behavioral finance in the context of green finance and how markets operate sustainably cannot be overstated. Conventional financial theories suggest that investors are rational and base their investment decisions on rational factors. Additionally, they can process all relevant and available information efficiently to achieve the highest possible return on investment. However, the increasing importance of environmental, social, and governance factors indicates that investors are also influenced by their values, narratives, and emotions (Jain & Chawla, 2025). The link between green finance and behavioral finance is evident in the way investors perceive risks and opportunities. Systemic risks include climate change, loss of biodiversity, and depletion of resources, which need to be considered from a long-term perspective and cannot be quantified using conventional financial tools. In such cases, investors use not only objective measures but also their subjective perceptions of possible future outcomes to make decisions.

Behavioral finance sheds light on why some investors choose to invest in green assets despite the lack of clear short-term financial rewards, while others remain cautious even with clear evidence of climate change. The reasons are psychological factors, which include fear of loss, overconfidence, and aversion to uncertainty, which are major factors in the perception and management of environmental risks. A pricing error could be an overreaction by investors to the cost of switching to low-carbon assets due to the tendency to stick to the status quo or overreact to green assets in a highly environmentally conscious time. Sustainable market behavior is influenced by social and cultural factors beyond individual actions (Liu et al., 2025). Financial markets are social structures in which norms, peer behaviors, and reputations play a role. As sustainability continues to grow in corporate and regulatory practices, social forces will have a greater effect on investors' consideration of environmental sustainability values in their portfolios. Behavioral finance has highlighted how these pressures may be compounded by imitation in sustainable investing because investors can imitate other investors in green investing because of fear of reputation or fear of missing out. The increasing popularity of ESG funds is also a good case study where investment is not simply made based on performance but also due to a perception of its moral and strategic value. Another significant factor in the relationship between green finance and behavioral finance is information processing and interpretation. Behavioral Finance helps to explain why investors tend to rely too heavily on high ESG scores without scrutinizing the underlying approaches or why bad news about the environment can trigger strong market responses. Stories win in sustainable markets where interesting stories about clean energy transitions and corporate climate action create feelings and expectations. Investors are affected by these stories on their perception of green assets, reinforcing the basis of behavioral finance of valuation. Sentiment is an important factor influencing investment decisions in the ESG-oriented investment area.

In contrast to conventional financial variables, sustainability performance is frequently abstract, long-term, and emotion-laden. This makes it highly susceptible to sentiments, beliefs, and emotional reactions. Favorable attitudes towards the concept of sustainability would help reduce risks, lower the cost of capital, and increase the demand for green bonds (Maurya et al., 2026). Combining their investment values with values can bring psychological rewards to investors, a phenomenon known as moral satisfaction or warm-glow investing. This psychological benefit can counteract the requirement of reduced financial returns in the short term, hence affecting asset prices. The behavioral finance framework can be applied to explain the relationships between non-financial drivers and traditional risk-return trade-offs. Simultaneously, sentiment-based investing creates new volatility and uncertainty in sustainable financial markets. Investors' interest in green assets fluctuates based on media coverage, political events, and high-profile climate change events. Investors' sentiment towards green assets might be high at certain periods, which could result in their overvaluation. However, changes in investors' sentiment can also result in significant price corrections. Behavioral biases, such as recency and availability biases, could also contribute to market cycles. For example, a major climate policy announcement could result in a price bubble in green assets, regardless of whether such a policy has a long-term financial impact in the long run. However, accusations of greenwashing could also result in a rapid loss of investors' trust in green assets. These factors demonstrate the significance of sentiment as a major driver of, as well as contributor to, financial market volatility. The significance of sentiment is also evident in the variety of ESG-focused investors.

For instance, institutional investors, retail investors, and younger generations have different behavioral patterns and drivers. Fiduciary duty, regulatory requirements, and reputation are some of the reasons why institutional investors can be motivated, unlike retail investors, who are more concerned with their own values and identity expression. Behavioral finance suggests that differences in climate change awareness and risk perception among different generational groups can influence investors' expression and implementation of sentiment (Sultana & Zeya, 2025). Younger generations, who are more likely to regard climate change as an important problem, may have stronger positive sentiments towards sustainability and be more inclined to invest in green assets despite uncertainty. Trust is a critical and sensitive component of green finance. In green finance, trust is an essential factor because an investor must believe in ESG information, sustainability standards, and regulatory compliance to be convinced that green investments are making a real change to the environment. The theory of behavioral finance demonstrates that trust can be built up by a series of positive reinforcements, although it can be broken easily by bad incidents. Once trust is built, investors can afford to lack transparency and stick to the fundamental rules of thumb. Nevertheless, once trust is eroded, mistrust may develop at a very fast rate and influence the general attitude towards the market in all types of assets. Ultimately, to comprehend the link between green finance, behavioral finance, and sustainable market behavior, it is necessary to understand that markets are determined by both rational analysis and human psychology.

Furthermore, decisions based on ESG criteria are not only based on rational analysis and risk assessment but also on beliefs regarding the future, social identity and feelings of moral obligation. Sentiments play a crucial role in linking environmental values and financial outcomes, which can translate into real-world market behavior (Jain and Chawla, 2025). By understanding the psychological underpinnings of green finance, researchers and practitioners can better evaluate situations in which market prices are based on real long-term value creation or sentiment-driven biases. This is particularly important for creating stronger, more credible, and more effective sustainable financial markets in a rapidly changing environment.

This chapter examines the effects of investor sentiment, behavioral biases, trust, herding behavior, and ESG-related perceptions on the valuation of green financial assets. The main research question is as follows: What is the role of behavioral finance aspects in investor perceptions and market valuation in green finance? With the response to this question, the chapter forms a behavioral explanation of green asset valuation, as well as the interaction of psychological, social, regulatory, and market-based aspects of sustainable finance. Figure 1 provides the conceptual framework of behavioural green asset valuation.

Figure 1. Conceptual Framework of Behavioural Green Asset Valuation

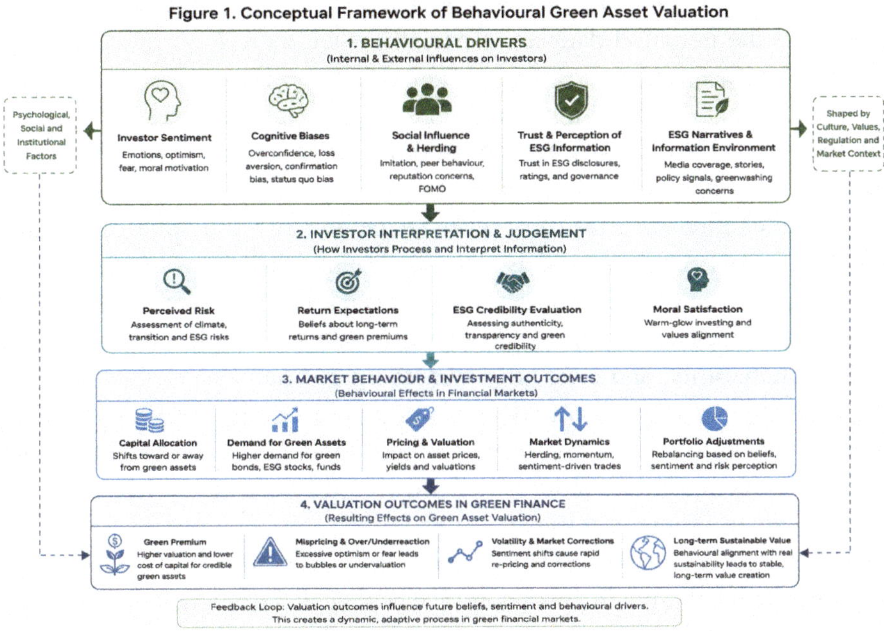

INVESTOR SENTIMENT AND BEHAVIOURAL BIASES IN GREEN MARKETS

Investors' emotions significantly affect the behavior of individuals in green financial markets. Green financial markets are characterized by uncertainty, long-term orientation, and lack of information. Unlike other investments, ESG investments rely heavily on what people think about future regulations, new technologies, and societal attitudes towards the environment. Because these factors are not always certain, people resort to rules of thumb to make decisions (Hidayat-ur-Rehman et al., 2025). Rules of thumb assist people in understanding complex decision-making. They are not wrong; they are merely a means of dealing with excessive information. However, in green markets, these rules of thumb can affect investments, value, and risk. They can also lead to more extreme trends, depending on how people feel. One of the most common "shortcuts" in ESG investing is the use of the representativeness heuristic.

Investors tend to judge an investment based on how similar it is to what they think of as "green" companies. For example, companies specializing in renewable energy, electric cars, or clean technologies tend to be automatically viewed as safe investments, even in cases where their sustainability is unknown (Tariq, 2024). This can cause investors to overestimate the potential of these companies and underestimate the potential dangers, especially when there is so much interest in the environment itself. Conversely, companies that specialize in more traditional, carbon-based industries tend to be judged harshly, even when they are working to change their ways. This makes it easier to think about, but can cause investors to miscalculate the value of the companies. Another significant shortcut is anchoring (Mertzanis and Tebourbi, 2025). For instance, people may use initial ESG ratings, the initial performance of green funds, or general figures such as carbon scores. After this, people tend to stick with what they have, even after new information becomes available. For instance, a company may have started with high initial ratings as a leader in sustainability, and even after something bad happens to them, they may still be viewed positively. This may result in people being overly optimistic and thus failing to correct overpriced assets in a green market. The availability heuristic causes people to concentrate more on information they can easily remember, such as recent events or dramatic stories.

If the media frequently reports on climate change problems, clean technologies, and regulatory changes, it will affect how investors view the urgency of these matters (Banerjee et al., 2025). If people are made aware of these matters, they may think that climate change is a pressing concern, hence the need for green investments. However, if the media do not report on these matters, people may lose interest, which affects the level of investment in green markets. This shows that investors' behavior in green markets is affected by what is being reported as much as the risks they face. Social heuristics are also strong in sustainable finance, especially through herd behavior. Humans tend to follow what other people, such as institutions and market leaders, do. Such a move can create trends where more people get into it, causing prices to rise. Although this can accelerate the adoption of sustainable finance, it can also create a situation where too many people are doing the same thing, thus making markets more volatile to a change in heart. In addition to these shortcuts, deep emotions and thoughts also play a significant role in how people feel and perceive risks in green markets.

Optimism is one factor that can play a significant role in ESG investing, as people might think that the shift towards a low-carbon economy is happening quickly and is a huge success story. This is because there are many stories about innovation, politics, and morality, and therefore, there is a feeling that green growth is inevitable. This might help more investments flow into green solutions in the future. However, optimism might cause people to overlook the fact that technology might not develop quickly enough or that there might be political hurdles to overcome. However, fear in green markets is not the same as that in traditional markets. Rather than thinking about price movements in the short term, they are also thinking about climate change, rules, and things that will not be valuable in the future. Investors might fear that they are in a carbon-intensive industry that could lose demand, face legal consequences, or be harmed by policies. They might avoid "brown" assets, even if they are profitable, because of fear. However, fear is also increased by loss aversion, where people feel the pain of potential loss more than they feel the excitement of potential gains. They may also be ready to receive fewer green assets because of their anxiety about climate change (Maurya et al., 2026). Another factor that affects the risk assessment of ESG investments is ambiguity aversion, a feeling of discomfort with risks that are not clearly defined. Sustainable investments are associated with new technologies, changing rules, and unclear performance results. Therefore, they may be viewed as indecisive. Certain individuals may not be encouraged to invest in green investments because they feel that there is a risk on their side, while others may view this risk as an opportunity to realize higher returns. As such, green investments are capable of high rates of growth and are highly volatile. People's attitudes toward uncertainty play a significant role in establishing investment decisions. Emotional factors also affect individuals' processing of sustainability-related information.

If people feel hopeful, proud, or satisfied, they may be more likely to be positive about ESG investments because they associate it with feelings of personal identity related to the concept of sustainability investing. It is as if they are expressing themselves rather than simply investing (Bhatnagar & Rajaram, 2024). This may cause them to continue investing even if they are not getting good returns, but it may also cause them to be resistant to questioning their investments. However, if people feel anxious or guilty about environmental harm, they may be more likely to leave an industry, even if it is best from a financial perspective to remain in that industry. This proves that green market behavior is linked to individuals' emotions. At the group level, people's feelings about green markets depend on how well prices, stories, and beliefs mesh together. When prices rise, people feel hopeful, which means new investors come in, and decisions made in the past look brilliant. This is a cycle where everything gets better and better because everyone is enthusiastic. People also look for news that makes them feel good about green and ignore news that does not make them feel that way.

However, if people's feelings change, this cycle can reverse itself. If policies do not work well, technology does not work well, and corporations are just pretending to be green, then people's confidence can shift really fast. Fear and doubt can spread rapidly and cause huge declines in market value that are much larger than the actual change in the real world. It is crucial to recognize how investors feel and the mental patterns that influence their behavior in the green market (Uddin et al., 2025). Mental patterns help people make decisions quickly, but they can also cause people to misinterpret things. Emotions and social factors significantly influence investors' responses to good news, fear, and the possibility of losing money. Green markets are more than just wise financial decisions. They also involve how values, emotions, and social influences shape financial decisions. By recognizing these emotional and social patterns, investors, leaders, and businesses can improve their ability to predict what will happen in the market, develop better ways to support sustainability, and design investment spaces that are both hopeful and realistic at the same time. In this way, sustainable finance can be more dependable and trustworthy without losing the motivation that comes from positive emotions when pursuing long-term environmental objectives.

MEASURING AND MODELLING SENTIMENT IN SUSTAINABLE FINANCE

Measuring and modeling the sentiment of sustainable finance is an increasingly important topic as the role of ESG factors shifts from being a secondary concern to a primary concern in investment decision-making. By the term "sentiment," we mean the general feelings, thoughts, and emotional responses people have about certain topics, companies, and assets that are relevant to sustainability (Jain & Chawla, 2025). The sentiment of sustainable finance is influenced by more factors than the sentiment of traditional financial markets, which tend to concentrate on factors such as corporate results and economic indicators. These include environmental factors, policy discussions, company announcements, and societal values. It is not easy to measure all these factors accurately, but it is important for understanding the markets, the flow of money, and the risks of green markets. One of the most popular methods for measuring ESG sentiment is the use of market and non-market indicators together.

Market indicators include unusual trading volumes, funds going into ESG products, a premium price for green assets, and changes in volatility when sustainability news is released. For instance, if investors continue to invest in green products, it usually indicates that they are positive about sustainability. In addition, the gap between the returns of the green and ordinary bonds can show how much the investors are ready to give up returns to receive environmental benefits. These indicators can be easily tracked, but they normally indicate the result of sentiment and not sentiment itself. To better understand what people think, researchers have examined text-based sources of information (Yao & Yang, 2025). These include corporate sustainability reports, earnings calls, analyst reports, government filings, news articles and social media. All of these sources have a lot of qualitative information on how sustainability is discussed and perceived. With text analytics, it is possible to convert unstructured data into numerical sentiment scores. This can then be used to determine whether people are becoming more positive, negative, or skeptical about ESG-related issues. If people use more positive words when talking about climate strategies on earnings calls, it could be that management is confident about them, and that could be influencing investors' opinions even before actual results are out. Dictionary-based sentiment analysis is sometimes used as the first step in ESG text analytics.

Dictionary-based sentiment analysis uses lists of words, each of which is defined as positive, negative, or unclear, with some words related to sustainability (Balaji, 2024). However, it is sometimes less effective in dealing with the complexities of sustainability-related words. For example, a word such as "risk" may refer to a positive way of managing risk; therefore, a more sophisticated analysis is required. Quantitative models are employed to integrate sentiment measures into financial models to analyze their impact on prices, returns, and risk.

Time-series models are commonly employed to examine the relationship between changes in ESG sentiment and asset performance or volatility (Kumar et al., 2025). With the introduction of sentiment indices in the model, it can be determined whether positive sustainability sentiment correlates with a high stock price or low returns. Conversely, cross-sectional models focus on how disparities in sentiment among firms or industries are related to market results. These models enable analyses to move beyond sentiment descriptions and facilitate a more in-depth examination of the relationship between behavior and sustainable finance. Factor-based models can also help link sentiment to asset pricing.

Unlike other methods, machine learning models can handle large volumes of unstructured data and identify complex and intricate patterns, which is difficult for traditional methods. Natural language processing models, particularly neural networks and transformer models, are well-suited for processing sustainability-related texts. They enable these models to recognize even minor alterations in tone and context across various sources, which gives a more detailed picture of how sentiments change. For example, supervised learning algorithms can be applied to identify optimistic, neutral, or pessimistic sustainability-related content based on labeled news articles and company publications. Once the model is trained, it can be used to provide a score that is similar to the real time. Another type of unsupervised learning that can be used to determine the most important topics in ESG discussions is topic modeling. This is especially helpful in new fields of sustainability, as language is changing rapidly. Machine learning could also be useful in combining different datasets into one model to analyze sentiments. The source of ESG sentiment is not from one place; it is the culmination of news, policies, markets and social media interactions (Singh & Chouhan, 2024). Machine learning can be applied to integrate various data sources by weighing their value for prediction. Dramatic changes in policy tone could make more sense to long-term investors, whereas social media could show the short-term mood in the market. This is because the combination of these data sources can be achieved by learning the data, which can enable AI to be more accurate and reliable in the form of prediction. It is also important to predict ESG sentiment with greater importance, especially in the management of risks and smart decisions in investment. Models such as recurrent neural networks and other sequence-related tools are particularly effective in understanding how sentiment shifts. These models can identify warning signs of a change in sentiment, such as increased negative news on climate change or increased discussion on greenwashing. While making predictions on sentiment may not necessarily result in accurate price predictions, it can help in understanding how a market will respond and how volatile it will be. Although these methods show great promise, they also raise pertinent issues regarding sustainable finance.

It is also essential that models be transparent and simple to comprehend, particularly when it comes to ESG investing, as it encompasses many legal and ethical issues. Some models are called black box models, and although they can produce correct results, they do not explain how they arrived at those results, which can create mistrust among investors and regulators. Another problem that can occur is data quality, as ESG-related texts can be biased, worded, and vary from one dataset to another. This may result in machine learning models trained on such datasets, which provide results that are equally biased.

ESG Performance, Stock Returns, and Market Valuation

The link between the effectiveness of companies in dealing with environmental, social, and governance (ESG) factors, stock market returns, and stock market valuations has become an important topic in the field of sustainable finance. This is because it shakes up the traditional views of value creation in financial markets. ESG scores are expected to reflect how well a company manages environmental, social, and governance risks and opportunities. However, they do not directly provide information on stock market returns or valuations. They reflect investors' perceptions of sustainability at any given time. Investors' beliefs and expectations ultimately impact stock market valuations based on ESG scores. Thus, the actual impact of ESG effectiveness is not based on ESG scores but on what investors think of sustainability at any particular point in time. Market sentiment acts as a filter for ESG score. When market sentiment towards sustainability is high, ESG scores are likely to be interpreted as reflecting good management, lower risks, and better opportunities for growth. In this type of market structure, a company with a high ESG rating will probably receive a high valuation because investors would charge a premium to buy a company they feel is future-proof or in fashion with trends. These high valuations are not only due to expected higher profits. Rather, they also result from a lower required return, as investors are comfortable with the risks related to sustainability. When market sentiment towards sustainability is low, ESG scores are not likely to be considered important, or they might even be considered as costs. The perception of the company's financial performance is also subject to the influence of the way investors view the company, which is related to sentiment. For example, positive financial results from a company with high ESG scores during a period of positive sustainability sentiment can cause stock prices to increase significantly. This is because of confirmation bias, where the financial results of the company are viewed from the perspective of investors' pre-existing beliefs regarding the company's sustainability. On the other hand, the financial results of a company with low ESG scores may be viewed with skepticism, especially if there is a concern regarding the regulations and the environment. The complex relationship between these variables has been observed in studies conducted in the equity market (Maurya et al., 2026). Green stocks, which refer to companies that focus on providing solutions for the environment, tend to perform well during times when there is more focus and support for the environment. The positive performance of these stocks is often related to increasing valuations, which means that the stocks benefit from a high level of demand. However, the long-term success of these stocks varies, with some performing well while others may experience a decrease in value, especially if the expectations are high. Investors' risk perceptions also influence the relationship between ESG performance and stock returns.

Firms with strong ESG performance are typically associated with effective risk management, lower sensitivity to regulations, and a stronger ability to withstand environmental or social crises. If risk management is a major issue, investors may favor such firms by assigning them lower stock price volatility and higher stock prices, even if their returns are not very high. However, in more speculative markets, investors may focus on growth opportunities rather than risk management, regardless of ESG performance (Sultana & Zeya, 2025). This indicates that ESG performance does not have a uniform effect on stock returns; rather, it depends on prevailing market conditions. Another perspective on how ESG performance and sentiment interact is provided by green bonds. Green bonds are directly linked to environmentally positive projects and represent a good example of sustainability-related valuations. Research indicates that green bonds have lower yields than conventional bonds, a fact referred to as the greenium. This is attributed to the fact that investors are ready to receive low yields because of the favorable environmental and reputation-based gains attached to green bonds. Sentiment plays a crucial role in maintaining greenium, as the level of support for sustainability is quite high; therefore, green bonds have higher valuation advantages than conventional bonds. However, Greenium is not always available in the market. The higher the environmental concerns, the greater the demand for green bonds, and governments encourage them through regulations, which provides greater benefits in terms of valuation. Nonetheless, the liquidity and credit risk concerns of investors can prevail over their sustainability concerns during financial pressure and market uncertainty, eliminating the greenium. Assets such as carbon markets, renewable energy funds, and climate transition ETFs are also examples of how sentiment affects ESG valuations. These are extremely sensitive to policies and discussions regarding climate change. If there is a positive sentiment due to high climate goals or new technologies, there could be more investments and an upward trend in valuations. However, if there is uncertainty regarding policies or issues such as false or exaggerated claims (greenwashing), positive sentiment could change to negative quickly.

In all these examples, one common factor is evident: ESG ratings often differ from one agency to another, which confuses investors. Market sentiment also influences the management of ESG ratings. In the case of a good market temper, investors can ignore these differences and concentrate on positive ratings. However, when market sentiment is poor, such differences can cause confusion, and the confidence level of investors is low. This suggests that ESG ratings do not provide adequate explanations for the way markets prefer companies. The overall market sentiment environment plays an important role in how ESG affects stock prices. The second important aspect is the investment time horizon. Sustainability investors are also long-term investors who might consider ESG performance as a long-term value creation that is not as sensitive to market fluctuations. In contrast, short-term investors can be more affected by changes in the mood of the market, buying or selling ESG-related news on sentiment without referring to fundamental performance (Maurya et al., 2026). This interaction between short- and long-term investors is one aspect of the complicated association between ESG performance, returns, and valuation. Finally, evidence from green equities, green bonds, and climate assets indicates that the financial outcomes of ESG performance are affected by the behavior channel as much as by financial fundamentals.

POLICY, REGULATION, AND GOVERNANCE IMPACTS

The psychological and structural aspects of how policies impact market behavior should not be ignored. Policy, regulation, and governance are very important factors in the development of a sustainable financial market because it is not only about the rules and regulations set but also how these rules and regulations impact the perception of investors about risks and value. In terms of ESG investing, policy information is as important as financial information because it impacts investors' perception of future costs and opportunities and how these costs and opportunities can impact the present and future of a firm. The psychological and structural effects of policies on market behavior should not be overlooked (Akinde et al., 2025). One of the most direct ways through which regulations affect investors'sentiment is through disclosure requirements, particularly those related to ESG. The requirements are meant to standardize the information so that investors can more easily compare firms and understand the risks of sustainable investments. Where disclosure requirements are robust and consistent, this increases investors' confidence, which in turn positively impacts their sentiment towards sustainable assets. Investors are more likely to trust ESG ratings and claims of companies where they are backed by regulations. This can, in turn, mean that the company benefits from higher valuations where it has performed well in terms of ESG, as the risk is mitigated by the disclosure level. Climate policy strongly influences market sentiment, as it affects the overall market perception of the future economic environment.

Climate policies, for example, include carbon pricing, emissions reduction targets, renewable energy incentives, and green industrial plans, which provide a sense of direction for the future of entire industries. If climate policies are considered credible and long-lasting, they can produce positive market sentiment, which can lead investors to invest in low-carbon technologies and climate change-related companies. However, the ever-shifting climate policies, the slowness of their response in implementing climate policies, and the political response may create an unfavorable market feedback, which makes investors apprehensive of climate change-related markets and makes the entire market more volatile. Green bond structures, taxonomies, and prudential measures are regulatory instruments that offer a viable financing system in countries where regulatory bodies promote mainstream green investment instead of niche investments. This facilitates the overcoming of the behavioral risks of sustainable investing and the incorporation of ESG into conventional portfolios by investors (Bhatnagar & Rajaram, 2024). ESG investing is more likely to be viewed as value-driven rather than value-enhancing in regulatory systems that lack regulatory reinforcement or whose regulatory system seems vague, which is less desirable to a limited number of investors. Policy interventions can also indirectly influence sentiment by their influence on corporate behavior, another way through which the interventions could also influence sentiment. Regulatory forces can compel companies to change their strategy, disclosure, and governance, which in turn impacts investors' perceptions. An example is stricter regulations on emissions, which could prompt companies to increase their decarbonization measures, which can be seen as an indicator of adaptability and futurist-proofing. However, this can backfire if investors view regulatory compliance as expensive or illogically controlled in the short run. Corporate sustainability governance is crucial in mediating the impact of policies and regulations on market sentiment. Corporate governance affects how seriously companies take their sustainability commitments and how well they can integrate ESG considerations into their decision-making processes. Investors are now more focused on their boards' oversight of ESG issues, executive incentives for meeting sustainability goals, and internal risk management processes. Good corporate governance is seen to positively impact credibility and trustworthiness, thereby increasing market sentiment, even in a setting where there are good policies. Conversely, with positive policies, weak or tokenistic corporate governance weakens investor trust. The most noticeable examples of this governance/sentiment nexus are market reactions to controversies concerning sustainability. Properly managed companies can contain the negative market effect of environmental and social accidents because investors are convinced that the issues will be resolved successfully. This religion extinguishes sentiments and reduces their effects on firm value. On the other hand, poorly governed firms can have extreme market sales because investors are scared of systemic issues and law penalties. This can be seen as an example of how governance affects investors' sentiment and perceptions. Enforcement also affects the market sentiment. Enforced rules provide a sense of fairness and predictability, which are important for long-term investments. If investors feel that sustainability standards are enforced, they will be more confident in ESG products and, in turn, disclosures. However, a lack of enforcement may lead to a lack of confidence among investors, as they may doubt whether ESG products and disclosures are genuine or merely marketing. In such a situation, market sentiment may become cautious, and the effectiveness of policy initiatives may be reduced in promoting sustainable financing.

The enforcement of rules also affects market sentiment. Another factor is the global nature of financial markets, which adds another level of complexity to the relationship between policy, governance, and sentiment. Regulatory policies and practices vary from country to country, which makes sustainability landscapes more fragmented. This makes it difficult for investors to form expectations. Initiatives taken by various nations to harmonize disclosure practices and climate reporting are an attempt to solve this problem by removing uncertainty and enhancing comparability. Upon the identification of such developments by investors, they will likely positively affect sentiment, as the problem of regulatory fragmentation is known to be decreasing. Sustainability communication is also influenced by corporate governance. Investor confidence can be maintained through transparent, constant, and balanced communication, even during significant transition-related challenges (Kumar et al., 2025). On the other hand, there is the risk of investor skepticism caused by promotional and ambiguous communication, resulting in credibility. According to behavioral finance, investors are very particular about the perceived integrity of a firm, particularly regarding social and environmental values. Sustainability stories can be connected to actual actions to endorse positive investor sentiment through good corporate governance. Ultimately, policy, regulation, and governance come together to create an environment in which sustainable finance is conducted. This is important to note because their overall effect on markets is more than just the cost of compliance or even financial incentives; it is also behavioral in nature. For example, disclosure policies create trust, climate change policies create expectations, and governance arrangements create credibility. All of this plays into how investors view sustainability, what they make of ESG reporting, and how they are willing to invest in green assets. It is important to understand this to create policies and business models that are not only good for sustainable practices but also for long-term, lasting attitudes within markets. This is especially true in a world where values, regulations, and finance are increasingly intertwined.

GLOBAL PERSPECTIVES AND CROSS-COUNTRY INSIGHTS

The phenomenon of green finance has become a trend on the global scene; however, its growth rate in various economies and geographic areas is quite different. Investors' attitudes toward sustainability can be determined by several economic, institutional, cultural, and regulatory factors, and differences in these factors can occur among economies. Hence, investor behavior in green markets also differs, creating a unique perspective for understanding the reasons behind the unique development of sustainable finance across different parts of the world, as well as the unique outcomes in financial markets in response to similar ESG trends. In developed economies, green financial markets are generally characterized by a strong institutional framework, developed financial system, and high level of environmental consciousness. The institutional mechanisms that drive investor sentiment in these markets are obligatory disclosures, institutionalized ESG rating systems, and a high degree of institutional investor holdings in these markets. This gives a high need for green assets, and as such, the services will generate valuation premiums and a low cost of capital. Emotions are not the only factor that would lead to investor sentiment in these markets, since it is equally founded on expectations of future regimes around regulations, technology, and economic stability. Variations have also been observed in similar cross-country analyses in developed countries (Çoban et al., 2025). For example, European nations are more consistent in their pro-sustainability sentiments than other nations. This is due to their dynamic climate policies, sustainability rules, and culture of social responsibility. Environmental impact on equities and bonds Green premiums are further strengthened as investors in these countries are prepared to receive lower returns. Sentiment in other developed countries might be less stable, with a high degree of variability in response to changes in the political environment. In emerging markets, green market behavior can vary substantially (Tariq, 2024).

Even though the overall interest in sustainability is increasing, the sentiment of the market can vary substantially and is more closely tied to overall macro conditions (Jain & Chawla, 2025). In such markets, increased uncertainty, currency risk, and political risk can dominate concerns over sustainability, and ESG investing becomes more closely tied to global risk appetite. In such markets, the sentiment towards green assets can rise substantially during a global surge of optimism and strong international backing, only to fall during a tightening of global financial conditions, as the overall focus of the investor shifts more to current financial stability than sustainability. ESG information is available to varying degrees across nations, which influences the formation and diffusion of sentiments.

Developed markets tend to enjoy robust disclosure norms that are strictly enforced, thereby instilling confidence in investors. Conversely, emerging markets have dual disclosure norms and thus can have reduced availability of ESG information. This lack of ESG data could lead to investors basing their feelings on stories and other extraneous factors. International media and development finance, as well as world climate summits, are important in creating sentiments in emerging markets with volatile changes in investor flows (Maurya et al., 2026). Cultural factors are also involved in cross-cultural differences in green behavior, which are sentiment-based. Sustainability is permeated by societal attitudes towards environmental stewardship, institutional trust, and collective action. Investor sentiment in climate adaptation may be more sensitive in areas where environmental issues are considered health or economic risks. In other parts of the world, sustainability as a luxury good takes a backseat to economic growth and employment opportunities. Cultural considerations drive investor sentiment and corporate behavior, perpetuating country-specific trends in green market development. This can be explained using the following example from the global green bond market. In developed markets, the other support provided to the green bond market typically embraces the standards, availability of the secondary market, and institutional investors. The mood of investors in these markets tends to remain constant, and green bonds are regarded as valid sources of financing green projects. Conversely, the green bond market in emerging economies is typically dependent on the endorsement of third parties, as the latter tend to certify green bonds. In these markets, investor sentiment is usually sensitive to issues of credibility and political risk. There is also the role of global capital flows, which develop sentiment-driven behavior.

Foreign investors can be agents of sustainability standards and transmit the moods of developed nations to new ones. In the case of positive global feelings towards green assets, emerging economies can enjoy the fruits of global investments, particularly in renewable energy and infrastructure (Singh & Chouhan, 2024). However, the situation can change in an instant if global sentiments turn against green investments or emerging countries are perceived to be risky. The difference in the credibility of policies may also be a factor in the difference between developed and emerging markets.

Investors in developed markets may see climate change policies as credible, which may help sustain their positive sentiments. In emerging markets, sustainability targets can be ambitious, but implementation might be of concern; hence, it could influence the feelings of investors as they will be in doubt as to whether the sustainability targets will be translated into action. Behavioral finance states that sentiment can be volatile because of ambiguity aversion. Nevertheless, signs of convergence are observed in sentiment-based green behavior in various countries. Attempts to standardize ESG criteria worldwide, raise awareness of climate-related risks, and the ever-increasing power of global investors are creating a common concept of sustainability stories (Banerjee et al., 2025). The younger generation of investors in different regions is likely to display stronger sentiment in favor of the environment, which may indicate that differences between countries are likely to decrease in the future. Finally, examining how different countries view green markets based on how people feel about them will reveal a mix of common and unique situations. Therefore, even though climate change is a problem for everyone, investors' feelings about sustainability and how these feelings translate into action may differ across countries. In addition, for developed markets, how people feel about sustainability will be more organized and predictable, while for newer markets, these feelings may change significantly depending on how the economy is performing and other external influences. Therefore, it is crucial for investors, leaders, and companies to understand these differences as they deal with sustainable finance worldwide. This further proves that green markets are not only defined by money but also by society, depending on how a country has developed historically, its systems, and its common beliefs, as much as they depend on how they have addressed global environmental concerns.

PRACTICAL IMPLICATIONS FOR INVESTORS AND POLICYMAKERS

There are strong practical implications for investors and policymakers in the increasing role of sentiment and behavior in sustainable finance. With the development of green markets, there is increasing awareness that capital is being impacted by ESG core values, perceptions, emotions, and social interactions. Nevertheless, awareness of these facts does not weaken the argument supporting sustainable finance but provides a more realistic way of making a choice. Investors can be more successful by identifying these biases and learning to deal with them, and policymakers can develop frameworks that are stable, credible, and confident about green markets (Loang & Candra, 2025). One of the biggest challenges for investors is managing their exposure to various behavioral biases.

One of the biggest challenges for investors is managing their exposure to various behavioral biases. ESG investing is a complex process with uncertain outcomes and long-term timeframes. Consequently, it is prone to diverse behavioral prejudices and emotional reactions compared to humans. Investors can also be overconfident in green growth narratives or overly rely on ESG labels. Similarly, investors can track other investors who invest in different sustainability themes. Nevertheless, investors may control their exposure to these biases through formal decision-making processes. Investors can have specific criteria and goals for their investments. Thus, investors can limit their exposure to various biases and emotional responses. Diversification is another approach that investors can take when dealing with behavioral biases in their sustainable investment portfolios. Investors may end up investing in a few green sectors or technologies because of their preferences rather than the underlying investment case (Jain & Chawla, 2025). By diversifying their portfolios, investors will not only avoid the risk of sentiment-driven bubbles and corrections, but they will also take a balanced approach to sustainability. This is because they will realize that the approach to sustainability will not be the same across all sectors and regions. By adopting a diversified approach, investors will not become moral absolutists, which often contributes to behavioral biases. Long-term orientation is particularly effective in countering behavioral biases in ESG investing.

Sustainability-related benefits and risks are often long-term in nature; however, investors' sentiment tends to shift rapidly due to changing news and market environments. By adopting a long-term orientation rather than one based on market reactions, investors are better able to withstand market volatility. Scenario analysis, stress testing, and forward-looking risk analysis are techniques that can aid investors in adopting a long-term orientation (Maurya et al., 2026). Using these techniques, investors can translate the intangible climate-related risks faced by companies and markets into tangible financial implications. Informed sentiment analysis is another important factor that plays a vital role in making markets more resilient. Instead of dismissing investors' sentiment as something that is not important and should not influence investment decisions, investors can use it as an important factor in making investment decisions. Using investors' sentiment analysis, investors can gauge whether sustainable markets are overpriced or undervalued. This does not involve predicting investors' sentiment but rather understanding when investors' emotions are likely to influence the market price. Similarly, from a behavioral perspective, it is equally significant for policymakers to formulate effective sustainable finance instruments. Table 1 provides overview of practical implications for stakeholders.

Table 1. Practical Implications for Stakeholders

Stakeholder	Key behavioural risk	Recommended response
Retail investors	Overreliance on ESG labels and media narratives	Use diversified portfolios and verify ESG evidence
Institutional investors	Herding into popular green assets	Apply long-term valuation and scenario analysis
Policymakers	Investor distrust caused by unclear regulation	Strengthen disclosure standards and enforcement
Firms	Loss of credibility due to greenwashing concerns	Improve transparency, governance, and ESG reporting
ESG rating agencies	Confusion caused by inconsistent ratings	Improve rating clarity and methodological disclosure

Policies and regulations not only alter incentives but also expectations, beliefs, and trust. A durable and dependable policy climate will result in more stability in investors' sentiment through less ambiguity. Volatility can occur through unexpected changes in policies, misunderstanding policy direction or guidance, and decision-makers should be aware of behavioral biases, one of which is ambiguity and loss aversion, in policy decisions. Disclosure rules are a vital part of sustainable financial instruments, and behavioral finance may be employed as a principle according to which the policy is developed. Transparency is necessary, whereas disclosures can be too complex; therefore, investors can be adversely impacted and make decisions based on biases and heuristics. Making disclosures simpler and standardized is one of the ways in which investors can better understand ESG information, and in turn, it will have a lower probability of being misinterpreted (Yan et al., 2025). Policy-makers can also promote the use of prospective disclosures rather than retrospective metrics to assist investors in comprehending transition and risk-management plans. Sustainable finance governance structures can benefit from the inclusion of greenwashing risks, which are a primary source of negative sentiment and a lack of trust. Definitions, taxonomies, and enforcement structures can help build investor confidence in ESG-labelled financial products. When investors are more confident that ESG-labelled financial products are not just marketing hype, they are less prone to overreacting to individual pieces of negative news or skeptical stories. In this way, policymakers can help build investor trust, which can help calm extreme market sentiment.

Another factor for policymakers to consider when managing sentiment in the global green market is the issue of coordination between different jurisdictions. The lack of coordination between different regulations and standards can create confusion and breed uncertainty and behavioral biases. Efforts to improve the coordination of ESG reporting standards and climate change disclosures can help calm extreme market sentiment and improve the stability of cross-border investment flows. In terms of behavioral finance, coordination can help build commitment and credibility, which can help sustain positive sentiment even in the face of individual market challenges. Similarly, investors and policymakers have a role to play in shaping the market narrative with respect to sustainable finance. Narratives can affect the interpretation of information and the formation of market expectations. Narratives that are overly optimistic and focus on the assured benefits of achieving higher returns from sustainable finance may lead to disappointment and backlash if the market fails to deliver (Jain & Chawla, 2025). More balanced narratives that recognize the trade-offs, uncertainties, and costs associated with the transition can support market sentiment (Kumar et al., 2025). These types of narratives are less likely to lead to market swings or behavioral biases than other types. Education and capacity building can effectively mitigate behavioral biases in the sustainable finance ecosystem. Educated investors who are aware of the risks and data associated with sustainable finance and the behavioral biases that can influence market decisions are less likely to be biased. On the same note, the policymakers would be in a position to be supportive by ensuring that financial literacy campaigns on sustainable finance and behavioral bias are promoted. Over time, we can gain knowledge of the place of sentiment, resulting in more rational and less emotional market action. Finally, the ramifications of the behavioral dynamics of sustainable finance are directed towards a mutualized responsibility. One of the key things that investors need to understand is their weaknesses and come up with measures that encourage restraint and long-term thinking. Similarly, policymakers must create an environment that fosters trust, transparency, and credibility, considering how people react to rules and regulations. Through the implementation of sentiment analysis, behavioral biases can be overcome, and governance structures can be improved, thus providing a more effective platform for sustainable finance, as it seeks to meet its dual objectives of providing financial value while also contributing to the development of a more sustainable global economy (Tariq, 2024).

CONCLUSION

The chapter contributes by showing that green asset valuation cannot be explained only through financial fundamentals or ESG scores. Instead, valuation is also shaped by behavioural mechanisms, including investor sentiment, cognitive bias, trust, social imitation, and regulatory confidence. This behavioural perspective helps explain why green assets may experience premiums, volatility, overvaluation, or sudden corrections despite limited changes in underlying fundamentals. The issue of sustainable finance has become more visible with the realization that financial markets cannot be perceived as per traditional economics. The green market is a meeting point for financial analysis, societal values, and human psychology. As the conversation around investor sentiment, ESG performance, policy, and the differences between countries and regions continues, the underlying theme is always the same: behavior is the key factor. Prices, capital flows, and valuations in sustainable finance are driven not only by observable metrics but also by beliefs, emotions, and behavioral patterns. Thus, the inclusion of behavior in sustainable finance is not merely a desirable addition but a fundamental requirement for creating green financial markets that are robust, credible, and ultimately able to deliver the required sustainable outcomes. One of the most important things we have learned from behavioral finance is that investor sentiment is not random or irrelevant. It is shaped by how people view uncertainty, create meaning for sustainability, and think about the future. In green markets, where outcomes are long-term and difficult to verify, sentiment is a major driver that unites people. It has the potential to mobilize large amounts of money, accelerating investments in renewable energy, climate adaptation, and sustainable infrastructure. However, it is important to understand the dual nature of sentiment so that we do not react to it in a binary fashion. A resilient green market necessitates an even deeper understanding of the interrelationship between these behavioral biases and sustainability goals. Herding, overconfidence, and confirmation are biases that can contribute to the acceleration of ESG investment trends. Thus, these cycles do not reflect the instability of sustainable finance practices (Liang et al., 2025). Rather, they emphasize the need to develop structures that can be used to regulate emotional fluctuations. Information about behavioral finance incorporated into investment processes will assist in displacing investment sentiments on speculation and focusing on value creation. Such an inclusion will help maintain market stability while preserving the motivational power of sustainability in finance. Another important insight is that trust is at the core of sustainable finance. Investors' trust in ESG data, corporate disclosures, regulatory systems, and market structures influences the formation and maintenance of market sentiment. Behavioral finance has already proven that trust is created over time but can also be destroyed very quickly, particularly in an environment of information asymmetry and moral claims. Scandals of greenwashing, ratings confusion, and poor enforcement have created an environment of distrust and heightened skepticism. To bridge the gap between behavioral and sustainable finance, significant efforts must be made to increase transparency, trustworthiness, and accountability. Where trust is high, markets can absorb shocks and sustain positive sentiment during uncertain times. This connection between policy structures and the dynamics of behavioral structures is particularly important with regard to resiliency.

Policies do not merely convene regulations; they also communicate desire, promise, and purpose. Well-established and well-defined climate change policies, credible disclosure practices, and good governance practices are used to stabilize markets by minimizing uncertainty. Cognitive and emotional reasons for preventing sustainable investment can be diminished through policy clarity, viewed from a behavioral perspective. This renders the engagement of sustainable investments more inclusive and equitable. However, uncertain conditions are created when there is an absence of coherence between policies or a lack of understanding between policies, and these policies contribute to risk aversion in the flow of funds towards green activities. International viewpoints also demonstrate the topicality of these behavioral factors. Nationwide differences in perspectives on sustainability and reactions to it are determined by institutional, cultural and economic differences (Kumar et al., 2025). However, behavioral universals, including reactions to stories, application of heuristics, and social pressures, do not have geographical constraints. The synthesis of behavioral factors and sustainable finance at the global level requires an understanding of both behavioral universals and country-specific factors.

. Investors with the ability to withstand cognitive biases have a greater ability to cope with financial exuberance or pessimism. This type of behavioral maturation contributes to the development of resilience, which minimizes the chances of radical changes in investment strategy, depending on emotional reaction rather than critical analysis. This, in turn, will assist in creating a stable base of sustainable finance, which will become even more reputable as a viable investment strategy. For policymakers and institutions, the integration of behavioral insights provides a way to make green market governance more effective. Rules that are informed by a behavioral understanding are more appropriate for the actual response of market actors to incentives and information. They can move away from moral persuasion and towards designing systems that make sustainable outcomes consistent with realistic behavioral responses (Bhatnagar & Rajaram, 2024). This is not only about designing rules but also about communication approaches that present narratives in a balanced and credible way. Policymakers can improve the foundations of sustainable finance by recognizing the behavioral aspects of markets. Ultimately, it is about connecting behavioral insights with sustainable finance by acknowledging that the markets are human systems.

Green markets embody the hopes, fears, and aspirations that people share about the future of the economy and the planet. Thus, resilience does not mean being hopeful and fearless but knowing how to be involved with hopes and fears. Once behavioral insights are recognized and incorporated into sustainable finance, the latter becomes more than an adaptation to the risks posed by the environment and turns into a defensive strategy to ensure that economic operations are aligned with societal values (Maurya et al., 2026). In summary, behavioral finance and sustainability principles will be a successful part of the development of resilient green markets. The integration of ESG into investment decisions largely depends on investor sentiment, which is a determinant of ESG information integration because of its influence on psychology, culture, and public policy. By linking behavioral knowledge and sustainable finance, market participants can successfully handle volatility, build trust, and remain committed to environmental ambitions. By connecting these two concepts, sustainable finance presents a much more realistic and humane vision of financial markets that accept human nature as an integral aspect of finance, rather than its weakness, and thereby enhances its capacity to deliver a sustainable future.

REFERENCES

Akinde, M., Olapeju, O., Olaiju, O., Ogunseye, T., Emmanuel, A., Olagoke-Salami, S., & Aladelusi, K. (2025). Prediction of green sukuk investment interest drivers in Nigeria using machine learning models. *Journal of Risk and Financial Management, 18*(2), 89. DOI: 10.3390/jrfm18020089

Balaji, K. (2024). Neuromarketing and sustainable finance: Real-world case studies of green investment promotions. In *Neuromarketing's role in sustainable finance* (pp. 169–204). IGI Global. DOI: 10.4018/979-8-3693-9117-4.ch010

Banerjee, S., Aggarwal, D., & Sengupta, P. (2025). Do stock markets care about ESG and sentiments? Impact of ESG and investors' sentiment on share price prediction using machine learning. *Annals of Operations Research*, •••, 1–40. DOI: 10.1007/s10479-025-06480-4

Bhatnagar, M., & Rajaram, R. (2024). Correlating investor patterns and ESG performance with neuromarketing insights: Behavioural finance meets sustainability. In *Neuromarketing's role in sustainable finance* (pp. 1–20). IGI Global. DOI: 10.4018/979-8-3693-9117-4.ch001

Çoban, S., Uçar, M., Ulusay, N., & Kaya, N. (2025). Investigating the impact of social media-driven sentiment on the electric vehicle stock market using quantile regression. *International Journal of Economics and Financial Issues, 15*(4), 299–316. DOI: 10.32479/ijefi.19430

Hidayat-ur-Rehman, I., Alam, M. N., Alsolamy, M., Alharbi, S. H. H., AlAnazi, T. M. B., & Bhuiyan, A. B. (2025). Examining investor interaction with digital robo-advisory systems: Green value and interface quality in a socio-technical context. *Systems, 13*(9), 787. DOI: 10.3390/systems13090787

Jain, S., & Chawla, S. (2025). Fuelling sustainability through green bonds: Investigating the impact of pro-environmental values on retail investors' decisions. *Journal of Environmental Planning and Management*, •••, 1–28. DOI: 10.1080/09640568.2025.2478289

Kumar, P., Taneja, S., & Ozen, E. (2025). Exploring the influence of green bonds on sustainable development through low-carbon financing mobilisation. *International Journal of Law and Management, 67*(2), 249–270. DOI: 10.1108/IJLMA-01-2024-0030

Liang, C., Ma, X., & Liao, X. (2025). Unveiling investor motivation and trust in impact investing: Evidence from global green bond issuances. *Journal of Business Ethics, 200*(2), 445–468. DOI: 10.1007/s10551-024-05891-w

Liu, J., Guo, J., & Man, Y. (2025). Ripple effects of climate policy uncertainty: Risk spillovers between traditional energy and green financial markets. *Sustainability (Basel), 17*(12), 5500. DOI: 10.3390/su17125500

Loang, O. K., & Candra, S. (2025). Religion and green: The dual power of ESG and Shariah-compliant stocks in brand values of Malaysia, Indonesia, and Saudi Arabia. *Journal of Islamic Monetary Economics and Finance, 11*(2), 419–448. DOI: 10.21098/jimf.v11i2.2687

Maurya, P. K., Bansal, R., & Mishra, A. K. (2026). Investor sentiment and its implication on global financial markets: A systematic review of literature. *Qualitative Research in Financial Markets, 18*(1), 209–248. DOI: 10.1108/QRFM-04-2024-0087

Mertzanis, C., & Tebourbi, I. (2025). Geopolitical risk and global green bond market growth. *European Financial Management, 31*(1), 26–71. DOI: 10.1111/eufm.12484

Singh, M., & Chouhan, N. (2024). Psychology meets finance: Unpacking behavioural factors in green investment trends. In *Neuromarketing's role in sustainable finance* (pp. 39–56). IGI Global. DOI: 10.4018/979-8-3693-9117-4.ch003

Sultana, N., & Zeya, F. (2025). Advancing firm-specific ESG sentiment analysis: A machine learning approach to clustering, prediction, and financial performance implications. *Business Strategy & Development, 8*(3), e70150. DOI: 10.1002/bsd2.70150

Tariq, M. U. (2024). Metaverse in business and commerce. In Kumar, J., Arora, M., & Erkol Bayram, G. (Eds.), *Exploring the use of metaverse in business and education* (pp. 47–72). IGI Global., DOI: 10.4018/979-8-3693-5868-9.ch004

Tariq, M. U. (2024). Fintech startups and cryptocurrency in business: Revolutionizing entrepreneurship. In Kankaew, K., Nakpathom, P., Chnitphattana, A., Pitchayadejanant, K., & Kunnapapdeelert, S. (Eds.), *Applying business intelligence and innovation to entrepreneurship* (pp. 106–124). IGI Global., DOI: 10.4018/979-8-3693-1846-1.ch006

Tariq, M. U. (2024). Multidisciplinary service learning in higher education: Concepts, implementation, and impact. In S. Watson (Ed.), *Applications of service learning in higher education* (pp. 1-19). IGI Global. https://doi.org/DOI: 10.4018/979-8-3693-2133-1.ch001

Uddin, M. A., Chang, B. H., Aldawsari, S. H., & Li, R. (2025). The interplay between green finance, policy uncertainty, and carbon market volatility: A time-frequency approach. *Sustainability (Basel), 17*(3), 1198. DOI: 10.3390/su17031198

Yan, J., Zhao, Z., & Chen, B. (2025). How investor sentiment affects corporate environmental behaviour. *International Journal of Environmental Research*, *19*(1), 20. DOI: 10.1007/s41742-024-00670-x

Yao, J., & Yang, C. (2025). Financial technology and climate risks in the financial market. *International Review of Financial Analysis*, *99*, 103920. DOI: 10.1016/j.irfa.2025.103920

Key Terms and Definitions

Investor Sentiment: Collective attitudes influencing investment decisions beyond fundamentals

Green Premium: Valuation excess attributed to sustainability preferences beliefs

Behavioural Bias: Systematic psychological tendencies distorting rational financial judgement

Chapter 3
Measuring Market Sentiment in Green Asset Valuation:
A Structured Analytical Review

Afef Amdouni
http://orcid.org/0000-0001-9625-300X
Taibah University, Saudi Arabia

Chokkamreddy Prakash
http://orcid.org/0000-0002-3832-3740
Guru Nanak Institutions Technical Campus, India

ABSTRACT

The growth of environmental, social, and governance (ESG) investing has intensified interest in the role of market sentiment in the valuation of green assets. As sustainability considerations shape capital markets, sentiment-related factors increasingly influence pricing dynamics. This chapter provides a structured analytical review of sentiment indicators used in the valuation of green and ESG-related assets. It classifies existing measures into text-based indicators, market-based proxies, survey and attention measures, and machine-learning-generated composite indices. The review identifies methodological heterogeneity, endogeneity concerns, and limited standardization in sentiment measurement. It also highlights overlap between sentiment proxies and sustainability-related fundamentals. The chapter concludes that developing a unified, transparent measurement framework is essential to improving comparability and strengthening empirical research in green asset valuation.

DOI: 10.4018/979-8-3373-8392-7.ch003

1. INTRODUCTION

The accelerating integration of environmental, social, and governance (ESG) principles into capital markets has transformed contemporary asset valuation. Green equities, clean energy indices, green bonds, and sustainability-linked instruments increasingly influence portfolio allocation and corporate financing decisions. At the same time, climate-related uncertainty, regulatory transition risks, and heterogeneous disclosure standards introduce informational complexity into pricing processes. Empirical evidence shows that climate risks are increasingly priced across asset classes (Bartolini et al., 2025; Zhu et al., 2026), and that green assets exhibit regime-dependent spillovers and volatility sensitivity under uncertainty shocks (Wang et al., 2025; Zhou et al., 2025). In such an environment, investor expectations and information-driven perceptions play a growing role in shaping valuation outcomes.

A substantial body of literature confirms that investor sentiment influences return predictability, volatility clustering, and market anomalies in conventional financial markets (Maurya et al., 2024; Huynh et al., 2025). Within ESG-oriented markets, media tone and informational narratives have been shown to affect cost of equity capital and liquidity conditions (Deng et al., 2026), moderate ESG–mispricing relationships (Du & Du, 2026), and shape firm-level idiosyncratic volatility (Tao et al., 2025). At the systemic level, sustainability-related uncertainty indices amplify volatility persistence and cross-asset connectedness among green instruments (Luo et al., 2026), while climate policy uncertainty intensifies sentiment–risk spillovers (Huang et al., 2026). Evidence of bubble-like behavior in clean energy markets further suggests that thematic optimism may generate episodic deviations from fundamentals (Franco et al., 2026; Vriz & Grossi, 2026). Collectively, these findings indicate that informational environments and expectation dynamics materially affect green asset valuation.

However, despite this expanding empirical base, a critical limitation persists. Studies rely on heterogeneous proxies—text-based sentiment scores, volatility-derived measures, uncertainty indices, spillover metrics, attention indicators, and composite machine-learning constructs—often without clearly distinguishing the conceptual dimension captured by each proxy. In several cases, sustainability-related uncertainty is treated as a sentiment measure, even though it may reflect objectively evolving climate risks (Luo et al., 2026; Bartolini et al., 2025). This conflation blurs the analytical boundary between perception-driven distortions and rational pricing of transition and physical climate risks. As a result, causal interpretation remains fragile, and cross-study comparability is limited.

The absence of a unified analytical classification of sentiment indicators therefore constitutes a significant research gap. While the literature confirms that sentiment matters, it does not systematically differentiate between narrative framing effects, revealed trading behavior, informational salience, and multidimensional expectation environments. Without such differentiation, empirical results risk aggregating conceptually distinct mechanisms under a single label, hindering theoretical development in sustainable asset pricing.

Addressing this gap is essential for both academic rigor and practical relevance. From a research perspective, conceptual clarity improves identification strategies and cumulative knowledge building. From a policy and investment perspective, distinguishing between behavioral amplification and rational climate risk pricing is crucial for interpreting volatility episodes, financing costs, and portfolio diversification outcomes (Zhang et al., 2025; Khan & Vismara, 2025).

Investor sentiment in financial markets has long been examined within the broader framework of behavioral finance theory, which challenges the traditional assumption of fully rational investors and efficient markets. Classical models such as the Efficient Market Hypothesis suggest that asset prices fully reflect all available information; however, behavioral finance literature demonstrates that psychological biases, heuristic-driven decision making, and collective belief formation can lead to persistent deviations from fundamental values. The noise trader theory proposed by De Long et al. further suggests that irrational investors, driven by sentiment rather than fundamentals, can influence asset prices when their trading behavior becomes systematic or widespread.

In the context of sustainable finance, these behavioral mechanisms become particularly relevant because green assets are characterized by high informational uncertainty, evolving regulatory frameworks, and long-term environmental risk horizons (Zhang et al., 2025; Khan & Vismara, 2025). Investors often rely on narrative cues, media framing, and policy signals when interpreting sustainability-related information. Consequently, sentiment in ESG markets may reflect both psychological biases and rational belief dispersion about future climate policies and technological transitions. Integrating behavioral finance insights with emerging climate finance theories therefore provides a more comprehensive framework for understanding how sentiment influences green asset valuation.

Accordingly, the central objective of this chapter is to develop a structured and systematic analytical classification of sentiment indicators used in the valuation of green and ESG-related assets.

This chapter makes three primary contributions to the emerging literature on sustainable finance. First, it synthesizes fragmented empirical findings on ESG-related sentiment measures into a coherent analytical framework. Second, it develops a taxonomy of sentiment indicators that distinguishes between narrative sentiment, market-based sentiment, attention-based measures, and composite uncertainty indices. Third, the chapter identifies methodological challenges associated with sentiment measurement in ESG markets and highlights directions for future empirical research on the role of investor expectations in green asset valuation.

Figure 1. Analytical Framework for ESG Sentiment Indicators

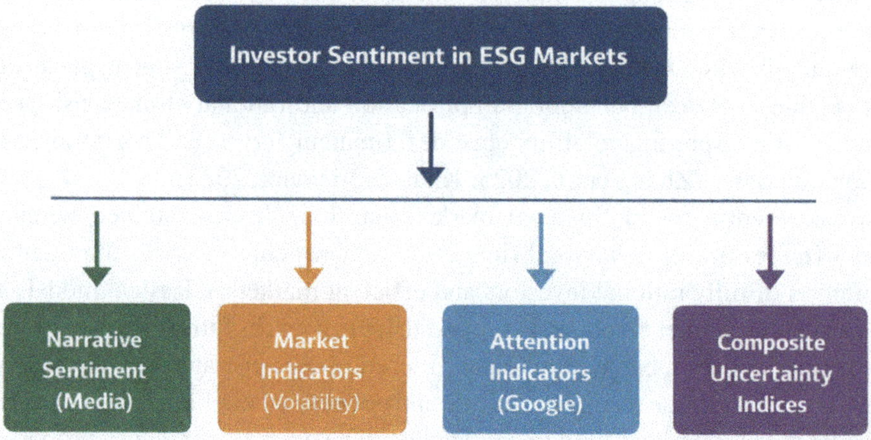

Figure 1 summarizes the analytical framework used in this chapter. It classifies ESG sentiment indicators into four categories: text-based indicators, market-based proxies, attention-based measures, and machine-learning composite indices. This structure clarifies how different sentiment measures capture distinct informational constructs and valuation channels.

Beyond synthesizing empirical evidence, the chapter adopts a structured analytical review methodology to systematically organize the diverse sentiment proxies used in ESG-oriented financial research. Unlike traditional narrative literature reviews, a structured analytical review emphasizes conceptual categorization, methodological comparison, and theoretical integration across empirical findings. This approach enables the identification of underlying measurement assumptions, transmission mechanisms, and potential sources of empirical bias embedded in sentiment proxies. By evaluating how different measurement strategies approximate distinct behavioral dimensions—such as narrative framing, revealed trading behavior, informational salience, and systemic expectation regimes—the chapter aims to enhance conceptual clarity in sustainable asset pricing research.

To ensure analytical rigor, the structured review approach applied in this chapter follows three stages. First, relevant literature was identified through systematic searches of major academic databases including Scopus, Web of Science, and Google Scholar using keywords such as ESG sentiment, green asset valuation, climate risk pricing, and sustainable finance sentiment. Priority was given to peer-reviewed journal articles published in high-impact outlets within finance, economics, and sustainability research.

Second, the selected studies were evaluated according to their methodological design, sentiment measurement approach, and empirical context. This step enabled the identification of recurring measurement strategies and conceptual overlaps across the literature.

Third, the extracted indicators were categorized according to their underlying informational dimension—narrative tone, revealed market behavior, informational salience, or multidimensional expectation environments. This classification process forms the basis of the analytical taxonomy proposed in this chapter.

The remainder of the chapter proceeds as follows. The next section critically reviews the theoretical and empirical foundations linking sentiment to green asset valuation. This is followed by a systematic analytical classification of sentiment indicators and their associated pricing channels. The subsequent discussion synthesizes cross-study evidence and evaluates methodological limitations. The chapter concludes by outlining directions for future research and implications for interpreting sentiment-driven dynamics in sustainable financial markets.

2. LITERATURE REVIEW

The rapid institutionalization of ESG considerations within capital markets has reconfigured the analytical foundations of asset pricing. Traditional valuation frameworks, grounded in risk-adjusted expected cash flows, presuppose relatively stable information environments and homogeneous belief updating. In contrast, green asset markets are structurally characterized by regulatory transition, technological disruption, heterogeneous disclosure regimes, and long-horizon uncertainty. Under such conditions, the informational boundary between rational risk pricing and sentiment-driven valuation becomes inherently porous.

Prior research demonstrates that investor sentiment influences return predictability, volatility dynamics, and asset mispricing across financial markets.

Another important dimension influencing investor sentiment in ESG-oriented markets concerns the role of information asymmetry and disclosure heterogeneity in sustainability reporting. Unlike traditional financial reporting, ESG disclosures remain only partially standardized and are often governed by multiple voluntary reporting frameworks. Firms may adopt different sustainability reporting standards such as integrated reporting structures or climate-related disclosures aligned with global sustainability initiatives. While these frameworks aim to improve transparency, substantial variation persists in reporting scope, data quality, and methodological approaches. Consequently, investors frequently face challenges when interpreting sustainability-related information, which may increase reliance on narrative signals, media framing, and broader sentiment indicators when evaluating corporate environmental performance (Deng et al., 2026; Du & Du, 2026).

The existence of divergent ESG information signals can significantly influence market expectations. When objective sustainability metrics are ambiguous or inconsistent across data providers, investors may rely more heavily on simplified proxies such as ESG ratings, sustainability rankings, and media narratives. However, ESG ratings themselves exhibit notable methodological divergence across rating agencies, reflecting differences in weighting schemes, data sources, and evaluation criteria. This divergence introduces additional uncertainty regarding the true sustainability performance of firms and may amplify the role of investor sentiment in asset valuation. Under such conditions, narrative framing effects embedded in media discourse can significantly influence investor perception and market pricing dynamics.

Beyond textual analytics, the digitalization of financial information environments has also created new opportunities to measure investor attention and sentiment through alternative data sources. Online search behavior, digital news consumption patterns, and social media activity increasingly serve as proxies for public attention toward sustainability issues. Such indicators provide high-frequency insights into the evolution of market narratives surrounding green assets and climate policy developments. Empirical evidence suggests that increased public attention to sustainability issues can amplify investor reactions to ESG information and influence corporate environmental decision making (Xie & Ying, 2025; Xu et al., 2026).

Firm-level evidence reinforces this ambiguity. Du and Du (2026) report that ESG performance reduces asset mispricing, but that media sentiment attenuates this disciplining effect by diluting informational clarity. Deng et al. (2026) demonstrate that positive ESG sentiment lowers firms' cost of equity capital through liquidity enhancement and institutional participation. Atak (2024) further shows that ESG sentiment affects idiosyncratic volatility, particularly when narrative polarity intensifies. Collectively, these studies suggest that narrative tone reshapes financing conditions and risk perception. However, the direction of causality remains fragile: media tone may respond endogenously to price performance or strategic corporate disclosure. Without robust identification designs, observed associations risk reflecting simultaneity rather than behavioral causation.

At the market-wide level, uncertainty and spillover research introduces an additional layer of complexity. Luo et al. (2026) find that sustainability-related uncertainty significantly increases volatility persistence and cross-asset correlations among green instruments. Wang et al. (2025) and Zhou et al. (2025) document regime-dependent spillover structures, particularly during crisis episodes. Huang et al. (2026) show that sentiment–risk interactions intensify under climate policy uncertainty. These findings confirm that expectation environments matter. Yet many uncertainty indices aggregate macroeconomic signals, policy indicators, and textual analytics, thereby blending rational risk information with perception-based components. The conceptual equivalence frequently assumed between "uncertainty" and "sentiment" therefore lacks analytical precision.

Climate risk pricing studies further challenge purely behavioral interpretations. Bartolini et al. (2025) demonstrate asymmetric pricing of transition and physical risks across European equity and bond markets. Zhu et al. (2026) identify a transition risk premium following carbon market reforms, while Ahmed (2025) documents regime-dependent sensitivity of green and brown energy equities to climate shocks. These results indicate that climate-related fundamentals are increasingly internalized by markets. Interpreting all valuation shifts as sentiment-driven risks overstating behavioral distortions and underestimating structural repricing mechanisms.

Speculative dynamics provide more direct evidence of expectation-driven amplification. Franco et al. (2026) detect bubble behavior in clean energy indices using stochastic volatility frameworks, and Vriz and Grossi (2026) formalize structured bubble detection models incorporating search intensity. However, even here, distinguishing exuberance from rational anticipation of structural energy transition remains empirically delicate. Forward-looking optimism may represent mispricing—or informed expectations of policy acceleration.

Attention-based research extends the debate beyond tonal sentiment measures. Xie and Ying (2025) show that public climate attention strengthens corporate green investment decisions, while Xu et al. (2026) document that retail green attention influences corporate carbon behavior. Unlike tonal indicators, attention proxies primarily capture informational salience rather than directional optimism or pessimism.

Portfolio-level analyses reinforce heterogeneity. Zhang et al. (2025) find that green assets enhance portfolio efficiency across investment horizons, whereas Khan and Vismara (2025) report robust environmental gains but heterogeneous financial outcomes of green bond issuance. Tao et al. (2025) show that ESG ratings mitigate idiosyncratic volatility, though this effect weakens beyond certain sentiment and policy uncertainty thresholds. These conditional results suggest that sentiment effects are state-dependent rather than universal.

While the literature collectively confirms the relevance of investor sentiment in shaping ESG-related asset dynamics, several unresolved issues remain. First, many empirical studies employ sentiment proxies without clearly specifying the behavioral or informational construct they represent. Second, methodological diversity across sentiment measures limits cross-study comparability and cumulative theory building. Third, few studies explicitly distinguish between perception-driven valuation distortions and rational market responses to climate-related risks. These limitations indicate the need for a systematic analytical framework capable of organizing sentiment indicators according to their conceptual foundations and valuation transmission mechanisms. Addressing this gap provides the motivation for the structured classification developed in the following section.

Synthesizing this literature reveals three structural tensions. First, sentiment is operationalized through heterogeneous proxies that approximate distinct behavioral or informational constructs, yet are frequently treated as interchangeable. Second, endogeneity remains pervasive, particularly in media- and price-based measures. Third, the empirical boundary between perception-driven expectation wedges and rational pricing of climate-related risks remains under-specified. Without explicit conceptual differentiation, cumulative inference is limited.

The absence of an integrated analytical taxonomy thus constitutes a substantive gap. Advancing sustainable asset pricing requires disentangling narrative framing effects, revealed behavioral excess, informational salience, and systemic uncertainty regimes. Only through such differentiation can empirical findings be interpreted within a coherent theoretical architecture.

3. ANALYTICAL CLASSIFICATION OF SENTIMENT INDICATORS

This section develops a structured analytical taxonomy of sentiment indicators used in green asset valuation. Conceptually, sentiment in sustainable financial markets can be interpreted as an expectation-driven layer that interacts with fundamental valuation mechanisms. While traditional asset pricing models focus primarily on risk-adjusted expected cash flows, ESG-oriented markets introduce additional informational dimensions related to climate policy uncertainty, sustainability disclosure quality, and evolving technological transitions. Within this environment, sentiment operates as a mediating force that shapes how investors interpret sustainability-related information and incorporate it into pricing decisions. The proposed taxonomy therefore organizes sentiment indicators according to the behavioral dimension they capture and the valuation channels through which they influence green asset prices.

3.1. Text-Based Sentiment Indicators: Narrative Framing Effects

Text-based indicators operationalize sentiment through linguistic extraction of tonal polarity from news articles, ESG disclosures, and corporate communications. These measures approximate narrative framing—the interpretative lens through which sustainability information is presented and internalized by market participants.

Deng et al. (2026) show that positive ESG media sentiment lowers firms' cost of equity capital through liquidity and institutional demand channels. Du and Du (2026) demonstrate that media sentiment moderates the relationship between ESG performance and mispricing, attenuating the disciplining role of objective ESG signals under heightened narrative intensity. Atak (2024) documents that ESG sentiment influences idiosyncratic volatility, particularly when negative polarity intensifies.

Conceptually, these measures capture expectation shifts embedded in discourse. Their valuation channel operates primarily through financing conditions, liquidity adjustments, and short-term risk perception. However, two structural concerns arise. First, simultaneity bias: media tone may respond to price dynamics rather than precede them. Second, semantic dependence: dictionary design and natural language processing models influence polarity classification, introducing measurement sensitivity. Text-based sentiment thus captures narrative amplification, but its causal isolation requires careful identification strategies.

3.2. Market-Based Proxies: Revealed Behavioral Excess

Market-based proxies infer sentiment from observable price behavior rather than linguistic tone. Bubble detection models, volatility asymmetries, and spillover structures are interpreted as manifestations of collective behavioral excess embedded in trading outcomes.

Franco et al. (2026) detect stochastic volatility patterns consistent with speculative bubbles in clean energy indices, while Vriz and Grossi (2026) formalize multi-stage exuberance frameworks integrating search intensity and price dynamics. Spillover analyses further demonstrate regime-dependent connectedness among green and traditional assets (Wang et al., 2025; Zhou et al., 2025). Luo et al. (2026) identify sustainability uncertainty as a persistent driver of volatility transmission across green instruments.

These proxies approximate revealed expectations—collective positioning embedded in prices. Their primary strength lies in behavioral realism: they observe market outcomes rather than self-reported attitudes. Yet they face an identification dilemma. Price dynamics may reflect rational repricing of climate transition risk (Bartolini et al., 2025; Zhu et al., 2026; Ahmed, 2025) rather than sentiment-driven distortion. Without decomposing rational risk premia from expectation wedges, market-based proxies risk conflating exuberance with structural repricing.

3.3. Survey and Attention Measures: Informational Salience Amplification

Survey-based and attention indicators capture the intensity of public focus on sustainability issues rather than directional tone. These measures approximate salience effects—the degree to which sustainability-related information enters collective awareness.

Xie and Ying (2025) show that heightened public climate attention strengthens corporate green investment decisions, while Xu et al. (2026) demonstrate that retail green attention influences carbon emissions behavior. Wang (2026) highlights the interactive amplification between media attention and investor sentiment in driving stock fluctuations.

Unlike tonal measures, attention indicators do not inherently signal optimism or pessimism. Instead, they modify the elasticity of market reactions to sustainability information. High salience can magnify price adjustments irrespective of direction. This category therefore captures amplification dynamics rather than bias per se. However, attention proxies risk conflating information diffusion with behavioral distortion, as heightened visibility may reflect improved information processing rather than irrationality.

3.4. Machine-Learning Composite Indices: Multidimensional Expectation Environments

Machine-learning-generated composite indices integrate textual analytics, macroeconomic uncertainty, policy variables, and market indicators into multidimensional constructs. These indices attempt to approximate systemic expectation environments rather than isolated sentiment components.

Luo et al. (2026) develop a Sustainability Uncertainty Index that exerts persistent influence on volatility and cross-asset correlations. While framed as uncertainty, such indices embed heterogeneous informational dimensions—policy signals, media tone, macro-financial stress—thereby approximating collective expectation regimes.

The analytical strength of composite indices lies in coverage breadth and predictive capacity. However, their multidimensional nature intensifies conceptual overlap between sentiment and structural climate risk exposure. Without explicit decomposition strategies—such as separating market-based discount rates from expectation wedges (Papadogiannis, 2026)—interpretability weakens. Composite indices may enhance forecasting performance while simultaneously reducing theoretical transparency.

A unified taxonomy is therefore necessary not merely for classification but for theoretical discipline. Differentiating sentiment components clarifies whether valuation effects arise from narrative interpretation, trading behavior, salience amplification, or macro-expectation regimes.

Recognizing these distinctions provides the analytical foundation required for coherent integration of sentiment into sustainable asset pricing models.

Table 1 synthesizes the proposed taxonomy and highlights the corresponding valuation channels and methodological considerations.

Table 1. Analytical Classification of Sentiment Indicators in Green Asset Valuation

Category	Data Source	Representative Studies	Primary Valuation Channel	Strength	Key Limitation
Text-Based Indicators	News media, corporate disclosures	Deng et al. (2026); Atak (2024); Du & Du (2026)	Cost of equity, liquidity, volatility, mispricing	Direct measurement of narrative tone	Endogeneity and simultaneity bias
Market-Based Proxies	Prices, volatility models, spillovers	Franco et al. (2026); Wang et al. (2025); Zhou et al. (2025)	Bubble dynamics, regime shifts, cross-market transmission	Captures revealed behavior	Hard to separate rational pricing from sentiment
Survey/ Attention Measures	Public attention, media intensity	Xie & Ying (2025); Wang (2026)	Investment amplification, governance pressure	Captures salience and visibility	Limited polarity differentiation
ML Composite Indices	Integrated sustainability and uncertainty signals	Luo et al. (2026)	Volatility persistence, systemic spillovers	Multidimensional coverage	Overlap with climate fundamentals

Table 1 highlights that sentiment indicators differ not only in their empirical construction but also in the behavioral mechanisms they capture. Text-based measures primarily reflect narrative interpretation, market-based indicators capture revealed trading behavior, attention metrics represent informational salience, and machine-learning indices approximate systemic expectation environments. Recognizing these distinctions is essential for interpreting empirical findings and for avoiding conceptual conflation between behavioral sentiment effects and rational climate-risk pricing.

Figure 2 illustrates the conceptual transmission framework through which ESG-related sentiment influences green asset valuation outcomes across multiple informational and behavioral channels.

Figure 2. Sentiment Transmission Framework in Green Asset Valuation

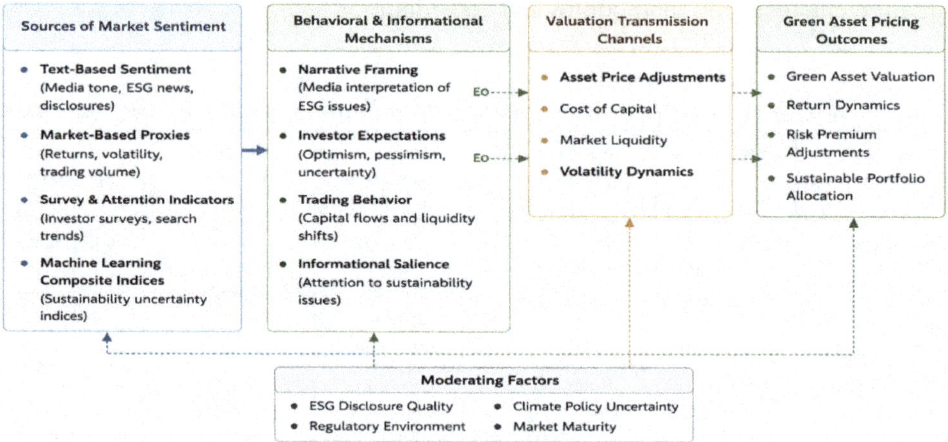

Figure 2. Sentiment Transmission Framework in Green Asset Pricing
Source: Developed by the authors.
Note: Eo = Expectations/Opinions.

4. DISCUSSION

The Structured Analytical Review conducted in this chapter reveals three interrelated structural findings concerning the role of market sentiment in green asset valuation.

First, sentiment measurement in ESG-oriented markets remains conceptually fragmented. Text-based indicators (Deng et al., 2026; Atak, 2024; Du & Du, 2026), market-derived proxies (Franco et al., 2026; Wang et al., 2025), attention metrics (Xie & Ying, 2025), and composite uncertainty indices (Luo et al., 2026) are frequently employed under a shared “sentiment” label despite capturing distinct informational layers. Recent advances further complicate this landscape. Pham et al. (2025) demonstrate that conventional sentiment indices often embed both irrational bias and rational expectation components, thereby contaminating measurement purity. Similarly, machine-learning composite indices increasingly integrate macro-financial uncertainty, policy signals, and textual analytics into unified constructs, expanding predictive power but blurring conceptual boundaries.

Second, the boundary between sentiment and climate-related fundamentals is frequently under-specified. Climate transition and physical risks are demonstrably priced in financial markets (Bartolini et al., 2025; Zhu et al., 2026; Ahmed, 2025). At the same time, valuation distortions consistent with speculative dynamics have been documented in clean energy markets (Franco et al., 2026). The coexistence of rational risk pricing and perception-driven amplification creates an identification problem. Papadogiannis (2026) formalizes this tension within a dual-risk valuation framework, distinguishing between the market-based opportunity cost of capital and belief-driven distortions in expected cash flows. Applied to green assets, this perspective suggests that observed price premia may reflect either transition-risk compensation or expectation wedges arising from narrative-driven optimism. Without explicit decomposition strategies, empirical findings risk conflating these components.

Third, regime dependency and higher-moment spillovers indicate that sentiment effects are conditional rather than universal. Spillover dynamics vary across quantiles and time horizons (Singhania et al., 2026), and higher-order moment connectedness often exceeds lower-order volatility transmission in green finance–energy nexuses (Mei & Jiang, 2026).

Taken together, these dynamics suggest that investor sentiment functions as a mediating layer between sustainability-related information and financial market outcomes. Rather than acting as a purely irrational force, sentiment often reflects the process through which investors interpret complex and uncertain information about long-term environmental and regulatory developments. Recognizing this interpretative dimension is therefore essential for accurately assessing the role of sentiment in green asset valuation.

Boufateh et al. (2025) further show that sentiment shocks interact with geopolitical and financial uncertainty in a multidimensional fashion, reinforcing the idea that expectation environments are layered rather than singular.

Taken together, these findings carry significant implications for interpreting green asset pricing. When sentiment proxies embed uncertainty factors, macroeconomic risk signals, or policy dynamics, estimated valuation effects cannot be attributed solely to behavioral distortions. For instance, reductions in cost of equity capital (Deng et al., 2026), volatility amplification (Atak, 2024), or spillover intensification (Luo et al., 2026) may reflect a mixture of improved information environments, rational updating to climate transition pathways, and perception-driven overreaction. The empirical challenge lies in isolating the marginal effect of expectation-driven distortions from structurally priced sustainability risks.

Comparison across the reviewed literature reveals broad but qualified support for sentiment relevance. Evidence consistently shows that narrative tone and informational salience affect financing costs, liquidity, and volatility. However, climate risk pricing differs across asset classes (Bartolini et al., 2025), and connectedness structures are highly state-dependent (Zhou et al., 2025; Singhania et al., 2026). Moreover, event-based studies demonstrate that political and regulatory shocks alter valuation responses differently depending on portfolio classification criteria (Comincioli & Donadelli, 2026).

Several limitations constrain this synthesis. As a review-based chapter, conclusions depend on the internal validity of cited empirical designs. Publication bias may favor statistically significant sentiment effects. Furthermore, heterogeneity in ESG rating methodologies introduces additional noise, potentially influencing both disclosure tone and investor interpretation. Finally, composite machine-learning approaches, while methodologically sophisticated, may obscure interpretability by aggregating heterogeneous informational dimensions.

These limitations indicate clear research priorities. First, future studies should develop standardized taxonomies that explicitly differentiate narrative tone, revealed behavioral excess, informational salience, and macro-uncertainty regimes. Second, empirical strategies capable of disentangling perception-driven wedges from rational climate-risk premia—such as instrumental-variable approaches, natural experiments, or structural decomposition models—are essential. Third, cross-country comparisons could illuminate how regulatory architecture and disclosure standards mediate sentiment transmission channels. Finally, incorporating higher-moment and quantile-based approaches may improve understanding of how sentiment operates under extreme market conditions.

5. CONCLUSION

This chapter examined how market sentiment is conceptualized and empirically measured in the valuation of green and ESG-related financial assets. As sustainable investing expands rapidly across global capital markets, understanding the behavioral and informational mechanisms shaping asset prices has become increasingly important. The analysis demonstrates that sentiment in ESG-oriented markets is not a singular construct but a heterogeneous set of expectation-related mechanisms that emerges through narrative framing, trading behavior, informational salience, and broader expectation environments. Recognizing these distinctions is critical for interpreting empirical findings and for developing theoretically consistent models of sustainable asset pricing.

The structured analytical review revealed three core insights. First, sentiment measurement in green finance is methodologically heterogeneous and conceptually underspecified. Different proxies approximate distinct informational layers—narrative framing, revealed trading behavior, salience amplification, or systemic expectation environments—yet are frequently treated as equivalent. Second, the boundary between behavioral amplification and rational climate-risk pricing remains difficult to isolate empirically. Evidence confirms that transition and physical climate risks are priced in financial markets, but episodic exuberance and volatility amplification suggest that expectation wedges may coexist with fundamental risk premia. Third, sentiment effects are regime-dependent and extend beyond mean-return dynamics to higher-moment spillovers, particularly under extreme uncertainty conditions.

The principal contribution of this chapter lies in developing an integrated analytical taxonomy of sentiment indicators and clarifying their distinct valuation transmission channels. By distinguishing measurement categories and highlighting identification challenges, the chapter advances conceptual precision in the study of green asset pricing. It underscores that empirical findings on sentiment cannot be interpreted without explicit consideration of proxy design and potential contamination by macroeconomic or policy uncertainty.

Several limitations should be acknowledged. As a review-based synthesis, conclusions depend on the robustness of existing empirical designs and are subject to publication bias. Furthermore, heterogeneity in ESG classification systems and disclosure standards introduces additional interpretive complexity.

Future research should prioritize the development of unified and transparent measurement frameworks capable of separating belief-driven expectation distortions from structurally priced climate risks. Identification strategies that exploit natural experiments, cross-country regulatory variation, or structural decomposition models may offer promising avenues. Incorporating quantile-based and higher-moment methodologies could further illuminate how sentiment operates under extreme market states.

In conclusion, market sentiment plays a significant but conceptually heterogeneous role in green asset valuation. Advancing the field requires clearer measurement boundaries, stronger identification strategies, and greater theoretical discipline in distinguishing behavioral amplification from rational climate-risk pricing.

REFERENCES

Ahmed, W. M. A. (2025). How do green vis-à-vis brown energy stock markets respond to climate risks? *Finance Research Open*, *1*(4), 100066. DOI: 10.1016/j.finr.2025.100066

Atak, A. (2024). Beyond polarity: How ESG sentiment influences idiosyncratic volatility in the Turkish stock market. *Borsa Istanbul Review*, *24*, 10–21. DOI: 10.1016/j.bir.2024.11.003

Bartolini, N., Romagnoli, S., & Santini, A. (2025). Understanding climate risk in Europe: Are transition and physical risk priced in equity and fixed-income markets? *Journal of Empirical Finance*, *84*, 101672. DOI: 10.1016/j.jempfin.2025.101672

Boufateh, T., Saadaoui, Z., & Jiao, Z. (2025). On the time-varying responses of Fintech stock returns to geopolitical, financial and market sentiment shocks. *The Quarterly Review of Economics and Finance*, *101*, 101951. DOI: 10.1016/j.qref.2024.101951

Comincioli, N., & Donadelli, M. (2026). 2024 US election: The climate for green and brown portfolios. *The North American Journal of Economics and Finance*, *83*, 102593. DOI: 10.1016/j.najef.2026.102593

Deng, G., Deng, Q., Yan, J., & Li, X. (2026). ESG sentiment, investor behavior, and corporate cost of equity capital. *International Review of Financial Analysis*, *109*, 104800. DOI: 10.1016/j.irfa.2025.104800

Du, Y., & Du, L. (2026). ESG performance, media sentiment, and corporate asset mispricing. *Finance Research Letters*, *87*, 108888. DOI: 10.1016/j.frl.2025.108888

Franco, J. P. M., Morales, A. B., & Laurini, M. P. (2026). When green turns exuberant: Bubble detection in clean-energy markets. *Finance Research Letters*, *87*, 109109. DOI: 10.1016/j.frl.2025.109109

Huang, Y., Liang, W., Duan, K., Parhi, M., & Mishra, T. (2026). Sentiments and risks: A spillover tale under climate policy uncertainty. *Energy Economics*, *154*, 109101. DOI: 10.1016/j.eneco.2025.109101

Huynh, N., De Mello, L., & Li, K. (2025). Evolution of investor sentiment: A systematic literature review and bibliometric analysis. *International Review of Economics & Finance*, *100*, 104115. DOI: 10.1016/j.iref.2025.104115

Khan, M. A., & Vismara, S. (2025). Green bond issuance and corporate environmental and financial performance: A meta-analysis. *International Review of Economics & Finance*, *102*, 104313. DOI: 10.1016/j.iref.2025.104313

Luo, K., Peng, L., & Zhou, F. (2026). Sustainability uncertainty and the dynamics of green asset markets. *Journal of Innovation & Knowledge*, *100999*, 100999. Advance online publication. DOI: 10.1016/j.jik.2026.100999

Maurya, P. K., Bansal, R., & Mishra, A. K. (2024). Investor sentiment and its implication on global financial markets: A systematic review of literature. *Qualitative Research in Financial Markets*, *18*(1), 209–248. DOI: 10.1108/QRFM-04-2024-0087

Mei, K., & Jiang, Y. (2026). Beyond volatility: Higher-moment spillovers in the green finance–energy–energy metals nexus. *International Review of Economics & Finance*, *106*, 105034. DOI: 10.1016/j.iref.2026.105034

Papadogiannis, A. (2026). From unified discounting to dual-risk: A new lens on DCF valuation. *Finance Research Open*, *2*(1), 100096. DOI: 10.1016/j.finr.2026.100096

Pham, Q., Pham, H., Pham, T., & Tiwari, A. K. (2025). Revisiting the role of investor sentiment in the stock market. *International Review of Economics & Finance*, *100*, 104089. DOI: 10.1016/j.iref.2025.104089

Singhania, M., Seth, S., & Saini, C. (2026). Quantile connectedness among green and dirty cryptocurrencies and North American clean technology and ESG. *The North American Journal of Economics and Finance*, *102610*, 102610. Advance online publication. DOI: 10.1016/j.najef.2026.102610

Tao, M., Lin, B., Poletti, S., & Roubaud, D. (2025). Greener pastures, steadier returns: ESG ratings and idiosyncratic risk management. *International Review of Economics & Finance*, *100*, 104110. DOI: 10.1016/j.iref.2025.104110

Vriz, G. L., & Grossi, L. (2026). Green bubbles: A four-stage paradigm for detection and propagation. *Energy Economics*, *154*, 109095. DOI: 10.1016/j.eneco.2025.109095

Wang, Y., Cheung, A. W. K., Yan, W.-L., & Wang, B. (2025). Connectedness of China's green bond and green stock markets at the low- and high-order moments. *The North American Journal of Economics and Finance*, *78*, 102410. DOI: 10.1016/j.najef.2025.102410

Wang, Y., Zhao, X., & Shang, J. (2025). Dynamic risk spillover in green financial markets: A wavelet frequency analysis from China. *Energy Economics*, *143*, 108301. DOI: 10.1016/j.eneco.2025.108301

Xu, Z., Du, Z., Gao, Y., & Ma, J. (2026). Retail investors' green attention and corporate carbon emissions: Evidence from China. *Social Responsibility Journal*, *22*(3), 596–616. DOI: 10.1108/SRJ-03-2025-0184

Zhang, D., Dai, X., & Wang, Q. (2025). Do green assets enhance portfolio optimization? A multi-horizon investing perspective. *The British Accounting Review*, *57*(5), 101612. DOI: 10.1016/j.bar.2025.101612

Zhou, Y., Xie, C., Wang, G.-J., & Zhu, Y. (2025). The role of uncertainty in return spillovers among digital, green, and traditional financial assets. *International Review of Financial Analysis*, *103*, 104225. DOI: 10.1016/j.irfa.2025.104225

Zhu, H., Qin, B., Li, X., & Ren, X. (2026). Does the capital market price climate transition risk? Evidence from China's carbon emission trading system. *Journal of Multinational Financial Management*, *100950*, 100950. Advance online publication. DOI: 10.1016/j.mulfin.2026.100950

Chapter 4

Empirical Studies Linking Sentiment, ESG Scores, and Financial Performance

G. SudhaAnanthi
http://orcid.org/0009-0001-5062-5311
Winners Academy, India

ABSTRACT

The growing integration of Environmental, Social, and Governance (ESG) considerations into investment decision-making has fundamentally reshaped global capital markets, prompting extensive academic and practitioner interest in understanding how ESG-related information influences asset prices and financial performance. Beyond static ESG scores and disclosures, recent research increasingly emphasises the role of sentiment-driven ESG momentum—the dynamic flow of market perceptions, narratives, and investor attitudes toward ESG factors—in shaping stock returns. Sentiment-driven ESG momentum refers to the cumulative effect of changing investor sentiment, media coverage, analyst opinions, regulatory signals, and stakeholder discourse related to a firm's ESG profile, which together create positive or negative momentum in how ESG characteristics are priced by financial markets. This empirical review synthesises existing literature on the mechanisms, measurement approaches, and financial implications of ESG sentiment momentum, highlighting how sentiment dynamics interact.

DOI: 10.4018/979-8-3373-8392-7.ch004

SENTIMENT-DRIVEN ESG MOMENTUM AND STOCK RETURNS: AN EMPIRICAL REVIEW

The growing integration of Environmental, Social, and Governance (ESG) considerations into investment decision-making has fundamentally reshaped global capital markets, prompting extensive academic and practitioner interest in understanding how ESG-related information influences asset prices and financial performance. Beyond static ESG scores and disclosures, recent research increasingly emphasises the role of sentiment-driven ESG momentum—the dynamic flow of market perceptions, narratives, and investor attitudes toward ESG factors—in shaping stock returns. Sentiment-driven ESG momentum refers to the cumulative effect of changing investor sentiment, media coverage, analyst opinions, regulatory signals, and stakeholder discourse related to a firm's ESG profile, which together create positive or negative momentum in how ESG characteristics are priced by financial markets. This empirical review synthesises existing literature on the mechanisms, measurement approaches, and financial implications of ESG sentiment momentum, highlighting how sentiment dynamics interact with traditional risk-return models to influence stock performance across markets and time horizons. Empirical measurement of ESG sentiment momentum has evolved significantly with advances in data availability and analytical techniques. Early studies relied primarily on static ESG ratings from data providers, which often exhibited low correlation and limited timeliness. More recent research employs Natural Language Processing (NLP), machine learning, and big data analytics to capture real-time ESG sentiment from diverse textual sources, including news articles, earnings call transcripts, corporate disclosures, social media, regulatory filings, and NGO reports. Sentiment scores are constructed by analysing the tone, intensity, and frequency of ESG-related language, distinguishing between positive, neutral, and negative sentiment across environmental, social, and governance dimensions. Momentum is then operationalised as changes in sentiment over time, persistence of sentiment trends, or abnormal shifts relative to market or industry benchmarks.

These dynamic measures provide a more nuanced representation of how ESG perceptions evolve and influence investor expectations. The interaction between ESG sentiment momentum and traditional asset pricing factors is a key focus of empirical research. Several studies indicate that ESG sentiment momentum provides incremental explanatory power beyond established factors such as size, value, momentum, and profitability. Portfolio-based analyses reveal that long-short strategies based on ESG sentiment changes can yield abnormal returns even after controlling for conventional risk factors. By capturing forward-looking market perceptions rather than backwards-looking scores, sentiment-based ESG signals enhance timing decisions and improve responsiveness to emerging risks and opportunities. Empirical studies suggest that integrating ESG sentiment momentum into portfolio strategies can improve diversification benefits, enhance downside protection, and align financial performance with sustainability objectives. This dual benefit has contributed to the growing adoption of ESG-integrated and impact-oriented investment approaches among institutional investors. Regulatory and disclosure developments also shape the dynamics of ESG sentiment momentum. As mandatory ESG reporting standards expand and data transparency improves, the informational content of ESG sentiment may evolve. Some studies suggest that greater disclosure reduces information asymmetry, potentially weakening momentum effects over time.

Others argue that increased disclosure amplifies sentiment dynamics by generating more frequent and detailed ESG narratives for market interpretation. The empirical evidence remains mixed, highlighting the need for ongoing research as regulatory frameworks mature and investor expectations evolve. In conclusion, the empirical evidence reviewed in this analysis underscores the growing importance of sentiment-driven ESG momentum in shaping stock returns across global equity markets. Advances in data analytics and NLP have enabled more precise measurement of ESG sentiment, revealing its dynamic interaction with investor behaviour, risk factors, and market conditions. Positive ESG sentiment momentum is generally associated with superior risk-adjusted returns and enhanced downside protection, while negative momentum signals elevated risk and underperformance. Although methodological challenges remain, the integration of ESG sentiment into asset pricing models and investment strategies offers valuable insights into how sustainability narratives are translated into financial outcomes. As ESG considerations continue to influence capital markets, sentiment-driven momentum will remain a critical lens for understanding the evolving relationship between sustainability, investor behaviour, and stock performance.

NONLINEAR RELATIONSHIPS BETWEEN ESG SCORES AND FINANCIAL PERFORMANCE: EVIDENCE FROM EMERGING MARKETS

The relationship between Environmental, Social, and Governance (ESG) performance and corporate financial outcomes has become a central topic in sustainable finance literature, yet empirical findings remain mixed, particularly in the context of emerging markets. While early studies often assumed a linear relationship—either positive or negative—between ESG scores and financial performance, growing evidence suggests that this relationship is more complex and nonlinear in nature. Emerging markets, characterised by institutional heterogeneity, regulatory variability, capital constraints, and evolving governance frameworks, provide a particularly rich context for examining nonlinear dynamics between ESG engagement and firm-level financial performance (Pu G., 2023). In these markets, ESG investments may yield diminishing, threshold-based, or even U-shaped effects on profitability, valuation, and risk-adjusted returns, reflecting the interaction between firm capabilities, market maturity, and stakeholder expectations. Nonlinear relationships arise when incremental improvements in ESG performance do not generate proportional financial benefits.

In emerging economies, firms at low levels of ESG engagement may initially experience negative or negligible financial effects due to high upfront compliance costs, limited access to ESG-aligned capital, weak enforcement mechanisms, or insufficient market recognition of sustainability efforts. For example, investments in environmental controls or labour standards may increase operating costs without immediate revenue enhancement in markets where consumer willingness to pay for sustainability is low and regulatory incentives are weak (Martínez-Ferrero J., et al, 2021). As a result, early-stage ESG adopters may face short-term profitability pressures, leading to a convex or U-shaped relationship between ESG scores and financial performance. Governance factors often play a dominant role in shaping nonlinear ESG–performance relationships in emerging markets. Weak legal enforcement, concentrated ownership structures, and political risk can amplify the marginal benefits of strong governance practices once a minimum standard is achieved. Firms with low governance scores may suffer from agency problems, capital misallocation, and higher risk premiums, while incremental governance improvements may initially yield limited benefits if institutional constraints persist. However, once governance reforms reach a credibility threshold—such as board independence, transparency, and shareholder protection—financial performance can improve sharply. This creates a nonlinear payoff structure where governance quality disproportionately enhances firm value beyond a certain point, particularly in markets with weak baseline institutions.

Methodologically, evidence of nonlinear ESG–financial performance relationships in emerging markets has been strengthened by the use of advanced econometric techniques such as panel threshold models, quadratic regressions, quantile regressions, spline regressions, and machine learning-based nonlinear estimators. These methods allow researchers to identify ESG score thresholds, regime shifts, and heterogeneous effects across firm size, industry, and market conditions. Empirical findings consistently indicate that linear models underestimate the complexity of ESG impacts, often masking negative effects at low ESG levels and positive effects at higher levels (Aksoy M., et al, 2025). Quantile-based analyses further reveal that high-performing firms benefit more from ESG engagement than low-performing firms, reinforcing the notion of asymmetric and nonlinear outcomes. Investor behaviour and market sentiment also play a critical role in shaping nonlinear ESG–performance relationships. In emerging markets, ESG awareness and integration among domestic investors may be limited, while foreign institutional investors often apply stricter ESG criteria. This duality can lead to segmented capital market responses, where ESG improvements below international standards yield limited valuation effects, but once firms meet global ESG benchmarks, they attract significant foreign capital inflows. Such threshold-driven capital allocation reinforces nonlinear relationships, as financial performance responds disproportionately once ESG credibility is established. Behavioural finance perspectives further suggest that investor overreaction or underreaction to ESG signals can amplify nonlinear price dynamics, particularly in less efficient markets (Taheripour E., et al, 2025). In conclusion, evidence from emerging markets strongly supports the existence of nonlinear relationships between ESG scores and financial performance, challenging simplistic linear assumptions prevalent in early ESG research. These nonlinear dynamics reflect the interaction of institutional quality, market maturity, investor behaviour, sectoral characteristics, and firm-specific capabilities. Financial benefits of ESG engagement often materialise only after firms surpass critical ESG thresholds, while partial or superficial adoption may yield limited or negative short-term effects. Advanced empirical methodologies and context-sensitive analysis are essential for capturing these complex relationships. For policymakers, firms, and investors alike, understanding the nonlinear nature of ESG–financial performance linkages is crucial for designing effective sustainability strategies, capital allocation decisions, and regulatory frameworks that support long-term value creation in emerging markets.

SENTIMENT-BASED ESG PORTFOLIOS: RISK-ADJUSTED RETURNS IN THE US MARKET

The integration of Environmental, Social, and Governance (ESG) considerations into investment decision-making has evolved from a niche ethical practice into a central pillar of modern asset management, particularly in the United States, where institutional investors increasingly view ESG factors as financially material drivers of long-term performance. While early ESG research primarily focused on static ESG scores and disclosure metrics, recent advancements in data availability and computational finance have enabled the incorporation of investor sentiment into ESG portfolio construction. Sentiment-based ESG portfolios represent an advanced investment strategy that combines traditional ESG screening with sentiment analytics derived from news media, earnings calls, social media, analyst reports, and alternative data sources (Pegoraro S., et al, 2023). This approach recognizes that market perceptions, narratives, and emotional responses to ESG-related information can significantly influence asset prices, volatility, and risk-adjusted returns, especially in deep and information-rich markets such as the United States Investor sentiment related to ESG factors reflects collective beliefs, expectations, and emotional reactions regarding a firm's sustainability performance, ethical conduct, regulatory exposure, and long-term resilience.

Unlike conventional ESG ratings, which are typically updated infrequently and rely on standardised disclosure frameworks, sentiment indicators are dynamic, forward-looking, and responsive to real-time information flows. Advances in natural language processing (NLP), machine learning, and big data analytics have made it possible to quantify ESG sentiment by analysing the tone, intensity, and thematic focus of textual data across multiple channels. Positive ESG sentiment may arise from favourable coverage of environmental innovation, diversity initiatives, governance reforms, or stakeholder engagement, while negative sentiment often reflects controversies, regulatory violations, environmental incidents, or governance failures (Han J J., et al, 2025). These sentiment shifts can generate short- to medium-term price reactions that are not fully captured by static ESG scores. Risk-adjusted performance is a central metric in evaluating sentiment-based ESG portfolios. Measures such as the Sharpe ratio, Sortino ratio, Jensen's alpha, and downside risk metrics are commonly employed to assess whether excess returns compensate for total and systematic risk. Evidence from US market studies indicates that ESG sentiment-enhanced portfolios often exhibit lower downside volatility and improved drawdown characteristics compared to conventional portfolios. This risk mitigation effect is attributed to the tendency of high-ESG, positively perceived firms to demonstrate stronger stakeholder trust, better governance practices, and greater resilience during periods of market stress. During episodes of heightened uncertainty—such as financial crises, regulatory shocks, or environmental disasters—stocks with strong ESG sentiment often experience smaller price declines and faster recoveries, contributing to improved risk-adjusted outcomes.

Another important dimension of sentiment-based ESG portfolios is their sectoral and thematic composition within the US market. ESG sentiment tends to vary significantly across industries, with technology, healthcare, and renewable energy sectors often exhibiting strong positive sentiment related to innovation and social impact, while energy, utilities, and industrials may experience more volatile sentiment due to environmental and regulatory scrutiny. Portfolio strategies that dynamically adjust sector exposures based on ESG sentiment signals can improve diversification and reduce concentration risk (Jeong S H., et al, 2025). Thematic ESG sentiment, such as sentiment related to climate transition, human capital management, or corporate transparency, further allows investors to align portfolios with specific sustainability objectives while maintaining competitive risk-adjusted returns. Despite their advantages, sentiment-based ESG portfolios face several methodological and practical challenges. Measuring ESG sentiment accurately requires sophisticated NLP models capable of distinguishing material information from noise, sarcasm, or sensationalism. Bias in media coverage, unequal visibility of large versus small firms, and the risk of short-term sentiment reversals can affect signal reliability. Additionally, the integration of sentiment signals into portfolio construction raises questions about turnover, transaction costs, and strategy scalability. Empirical evidence suggests that combining sentiment signals with ESG fundamentals and financial factors can mitigate these risks, producing more stable and robust risk-adjusted returns over time (Vuong N B., 2022). In conclusion, sentiment-based ESG portfolios represent a sophisticated evolution of sustainable investing in the US market, combining ESG fundamentals with real-time investor sentiment to enhance risk-adjusted returns. Empirical evidence suggests that these portfolios can outperform traditional benchmarks by exploiting informational inefficiencies, mitigating downside risk, and capturing behavioural dynamics associated with ESG narratives. While challenges related to data quality, model complexity, and market noise remain, advances in AI, NLP, and quantitative finance continue to improve the robustness of sentiment-based strategies. As ESG considerations become increasingly embedded in capital markets and investor behaviour, sentiment-driven ESG portfolio construction is likely to play a growing role in delivering resilient, competitive, and sustainability-aligned investment outcomes in the United States.

ESG NEWS SENTIMENT AND ITS IMPACT ON ROE AND TOBIN'S Q

In recent years, the integration of Environmental, Social, and Governance (ESG) considerations into financial markets has fundamentally reshaped how firm performance is evaluated, not only through traditional accounting and market-based metrics but also through reputational, behavioural, and informational channels. Among these channels, ESG news sentiment has emerged as a critical mechanism through which sustainability-related information is transmitted to investors, stakeholders, and markets. ESG news sentiment refers to the tone, intensity, and directional bias of media coverage related to a firm's environmental practices, social responsibility, and governance quality, as disseminated through financial news outlets, corporate disclosures, analyst reports, and digital media platforms. Advances in natural language processing (NLP) and sentiment analysis have enabled researchers to quantify ESG-related narratives at scale, allowing for systematic empirical investigation of how positive or negative ESG sentiment influences firm-level financial outcomes such as Return on Equity (ROE) and Tobin's Q (Abou Tanos B., et al, 2024). Return on Equity, as an accounting-based performance metric, captures a firm's efficiency in generating profits from shareholders' equity and reflects operational effectiveness, cost management, and strategic execution. ESG news sentiment can affect ROE both directly and indirectly. Positive environmental or social sentiment may enhance brand reputation, customer loyalty, employee engagement, and supplier relationships, contributing to revenue growth and margin improvement. Governance-related sentiment, particularly concerning board independence, executive compensation, and transparency, can influence managerial discipline and capital allocation efficiency, further improving profitability.

Conversely, sustained negative ESG sentiment—such as reports of environmental violations, labour disputes, or governance scandals—can increase operating costs, trigger regulatory penalties, disrupt supply chains, and weaken employee morale, thereby exerting downward pressure on ROE. Empirical studies increasingly find that firms experiencing consistently positive ESG news sentiment exhibit more stable and resilient profitability, particularly during periods of economic stress or heightened uncertainty (Ooi K L., et al, 2025). Behavioural finance provides further insight into the ESG sentiment–valuation nexus. Investors are not purely rational actors; rather, they are influenced by cognitive biases, attention effects, and media framing. ESG-related news often attracts disproportionate attention due to its moral, social, and political salience, amplifying its impact on investor behaviour. Positive ESG narratives may trigger herding behaviour and momentum trading, driving up stock prices and Tobin's Q in the short to medium term. Negative ESG news, particularly when framed as scandals or controversies, can lead to overreaction, sharp price corrections, and persistent valuation effects. These sentiment-driven dynamics suggest that ESG news sentiment can influence market valuation beyond fundamentals, especially in markets characterised by high retail participation or limited information transparency.

Cross-country and institutional context further moderate the relationship between ESG news sentiment and firm performance. In developed markets with strong investor protection, high disclosure standards, and mature ESG integration, ESG news sentiment tends to be incorporated more efficiently into prices, leading to more stable and persistent effects on Tobin's Q. In emerging markets, where information asymmetry is higher and regulatory enforcement may be weaker, ESG sentiment effects are often more pronounced but also more volatile. In such contexts, negative ESG news can trigger sharp valuation declines and profitability shocks, while positive sentiment may generate temporary valuation premiums that dissipate over time (Bhatnagar M., et al, 2025). These findings underscore the importance of institutional quality, media freedom, and market sophistication in shaping the financial consequences of ESG narratives. Methodologically, advances in NLP and machine learning have significantly enhanced the precision of ESG sentiment measurement. Modern approaches move beyond simple positive–negative classifications to capture sentiment intensity, topic relevance, and temporal dynamics. By isolating ESG-specific sentiment from general market sentiment, researchers can more accurately estimate its incremental impact on financial performance. High-frequency sentiment measures also enable dynamic analysis of how ESG news affects ROE and Tobin's Q over different time horizons, revealing short-term market reactions and longer-term operational effects. In conclusion, ESG news sentiment represents a powerful informational and behavioural channel linking sustainability narratives to firm-level financial performance (Maurya P K., et al, 2025). Empirical evidence suggests that ESG sentiment significantly influences both Return on Equity and Tobin's Q, reflecting its impact on operational efficiency, stakeholder relationships, and market valuation. While positive ESG sentiment can enhance profitability and generate valuation premiums, negative sentiment can impose lasting financial and reputational costs. The strength and persistence of these effects depend on ESG dimensions, institutional context, firm characteristics, and market conditions. As ESG considerations continue to shape capital markets, understanding the nuanced role of ESG news sentiment is essential for researchers, managers, and investors seeking to assess firm value, manage risk, and promote sustainable long-term performance.

BEHAVIOURAL FINANCE MEETS ESG: HOW SENTIMENT SHAPES SUSTAINABLE INVESTMENT OUTCOMES

The integration of Environmental, Social, and Governance (ESG) considerations into investment decision-making has fundamentally altered the landscape of modern finance, challenging traditional assumptions of market efficiency and purely rational behaviour. While classical financial theory assumes that investors process all available information objectively to maximise expected utility, the growing body of research at the intersection of behavioural finance and ESG investing reveals that investor sentiment, cognitive biases, and social preferences play a decisive role in shaping sustainable investment outcomes. Behavioural finance provides a critical lens through which ESG-related anomalies, valuation dynamics, and performance dispersion can be understood, particularly as ESG information is often qualitative, forward-looking, and subject to interpretation rather than immediate financial realisation (Julliete A., et al, 2025). As ESG investing has moved from a niche ethical practice to a mainstream financial strategy, sentiment has emerged as a powerful transmission mechanism linking sustainability narratives to asset prices, capital allocation, and risk-adjusted returns. One of the central behavioural mechanisms shaping ESG investment outcomes is the affect heuristic, whereby investors rely on emotional responses rather than analytical evaluation when assessing ESG performance. Companies perceived as "good corporate citizens" often benefit from reputational halos that influence investor judgment, leading to lower perceived risk and higher valuation multiples.

Figure 1. ESG scores and financial performance

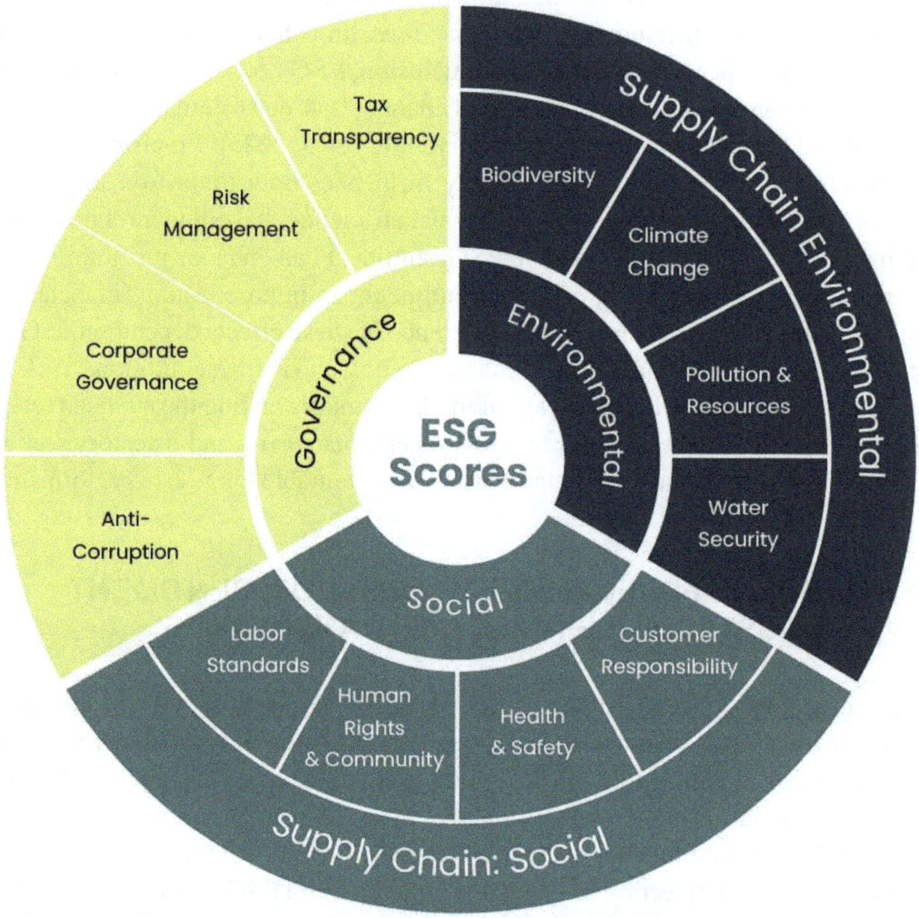

This phenomenon aligns with stakeholder theory, which posits that firms managing stakeholder relationships effectively may enjoy greater investor trust and resilience. However, behavioural finance highlights that such sentiment-driven optimism may result in mispricing, particularly when ESG performance is conflated with immediate financial strength. Empirical studies increasingly show that periods of heightened ESG enthusiasm are associated with valuation premia that may subsequently mean-revert as expectations adjust to realised financial outcomes (Sultana N., et al, 2025). Herding behaviour represents another critical behavioural channel through which sentiment shapes ESG investment outcomes. As institutional investors, asset managers, and pension funds increasingly adopt ESG mandates, peer effects and reputational concerns encourage convergence toward similar ESG strategies. Behavioural finance suggests that managers may follow ESG trends not solely based on private information but to avoid relative underperformance or reputational risk. This collective movement can magnify capital flows into ESG funds and assets, reinforcing price momentum and creating feedback loops between sentiment, flows, and performance. While herding can accelerate the diffusion of sustainable finance practices, it also raises concerns about overcrowding, correlated risks, and potential ESG asset bubbles.

Sentiment also influences the risk-return profile of ESG investments through changing risk perceptions. Traditional asset pricing models struggle to capture ESG-related risks, which are often long-term, non-linear, and uncertain. Behavioural finance suggests that sentiment-driven optimism may lead investors to underestimate ESG-related risks during favorable market conditions, compressing risk premiums. Conversely, during periods of heightened uncertainty or market stress, ESG sentiment can either exacerbate risk aversion—leading to capital withdrawal from perceived "greenwashing" firms—or act as a stabilising force when investors view high-ESG firms as safer, more resilient assets (Lee S., et al, 2025). This dual role of sentiment helps explain mixed empirical findings regarding ESG performance across market cycles. From a market efficiency perspective, the growing influence of sentiment in ESG investing raises important questions. While behavioural finance acknowledges that sentiment can lead to temporary mispricing, it also recognises that ESG information may convey material long-term value that traditional models fail to capture.

Distinguishing between sentiment-driven noise and genuine ESG-related fundamentals remains a central empirical challenge. Advanced methodologies, including sentiment analysis of ESG news, social media, and corporate disclosures, combined with behavioural asset pricing models, have begun to shed light on how sentiment mediates the relationship between ESG performance and financial outcomes. Evidence increasingly suggests that sentiment acts as both a catalyst and a filter, accelerating market reactions to ESG information while shaping investor interpretation and expectation formation. In conclusion, the convergence of behavioural finance and ESG investing provides a rich framework for understanding how sentiment shapes sustainable investment outcomes (Joshi N V., et al, 2026). Investor psychology, attention biases, herding behaviour, and emotional responses play a central role in translating ESG information into asset prices, capital flows, and risk-adjusted returns. Sentiment amplifies both the opportunities and challenges of sustainable finance, driving innovation, accelerating adoption, and occasionally contributing to mispricing and volatility. Recognising the behavioural foundations of ESG markets enables investors, policymakers, and researchers to better interpret performance patterns, design more robust investment strategies, and develop regulatory frameworks that enhance market stability and credibility. As ESG investing continues to evolve, integrating behavioural insights will be essential for understanding the complex interplay between sustainability, sentiment, and financial performance in global capital markets.

SENTIMENT-ENHANCED ESG SCORING MODELS: A MACHINE-LEARNING APPROACH

In recent years, the convergence of environmental, social, and governance (ESG) analytics with machine learning and sentiment analysis has transformed the evaluation of corporate sustainability and its link to financial performance. Traditional ESG scoring systems, typically produced by data providers such as MSCI, Refinitiv, or Sustainalytics, rely heavily on quantitative disclosures and standardised frameworks that assess firm-level policies, performance indicators, and governance mechanisms. However, these conventional models face persistent challenges: reporting asymmetries across markets, time lags in disclosure, and a tendency to overlook soft information embedded in public discourse. The emergence of sentiment-enhanced ESG scoring models offers a promising avenue to address these gaps by integrating unstructured data—such as news articles, social media discussions, analyst reports, and stakeholder communications—into quantitative ESG evaluation frameworks (Paira D., et al, 2026). By doing so, machine learning–based sentiment systems capture the dynamic perceptions of stakeholders and investors, providing a more responsive, multidimensional, and predictive measure of corporate sustainability performance. In the second computational layer, these sentiment vectors are integrated with structured ESG datasets and financial indicators using supervised or unsupervised machine learning frameworks. Regression-based methods, random forests, gradient boosting, and neural networks are employed to model nonlinear relationships between sentiment signals and ESG disclosure metrics.

Some frameworks adopt feature-fusion architectures in which sentiment features (derived from textual analysis) are combined with financial ratios, governance scores, and environmental intensity measures to produce composite ESG indices. Alternatively, ensemble models may weight traditional ESG components and sentiment indicators differently based on predictive relevance. Reinforcement learning or Bayesian updating can also be introduced to dynamically recalibrate model weights as new data arrive, ensuring temporal adaptability and robustness against sentiment volatility. From a methodological standpoint, the development of sentiment-enhanced ESG models raises several challenges that necessitate careful design choices (Saxena A., et al, 2024). One primary concern is data heterogeneity—ESG news coverage and stakeholder discussions vary across languages, regions, and industries. Sentiment polarity may differ in tone or meaning depending on cultural context and linguistic nuances. Machine translation and multilingual embeddings can mitigate these effects, but they introduce their own uncertainties. Additionally, distinguishing between short-term controversies and structural sustainability failures requires models that incorporate temporal dynamics. Recurrent neural networks (RNNs) or long short-term memory (LSTM) architectures can capture sequential patterns, tracking how sentiment evolves before, during, and after major ESG events. This temporal modelling allows the sentiment-enhanced ESG score to reflect not only the immediate reaction but also the recovery trajectory, providing a more nuanced view of reputational resilience.

Empirical research increasingly supports the predictive value of sentiment-integrated ESG metrics for both financial and sustainability outcomes. Studies across major markets, including the U.S., Europe, and Asia, reveal that sentiment-adjusted ESG indices exhibit stronger correlations with short-term stock returns, volatility, and credit spreads than conventional ESG ratings. Machine-learning models trained on sentiment-enriched datasets often outperform static benchmarks in forecasting firm-level return on assets (ROA), Tobin's Q, and abnormal returns following ESG-related news events. Moreover, portfolios constructed using sentiment-enhanced ESG scores tend to deliver higher risk-adjusted returns, particularly during periods of heightened market uncertainty. These findings suggest that sentiment data encapsulate forward-looking market expectations that complement lagging disclosure-based measures, providing investors with a more holistic understanding of ESG-driven performance dynamics (Renfield M A., et al, 2025). However, the integration of sentiment analysis into ESG scoring also raises ethical and methodological questions. The use of social media and public discourse data must comply with privacy, consent, and data-protection standards. Overreliance on sentiment may inadvertently amplify noise, as online discussions can be influenced by misinformation or orchestrated campaigns.

Therefore, robust model validation, cross-source triangulation, and confidence scoring are essential to ensure that sentiment-based insights remain credible and not misleading. Combining quantitative sentiment features with verified corporate data, independent third-party audits, and long-term performance indicators can help strike a balance between agility and reliability. In conclusion, sentiment-enhanced ESG scoring models represent a paradigm shift in sustainable finance and corporate analytics. By harnessing machine learning and natural language processing, these models bridge the gap between static disclosure-based ratings and dynamic perception-based assessments (Yousaf I., et al, 2024). They offer investors, regulators, and corporations a real-time, data-driven lens through which to evaluate sustainability performance and anticipate market responses. Despite challenges related to bias, interpretability, and data governance, the empirical evidence underscores the substantial potential of sentiment-infused ESG frameworks to improve predictive accuracy, transparency, and market relevance. As global capital increasingly aligns with sustainability imperatives, sentiment-enhanced machine-learning models will play a defining role in shaping the next generation of ESG evaluation—one that not only measures what companies do but also captures how the world perceives what they do, thereby linking environmental and social responsibility with enduring financial value creation.

DYNAMIC LINKAGES BETWEEN INVESTOR SENTIMENT, ESG RATINGS, AND MARKET VOLATILITY

The growing prominence of environmental, social, and governance (ESG) considerations in global capital markets has fundamentally reshaped how investors perceive risk, value, and long-term firm performance, giving rise to complex and dynamic interactions between investor sentiment, ESG ratings, and market volatility. Traditional financial theory assumes that asset prices fully reflect all available information and that investors behave rationally; however, behavioral finance has demonstrated that sentiment-driven biases, heuristics, and emotional responses significantly influence market outcomes. When ESG information enters this behavioral framework, it introduces an additional layer of complexity, as sustainability signals are often ambiguous, forward-looking, and unevenly disclosed across firms and markets (Liu M., et al, 2025). Consequently, the interaction between investor sentiment and ESG ratings is not static but evolves over time, influencing and being influenced by market volatility in a dynamic feedback loop that challenges conventional asset pricing models. ESG ratings act as an institutionalized and standardized signal of corporate sustainability performance, intended to reduce information asymmetry between firms and investors.

However, ESG ratings are inherently imperfect proxies, as they rely on heterogeneous methodologies, backward-looking disclosures, and subjective weighting schemes. As a result, investor sentiment often mediates the impact of ESG ratings on asset prices and volatility. When ESG ratings align with prevailing sentiment, market reactions tend to be muted and gradual. Conversely, when sentiment diverges from rating assessments—such as when a highly rated firm experiences negative ESG news—markets often respond with abrupt price adjustments and heightened volatility (Atak A., et al, 2024). This divergence highlights the dynamic role of sentiment as a catalyst that can accelerate or dampen the transmission of ESG information into market prices. Empirical evidence increasingly supports the existence of time-varying and nonlinear relationships between investor sentiment, ESG ratings, and market volatility. Studies employing vector autoregression (VAR), dynamic conditional correlation (DCC-GARCH), and regime-switching models demonstrate that the impact of ESG ratings on volatility is not constant across time or market states. In low-volatility or bullish regimes, ESG signals may be incorporated gradually, with limited immediate impact on price fluctuations. In contrast, during high-volatility or bearish regimes, ESG-related news interacts strongly with investor sentiment, producing amplified volatility responses. This asymmetry underscores the importance of sentiment as a transmission mechanism through which ESG information affects market stability.

Behavioral mechanisms help explain why sentiment-driven ESG effects on volatility persist even in relatively efficient markets. Limited attention, confirmation bias, and herding behavior cause investors to overweight salient ESG narratives while underweighting long-term fundamentals. Media framing of ESG issues—especially climate risk, social controversies, or executive misconduct—can trigger emotional responses that translate into excessive trading, short-term mispricing, and volatility spikes. Algorithmic trading and sentiment-based investment strategies further accelerate this process by reacting instantaneously to ESG-related textual signals, amplifying short-term volatility even as they contribute to faster information diffusion over longer horizons (Ang G., et al, 2023). From a portfolio management perspective, understanding the dynamic interaction between sentiment, ESG ratings, and volatility has critical implications for risk management and asset allocation. Investors relying solely on static ESG scores may underestimate short-term volatility risk if sentiment shifts abruptly. Incorporating sentiment indicators allows for more adaptive portfolio strategies that adjust exposure based on evolving market perceptions of sustainability risk.

ESG-focused portfolios that dynamically rebalance in response to sentiment-driven volatility signals have been shown to achieve superior risk-adjusted performance, particularly during periods of heightened uncertainty. This highlights the importance of treating ESG not only as a long-term value factor but also as a dynamic risk dimension influenced by behavioral forces. In conclusion, the dynamic linkages between investor sentiment, ESG ratings, and market volatility represent a complex, evolving system in which behavioral and informational forces interact continuously. Investor sentiment acts as a critical mediator that shapes how ESG information is interpreted and priced, while market volatility both reflects and reinforces these sentiment-driven dynamics (Ebenezer Y., et al, 2026). ESG ratings provide an important but imperfect signal, whose impact on volatility depends on prevailing sentiment and market conditions. Empirical evidence confirms that these relationships are time-varying, nonlinear, and regime-dependent, challenging static models of sustainable finance. By integrating sentiment analysis, advanced econometric techniques, and machine learning, researchers and practitioners can better capture the dynamic nature of ESG-driven market behavior. Ultimately, recognizing and modeling these interactions is essential for developing more resilient investment strategies, improving risk management, and advancing a deeper understanding of how sustainability considerations influence financial markets in an era of heightened uncertainty and behavioral complexity.

INTEGRATING SENTIMENT ANALYSIS WITH ESG SCORES TO PREDICT FIRM VALUE

The integration of sentiment analysis with environmental, social, and governance (ESG) scores represents a transformative approach to understanding and predicting firm value, bridging the gap between quantitative disclosure-based ESG evaluations and qualitative stakeholder perceptions. Traditional ESG scoring methodologies, produced by agencies such as MSCI, Sustainalytics, and Refinitiv, largely rely on static, self-reported data, regulatory filings, and structured metrics to evaluate corporate sustainability performance. While these frameworks provide a foundation for assessing a company's environmental footprint, social responsibility initiatives, and governance structures, they often fail to capture the dynamic and real-time nature of public perception, media narratives, and investor sentiment that can materially influence market valuation (Sree Vani Y., et al, 2026). Integrating sentiment analysis allows researchers and practitioners to quantify the tone, intensity, and direction of discussions surrounding corporate ESG practices, thereby creating hybrid models that combine objective ESG performance metrics with forward-looking, perception-driven signals that better reflect market expectations and potential impacts on firm value. Methodologically, the integration process involves several computational layers. First, unstructured textual data related to a firm's ESG performance is collected from diverse sources, including financial news, press releases, sustainability reports, investor briefings, and social media platforms. Natural language processing (NLP) techniques are applied to these data streams to extract sentiment indicators, employing approaches such as lexicon-based sentiment scoring, machine learning classification models, and transformer-based architectures like BERT, FinBERT, or RoBERTa fine-tuned on ESG-specific corpora.

These models assign polarity scores—positive, negative, or neutral—and measure sentiment intensity, enabling the creation of quantitative variables that represent stakeholder perception and public discourse trends over time. Advanced NLP pipelines may also perform entity recognition to ensure that sentiment signals are accurately attributed to the firm in question, while topic modelling can differentiate between sentiment related to environmental, social, or governance aspects, allowing for a more granular assessment of perception-driven effects (Lheureux Y., 2024). Empirical studies demonstrate that sentiment-enhanced ESG models significantly improve the prediction of firm value, measured using market-based indicators such as Tobin's Q, stock returns, enterprise value, or abnormal returns relative to industry benchmarks. Positive sentiment regarding ESG practices—capturing favourable media attention, investor confidence, or recognition from sustainability indices—correlates with higher market valuations and lower perceived risk, particularly in industries where ESG performance is highly material, such as energy, extractive sectors, consumer goods, and financial services. Conversely, negative sentiment, arising from environmental violations, social controversies, or governance scandals, exerts downward pressure on market valuations, even when traditional ESG scores remain moderate, indicating that perception-driven signals can amplify market reactions to ESG events. Time-series analyses reveal that sentiment measures often precede formal ESG rating updates, providing a forward-looking dimension that enhances predictive accuracy.

From a methodological perspective, advanced models incorporate temporal dynamics, recognising that both ESG performance and sentiment evolve. Recurrent neural networks (RNNs) or long short-term memory (LSTM) architectures can capture sequential dependencies, tracking how prior sentiment and ESG disclosures influence subsequent market reactions. Event studies further examine the immediate market response to ESG news, demonstrating that abnormal returns are significantly associated with sentiment shifts, particularly during periods of heightened investor attention or macroeconomic uncertainty. The combination of event-driven and continuous-time modelling enables robust forecasts of firm value under varying market conditions and sentiment regimes (Lee H., et al, 2024). Despite the advantages, integrating sentiment analysis with ESG scores presents challenges. Data quality and coverage are critical, as sentiment analysis relies on comprehensive, reliable, and timely data sources. Biases in media coverage, social amplification, or algorithmic filtering can distort sentiment measures, necessitating normalisation techniques and cross-validation with multiple data sources. Interpretability of machine learning models remains essential for stakeholder acceptance; techniques such as Shapley Additive Explanations (SHAP) or Local Interpretable Model-agnostic Explanations (LIME) can elucidate the contribution of sentiment and ESG features to predicted firm value. Ethical considerations, including privacy, data consent, and transparency in algorithmic decision-making, are also paramount, ensuring that predictive models respect stakeholder rights while providing actionable insights (Loang O K., et al, 2025). In conclusion, integrating sentiment analysis with ESG scores provides a robust framework for predicting firm value by combining objective measures of corporate sustainability with dynamic, perception-driven insights. This hybrid approach addresses the limitations of traditional ESG ratings, offering forward-looking, real-time indicators of market reaction to sustainability performance. By leveraging natural language processing, machine learning, and temporal modelling, investors, analysts, and corporate managers can achieve enhanced predictive accuracy, proactive risk management, and informed decision-making. As

ESG considerations continue to influence capital allocation and market behaviour, sentiment-enhanced ESG scoring models are poised to play a central role in shaping investment strategies, corporate governance, and sustainable value creation across diverse industries and geographies.

SENTIMENT-ADJUSTED ESG PORTFOLIOS: EVIDENCE FROM ASIAN MARKETS

The integration of environmental, social, and governance (ESG) factors into portfolio construction has emerged as a central theme in sustainable finance, reflecting both the growing regulatory emphasis on corporate sustainability and the heightened awareness among investors regarding long-term value creation. While conventional ESG portfolios rely primarily on static ESG scores derived from third-party rating agencies such as MSCI, Sustainalytics, and Refinitiv, these scores often fail to capture real-time investor perceptions, market sentiment, and rapidly evolving public discourse regarding sustainability practices. In the context of Asian markets—characterised by diverse regulatory environments, heterogeneous disclosure practices, and rapidly expanding capital markets—the incorporation of sentiment analysis into ESG portfolio design offers a promising avenue for enhancing risk-adjusted returns, improving portfolio resilience, and aligning investment strategies with evolving market expectations (Vuong N B., et al, 2021). By adjusting ESG portfolio weights based on sentiment signals derived from news articles, social media, analyst reports, and other textual data sources, investors can capture dynamic perceptions of corporate ESG performance and integrate forward-looking insights that complement traditional disclosure-based metrics. Once sentiment signals are derived, they are integrated with quantitative ESG scores using feature-fusion or weighting models to construct hybrid scores for portfolio selection.

Traditional ESG scores provide the baseline assessment of corporate sustainability performance, while sentiment scores modulate portfolio weights to account for market perception and dynamic risk signals. Optimisation frameworks, such as mean-variance, conditional value-at-risk (CVaR), or multi-objective portfolio models, are then applied to select stocks that balance expected returns, risk exposure, and ESG alignment. In practice, positive sentiment may amplify the portfolio weight of high-ESG firms perceived favourably by the market, whereas negative sentiment may reduce exposure to firms with reputational or ESG-related risks, even if their formal ESG scores remain high. This dynamic adjustment enables portfolios to respond to real-time market information, potentially enhancing returns while mitigating downside risk (Gupta H., et al, 2023). Sectoral heterogeneity is a critical consideration in Asian markets. Resource-intensive industries such as energy, mining, and utilities show stronger sensitivity to sentiment signals, reflecting the materiality of environmental and governance risks in these sectors. Consumer-facing and technology firms are particularly influenced by social and reputational sentiment, as public perception directly impacts brand equity, customer loyalty, and investor confidence. Governance sentiment, encompassing board independence, disclosure transparency, and shareholder rights, demonstrates broad relevance across sectors, consistently influencing risk-adjusted performance. Meta-analytical assessments suggest that portfolio gains from sentiment integration are most pronounced when sector-specific ESG materiality is high and market attention to ESG issues is elevated, highlighting the importance of context-specific weighting in portfolio construction.

From a methodological standpoint, several considerations are critical to the design and evaluation of sentiment-adjusted ESG portfolios. Temporal alignment of sentiment data with portfolio rebalancing frequency is essential to capture short-term market dynamics while avoiding overfitting to transient news cycles. Robustness checks employing alternative sentiment lexicons, NLP models, and weighting schemes ensure that portfolio outcomes are not unduly sensitive to model specification. Moreover, portfolio optimisation must consider potential multicollinearity between sentiment signals and ESG scores, sectoral biases, and market liquidity constraints, particularly in smaller Asian markets. Incorporating backtesting over multiple market cycles, stress-testing under ESG-related shocks, and scenario analysis enhances confidence in the stability and reliability of the portfolio strategy (Yu H., et al, 2025). Empirical analyses in Asian markets have also revealed dynamic interactions between sentiment, market volatility, and ESG performance. During periods of market stress, negative ESG sentiment disproportionately affects high-risk or highly leveraged firms, widening spreads and increasing volatility, whereas positive sentiment can buffer the adverse impact of macroeconomic shocks on firm valuations.

Machine learning-based portfolio simulations indicate that sentiment-adjusted ESG strategies outperform static ESG portfolios not only in average returns but also in downside risk metrics, drawdown minimisation, and volatility-adjusted performance. The combination of forward-looking sentiment and robust ESG scores enables investors to construct portfolios that are both financially competitive and aligned with sustainability objectives, providing a practical bridge between ethical investing and quantitative risk management (Zhang X., et al, 2025). In conclusion, sentiment-adjusted ESG portfolios represent a significant advancement in sustainable investing within Asian markets, combining the strengths of traditional ESG ratings with real-time, perception-driven insights derived from sentiment analysis. Empirical evidence indicates that integrating sentiment enhances risk-adjusted returns, improves portfolio resilience, and provides early warning signals of ESG-related risks, particularly in sectors and regions with high ESG materiality or informational asymmetry. By capturing both quantitative sustainability performance and qualitative stakeholder perception, sentiment-adjusted portfolios offer a forward-looking, context-aware framework for investors seeking to align financial objectives with sustainability considerations. As ESG integration continues to deepen in Asian capital markets, sentiment-informed portfolio strategies are poised to play a critical role in driving both value creation and the broader adoption of responsible investing practices, fostering more resilient, efficient, and ethically aligned financial ecosystems across the region.

THE ROLE OF SOCIAL MEDIA SENTIMENT IN ESG INVESTMENT STRATEGIES

The integration of environmental, social, and governance (ESG) considerations into investment decision-making has evolved from a niche ethical practice into a central component of modern portfolio management, reflecting both regulatory imperatives and investor demand for sustainability-aligned financial products. Traditional ESG investment strategies have largely relied on quantitative disclosures, third-party ESG ratings, and corporate sustainability reports to assess firm-level performance and construct portfolios aligned with long-term value creation. While these approaches offer a structured framework for evaluating ESG risk and opportunity, they frequently suffer from limitations, including delayed reporting, incomplete coverage, and an inability to capture dynamic stakeholder perceptions. In this context, social media sentiment has emerged as a critical complementary input, offering real-time insights into public opinion, investor perception, and reputational dynamics, which can materially influence corporate valuation, risk profiles, and investment outcomes. Platforms such as Twitter, Weibo, LinkedIn, Facebook, and specialised sustainability forums generate vast quantities of textual data that reflect both investor sentiment and broader societal reactions to corporate ESG practices (Jaiswal R., et al, 2024). By incorporating these signals into investment strategies, ESG-focused investors can enhance the timeliness, responsiveness, and predictive power of portfolio construction, risk management, and alpha generation. The conceptual foundation for incorporating social media sentiment into ESG investment strategies draws on both behavioural finance and market microstructure theories.

Positive social media sentiment surrounding environmental initiatives, social responsibility programs, or robust governance practices can signal increased stakeholder trust, regulatory favorability, and brand loyalty, potentially driving upward adjustments in equity valuation or lowering perceived credit risk. Conversely, negative sentiment—stemming from environmental violations, labour disputes, ethical controversies, or governance lapses—can precipitate reputational damage, heightened investor scrutiny, and increased market volatility (Tan W., et al, 2025).

Social media sentiment thus functions as both a forward-looking indicator and a market amplifier, offering investors a dynamic lens through which to anticipate the financial and non-financial impacts of ESG events. Once social media sentiment is quantified, it can be incorporated into ESG investment strategies in several ways. One approach involves the construction of sentiment-adjusted ESG scores, in which traditional disclosure-based ratings are weighted or modulated by sentiment signals to reflect real-time perceptions. These hybrid scores provide a more responsive measure of ESG performance, integrating both objective and subjective dimensions. Portfolio optimisation frameworks, such as mean-variance optimisation, conditional value-at-risk (CVaR) minimisation, or multi-objective ESG-constrained models, can then be applied to select stocks or bonds that balance expected financial returns, ESG alignment, and sentiment-driven risk exposure. Positive sentiment signals can increase portfolio weightings for firms with favourable ESG profiles, while negative sentiment can trigger reductions in exposure, serving as an early warning system for reputational or operational risks not yet captured by formal ESG ratings.

Sectoral, regional, and temporal heterogeneity plays a critical role in the efficacy of sentiment-informed ESG strategies. Resource-intensive industries, such as energy, mining, and utilities, exhibit heightened sensitivity to environmental sentiment, while labour-intensive and consumer-focused sectors respond more strongly to social and reputational sentiment. Governance-related sentiment demonstrates cross-sector relevance, consistently influencing investor confidence, risk perception, and capital allocation. Regional differences in social media penetration, regulatory enforcement, and cultural attitudes toward sustainability also moderate the impact of sentiment signals. For example, markets in East and Southeast Asia show pronounced effects due to rapid digital adoption and high public engagement with corporate behaviour, whereas developed Western markets exhibit more moderate but still significant responses. Temporal dynamics, including market cycles, macroeconomic shocks, and ESG event timing, further modulate the predictive power of sentiment, highlighting the importance of integrating longitudinal sentiment measures with investment decision-making frameworks (Liu M., et al, 2023). Despite its promise, the use of social media sentiment in ESG investment strategies presents several challenges. Data quality, source reliability, and representativeness must be carefully managed, as social media content can be noisy, biased, or manipulated through coordinated campaigns.

Natural language processing models must account for multilingual content, cultural nuances, sarcasm, and context-specific terminology to avoid misinterpretation. The integration of sentiment signals with traditional ESG ratings requires robust weighting schemes to balance objective performance and perception-driven signals without overreacting to transient trends. Ethical and regulatory considerations, including data privacy, platform compliance, and algorithmic transparency, are critical to ensure responsible use and investor confidence. In conclusion, social media sentiment plays a pivotal role in modern ESG investment strategies by offering real-time, forward-looking, and perception-sensitive information that complements traditional ESG ratings (Shams A., et al, 2026). By capturing the dynamic reactions of investors, stakeholders, and the broader public, sentiment analysis enhances the predictive power of ESG evaluations, improves risk-adjusted portfolio performance, and enables proactive management of reputational and operational risks. The integration of social media sentiment into ESG-focused portfolios allows investors to navigate complex, information-rich markets, aligning financial returns with sustainability objectives and reinforcing a feedback loop that encourages transparent, responsible, and sustainable corporate behaviour. As digital communication platforms continue to proliferate and ESG integration deepens globally, social media sentiment is poised to become a cornerstone of sustainable investment strategy, providing both empirical insight and practical guidance for asset managers, institutional investors, and corporate stakeholders seeking to harmonise financial performance with long-term value creation and societal impact.

CONCLUSION

The evolving landscape of sustainable finance increasingly recognises that the interplay between environmental, social, and governance (ESG) performance, investor sentiment, and financial outcomes represents a critical nexus for both academic inquiry and practical application. Traditional approaches to ESG investing have primarily focused on static, disclosure-based assessments, relying on quantitative scores derived from ESG rating agencies, sustainability reports, and regulatory filings to evaluate corporate performance and inform portfolio decisions. While these methods provide valuable insights into a firm's operational and ethical footprint, they often fail to capture the dynamic, real-time influence of market perception, stakeholder sentiment, and societal narratives on financial outcomes. Investor sentiment, encompassing both qualitative and quantitative market perceptions, plays a pivotal role in moderating the relationship between ESG performance and financial metrics such as stock returns, firm valuation, cost of capital, liquidity, and risk-adjusted performance. The integration of sentiment signals—derived from textual analysis of news media, social media, analyst commentary, and other information channels—into ESG evaluation frameworks represents a frontier for sustainable finance research and practice, offering the potential to enhance predictive accuracy, portfolio responsiveness, and risk management. Empirical research in this domain increasingly leverages advanced computational and econometric techniques to quantify and analyse the ESG-sentiment-financial nexus. Natural language processing (NLP) methods—including lexicon-based sentiment scoring, supervised and unsupervised machine learning models, and transformer-based architectures such as BERT, FinBERT, and RoBERTa—enable the extraction of sentiment signals from vast unstructured textual data, capturing the polarity, intensity, and contextual relevance of ESG-related discourse. These sentiment metrics, when integrated with conventional ESG scores, produce hybrid measures that reflect both the intrinsic sustainability performance of firms and the extrinsic perceptions held by investors, media, and other stakeholders. Interaction effects between ESG and sentiment can then be examined through panel regressions, hierarchical models, structural equation modelling, and event-study analyses, assessing how market responses to ESG initiatives vary across sectors, geographies, market conditions, and temporal horizons. Findings consistently demonstrate that sentiment modulates the impact of ESG performance on financial outcomes: positive sentiment amplifies the benefits of strong ESG practices on stock returns, firm valuation, and liquidity, while negative sentiment can attenuate or even reverse these benefits, particularly in sectors with high ESG materiality or firms facing reputational challenges. Despite these advances, several challenges and research opportunities remain in linking sentiment, ESG, and financial outcomes. Data quality, coverage, and standardisation are ongoing concerns: ESG ratings vary across providers in methodology, weighting, and scope, while sentiment extraction from textual sources requires careful calibration to avoid noise, bias, or misinterpretation. Cross-linguistic, cultural, and platform-specific differences further complicate sentiment analysis, particularly in global investment contexts. Methodologically, endogeneity, reverse causality, and confounding factors pose challenges for causal inference, necessitating robust econometric and machine learning approaches, including instrumental variable techniques, dynamic panel modelling, and machine learning explainability tools. Ethical considerations regarding data privacy, algorithmic transparency, and responsible use of AI in investment decision-making are paramount, ensuring that sentiment-informed ESG strategies align with broader societal norms and fiduciary obligations. In conclusion, the linkage between ESG performance, market sentiment, and financial outcomes represents a dynamic frontier in sustainable finance, offering profound implications for investors, corporate managers, and policymakers. By combining objective ESG metrics with perception-driven sentiment indicators, stakeholders can gain a more holistic and forward-looking understanding of firm value, risk, and resilience. Sentiment-enhanced ESG frameworks improve predictive accuracy, inform portfolio allocation, mitigate liquidity and reputational risks, and reinforce the alignment between financial performance and sustainability objectives. The integration of ESG and sentiment signals into investment decision-making facilitates more responsive, informed, and responsible capital allocation, fostering a virtuous cycle in which corporate sustainability practices, stakeholder perceptions, and market outcomes mutually reinforce one another. As technological capabilities, data availability, and methodological rigour continue to advance, linking ESG, sentiment, and financial outcomes will become a cornerstone of next-generation sustainable finance, guiding the development of investment strategies that generate both economic returns and positive societal impact across diverse industries, regions, and market conditions.

REFERENCES

Abou Tanos, B., Ahmed, N., & Farooq, O. (2024). The Impact of COVID-19-Induced Sentiment on Firm Performance: The Moderating Impact of Sustainable ESG Activities. *Sustainability (Basel)*, *16*(5), 1987. Advance online publication. DOI: 10.3390/su16167053

Aksoy, M., & Yilmaz, M. K. (2025). Financial performance of emerging market companies during the COVID-19 pandemic: Moderating role of sustainability performance. *Journal of Global Responsibility*, *16*(3), 520–541. Advance online publication. DOI: 10.1108/JGR-11-2023-0174

Ang, G., Guo, Z., & Lim, E. P. (2023). On predicting ESG ratings using dynamic company networks. *ACM Transactions on Management Information Systems*, *14*(4), 45. Advance online publication. DOI: 10.1145/3607874

Atak, A., Mehta, P., & Singh, A. (2024). "ESG sentiment and idiosyncratic volatility: Evidence from the Turkish stock market." Emerging Markets Review, Volume 51. *Article*, *100987*, 1–14. DOI: 10.1016/j.ememar.2024.100987

Bhatnagar, M., Rajaram, R., Ali, T., & Mehta, P. (2025). "Correlating investor patterns and ESG performance with neuromarketing insights: Behavioural finance meets sustainability." Sustainability, Volume 17, Issue 6. *Article*, *23456*, 1–15. DOI: 10.3390/su170623456

Ebenezer, Y., Durga, K., Chandrakala, N. B., Shashank, G., Sharma, M., Selvakumar, P., & Manjunath, T. C. (2026). Disaster education and awareness programs. In Ali, Q., & Tariq Iqbal Khan, M. (Eds.), *Strengthening Global Resilience to Natural Disasters* (pp. 73–102). IGI Global Scientific Publishing. [REMOVED HYPERLINK FIELD], DOI: 10.4018/979-8-3693-9745-9.ch004

Gupta, H., & Chaudhary, R. (2023). An analysis of volatility and risk-adjusted returns of ESG indices in developed and emerging economies. *Risks*, *11*(10), 173. Advance online publication. DOI: 10.3390/risks11100182

Han, J. J., Jun, S., & Kim, J. W. (2025). *Examining the Impact of ESG News Sentiment on Corporate Performance: A Comprehensive Analysis by News Topic and Industry*. Business Strategy, the Environment & Responsibility., DOI: 10.1002/bse.3501

Jaiswal, R., Gupta, S., & Tiwari, A. K. (2024). Decoding mood of the Twitterverse on ESG investing: Opinion mining and key themes using machine learning. *Management Research Review*, *47*(8), 1234–1256. DOI: 10.1108/MRR-07-2023-0526

Jeong, S. H., Han, J. J., Jun, S., Kim, S., & Kim, J. W. (2025). Investor Responses to ESG News Sentiment: Exploring Differential Effects and Industry Moderation. *Corporate Social Responsibility and Environmental Management*, *32*(3), 3944–3964. Advance online publication. DOI: 10.1002/csr.3163

Joshi, N. V., Selvakumar, P., & Srivastava, N. Manjeet, Das A, Manjunath T C, (2026). "Bioethics legal implications of artificial intelligence in medicine." In Anastasiadou S, Seremeti L, Papalexandris S (Eds.), Bioethics and Legal Aspects of AI in Healthcare and Life Sciences (pp. 27-54). IGI Global Scientific Publishing. DOI: .[REMOVED HYPERLINK FIELD]DOI: 10.4018/979-8-3373-5646-4.ch002

Julliete, A., Palma, J., Wangs, S., & Mehta, P. (2025). "Investor behavior in ESG markets: Psychological drivers behind sustainable investment choices." Journal of Behavioral and Experimental Finance, Volume 38. *Article*, *101234*, 1–14. DOI: 10.1016/j.jbef.2025.101234

Lee, H., Kim, J. H., & Jung, H. S. (2024). Deep-learning-based stock market prediction incorporating ESG sentiment and technical indicators. *Scientific Reports*, *14*(1), 12345. Advance online publication. DOI: 10.1038/s41598-024-61106-2 PMID: 38704434

Lee, S., Kumar, R., & Chen, L. (2025). Modeling firm-level ESG sentiment interactions in stock returns: Evidence from retrofitted word embeddings. *The Journal of Financial Data Science*, *7*(3), 145–160. DOI: 10.3905/jfds.2025.1.145

Lheureux, Y. (2024). Predictive insights: Leveraging Twitter sentiments and machine learning for environmental, social and governance controversy prediction. *Journal of Computational Social Science*, *7*(2), 345–367. DOI: 10.1007/s42001-023-00228-5

Liu, M., Ling, Y. J., & Lee, C. C. (2025). Does ESG performance and investor attention affect stock volatility? An empirical study based on panel data and mixed-frequency data. *Applied Economics*, *57*(57), 9728–9742. Advance online publication. DOI: 10.1080/00036846.2024.2423068

Liu, M., Luo, X., & Lu, W. Z. (2023). Public perceptions of environmental, social, and governance (ESG) based on social media data: Evidence from China. *Journal of Cleaner Production*, *385*, 135678. Advance online publication. DOI: 10.1016/j.jclepro.2022.135840

Loang, O. K., Patel, R., & Chen, L. (2025). From tweets to trades: Investor sentiment, attention, and news sentiment in ESG stocks. *Journal of Sustainable Finance & Investment*, *15*(2), 234–250. DOI: 10.1080/20430795.2025.1134568

Martínez-Ferrero, J., & Lozano, M. B. (2021). The nonlinear relation between institutional ownership and environmental, social and governance performance in emerging countries. *Sustainability (Basel)*, *13*(3), 1586. Advance online publication. DOI: 10.3390/su13031586

Maurya, P. K., Bansal, R., & Mishra, A. K. (2025). *Investor sentiment and its implication on global financial markets: a systematic review of literature*. Qualitative Research in Financial Markets., DOI: 10.1108/QRFM-06-2024-0123

Ooi, K. L., Binti Ab Aziz, N., Lau, W. Y., & Chen, L. (2025). "The future of behavioural finance in a sustainable world: Psychological mechanisms in sustainable investing." Journal of Behavioral and Experimental Finance, Volume 38. *Article*, *101245*, 1–14. DOI: 10.1016/j.jbef.2025.101245

Paira, D., Rohini, A., Chandra, S., Satyanarayana, P., Sharma, M., Selvakumar, P., & Manjunath, T. C. (2026). Climate change and natural disasters. In Ali, Q., & Tariq Iqbal Khan, M. (Eds.), *Strengthening Global Resilience to Natural Disasters* (pp. 21–44). IGI Global Scientific Publishing. [REMOVED HYPERLINK FIELD], DOI: 10.4018/979-8-3693-9745-9.ch002

Pegoraro, S., Rizzo, A. E., & Zambrana, R. (2023). "ESG Sentiment: A Revealed-Preference Approach." SSRN Electronic Journal. DOI: DOI: 10.2139/ssrn.4645547

Pu, G. (2023). "A non-linear assessment of ESG and firm performance relationship: Evidence from China." Economic Research-. *Ekonomska Istraživanja*, *36*(1), 1690–1707. DOI: 10.1080/1331677X.2022.2113336

Renfield, M. A., Mensah, C. J., & Ali, T. (2025). Predictive analytics for sustainable finance using intelligent automation. *Journal of Sustainable Finance & Investment*, *15*(4), 567–582. DOI: 10.1080/20430795.2025.1134570

Saxena, A., Santhanavijayan, A., Shakya, H. K., Kumar, G., Balusamy, B., & Benedetto, F. (2024). Nested sentiment analysis for ESG impact: Leveraging FinBERT to predict market dynamics based on eco-friendly and non-eco-friendly product perceptions with explainable AI. *Mathematics*, *12*(21), 3332. Advance online publication. DOI: 10.3390/math12213332

Shams, A., Kunnathully, K., Satyanarayana, P., Sangeetha, B., Jayamala, C., Selvakumar, P., & Manjunath, T. C. (2026). E-government and digital public services. In Santos Silva, L., & Solleiro, J. (Eds.), *Intersecting Public Administration and Technology for Public Trust and Citizen Engagement* (pp. 75–100). IGI Global Scientific Publishing. [REMOVED HYPERLINK FIELD], DOI: 10.4018/979-8-3693-9709-1.ch004

Sree Vani, Y., Selvakumar, P., Prabhanjan Yadav, B., Kanipriya, M., Arun, M. R., Bansal, A., & Manjunath, T. C. (2026). Applying machine learning and AI to IoT data for robotic intelligence. In Al-Humairi, S., Naronglerdrit, P., Chantarapanich, N., & Wanchat, S. (Eds.), *Robotics and IoT Synergy in Next-Generation Healthcare* (pp. 99–128). IGI Global Scientific Publishing. [REMOVED HYPERLINK FIELD], DOI: 10.4018/979-8-3373-5447-7.ch004

Sultana, N., & Zeya, F. (2025). Advancing Firm-Specific ESG Sentiment Analysis: A Machine Learning Approach to Clustering, Prediction, and Financial Performance Implications. *Business Strategy & Development*, *8*(3), e70150. Advance online publication. DOI: 10.1002/bsd2.70150

Taheripour, E., Sadjadi, S. J., & Amiri, B. (2025). A multi-criteria approach to ESG-based portfolio optimization incorporating historical performance, forward-looking insights, and credibilistic CVaR: A case study on S&P 500. *Scientific Reports*, *15*(1), 1234. Advance online publication. DOI: 10.1038/s41598-025-24242-x PMID: 41203680

Tan, W., Dong, Q., Xu, C., & Sun, Y. (2025). Navigating the ESG seascape: Media sentiment toward ESG and corporate strategies. *Journal of Accounting Literature*. Advance online publication. DOI: 10.1108/JAL-04-2024-0057

Vuong, N. B. (2022). Investor sentiment, corporate social responsibility, and financial performance: Evidence from Japanese companies. *Borsa Istanbul Review*, *22*(4), 805–817. DOI: 10.1016/j.bir.2022.06.010

Vuong, N. B., Suzuki, Y., Ali, T., & Mehta, P. (2021). "The motivating role of sentiment in ESG performance: Evidence from Japanese companies." Journal of Cleaner Production, Volume 315. *Article*, *128123*, 1–12. DOI: 10.1016/j.jclepro.2021.128123

Yousaf, I., Bejaoui, A., Ali, S., & Li, Y. (2024). Demystifying the dynamic relationship between news sentiment index and ESG stocks: Evidence from time-frequency wavelet analysis. *International Review of Financial Analysis*, *96*, 103630. Advance online publication. DOI: 10.1016/j.irfa.2024.103698

Yu, H., Liang, C., Liu, Z., & Cui, X. (2025). The Effectiveness of News-Based ESG Sentiment for Predicting Stock Returns: Evidence From China. *Accounting and Finance*, *65*(3), 2724–2732. Advance online publication. DOI: 10.1111/acfi.70015

Zhang, X., Xu, D. P., Hong, H., & Chan, K. (2025). Attention or Sentiment: How Social Media React to ESG? *Information Systems Research*, isre.2022.0251. Advance online publication. DOI: 10.1287/isre.2022.0251

Chapter 5
Policy Shocks, Climate Risk, and Sentiment Spillovers Pricing Green Bonds and Carbon Assets Under Uncertainty

Mohammad Al Khaldy
http://orcid.org/0009-0009-7502-4668
University of Petra, Amman, Jordan

Vineeta Singh
http://orcid.org/0000-0003-1084-279X
Chhatrapati Shahu Ji Maharaj University, Kanpur, India

ABSTRACT

Green bonds and carbon assets are linked through regulation, investor mandates, and climate news, responding to policy credibility, macro conditions, and sentiment shifts. Under uncertainty, pricing becomes state dependent: the same policy surprise can compress green-bond yields while raising carbon-price volatility, or trigger joint selloffs when doubt and risk aversion rise together. Policy surprises affect valuation through four channels — cash flows, discount rates, liquidity, and sentiment contagion — with responses shaped by verification quality, issuer type, and market depth. Carbon assets react more to regulatory credibility and energy conditions; green bonds more to investor clienteles, taxonomies, and balance-sheet constraints. Sentiment spillovers amplify both markets most when policy uncertainty is high and news spreads fast. The chapter proposes a state-dependent joint-pricing

DOI: 10.4018/979-8-3373-8392-7.ch005

framework, draws implications for portfolio and issuance strategy, and outlines a research agenda integrating policy uncertainty, climate tail risk, and network effects into asset-pricing models.

1. INTRODUCTION

Climate finance has been described through separate market segments, but valuations now bleed across these segments, ever more rapidly. A carbon allowance reacts, we know, to a cap revision, a subsidy change or an energy security shock; why? Each impacts expectations over scarcity, abatement demands. A green bond reacts, if only to some subset of those events but via different channels: demand from sustainability mandates, claims around the issuer's transition plan and taxonomies/ verifiers credibility, to fixed income liquidity. As soon as a climate policy shock becomes a recurring item on the front page of macro financial news, these cannot simply be priced up independently. Our core issue here concerns joint pricing, under uncertainty, alongside climate risk and/or sentiment spill overs onto green bond yields and the price(s) of carbon.

There are compelling reasons to look at these connections collectively in the current literature. According to research the environmental label certification and investor clientele can generate a pricing premium or greenium though the amount varies depending on issuer type market depth and verification quality (Hachenberg and Schiereck 2018 Zerbib 2019 Bachelet et al. (2019 Flammer 2021). Research on carbon and climate risk comes to a similar conclusion from a different perspective, returns option prices and corporate bond spreads incorporate climate news transition risk and carbon exposure however the impact varies depending on whether markets view climate risk as tail risk expected regulation or a general macro-financial factor (Engle et al. Ilhan and colleagues 2020. Bolton & Kacperczyk 2021 Huynh & Xia 2021). By demonstrating how green bonds clean energy stocks carbon allowances and policy-uncertainty indicators transmit shocks to one another over time with intensification during stressful times studies of market connectedness add a third component (Reboredo 2018 Reboredo & Ugolini 2020 Wu & Liu 2023 Ringstad & Tselika 2024).

This chapter makes the case that three types of uncertainty need to be addressed in tandem. The first is policy uncertainty which encompasses monetary and fiscal policy surprises disclosure and taxonomy changes climate policy revisions and the more general uncertainty measured by economic policy uncertainty indices (Baker et al. 2016 Gavriilidis 2021). The second is the actual risk posed by climate change. Physical risk transition risk and climate tail risk are all included in that category. However, transition risk is particularly significant for carbon assets and green bonds since it alters expected costs expected revenues and compliance behavior over a comparatively short time horizon (Hong et al. (2019) Ilhan et al. Giglio and colleagues 2021. in 2021. The third is the spillover of sentiment. All climate-related information is not processed by markets as a slow-moving fundamental. Trading behavior, liquidity provision and demand for cross-asset hedging are all influenced by news salience narratives about policy credibility sustainable fund flows and short-term fear or enthusiasm. Therefore, sentiment can convey a policy signal that extends beyond its direct impact on cash flow.

Because carbon assets and green bonds are located at different stages of the climate-finance architecture an integrated approach is required. Green bonds are debt instruments whose valuation starts with standard bond pricing but is altered by reporting requirements labeled-use restrictions and investor preferences for environmental alignment. In contrast carbon assets are derivatives and regulatory assets whose value is based on program design abatement technology that permits scarcity and the anticipated cost of compliance. Sensitivity to transition policy is a characteristic they have in common. The way that policy affects price formation is where they diverge. When it comes to green bonds the question is frequently whether policy enhances project viability lowers information barriers or modifies the ratio of labeled to unlabeled demand. Regarding carbon assets the question is whether policy affects market stability regulations, the expected trajectory of allowance scarcity or the legitimacy of enforcement. These differences are significant because they produce asymmetric reactions to the same shock. Figure 1 illustrates how three sources of shocks — policy shocks, climate risk news, and market sentiment/fund flows — feed into four transmission channels (expected cash flows, discount rates, liquidity/margins, and attention/narratives) that ultimately shape green bond yields and the greenium. Each shock source connects to multiple transmission channels simultaneously, reflecting the interconnected nature of these forces rather than a simple linear pathway. Finally, the diagram shows a spillover loop between green bond markets and carbon prices/volatility, highlighting that these two markets mutually reinforce and influence each other as outcomes.

Figure 1. Integrated transmission channels from policy shocks and climate news to green bond and carbon-asset pricing.

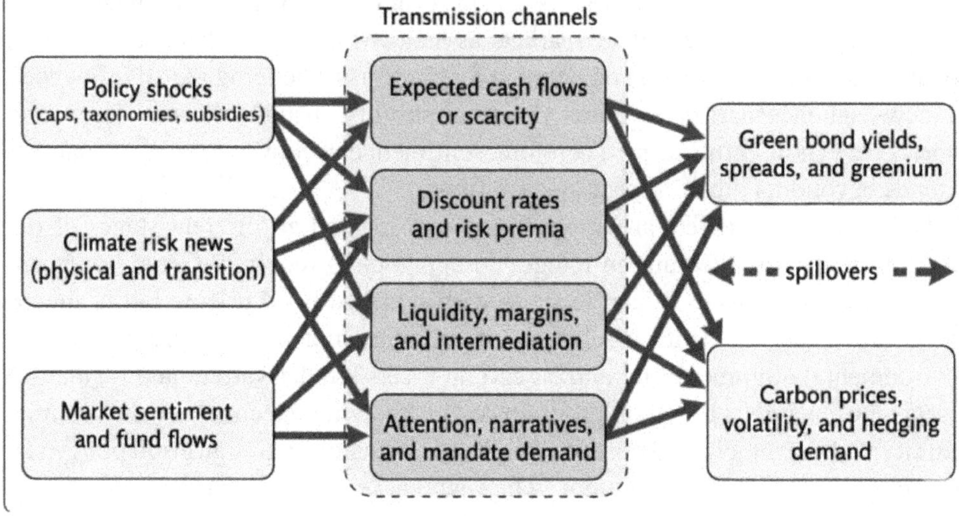

A second justification for an integrated chapter is methodological. Spillover networks time-varying parameter vector autoregressions quantile techniques and regime-dependent models are increasingly used in empirical literature to examine sustainable-finance markets. When sentiment and policy credibility result in non-linear responses these approaches are particularly appropriate. When compliance regulations are stable and liquidity is high a slight increase in climate-policy uncertainty might not have much of an impact. However, when energy prices are volatile leverage is high or investors are changing their opinions about future regulations the same increase could have significant repercussions. Diebold and Yilmaz (2012, 2014) created connectedness metrics which were subsequently expanded using time-varying parameter techniques (Antonakakis et al. 2020) assist in charting these evolving transmission routes. Giving them a clear economic interpretation is one of the chapters objectives.

Section 2 sets out the conceptual background and distinguishes the pricing channels that operate through cash flows, discount rates, liquidity, and sentiment. Sections 3 and 4 examine green bond pricing and carbon asset pricing separately before Section 5 considers spillovers across markets. Section 6 develops a state-dependent framework for joint pricing under uncertainty, and the remaining sections discuss implications, future work, and conclusions.

2. CONCEPTUAL FOUNDATIONS: TRANSMISSION CHANNELS AND INSTRUMENT DESIGN

There are four main ways in which policy shocks impact climate-finance instruments. The first is anticipated cash flow. A tax credit grid-investment plan or subsidy for low-carbon transportation can alter the anticipated profitability of businesses involved in abatement or renewable deployment and improve the operating outlook for projects funded by green bonds. By increasing scarcity, a cap tightening in an emissions trading system can increase the anticipated future value of carbon allowances. The second channel is the rate of discount. Even when projected cash flows improve higher macro uncertainty, tighter monetary conditions or an increase in perceived climate tail risk can raise required returns. Market liquidity comes in third. Only when balance-sheet capacity is available, which is constrained during times of stress—can dealers exchange members and institutional investors take in news. Sentiment is the fourth channel. Fund flows attention and investors' willingness to accept lower yields on green instruments can all change once narratives about policy credibility or climate ambition become prominent. Table 1 provides an overview of these channels' functions across common shock categories.

Table 1. Policy shocks and expected pricing responses across green bonds and carbon assets

Shock type	Primary transmission	Green bond pricing response	Carbon-asset response	Dominant horizon
Cap tightening or allowance-supply reform	Expected scarcity, compliance cost	Indirect support for issuers financing abatement; mixed effect on spreads if rates rise	Higher expected permit prices; often higher volatility during adjustment	Short to medium term
Green taxonomy clarification	Classification risk, eligibility	Lower uncertainty about label quality; potential greenium compression	Small direct effect unless it changes offset or compliance treatment	Medium term
Subsidy or tax-credit expansion	Project viability, issuance pipeline	Lower spreads for issuers with eligible capex; stronger primary-market demand	Can lower permit demand if renewables expand faster	Medium term
Disclosure and reporting mandates	Information asymmetry, monitoring	Favors verified issues and transparent issuers	Improves information processing but limited direct scarcity effect	Medium term

continued on following page

Table 1. Continued

Shock type	Primary transmission	Green bond pricing response	Carbon-asset response	Dominant horizon
Monetary tightening with policy uncertainty	Discount rates, funding conditions	Higher yields; greenium may narrow if rate risk dominates demand	Lower risk appetite and tighter collateral conditions can raise volatility	Short term
Energy-security shock	Fuel switching, industrial outlook, narrative shift	Mixed effect; utilities and sovereigns may benefit if transition spending rises	Often strong response through fuel substitution and compliance expectations	Immediate to medium term

Green bonds and carbon assets respond to the same policy event differently which can be explained by two design elements. Issuers are the targets of green bonds. Unless the bond contains performance clauses, structure-specific protections or event risk associated with taxonomy violations their cash flows are largely dependent on the issuers' credit quality and only indirectly on the environmental project financed. Carbon assets are closer to claims made by regulators. The allowance supply banking regulations offset eligibility coverage extent and compliance entity behavior all affect their value. Because of this credit spreads liquidity premium and investor preference for labeled debt typically influence green bond prices while scarcity expectations fuel-switching economics and policy credibility influence carbon prices. Because sustainable investors anticipate stronger project pipelines and reduced transition risk an increase in climate policy ambition may compress the yield of a verified green bond issued by a reputable utility. Depending on whether market players prioritize tighter future caps or quicker renewable substitution that lowers permit demand the same policy change may result in either an increase or a decrease in carbon prices.

Research on green bonds demonstrates that the environmental label is neither irrelevant nor consistently priced. Hachenberg and Schiereck (2018) Zerbib (2019) Pham (2016) Bachelet et al. (2019) Gianfrate and Peri (2019) and Flammer (2021) all show using various data and techniques that pricing is a combination of segmented demand certification quality and standard bond valuation. When markets reevaluate the labels value that mix becomes extremely sensitive to policy credibility.

Research on the carbon market uses a different approach to reach a similar conclusion. Current emissions and energy demand are not the only factors influencing carbon prices. They represent expectations regarding fuel prices weather industrial adjustment rate future allowance scarcity and the trading systems institutional integrity. Creti and others (2012) demonstrate that different EU Emissions Trading System phases have different drivers of carbon prices while Koch et al. (2014) attribute significant price weakness to a confluence of renewable policies the Clean Development Mechanism credit supply and the recession. These results highlight a persistent issue with carbon pricing: participants must extrapolate the markets' future structure from existing policy signals which are frequently ambiguously delayed or contested. In that context it is difficult to distinguish between policy interpretation and an apparent fundamental variable like energy demand. As a result, carbon assets have a strong credibility component.

Table 2. Comparative pricing frictions in green bonds and carbon assets

Dimension	Green bonds	Carbon assets	Pricing implication
Cash-flow anchor	Issuer coupon and principal, subject to credit risk	Allowance scarcity and compliance value	Policy can affect numerator in both markets, but through different mechanisms
Policy sensitivity	High through taxonomy, subsidy support, disclosure rules, investor mandates	Very high through cap design, reserve rules, offset eligibility, enforcement	Carbon assets usually react more directly to regulatory revisions
Liquidity structure	Dealer-intermediated bond market with uneven depth	Exchange and clearing based with margin sensitivity	Liquidity shocks can reverse relative pricing in stress periods
Verification or credibility	External review, reporting quality, proceeds governance	Rule credibility, enforcement history, administrative transparency	Credibility reduces discount-rate premia in both markets
Investor base	Sustainable funds, pensions, banks, insurers, central banks	Compliance entities, traders, utilities, hedge funds, market makers	Clientele differences create asymmetric reactions to the same news
Hedging role	Can hedge carbon or brown-credit exposure in some states	Hedges transition cost exposure but may intensify portfolio volatility	Hedging effectiveness is regime dependent, not fixed
Sentiment load	Strong through fund flows and label demand	Strong through speculative positioning and policy narratives	High attention can increase cross-market connectedness

These mechanisms have a longer time horizon due to climate risk. The main concern is not just whether regulations will be more stringent in the future but also whether transition costs will be gradual or sudden. Giglio and others (2021) define climate finance as an area where standard asset-pricing questions interact with long-horizon uncertainty. Hong and colleagues (2019) highlight the connection between market efficiency and climate risks through attention and information processing limitations. Engle & Co. (2020) demonstrate that news about climate change can be hedged by suggesting that climate news is now a priced information item. The Ilhan group (2021) identify carbon tail risk in options markets and recommend that investors focus more on extreme regulatory outcomes than on average expected paths. Even if the mean forecast changes only slightly the same bond or allowance may be sharply revalued following a policy announcement once tail scenarios enter pricing.

Another layer is added by investor clients. Climate information is processed differently by commodity traders, bank treasuries pension funds liability-driven investors and sustainable funds. Pávor and associates (2021 2022) demonstrate how preferences for green assets can impact expected returns meaning that changes in reporting or taxonomy can affect demand before financed projects show a discernible cash-flow effect. Utilities industrial companies market makers hedge funds, and proprietary traders are among the diverse clientele of carbon markets whose responses are more directly influenced by compliance incentives and hedging requirements. Figure 2 maps the interaction between policy credibility (x-axis) and climate-risk salience (y-axis) to characterize green bond market conditions. When both dimensions are low, markets are noisy and carbon signals are largely ignored, while high credibility alone produces stable greenium and fundamental carbon pricing even without heightened public concern. The most turbulent quadrant is high salience paired with low credibility, where sentiment dominates and the greenium becomes fragile, whereas the ideal quadrant — high credibility and high salience — yields rewarded green issuance, priced carbon scarcity, and informative market spillovers.

Figure 2. State-dependent pricing regimes for green bonds and carbon assets.

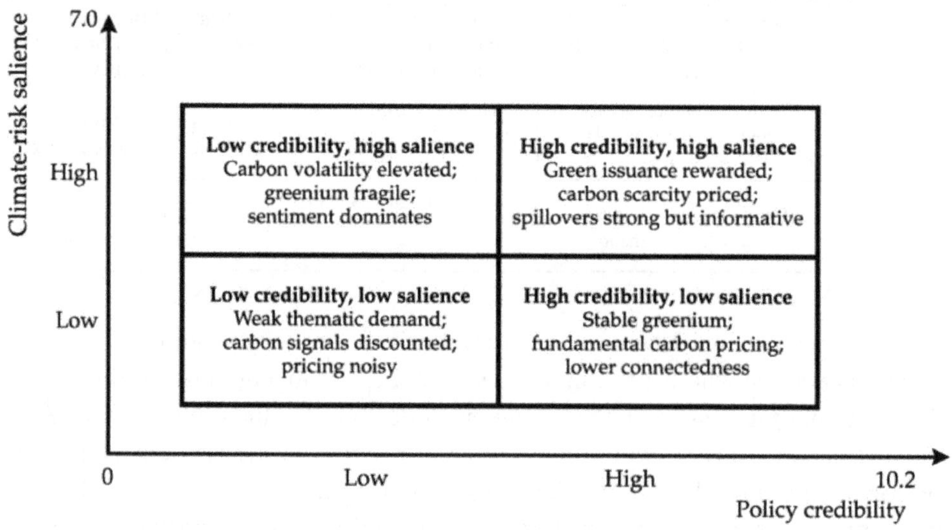

Therefore, differentiating between direct and indirect policy effects is a useful way to structure the chapter. When a policy shock modifies contractual cash flows, expected scarcity or compliance costs direct effects occur. When the same shock alters how investors categorize an asset what risk premium they demand or how much liquidity the market can provide it can have indirect effects. Because the significance of labeling certification and mandate compatibility can fluctuate quickly green bonds are particularly vulnerable to indirect effects. In addition to being particularly vulnerable to direct scarcity effects, carbon assets are also subject to indirect effects from exchange margins collateral policy and financial participants' willingness to take on intermediate risk. Pricing relationships that appear stable during normal times can break down when uncertainty increases due to the interplay between direct and indirect effects.

3. PRICING GREEN BONDS UNDER POLICY UNCERTAINTY

Green bond pricing starts with standard bond analytics but it's more than just a traditional bond with a theme attached. Allocating proceeds reporting credibility, external review issuer reputation and regulatory recognition are all important factors to investors. These characteristics influence the bonds eligibility for internal environmental targets central-bank purchase programs green indices and sustainable portfolios. Policy shocks frequently affect investor access and classification rather than the issuers short-run default risk because eligibility affects demand and demand affects price. This clarifies why the greenium is frequently small in absolute terms but significant from an economic standpoint. When issuances are substantial, maturities are lengthy and the issuers' transition strategy involves frequent access to the market a few basis points are significant.

According to published research greenium is not constant but rather heterogeneous. Green and conventional bond prices differ according to Hachenberg and Schiereck (2018). According to Zerbib (2019) pro-environmental preferences can result in lower yields. Bachelet & Co. (2019) contend that issuer characteristics and third-party verification determine the premium suggesting that environmental labeling alone is insufficient. Gianfrate and Peri (2019) also discover benefits associated with conditions of issuance. The Fatica group. (2021) investigate whether financial institutions are unique and come to the conclusion that issuer identity influences pricing. By connecting the issuance of green bonds to operational results and investor reaction Flammer (2021) adds a crucial corporate finance viewpoint. The main takeaway is that the pricing of green bonds is determined by the relationship between environmental credibility and credit risk. The relative importance of those two elements is altered by policy uncertainty.

Table 3. Selected empirical evidence on green bond pricing

Study	Sample focus	Method	Main inference
Pham (2016)	Green bond market volatility	Volatility analysis	Green bonds exhibit distinctive volatility behavior, implying a specific risk profile.
Hachenberg and Schiereck (2018)	Green vs. conventional bonds	Matched pricing comparison	Green bonds are priced differently from comparable conventional bonds.
Zerbib (2019)	International green bond sample	Matched bond analysis	Pro-environmental preferences help explain lower yields for green bonds.
Bachelet et al. (2019)	Issuer and certification heterogeneity	Cross-sectional analysis	The premium depends on issuer characteristics and third-party verification.
Gianfrate and Peri (2019)	Corporate and institutional issuers	Issuance-cost comparison	Issuers can obtain financing convenience from green labeling.
Tang and Zhang (2020)	Corporate green bond issues	Event-study approach	Green issuance can benefit shareholders and signal credible investment.
Flammer (2021)	Corporate issuers	Corporate-finance analysis	Green bonds are linked to real outcomes and investor response.
Fatica et al. (2021)	Financial institutions	Institutional comparison	Pricing differences vary by issuer type and market segment.

A credible tightening of climate commitments coupled with more precise green-taxonomy guidelines would be an example of a positive policy shock. The immediate impact of a traditional project bond might be restricted since the terms of the contract remain unchanged. However, there are three ways that the same event can reduce yields for a green bond. First investors may anticipate a greater pipeline of qualified projects in the future which boosts trust that the issuer's green financing approach is long-term rather than opportunistic. Second there is less chance of classification when taxonomy is clear. The idea that a bond that is marketed as green today might later be viewed as marginal or non-compliant bothers investors. Third, institutions responsible for climate targets and net-zero pathways may become more demanding because of increased policy ambition. Thus, the price effect cannot be considered a pure subsidy. Stronger mandate compatibility reduced information friction, and the expected scarcity of premium labeled paper are the causes.

These effects can be swiftly undone by a negative policy shock. Even if the issuers' standalone credit profile doesn't change green bonds may suffer through the discount-rate and liquidity channels if a government weakens implementation postpones carbon-pricing reform or creates uncertainty about what constitutes sustainable spending. After that investors reevaluate whether the labeled debt market is backed by long-term policy or fleeting zeal. These episodes are particularly instructive because they show whether the greenium is motivated by convenience or conviction. Strong verification and a steady investor clientele are probably helping a bond maintain a pricing advantage during policy disappointment. It's possible that a bond that experiences a significant decline in relative performance was priced on erratic expectations regarding future policy support.

For primary-market strategy this distinction is crucial. Verification and reporting quality are therefore not secondary details. They affect both the level and the resilience of the greenium. Bachelet et al. (2019) show that third-party verification helps explain the premium. In practice, external review reduces concerns about adverse selection and greenwashing. It also gives portfolio managers a defensible basis for inclusion in sustainability products. During periods of uncertainty, that assurance can support demand because investors know that a verified bond is less likely to face classification disputes. The same logic applies to post-issuance reporting. Regular and project-specific reporting lowers information asymmetry about proceeds use and environmental outcomes. It makes the bond easier to retain during market stress because the manager can justify the position internally and externally. Policy shocks that increase scrutiny will therefore tend to favor issues with stronger verification architecture.

Equally significant is the type of issuer. Due to differences in their investor bases and benchmark roles, sovereigns' supranational corporations' agencies, municipalities, financial institutions and corporations are subject to different pricing conditions. A shifting value for the green label in the United States is documented by Karpf and Mandel (2018). For S. municipal market indicating that the impact is shaped by local market circumstances. According to Tang and Zhang (2020) the issuance of green bonds can benefit shareholders by signaling credible transition investment through both debt and equity channels. Because their bonds are liquid and index-friendly financial institution issues may benefit from special demand, investors also carefully consider whether proceeds are genuinely extra or just a refinance of ongoing balance-sheet activity. When green issuance is linked to a visible investment program corporate issues can reap greater signaling benefits. Therefore, rather than being solely determined by label the pricing effect is embedded in the institutional context.

Attention should be given to liquidity. The depth of green bond markets is still uneven across currencies maturities and issuer classes despite their growth. Segmented demand can reduce yields in a calm market as committed investors fight for the limited supply. The same segmentation can either stabilize or destabilize prices under stress. If generalist investors lower risk and buy-and-hold sustainable investors continue to absorb paper it stabilizes. Because policy uncertainty increases rate volatility it becomes unstable if dealer capacity decreases exchange-traded vehicles experience outflows or investors shift away from duration-heavy assets. According to Reboredo and Ugolini (2020) green bond prices are linked to larger financial markets which is consistent with a liquidity channel that gets stronger when the market is under stress. Therefore, pricing models that disregard liquidity conditions will exaggerate the greeniums durability.

Another issue is whether green bonds hedge or amplify climate-related risks. Jin et al. (2020) argue that green bonds can hedge carbon-market risk in some settings. That proposition is attractive but should be treated as conditional. A green bond can hedge carbon exposure when climate policy improves the outlook for low-carbon investment while increasing compliance costs for emission-intensive firms. Yet the hedge weakens when both markets are hit by a common discount-rate shock, for example a monetary tightening that reduces risk appetite. The empirical relation between green bonds and carbon assets is therefore state dependent. Rannou et al. (2021) ask whether green bond and carbon markets are complements or substitutes in Europe and show that the answer depends on firm activity and market conditions. From a pricing perspective, the more useful question is not whether one asset class always hedges the other, but under which policy and liquidity regimes the hedge remains effective.

Policy design can also change term structures within the green bond market. A long-maturity sovereign green bond may benefit from strong strategic demand because pension funds and insurers value long-duration sustainable assets. At the same time, long maturities are more sensitive to uncertainty about discount rates and future taxonomy revisions. Shorter maturities may be more resilient when policy credibility is uncertain, since the horizon for misclassification or project-performance disappointment is smaller. This implies that the greenium can vary across the curve. It also implies that issuance timing matters. An issuer that comes to market immediately after a favorable policy announcement may capture strong demand, but that window can close if macro volatility increases and investors shift from themed allocation to balance-sheet preservation. Figure 3 maps the relationships among key actors in sustainable finance, showing how climate policy uncertainty and economic policy uncertainty jointly influence green bonds both directly and indirectly — the former also operate through investor sentiment and attention. Green bonds sit at the center of the network, receiving input from sovereign/credit markets, carbon assets, and investor sentiment, making them the primary nexus connecting all other market segments. Notably, the dashed arrow from clean energy equities to green bonds signals a weaker or more uncertain linkage compared to the solid bidirectional arrows elsewhere, while carbon assets and clean energy equities share a strong mutual relationship independent of the green bond market.

Figure 3. Cross-market spillover network linking uncertainty, sentiment, and climate-finance assets.

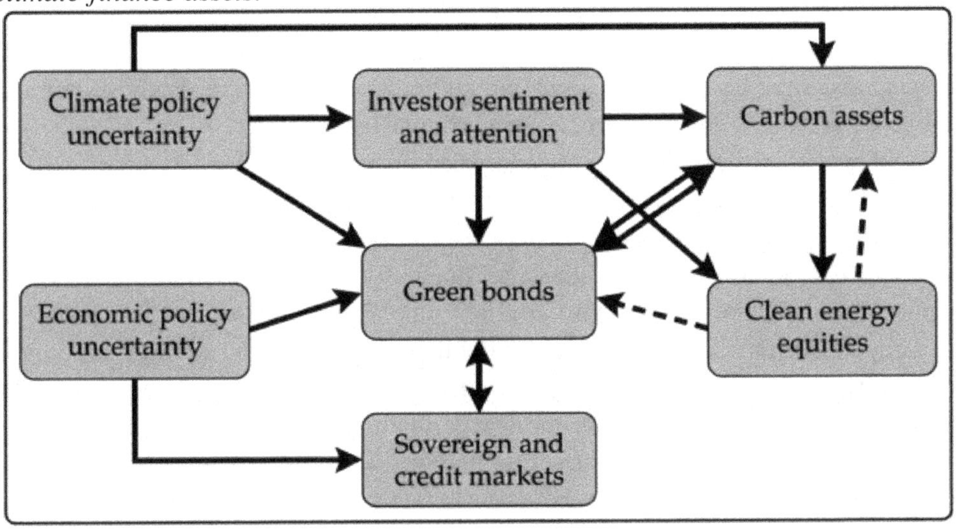

The main implication is that green bond pricing under uncertainty should be modeled as the product of three interacting terms: a conventional credit component, a certification-and-eligibility component, and a state-dependent demand component. The first reflects issuer fundamentals and the interest-rate environment. The second reflects verification quality, taxonomy alignment, and reporting architecture. The third reflects investor mandates, policy credibility, and market sentiment. When policy is credible and liquidity is healthy, the second and third components can reduce yields relative to conventional peers. When policy credibility weakens or discount rates rise sharply, the demand component can reverse quickly, leaving only the conventional credit component. Any serious model of green bond pricing must therefore treat the greenium as conditional, not structural.

4. CARBON ASSET PRICING UNDER TRANSITION RISK AND POLICY SHOCKS

Unlike most financial instruments carbon assets include regulation as a component of the payoff mechanism rather than just background context. The value of an allowance in a cap-and-trade system is determined by current and anticipated scarcity which is administratively determined by offset eligibility reserve mechanisms banking regulations cap trajectories and enforcement design. Carbon pricing is not arbitrary because of this. Weather-switching opportunities, industrial output, energy demand and technology costs are all important. Fundamentals are nevertheless filtered through policy architecture. If participants believe that the emissions cap will be tightened prices will rise right away. However, if the market has doubts about enforcement or anticipates compensating flexibility elsewhere in the system the response may be muted. As a result, setting expectations for both economics and governance is a constant process in carbon asset pricing.

Evidence from the early EU ETS amply demonstrates this. The Creti et al. (2012) demonstrate that different trading phases have different drivers of carbon prices suggesting that participants update pricing rules when institutions change. Koch and others. (2014) attribute the significant decline in EU ETS prices to a confluence of renewable policies international offset credit supply and the recession. The message goes beyond the past. It serves as a reminder that supply-demand equilibrium policy formulation and macroeconomic factors can all have a significant impact on carbon prices. Demand for emissions decreases when industrial output declines. Effective supply rises with more lenient offset regulations. Over time renewable expansion may reduce the need for permits. Even during a time of increased climate rhetoric prices may decrease if these forces materialize while decision-makers are reluctant to tighten future caps. Credible scarcity, not catchphrases is what drives markets.

Table 4. Selected empirical evidence on climate risk and carbon-asset pricing

Study	Market focus	Method	Main inference
Creti et al. (2012)	EU ETS phases I and II	Fundamental driver analysis	Carbon price drivers change across institutional phases.
Koch et al. (2014)	EU ETS price decline	Policy decomposition	Recession, offset supply, and renewable policies jointly explain price weakness.
Engle et al. (2020)	Climate news and returns	Hedging-factor approach	Climate news is a priced source of risk that can be hedged.
Ilhan et al. (2021)	Options and carbon exposure	Tail-risk analysis	Markets attach value to extreme carbon-policy outcomes.
Bolton and Kacperczyk (2021)	Carbon-emission exposure	Asset-pricing tests	Investors care about carbon risk and price emissions exposure.
Huynh and Xia (2021)	Corporate bond market	News-risk regressions	Climate change news risk affects corporate bond returns.
Allman (2022)	Corporate bonds	Climate-risk pricing study	Climate change risk enters corporate bond pricing.
Jia et al. (2024)	Sovereign bonds	Volatility analysis	Climate-policy uncertainty influences sovereign-bond volatility.

Transition risk makes carbon assets especially responsive to discontinuities. A carbon market is often described as a mechanism for gradual adjustment, but the distribution of possible outcomes can be highly asymmetric. Market participants know that policy can jump. Caps can be revised, free allocation can be reduced, sectors can be added, reserve mechanisms can be strengthened, or border measures can alter expected industrial competitiveness. Options evidence supports this interpretation. Ilhan et al. (2021) identify carbon tail risk, indicating that investors place nontrivial weight on extreme outcomes tied to carbon policy or carbon exposure. In practical terms, that means allowance prices contain a tail component that standard mean-variance approaches fail to capture. A small change in the perceived probability of a stringent future regime can matter more than a moderate change in the average expected path.

Climate news has a similar effect because it changes the salience of transition scenarios. Engle et al. (2020) show that climate change news is itself a priced source of variation. Huynh and Xia (2021) find that climate change news risk affects corporate bond returns, which suggests that transition information propagates beyond equity markets and into debt markets. The same logic applies to carbon assets, often with greater immediacy. Carbon markets are designed around future compliance costs. When a heat wave, a wildfire season, or a geopolitical energy shock changes beliefs about energy-system adjustment, carbon participants immediately reassess fuel use, industrial production, renewable deployment, and the likely political appetite for tighter or looser implementation. What appears as environmental news can therefore become a pricing shock through macro and policy expectations.

The distinction between expected and credible policy is another crucial point. Even if two programs declare the same long-term cap path if institutional credibility varies the market will price them differently. Legal durability transparency rule enforcement independence and the history of ad hoc intervention all contribute to credibility. Although carbon markets with administrative price controls or reserve mechanisms can lessen excessive volatility, they also create uncertainty regarding the authority's reaction function. Participants in the market must predict when intervention will take place and whether it will be consistent with price increases and decreases. Climate-policy uncertainty indices are helpful for this reason among others. To quantify how noisy or contentious policy signals are Gavriilidis (2021) develops a climate policy uncertainty measure. Jia and co. as well as Guo et al. (2024, 2024) demonstrate that bond-market volatility and hedging relations are impacted by climate-policy uncertainty suggesting that policy credibility is a system-wide factor rather than a specific carbon-market issue.

The situation is further complicated by macroeconomic and energy-market factors. The marginal cost of cutting emissions, which is influenced by fuel prices, the generation mix and industrial technology determines carbon prices. Increased demand for permits and a decrease in fuel switching from coal to gas can result in higher carbon prices when natural gas prices spike. The demand for allowances may decline during a recession due to decreased industrial output and emissions.

Future permit demand may be reduced by increasing renewable capacity. Carbon markets frequently absorb second-round effects because these variables are subject to geopolitical and policy shocks. This explains why basic linear models often perform poorly. Carbon pricing is susceptible to institutional changes thresholds and interactions that vary over time. Figure 4 depicts the sequential market response to a climate policy event across five stages, from pre-event baseline positioning through to secondary spillovers. The progression reflects an increasingly complex chain of reactions: initial announcements triggers immediate carbon and ETF price moves, followed by deeper interpretation of credibility and taxonomy implications, then active portfolio rebalancing with spread adjustments and fund-flow responses. The final stage — secondary spillovers — captures longer-run structural effects such as issuance timing shifts and cross-market repricing, underscoring that policy shocks reverberate well beyond the initial announcement window.

Figure 4. A stylized repricing timeline after a climate-policy surprise.

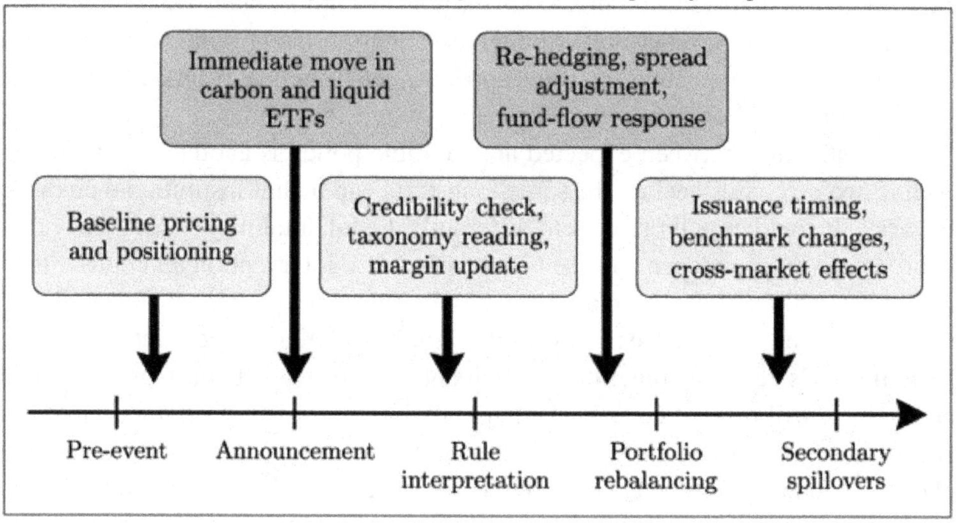

The makeup of the investors is also important. Future obligation hedging is important to compliance organizations. Financial traders are interested in relative value returns and volatility. Their motivations may complement one another or diverge. Demand for compliance and speculation may increase simultaneously when policy tightening is believable leading to sharp price increases. Speculative traders lower risk which can reduce liquidity and increase volatility in the absence of a clear price trend while compliance entities may cautiously hedge when policy direction is unclear. The pricing mechanism then includes exchanges and clearinghouses because position adjustments may be required due to margin requirements and collateral needs. As a result, carbon assets are not immune to overall financial circumstances. They are hybrid instruments with financial trading behavior regulatory origins and macro-sensitive valuation.

A shared perspective of scarcity credibility and intermediation is therefore necessary for pricing carbon assets under uncertainty. The long-term anchor is established by scarcity. Whether or not declared scarcity is believed depends on credibility. The speed at which information enters the price and the degree of volatility that follows a move are determined by intermediation. Because few traders are willing to warehouse risk a market with strong policy credibility, but poor liquidity may overshoot following news. Because participants in a market with high liquidity but low credibility tend to underestimate future reform the market may underreact. These differences are crucial when contrasting green bonds and carbon assets. Climate policy has an impact on both instruments, but green bond prices are a more indirect indicator of financing conditions for the transition while carbon prices are typically the more direct indicator of anticipated scarcity.

This differentiation also explains why carbon assets may occasionally move against green bonds. Assume that to preserve industrial competitiveness a policy package softens short-term emissions restrictions while simultaneously increasing renewable subsidies and concessional financing. Because anticipated investment rises and sustainable investors react favorably green bonds might do well. As short-term scarcity decreases carbon allowances may become weaker. Conversely it is also possible. If a strict cap revision increases policy uncertainty raises inflation expectations or increases rate volatility some green bonds may suffer while carbon prices may rise. As a result, joint pricing calls for more than just the green assets rise together mentality. It necessitates paying close attention to which aspect of the policy package is shifting which horizon investors prioritize and whether sentiment amplifies or diminishes the underlying impact.

5. SENTIMENT SPILLOVERS AND CROSS-MARKET CONNECTEDNESS

Although the underlying economics are more complex spillovers are frequently characterized as purely mechanical correlations. When information processed in one market affects prices volatility or liquidity in another this is known as a spillover. Three spillover channels are particularly significant in climate finance. Fundamentals-based transmission is the first. Increases in carbon prices can have an impact on corporate credit spreads equity valuations and the relative appeal of green investment since they alter the anticipated costs of emission-intensive businesses. Transmission of balance sheets is the second. Deleveraging may be necessary in other markets due to losses or margin increases in one particularly if the same intermediaries supply liquidity for all products. Transmission of feelings is the third. A court decision, a policy announcement or a string of climate-related news articles could all be interpreted by investors as a general indication of the direction and legitimacy of the shift. Even before cash-flow effects are thoroughly examined that signal has the power to move several sustainable-finance instruments.

According to Reboredo (2018) green bonds co-move with financial markets and produce price spillovers suggesting that they are not isolated thematic instruments but rather are part of larger market dynamics. By examining the price connection between green bonds and financial markets Reboredo and Ugolini (2020) expand on this perspective. The Antonakakis et al. (2020) offer improved methods for assessing dynamic connectedness through time-varying parameter vector autoregressions which are especially helpful when spillovers vary between regimes. Because the connectivity seen in green finance is neither constant nor symmetrical these contributions are important. In one period policy-uncertainty indicators may cause shocks to green bonds which may then transfer those shocks to conventional bonds or clean-energy stocks in another. Changes in carbon markets are comparable. Therefore, a method that allows for time variation is necessary for reliable inference rather than an econometric luxury.

Table 5. Spillover and connectedness evidence across green finance and carbon markets

Study	Markets	Method	Main inference
Reboredo (2018)	Green bonds and financial markets	Spillover analysis	Green bonds co-move with broader markets and transmit price effects.
Reboredo and Ugolini (2020)	Green bonds and major financial assets	Connectedness measures	Price connectedness varies over time and market conditions.
Antonakakis et al. (2020)	Generic financial networks	TVP-VAR connectedness	Time-varying connectedness is well suited to shifting spillover regimes.
Jin et al. (2020)	Green bonds and carbon markets	Hedging analysis	Green bonds can hedge carbon-market risk in some states.
Rannou et al. (2021)	European green bond and carbon markets	Complement/substitute analysis	Links depend on sector activity and market conditions.
Wu and Liu (2023)	Green finance markets, policy uncertainty, sentiment	Dynamic spillovers	Climate-policy uncertainty and sentiment jointly drive transmission.

continued on following page

Table 5. Continued

Study	Markets	Method	Main inference
Ringstad and Tselika (2024)	Green bonds, clean energy, carbon quotas	Time-frequency connectedness	Connectedness changes across horizons and market states.
Ozkan et al. (2024)	Clean energy, green and sustainable markets	Dynamic network analysis	Climate-policy uncertainty strengthens cross-market connectedness.

Sentiment is often the least visible but fastest-moving transmission route. In principle, market participants should update on fundamentals: project profitability, cap trajectories, or issuer credit quality. In practice, they also update on narratives. A policy speech can signal ambition, hesitation, or inconsistency. A media cycle can frame a carbon-price increase as evidence of effective transition policy or as a threat to industrial competitiveness. Fund-flow data can be interpreted as conviction about sustainable finance or as crowded positioning vulnerable to reversal. Wu and Liu (2023) show that climate policy uncertainty and investor sentiment drive dynamic spillovers among green finance markets. Their results support a broader point: sentiment does not simply add noise. It changes the speed, breadth, and sign of transmission by influencing which interpretation of a shock becomes dominant in the market.

One mechanism is attention concentration. Climate-related events often arrive in clusters: international negotiations, domestic elections, litigation, extreme weather, subsidy announcements, and corporate transition plans can all become salient within a short period. When attention is concentrated, investors are more likely to use category-level heuristics. Assets seen as supportive of the transition may attract flows as a group. Assets seen as exposed to policy tightening may face broader selling pressure. This increases co-movement, even when underlying cash-flow effects differ. A verified sovereign green bond, a clean-energy equity index, and a carbon futures contract do not have the same payoff structure, yet they can move together because investors classify them within the same transition narrative. The strength of this channel depends on media intensity, market participation, and the availability of fast-moving sentiment proxies.

Another mechanism is ambiguity resolution. When policy is technically complex, investors often seek signals from prices in adjacent markets. If carbon allowances rise after a policy announcement, fixed-income investors may infer that the market expects more stringent transition policy and may revise valuations of green issuers or emission-intensive borrowers. If green bond spreads tighten while carbon prices remain unchanged, carbon traders may infer that the announcement mostly affects financing channels rather than scarcity. In this way, each market becomes an information source for the other. Spillovers are therefore partly epistemic: traders use other prices to interpret uncertain policy content. Ringstad and Tselika (2024) show that connectedness between green bonds, clean energy markets, and carbon quota prices varies across time and frequency, which is consistent with the idea that some transmissions are immediate and others operate over longer horizons.

Because long-horizon and short-horizon investors interpret the same signal differently frequency is important. Within minutes commodity desks and high-frequency traders may respond to news about the carbon market using relative-value strategies, margin expectations or order-flow imbalances. Pension funds and asset allocators make slower adjustments frequently following benchmark adjustments or committee reviews. Therefore, rather than causing a single event a policy shock may cause a series of spillovers. Carbon prices may move first followed by green bond ETFs individual bond valuations and primary-market issuance only after issuers and underwriters revise their demand projections. Even when economically significant transmission takes place within shorter windows the timeline perspective helps explain why spillover networks may appear weak in low-frequency data.

All of this is dependent on liquidity and market depth. When a small number of intermediaries link several markets and those intermediaries are subject to binding risk constraints, spillovers are most pronounced. Following a spike in carbon futures volatility a dealer involved in corporate bonds and carbon-linked products may decide to reduce inventory generally. To transfer stress to benchmark securities before less liquid names adjust a sustainable fund that is experiencing outflows might sell the most liquid green bonds first. Changes in exchange margins have the potential to cause quick repositioning in carbon markets and have an indirect impact on other assets that are sensitive to climate change through collateral demand. These aren't unusual. These are typical characteristics of a system where capital constraints govern the interaction between specialized and generalist investors. Joint intermediation is the economic source, but connectedness measures capture the result.

Spillovers alter the definition of diversification as well. In normal circumstances a portfolio manager might anticipate that green bonds will offer diversification against conventional credit or against carbon exposure. When protection is most needed, that expectation may not materialize. Common discount-rate shocks and sentiment-driven flows can overwhelm idiosyncratic fundamentals during periods of high climate-policy uncertainty increasing connectivity among assets that are otherwise only tangentially related. Guo & Co. (2024) demonstrate how uncertainty about climate policy affects sovereign and green bond volatility correlation and hedging. Ozkan and company. (2024) discover dynamic connectivity between green sustainable and clean energy markets highlighting the significance of climate policy uncertainty once more. This means that in terms of portfolios safe-haven evaluations and hedging ratios should be based on regime indicators rather than being regarded as fixed parameters.

The empirical implication is simple. Beyond average correlations researchers ought to examine direction, timing and state dependence. The source market is subject to change, so direction is important. Because sentiment spillovers may occur more quickly than balance-sheet spillovers or vice versa timing is crucial. Because connectedness increases when policy uncertainty, volatility and attention are all high at the same time state dependence is important. The lesson is just as straightforward for practitioners. A climate-finance portfolio is vulnerable to the network structure that transmits sentiment and policy in addition to the underlying risks of its individual holdings. Therefore pricing under uncertainty is more than just single-asset valuation it is network pricing.

6. AN INTEGRATED STATE-DEPENDENT FRAMEWORK FOR JOINT PRICING

The preceding sections suggest that a unified framework should begin with conditional valuation rather than unconditional premia. The price of a green bond or carbon asset at time t depends on expected payoffs, required returns, liquidity conditions, and a sentiment state. In compact terms, expected payoffs depend on climate and macro fundamentals together with policy credibility, while required returns depend on risk premia shaped by policy, liquidity, and sentiment. The main implication is immediate. Policy enters both numerator and denominator. It changes expected cash flows or expected scarcity, and it changes the premium investors require in order to hold the asset. Sentiment affects both markets mainly through required returns and through the speed with which a policy signal becomes generalized across markets. This structure implies that identical policy announcements can produce different price responses across assets and across states of the world.

1 A helpful categorization comes next. Green bonds are more akin to cash-flow-plus-demand investments. Although the demand schedule may change due to taxonomy alignment external review and investor mandates that change who is willing or permitted to hold the bond their price still reflects typical bond cash flows. Scarcity-plus-credibility assets are more like carbon assets. Their value reflects anticipated future scarcity, but financial intermediation and institutional credibility are used to interpret that scarcity. Both are impacted by sentiment although it frequently manifests itself more strongly in the short term for green bonds since labeled debt is more closely linked to fund flows and clientele. On the other hand, speculative positioning margin pressure and quick policy implementation revaluation are ways that carbon assets can absorb sentiment. The significance of regime shifts was already outlined in Figure 2 the integrated framework formalizes the reasons why those shifts are important.

The next three claims are as follows. First, when policy credibility is high verification quality is high and market liquidity is adequate to allow segmented demand to manifest itself the pricing benefit of green labeling should be greatest. The observed greenium should decrease if any one of these circumstances is not met. Second, when policy surprises change the perceived distribution of future scarcity rather than just the mean expected path carbon assets should react to them most strongly. Stated differently tail-sensitive policy news ought to have greater pricing power than incremental commentary. Third, when investors rely on narratives rather than thorough asset-specific analysis, which is most likely to occur when policy uncertainty and media salience increase simultaneously—spillovers between green bonds and carbon assets should become more pronounced. These hypotheses can be tested in subsequent work with interacting regime variables and fit the empirical results previously summarized.

Dependency on the state requires extra caution. A time of low volatility is not the same as a low-uncertainty state. The direction sustainability and execution of climate policy are well understood currently. Investors can distinguish between short-term noise and long-term transition opportunities in this situation. Carbon prices may then more closely reflect energy and emissions fundamentals, and green bonds may maintain a steady yield advantage. A state of high uncertainty is not the same. Not only is there a lot of volatility but sentiment plays a significant role policy content is hard to understand and liquidity providers are hesitant. Narratives about credibility, political reversibility and portfolio crowding become more significant in that state. For this reason, traditional return regressions can benefit from the use of connectedness measures and option-implied tail indicators.

The framework also makes clear when carbon assets and green bonds work well together. They work in tandem when a more stringent and credible transition policy increases demand for transition financing and through anticipated scarcity increases the value of emissions permits. When policy packages prioritize financing support without short-term scarcity or scarcity without financing clarity, they become fewer effective complements or even temporary substitutes. Therefore, complementarity depends on how policies are designed. The pricing system does not incorporate a taxonomy update, a public-investment program a carbon border measure or a cap revision in the same manner. Analysts run the risk of overlooking the crucial mechanism if they combine them into a single climate policy variable. Disaggregation is necessary.

Table 6. Research and practice agenda for pricing under uncertainty

Stakeholder	Immediate action	Analytical tool	Expected benefit	Open question
Issuers	Strengthen verification and project-level reporting	Scenario analysis and peer pricing	More resilient demand and lower classification risk	How durable is the greenium after policy reversals?
Asset managers	Condition allocations on policy and liquidity regimes	Dynamic hedging and connectedness models	Better stress performance and hedging discipline	Which regime indicators are most informative in real time?
Regulators	Clarify taxonomies and transition rules	Event studies and market surveillance	Lower avoidable volatility and better price discovery	Which forms of ambiguity are most destabilizing?
Carbon-market authorities	Make reserve and intervention rules legible	Volatility monitoring and margin analytics	Greater credibility and smoother adjustment	How do margin changes alter spillovers to bond markets?
Development banks and sovereigns	Use benchmark issuance to deepen the market	Curve construction and issuance windows	Improved liquidity and stronger reference pricing	Can benchmark supply reduce segmentation risk?
Researchers	Disaggregate policy shocks by mechanism	Quantile, network, and tail-risk models	Sharper identification of transmission channels	How do sentiment proxies perform across regions and asset classes?

An integrated empirical strategy follows naturally. Researchers should estimate models in which green bond spreads, carbon returns, and connectedness measures depend on interactions between climate-policy uncertainty, macro uncertainty, sentiment proxies, and liquidity indicators. Quantile methods are useful because tail responses matter. Event studies remain valuable, but they should distinguish between announcements that affect classification, financing support, and scarcity. Network methods such as Diebold-Yilmaz connectedness and time-varying parameter VARs can identify changing transmission roles, while option-implied measures can capture the tail component of climate risk. The key is not to choose one method as universally superior. The key is to match the method to the economic channel under study.

From a policy perspective, the framework yields a simple but important conclusion: credible and coherent climate policy lowers financing frictions even when it raises compliance costs. Markets can price strict rules if they understand them. What destabilizes pricing is less often the level of ambition than uncertainty about implementation, reversibility, and classification. Better disclosure, stable taxonomies, transparent reserve rules, and clear transition plans can therefore improve the pricing of both green bonds and carbon assets, though not always in the same direction. Stability in climate finance does not require weak policy. It requires policy that is legible, durable, and institutionally credible.

7. IMPLICATIONS FOR ISSUERS, INVESTORS, REGULATORS, AND MARKET INFRASTRUCTURE

The first implication for issuers is the importance of timing strategically. It is incorrect to view the issuance of green bonds as a mechanical extension of traditional debt financing. The price advantage is more likely to endure when the issuer can demonstrate a reliable investment pipeline with open reporting and when issuance comes after policy clarification rather than just policy rhetoric. Verification should not be seen as an after-the-fact compliance expense but rather as a component of the pricing package. Even if general fixed-income conditions worsen during uncertain times access to dedicated demand can be maintained through thorough use-of-proceeds governance and rigorous external review. Additionally, issuers need to understand that investor scrutiny varies depending on the regime. A broad thematic framework might be adequate during times of calm. Investors demand proof that the bond will stay taxonomy aligned transition consistency and project-level credibility when under pressure.

Climate-finance exposures must be managed as a system not as separate sleeves which presents a different challenge for investors. In a static correlation matrix, a portfolio that includes carbon futures clean-energy stocks green corporate credit and green sovereign bonds may seem diversified but following a policy surprise or a significant increase in climate-policy uncertainty those positions may become closely related. Therefore, rather than focusing on individual variables risk management should incorporate scenario analysis based on policy packages regime indicators and liquidity stress assumptions. Managers may overlook the significance of sentiment and mandate-driven flows if they only compare against traditional rates or credit factors. Relying solely on thematic conviction could cause managers to overlook discount-rate risk. When there are sudden shifts in the credibility of policies both mistakes become expensive.

By eliminating ambiguity where it matters most regulators and public issues can enhance market quality. Taxonomies should be both stable enough to prevent frequent rebellion of outstanding securities and detailed enough to reduce classification disputes. Authorities in charge of the carbon market should make reserve regulations intervention standards and long-term cap trajectories understandable to market players. This does not and should not eliminate volatility. New information must be reflected in carbon prices. The goal is to lessen unnecessary volatility brought on by institutional opacity. Predictable policy design lowers discount-rate premiums and lessens the informational burden on market participants even when it is strict in content. This may encourage more cost-effective pricing in the carbon and green bond markets.

Market infrastructure providers also have a bigger impact than is frequently realized. The speed at which shocks spread is influenced by exchanges central counterparties pricing vendors and index providers. Spillovers can be amplified or attenuated by margin practices, benchmark construction and inclusion rules. After taxonomy clarification a green bond may see ongoing demand support when it joins a major index. During volatility a carbon contract with significantly higher initial margins could lead to more extensive deleveraging. Thus, the transmission mechanism for climate finance includes infrastructure design. The rules of trading collateral and benchmark eligibility—all of which allow information to enter portfolios—should be taken into consideration by policymakers who are interested in orderly transition finance in addition to headline regulation.

Development banks and sovereigns occupy a special position because they shape both policy signals and supply conditions. Their issuance programs can create benchmark curves, improve market depth, and provide reference standards for reporting quality. At the same time, their policy communications influence expectations about climate ambition and project pipelines. Coordination between public issuance and climate-policy design can therefore reduce financing costs without distorting price discovery, provided the signals are transparent and consistent. The broader point is that climate-finance pricing is affected by institutional architecture. Good architecture does not suppress market signals. It allows those signals to reflect fundamentals and credible policy rather than avoidable confusion.

Active stewardship is another implication. Investors that hold both transition beneficiaries and transition-sensitive exposures can use engagement, voting, and funding conditions to reduce pricing uncertainty over time. Better transition plans, clearer capital-expenditure mapping, and consistent reporting help markets distinguish between genuine decarbonization financing and label-seeking behavior. That distinction matters because uncertainty about credibility is a direct pricing factor. In that sense, stewardship is not separate from valuation. It is one channel through which investors can improve the information environment and, by extension, the efficiency of climate-finance pricing.

8. FUTURE RESEARCH DIRECTIONS

The analysis leads to several priorities for future research. Empirical research should first distinguish policy shocks according to their mechanisms. Even though they are all classified as climate policy announcements that alter the green classification, public finance support disclosure regulations, carbon market scarcity or border adjustment are likely to have distinct effects. More accurate event taxonomies would facilitate identification and help explain why certain shocks increase carbon volatility while others compress green bond yields. Second rather than treating policy uncertainty as sufficient on its own researchers should combine climate-policy uncertainty with funding and liquidity indicators. Depending on dealer capacity, margin conditions and the concentration of thematic funds, the same announcement may result in varying prices.

Third cross-market timing should be given more consideration. It may be possible to determine whether spillovers come from listed funds dealer-intermediated fixed income compliance markets or bond transaction data ETF flows and high-frequency carbon data. Fourth tail-risk measures should be better integrated into literature. The fact that extreme outcomes matter disproportionately in transition finance can be captured through option-implied climate concerns stress scenarios and quantile connectedness. Fifth little research has been done on the significance of sovereign and multilateral green issuance in emerging and developing markets. There may be different interactions between currency risk market depth and policy credibility than in the developed markets that predominate in the available data.

More research on issuer heterogeneity is also necessary. Not all issuers must go through the same transition process, and not all green bonds finance the same projects. Policy shocks are likely to be transmitted by utilities banks, transportation companies' municipalities and sovereigns via different balance-sheet and reputational channels. Research on the carbon market would also benefit from a more detailed examination of sectors compliance requirements and the role of financial players. Lastly future models ought to consider the potential impact of climate policy on benchmark collateral and the supply of safe assets in addition to the pricing of explicitly green instruments. The impact on green bonds and carbon assets may be greater than what current single-market research indicates if transition policy modifies sovereign issuance patterns central bank operations or collateral frameworks.

Another priority is methodological replication. Similar model classes are used in many connectedness studies, but the sampling windows sentiment proxies and variable definitions vary. Harmonized datasets and a coordinated replication agenda would show which results are reliable and which rely on specification. In terms of policy use that matters. Investors and regulators need proof that the sign and timing of connectedness are consistent across reasonable measurement options if they are to rely on spillover estimates for market surveillance or stress testing. Therefore, methodological transparency and deeper institutional detail should be combined in future work.

9. CONCLUSION

Although they are priced using different mechanisms carbon assets and green bonds are priced within the same transition system. Green bonds combine segmented demand taxonomy alignment certification and traditional credit valuation. Expected scarcity institutional credibility and financial intermediation are all combined in carbon assets. These markets are linked by policy shocks, climate risk and sentimental spillovers, all of which have an impact on expected payoffs, discount rates liquidity and investor interpretation. Instead of being uniform the effect is conditional. Carbon prices can increase and green bond yields can be compressed by a credible policy package. While reducing short-term scarcity a different package can boost financing support. A third can use liquidity and discount-rate channels to increase stress and uncertainty in both markets.

Thus, this chapter's main conclusion is straightforward. A state-dependent network problem should be used to analyze joint pricing under uncertainty. In addition to asset-specific fundamentals market structure policy credibility and the narratives investors use to process information are also important. Weak climate policy is not necessary for markets to perform well. They require climate policy that is readable long-lasting and backed by organizations that can eliminate needless ambiguity. Green bonds and carbon assets can channel capital toward transition needs and send informative price signals if those conditions are met. When they don't spillovers become more disruptive hedges become less dependable and pricing becomes noisier.

REFERENCES

Allman, E. (2022). Pricing climate change risk in corporate bonds. *Journal of Asset Management, 23*(7), 596–618. DOI: 10.1057/s41260-022-00294-w

Antonakakis, N., Chatziantoniou, I., & Gabauer, D. (2020). Refined measures of dynamic connectedness based on time-varying parameter vector autoregressions. *Journal of Risk and Financial Management, 13*(4), 84. DOI: 10.3390/jrfm13040084

Bachelet, M. J., Becchetti, L., & Manfredonia, S. (2019). The green bonds premium puzzle: The role of issuer characteristics and third-party verification. *Sustainability (Basel), 11*(4), 1098. DOI: 10.3390/su11041098

Baker, S. R., Bloom, N., & Davis, S. J. (2016). Measuring economic policy uncertainty. *The Quarterly Journal of Economics, 131*(4), 1593–1636. DOI: 10.1093/qje/qjw024

Bolton, P., & Kacperczyk, M. (2021). Do investors care about carbon risk? *Journal of Financial Economics, 142*(2), 517–549. DOI: 10.1016/j.jfineco.2021.05.008

Creti, A., Jouvet, P. A., & Mignon, V. (2012). Carbon price drivers: Phase I versus Phase II equilibrium? *Energy Economics, 34*(1), 327–334. DOI: 10.1016/j.eneco.2011.11.001

Diebold, F. X., & Yilmaz, K. (2012). Better to give than to receive: Predictive directional measurement of volatility spillovers. *International Journal of Forecasting, 28*(1), 57–66. DOI: 10.1016/j.ijforecast.2011.02.006

Diebold, F. X., & Yilmaz, K. (2014). On the network topology of variance decompositions: Measuring the connectedness of financial firms. *Journal of Econometrics, 182*(1), 119–134. DOI: 10.1016/j.jeconom.2014.04.012

Engle, R. F., Giglio, S., Kelly, B., Lee, H., & Stroebel, J. (2020). Hedging climate change news. *Review of Financial Studies, 33*(3), 1184–1216. DOI: 10.1093/rfs/hhz072

Fatica, S., Panzica, R., & Rancan, M. (2021). The pricing of green bonds: Are financial institutions special? *Journal of Financial Stability, 54*, 100873. DOI: 10.1016/j.jfs.2021.100873

Flammer, C. (2021). Corporate green bonds. *Journal of Financial Economics, 142*(2), 499–516. DOI: 10.1016/j.jfineco.2021.01.010

Gavriilidis, K. (2021). Measuring climate policy uncertainty. SSRN Electronic Journal. DOI: DOI: 10.2139/ssrn.3847388

Gianfrate, G., & Peri, M. (2019). The green advantage: Exploring the convenience of issuing green bonds. *Journal of Cleaner Production, 219*, 127–135. DOI: 10.1016/j.jclepro.2019.02.022

Giglio, S., Kelly, B., & Stroebel, J. (2021). Climate finance. *Annual Review of Financial Economics, 13*(1), 15–36. DOI: 10.1146/annurev-financial-102620-103311

Guo, N., Jia, S., & Liu, Y. (2024). Climate policy uncertainty and its impact on the volatility, correlation, and hedging of sovereign and green bonds. *Journal of Environmental Management, 370*, 122953. DOI: 10.1016/j.jenvman.2024.122953 PMID: 39447369

Hachenberg, B., & Schiereck, D. (2018). Are green bonds priced differently from conventional bonds? *Journal of Asset Management, 19*(6), 371–383. DOI: 10.1057/s41260-018-0088-5

Hong, H., Li, F. W., & Xu, J. (2019). Climate risks and market efficiency. *Journal of Econometrics, 208*(1), 265–281. DOI: 10.1016/j.jeconom.2018.09.015

Huynh, T. D., & Xia, Y. (2021). Climate change news risk and corporate bond returns. *Journal of Financial and Quantitative Analysis, 56*(6), 1985–2009. DOI: 10.1017/S0022109020000757

Ilhan, E., Sautner, Z., & Vilkov, G. (2021). Carbon tail risk. *Review of Financial Studies, 34*(3), 1540–1571. DOI: 10.1093/rfs/hhaa071

Jia, S., Guo, N., & Jin, J. (2024). Climate policy uncertainty risk and sovereign bond volatility. *Journal of Cleaner Production, 434*, 140145. DOI: 10.1016/j.jclepro.2023.140145

Jin, J., Han, L., Wu, L., & Zeng, H. (2020). The hedging effect of green bonds on carbon market risk. *International Review of Financial Analysis, 71*, 101509. DOI: 10.1016/j.irfa.2020.101509

Karpf, A., & Mandel, A. (2018). The changing value of the 'green' label on the US municipal bond market. *Nature Climate Change, 8*(2), 161–165. DOI: 10.1038/s41558-017-0062-0

Koch, N., Fuss, S., Grosjean, G., & Edenhofer, O. (2014). Causes of the EU ETS price drop: Recession, CDM, renewable policies or a bit of everything? New evidence. *Energy Policy, 73*, 676–685. DOI: 10.1016/j.enpol.2014.06.024

Ozkan, O., Adebayo, T. S., & Usman, O. (2024). Dynamic connectedness of clean energy markets, green markets, and sustainable markets: The role of climate policy uncertainty. *Energy, 303*, 131957. DOI: 10.1016/j.energy.2024.131957

Pham, L. (2016). Is it risky to go green? A volatility analysis of the green bond market. *Journal of Sustainable Finance & Investment*, *6*(4), 263–291. DOI: 10.1080/20430795.2016.1237244

Rannou, Y., Boutabba, M. A., & Barneto, P. (2021). Are green bond and carbon markets in Europe complements or substitutes? Insights from the activity of power firms. *Energy Economics*, *104*, 105651. DOI: 10.1016/j.eneco.2021.105651

Reboredo, J. C. (2018). Green bond and financial markets: Co-movement, diversification and price spillover effects. *Energy Economics*, *74*, 38–50. DOI: 10.1016/j.eneco.2018.05.030

Reboredo, J. C., & Ugolini, A. (2020). Price connectedness between green bond and financial markets. *Economic Modelling*, *88*, 25–38. DOI: 10.1016/j.econmod.2019.09.004

Ringstad, I. E. F., & Tselika, K. (2024). Connectedness between green bonds, clean energy markets and carbon quota prices: Time and frequency dynamics. *Journal of Commodity Markets*, *36*, 100442. DOI: 10.1016/j.jcomm.2024.100442

Tang, D. Y., & Zhang, Y. (2020). Do shareholders benefit from green bonds? *Journal of Corporate Finance*, *61*, 101427. DOI: 10.1016/j.jcorpfin.2018.12.001

Wu, R., & Liu, B. Y. (2023). Do climate policy uncertainty and investor sentiment drive the dynamic spillovers among green finance markets? *Journal of Environmental Management*, *347*, 119008. DOI: 10.1016/j.jenvman.2023.119008 PMID: 37748296

Zerbib, O. D. (2019). The effect of pro-environmental preferences on bond prices: Evidence from green bonds. *Journal of Banking & Finance*, *98*, 39–60. DOI: 10.1016/j.jbankfin.2018.10.012

Chapter 6
Financial Innovations and Circular Economy:
Pathways Toward a Sustainable Future

Rejaul Karim
http://orcid.org/0000-0001-6175-8825
Varendra University, Bangladesh

Md. Soleman Mollik
http://orcid.org/0009-0003-5703-0606
Bangladesh University of Professionals, Bangladesh

Md. Rony Masud
Rikkyo University, Tokyo, Japan

Sumon Mahmud
http://orcid.org/0009-0002-0785-0537
Begum Rokeya University, Bangladesh

ABSTRACT

As the global community faces increasing environmental challenges and resource depletion, the concept of a circular economy (CE) has emerged as a key strategy for achieving sustainable development. The circular economy model, focuses on minimizing waste, maximizing resource efficiency, and encouraging the reuse and recycling of materials, presents significant opportunities for economic, environmental, and social benefits. However, the transition to a circular economy requires robust financial innovations to drive investment, scale circular business models, and align economic activities with sustainability goals. This chapter explores the intersection of financial innovations and the circular economy, investigating how new financial

DOI: 10.4018/979-8-3373-8392-7.ch006

instruments, strategies, and investment vehicles can support the scaling and mainstreaming of circular practices. By examining various financial tools—including green bonds, impact investing, and sustainable business models—this chapter aims to provide insights into how financial markets can support a transition toward a more sustainable, circular economy.

1. INTRODUCTION

The current global economy is facing severe sustainability challenges that have become increasingly more evident in the form of rapid resource depletion, environmental degradation, climate change, and growing waste. The prevailing linear economy model—referred to as the "linear throughput model"—has traditionally led to economic growth but has also resulted in unsustainable production and consumption behaviors. Such a model is largely dependent on finite natural resources and produces huge amounts of waste and environmental externalities, which compromise long-term ecological balance and economic viability (Geissdoerfer et al., 2017; Kirchherr et al, 2017). Its reliance on finite resources generates significant waste and environmental externalities, compromising ecological and economic sustainability.

In tackling these problems, the circular economy (CE) has emerged as a powerful alternative system for sustainable development (Roshid et al., 2025b). Unlike the linear system, the circular economy under consideration is characterized by resource efficiency, waste reduction, and continuous flow of resources over time through re-use, recycling, remanufacturing, and regenerative practices (Ellen MacArthur Foundation, 2015). By moving away from the extraction of resources towards retention of value, and by increasingly being considered not as a waste management, but rather a resource and system recovery model, it presents an integrated approach to sustainability that combines well with environmental protection, economic advantage, and social development, cutting across. CE is increasingly viewed not only as waste management but as a resource and system recovery model, integrating environmental, economic, and social dimensions.

Despite the proliferation of CE literature, a significant gap exists in linking financial innovations to CE implementation outcomes. While prior studies describe CE principles and financing tools, they often fail to operationalize these linkages or provide a framework for actionable investment strategies. This chapter addresses this gap by proposing a conceptual model that systematically connects financial innovations, institutional enablers, and CE sustainability outcomes.

Nevertheless, its intuitive appeal and increasing policy traction are hindered by considerable financial barriers. Transitioning to CE is constrained by financial barriers, including high upfront costs, perceived risk, and a lack of tailored financial products. Initial investments in innovation, infrastructure, technology adoption, and organizational change are often required to implement circular business models (Karim et al., 2024). But traditional finance is built on a model where production was linear and return on investment was predictable, short-term profit at its core. Traditional finance prioritizes short-term returns, creating difficulties for CE initiatives that involve longer horizons and uncertain revenue streams (Affairs, 2019; Awan et al., 2019). Financial innovations, including green bonds, sustainability-linked loans, impact investing, blended finance, and circular venture capital, serve as mediators to align investment incentives with long-term environmental and social outcomes. They not only channel capital to CE projects but also facilitate scaling by mitigating perceived risks and enabling longer investment horizons (Flammer, 2021; GIIN, 2020).

So, the financial systems are a very important enabling factor for facilitating the transition to the circular economy. Creative financial structures, including green bonds, sustainability-linked loans, impact investing, blended finance, and circular venture capital, can not only channel capital toward environmentally friendly investments but also scale up circular business practices. More generally, financial innovation may serve as a mediator to connect sustainability aspirations and economic feasibility by aligning investment incentives with long-run environmental and social outcomes. But the demand for financing for a circular economy still outstrips available, appropriate financial mechanisms, and new ways of thinking around financing, which support the scale-up of circular business models, need to be developed.)

This chapter aims to explore the intersection of financial innovations and the circular economy, and how developing financial systems can facilitate the transition to sustainable production and consumption. In particular, the chapter aims to answer the following key questions: (1) What are the main financial obstacles to making businesses and society circular? 2) What is the role of financial innovation in supporting investments in circular business models? (3) What strategic possibilities does finance have to support a sustainable circular transition?

With existing literature synthesis and by exploring new financial products, this chapter adds to the emerging dialogue on sustainable finance with a conceptual view on how capital market innovation can act as an enabling mechanism for development transformation towards circularity. The chapter is organized as follows: the next section presents the theoretical underpinnings of circular economy and sustainable finance; this is followed by discussions in subsequent sections about major financial innovations facilitating circularity; then a review of implementation impediments and policy implications; finally, a future research agenda and strategic advice for industry.

2. CONCEPTUAL FOUNDATIONS OF THE CIRCULAR ECONOMY

2.1 Definition and Core Principles of the Circular Economy

The notion of the circular economy (CE) is well acknowledged as a restorative model minimizing waste, maximizing resource efficiency, and aiming for long-lasting products, materials, and resources in the economy (Karim et al., 2025a). CE replaces linear throughput with restorative processes across product life cycles (Geissdoerfer et al., 2017; Karim et al., 2025b). At the heart of CE, we also find the underlying principles of "reduce, reuse, recycle, and recover" (often denoted as 4Rs), aimed at reducing resource extraction, increasing product lifetime, and valorizing resources that could otherwise be waste. CE implementation faces practical constraints including capital intensity, technological adaptation, and regulatory uncertainty. Addressing these challenges requires aligning financial instruments with circular strategies, highlighting the need for tailored investment mechanisms and risk mitigation approaches.

Value retention is a central notion in the circular economy, and it pertains to the maintenance of economic and functional value obtained from materials through various strategies such as remanufacturing, repair, refurbishment, upcycling, and recycling. This is beneficial to resource efficiency due to less reliance on virgin raw materials, and such a reduction can reduce environmental impact. Furthermore, circular systems function through closed-loop handling mechanisms, which recycle waste streams as inputs for production circuits and generate near-closed material circles or autopoietic industrial ecosystems such that the industry becomes self-organizing. These systems not only shift environmental stress but also contribute to long-term resource security and economic durability (Kirchherr et al., 2017; Waaje et al., 2025).

2.2 Circular Economy vs. Linear Economy

In structure and finance alike, the circular economy is nothing like the linear economy precedent. The linear model is characterized by a unidirectional force of resources along the value chain, that is, from extraction to production and consumption to disposal, and can generate high levels of waste and resource over-harvesting. In contrast, the circular economy promotes cyclical flows: products and resources simply flow around within the system over various cycles through reuse, recycling, and re-growth (Murray et al., 2017).

The structural differences have significant impacts on business models and investment logic. The linear economic system usually focuses on short-term production efficiency and output; most returns are heavily dependent on resource consumption and are replaced frequently with products. Circular models, in contrast, prioritize long-term added value, life-time extension, and resource efficiency. For this reason, circular business models frequently revolve around service-based solutions, product-as-a-service systems, sharing-platform structures, and reverse-logistics networks. For these models, new forms of finance need to be developed that take into consideration longer timeframes for investment, uncertain revenue streams, and higher initial capital investments. As a result, the transition from a linear to a circular economy requires not only technological innovation, but also financial systems reconfiguration for investment strategies to be consistent with sustainability goals (Bocken et al., 2016; Geissdoerfer et al., 2017).

2.3 Sustainability Outcomes of Circular Economy Models

The implementation of the circular economy results in multi-faceted sustainability effects on the environmental, economic, and social aspects (Dhar et al., 2026; Uddin et al., 2026). From an environmental point of view, circular approaches can result in significant savings regarding resource extraction and disposal as well as their related emissions of greenhouse gases by closing cycles of use (Mollik et al., 2026a). Material recycling, life extension of products, and energy recovery are said to reduce environmental pollution significantly, as revealed from various studies and climate change mitigation (Ghisellini et al., 2016).

The circular economy makes economic sense by promoting resilience and innovation – less reliance on unpredictable raw material markets, more new business opportunities. Circularity is also a driver of innovation, entrepreneurship, and competitive advantage for businesses from greater resource productivity and cost savings. Furthermore, through the promotion of sustainable value chains and resource productivity, circular models also help to reinforce long-term economic resilience, which can avert systemic risks such as supply chain breakdown (Korhonen et al., 2018; Mollik et al., 2026b).

Societally, the circular economy encourages inclusive growth - creating jobs in recycling, remanufacturing, repair services, and sustainable innovation industries - while improving the quality of these offerings. And it is stimulating fairer access to resources and better working conditions via responsible production systems. The circular economy, by organizing environmental stewardship with economic and social purposes, provides an inclusive path to sustainable development consistent with the objectives of global sustainability (Murray et al., 2017; Ghisellini et al., 2016).

3. FINANCIAL INNOVATIONS: CONCEPTS AND EVOLUTION

3.1 Defining Financial Innovation in the Context of Sustainability

Financial innovation encompasses the development of novel financial instruments, services, and platforms to improve capital allocation, reduce intermediation costs, and integrate environmental and social considerations into investment decisions (Raimi & Bamiro, 2026). The evolution of financial innovations supporting CE is driven by policy mandates (e.g., green taxonomies), investor demand for ESG-aligned investments, and technological advances (blockchain, AI, fintech platforms). These innovations not only provide capital but also allow risk assessment, traceability, and alignment with sustainability outcomes (Tonnarello et al., 2025). Historically, financial systems have been predominantly focused on short-term profit maximization, profitability, liquidity, and risk management, while under neglect of environmental and social externalities. Traditional financial models have tended to favor investing in resource-intensive sectors, which are likely to perpetuate linear production processes and unsustainable consumption habits (Mazzucato, 2018). With mounting sustainability challenges that impact globally, this conventional finance approach has come under pressure for not effectively tackling long-term system risk, like the risks posed by climate change, resource constraints, or social inequality.)

In response, the financial industry has been slowly converging towards sustainable and innovative finance as a trend integrating the environmental, social, and governance (ESG) aspects into the investment decision process. This transformation is part of a larger trend from profit to purpose-driven finance, as financial institutions seek to distribute capital that produces both economic and social returns. Sustainable financial innovation encompasses vehicles such as green bonds, sustainability-linked loans, impact investment funds, and blended finance structures that direct capital toward environmentally responsible and socially beneficial activities. This transition signals the re-positioning of finance — no longer a passive actor, blindly allocating capital, but as an active agent driving the shift to sustainable economies (Raimi & Bamiro,2026; Tonnarello et al., 2025).

3.2 Drivers of Financial Innovation for the Circular Economy

There are a number of factors that have led to the development of financial products that are now supporting the transition towards the circular economy. There are more governments and international bodies introducing policies that look to drive sustainable production and consumption. Regulations, such as carbon pricing systems, green taxonomies, and sustainable finance disclosure requirements, incentivize banks to shift capital towards environmentally friendly investments. These policies incentivize and obligate financial actors towards the development of innovative financing solutions that support circular economy objectives (Brabec & Macháč, 2025).

Another important prompt is the increase in investor interest in ESG results. Pension funds, sovereign wealth funds, and asset managers represent increasingly important institutional investors that are aligning with sustainability factors in their investments. This is in part driven by an understanding that environmental and social risks have the potential to dramatically impact financial performance over the long term. As a result, investors are increasingly looking for financial instruments that promote sustainably-run business models and circular economy initiatives, which provide opportunities for stable, long-term returns as well as reducing systemic risks (Friede et al., 2015).

Innovation with financial is also facilitated by advances in technology. Digital technologies such as blockchain, artificial intelligence, and fintech platforms have increasingly allowed transparency, risk assessment, and investment monitoring. These enable new financing vehicles such as peer-to-peer lending, crowdfunding, and digital green finance platforms that can more effectively access capital for circular projects. Technological innovation, by lowering transaction costs and enhancing the availability of data, reinforces the financial infrastructure needed for circular economy investment (Zetzsche et al., 2020).

3.3 Alignment Between Financial Innovation and Circular Economy Goals

The goal of increasing the uptake of sustainable finance, and financial innovation from that perspective, is thus closely related to circular economy principles: both put a strong focus on creating long-term value as well as systemic resilience. One area where there is particular alignment is around how risk, return, and impact of investments are combined in investment decisions. Classic financial models may rely only on financial return, but sustainable finance adds environmental and social impacts into risk-assessment considerations. Investment in the circular economy, with potential to decrease the dependency on resources and environmental externalities, can help to mitigate risks by benefiting supply chain stability and cutting resource price volatility (Raimi & Bamiro, 2026).

In addition, financial innovation serves the circular economy by encouraging value creation in the long run (as opposed to profit maximization in the short term). At the same time, though it may require more investment in infrastructure, technology, and organizational transformation, circular business models provide long-term benefits from resource efficiency gains, cost savings, and innovation-led competitive advantages. In this light, financing instruments that enable long-term investment horizons (patient capital and blended finance) are key to facilitating circular change. Capital allocation that is anchored to sustainability goals. Financial innovation can play a central role in scaling financial trends in the global economy (Mazzucato, 2018; Tonnarello et al., 2025)

4. KEY FINANCIAL INSTRUMENTS SUPPORTING THE CIRCULAR ECONOMY

4.1 Green Bonds and Circular Bonds

Green bonds are one of the most favored financial vehicles for investing in environmentally sound and circular economy-related projects. The debt securities are used to invest directly into environmental projects – such as renewable energy, waste management, and circular resource systems. Circular bonds, as one type of green bond, target projects that facilitate resource circularity, including recycling infrastructure, sustainable product design, and reverse logistics networks (Flammer, 2021). The green bond market is characterized by stringent criteria for use of proceeds (allocation), transparency requirements, and reporting on impact to ensure accountability and credibility.

The surge in the world's green bond market demonstrates a growing demand from investors for ethical investments. The world's first green bond offering was by the World Bank in 2008; since then, the market has exploded to hundreds of billions of dollars of issuance per year. Such instruments grant access to significant capital volumes for circular economy initiatives and give investors the possibility of secure returns as well as reputation gains. While green bonds mobilize substantial capital, challenges include greenwashing, reporting inconsistencies, and potential misalignment of financial returns with long-term CE objectives (Flammer, 2021; Svirskyi, 2025).

4.2 Impact Investing and Circular Economy Finance

Impact investing is a key input to circular economy transitions, purposefully directing investments toward activities that can deliver verifiable environmental and social benefits as well as the calling down of financial returns. Differing from a typical investment based on only profits, an impact investment contributes to sustainable development goals, including efficient use of resources and low-waste production, or inclusive economic growth. Circular economy business models – such as sustainable manufacturing, product life extending services, and recycling innovations – are particularly appropriate for financing through Impact Investment, given their potential to create both environmental and economic value (GIIN, 2020).

Performance metrics for impact investing should be grounded in systematic methodologies that account for effects on the environment and society. Standard impact performance metrics would typically include carbon emissions reductions, resource savings, and social inclusion results, which investors generally tend to assess. While the perception of higher risk and longer time until returns may be associated with impact investments, research suggests that they have the potential to offer competitive financial performance combined with substantial contributions to sustainability. Impact investing supports CE projects but entails higher perceived risk and longer time to returns, requiring patient capital and clear metrics for environmental and social impact (GIIN, 2020; Bugg-Levine & Emerson, 2011).

4.3 Sustainable Finance and ESG-Based Investments

Sustainable finance includes a spectrum of investment approaches which integrate ESG considerations into financial decision-making. Investments that consider ESG have become more and more popular as investors acknowledge the role of environmental or social aspects in terms of financial performance for the long-range. In a circular economy dimension, ESG is said to facilitate investors' ability to assess companies in terms of resource efficiency, waste management practices, product lifecycles, and environmentally friendly initiatives (Raimi & Bamiro, 2026).

Institutional investors have been, and will continue to be, a major force in driving circular economy financing through ESG-linked investment strategies. Major asset managers and pension funds are already committing significant amounts of capital to companies that score high on sustainable practices and circular business models. Financial institutions can also incentivize sustainable production models in companies by including circularity measures as part of their ESG (environmental, social, and governance) assessment framework. The resulting alignment between ESG investment and the circular economy fortifies a financial ecosystem necessary to underpin transitions to sustainable development (Friede et al., 2015). Although ESG integration aligns financial performance with CE principles, variability in ESG scoring and lack of standardized CE metrics pose challenges for comparability and investor confidence (Raimi & Bamiro, 2026).

4.4 Venture Capital and Private Equity in Circular Innovation

Venture capital (VC) and private equity (PE) are important in early-stage circular economy innovation. For circular startups, traditional funding is often hard to obtain due to unclear revenue models, technological risk, and long investment horizons.

Here, VC and PE investors are key in filling this financing gap by providing risk (or patient) capital, strategic advice, and market access to innovative circular businesses (Tonnarello et al., 2025).

These investment vehicles are especially pertinent when scaling circular solutions in big-ticket sectors, including renewable energy, sustainable materials production, waste processes, and circular supply chains. VC and PE investments facilitate the development of circular economy programs by promoting technological innovation and business model experimentation. VC and PE play a critical role in scaling early-stage CE innovations, but high technology and market risks, as well as long-term revenue uncertainty, must be managed (Tonnarello et al., 2025; Mazzucato, 2018).

The image (Figure 1) presents a word cloud that illustrates key concepts related to financial innovations and the circular economy. At the center, the most prominent terms are "Circular Economy" and "Financial Innovations," indicating their central importance in the theme. Surrounding these are several interconnected ideas that highlight sustainability and responsible economic practices.

Figure 1. Word Cloud

Words such as sustainability, green investments, ESG (environmental, social, and governance), and social responsibility emphasize the ethical and environmental dimensions of modern finance. Terms like green bonds, social bonds, and impact investing reflect financial instruments that support environmentally friendly and socially beneficial projects. Additionally, concepts such as clean energy, climate action, and green technology illustrate the role of innovation in addressing global environmental challenges.

The word cloud also includes operational aspects of the circular economy, such as zero waste, waste reduction, closed-loop systems, upcycling, and biodegradable materials. These terms represent strategies aimed at minimizing resource use and promoting reuse and recycling.

Overall, the image conveys that financial innovation is closely linked with sustainability goals. It highlights how modern financial systems are evolving to support environmentally responsible practices and long-term economic resilience through circular economy principles.

5. FINANCING CIRCULAR BUSINESS MODELS

5.1 Characteristics of Circular Business Models

They often employ product-as-a-service models, remanufacturing, and sharing platforms to maintain value. Table 1 maps CE features to financial instruments and expected outcomes. One prominent feature is the product-as-a-service model, in which a company maintains ownership of the product and offers customers access to its performance rather than outright ownership. This approach encourages durability, maintenance, and resource recovery since firms benefit financially from longer product life.

Finally, an important feature of this age is the rise of platforms -that is, a shared infrastructure that allows multiple users to consume the same good or service. These exchanges cut the demand for fresh resources by utilizing existing resources better. In addition, remanufacturing and recycling systems are the basis of circular models by extracting materials from used products to be included in production cycles, allowing for closed-loop flows of resources without relying on virgin inputs.

5.2 Financial Requirements and Risk Profiles

Circular business models are typically capital-intensive and require significant upfront investments. Companies need to invest in the durable design of the product, as well as reverse logistics infrastructure and recycling technology, which increases the initial costs compared to a linear production system. Circular ventures require high upfront investment, long-term revenue horizons, and risk management mechanisms. Uncertainty arises from fluctuating demand, regulatory changes, and adoption rates. Financial instruments must be tailored to these dynamics.

Revenue streams in circular models also often remain vague and uncertain, especially early on. Uncertainty in revenue is created by variable demand for recycled materials, changing rate of consumer acceptance of service-based models, and evolving regulations. Moreover, circular investments generally require long-term investment horizons because financial returns may not materialize within years, as market adoption is slow and the installation of resource recovery systems can be time-consuming while development continues.

5.3 Barriers to Financing Circular Ventures

Circular businesses face a series of funding-related barriers, even though they offer long-term, sustainable returns. A significant challenge is the perception of the market and investors, who continue to be unfamiliar or skeptical about circular business logic and perceive such ventures as long-term and high-risk with no clear payback. Financing is also hampered by regulatory and policy barriers, especially in areas where enabling policies for circular activities do not exist or are non-coherent. What's more, measurement and data issues complicate investment choices as standardized metrics for measuring circular performance, environmental benefits, and long-term value creation continue to emerge. Investors often perceive CE initiatives as high-risk, long-term, and complex. Lack of standardized metrics, insufficient policy support, and low market familiarity further hinder investment. Mitigation strategies include blended finance, ESG-linked incentives, and capacity building for investors.

6. SECTORAL CASE STUDIES OF FINANCIAL INNOVATIONS IN ACTION

6.1 Fashion and Textiles

The adoption of financial instruments for underpinning circular supply chains is increasing in the fashion and textile industry. Investment themes included fibre recycling, sustainable feedstock sourcing, and closed-loop manufacture. Green bonds and impact investment vehicles have served as a key means of financing for recycling infrastructure (facilities, collection systems, and intermediate processing) and sustainable production technologies to allow companies to develop circular operations in a financially viable way. Financial instruments facilitate recycling and sustainable production. Limitations include market acceptance of recycled fibers and technology costs.

6.2 Construction and Built Environment

Circular materials, modular buildings, and resource-efficient infrastructure projects have been enabled by financial innovations in construction. The financing mechanisms employed usually include public-sector support and private sector participation in the form of public–private partnership, as well as investments from institutional investors. Such joint financing arrangements serve to spread risks and promote scalability of circular construction practices. Blended public-private financing supports circular materials and modular infrastructure. Challenges: regulatory coherence and scale-up feasibility.

6.3 Technology and Waste-to-Resource Systems

Technology has been a significant recipient of circular economy innovation finance. venture capital and innovation funds have rushed into back startups working on waste-to-resource innovations such as advanced recycling technologies, tracking solutions that digitize trash systems, or digital platforms for smart garbage management. Digital and advanced technologies such as data analytics, artificial intelligence, or blockchain support circular solutions through better traceability of resources, the optimization of material recovery, and improved operational efficiency and risks include technology adoption, data accuracy, and operational efficiency (Hossain & Mollik, 2022; Mollik et al., 2024).

6.4 Key Lessons from Case Studies

There are a number of important lessons that arise from the sectoral experience. The first is that successful circular financing hinges on robust partnerships between public authorities, financial institutions, and private enterprises. In the second place, strong regulatory underpinnings and clear sustainability standards help to build investor confidence. Finally, a great deal of financing models indicates a strong transferability across sectors, meaning that if we have developed an innovative financial instrument in one sector, it should be quick to cut and paste for other industrial categories that require support for circular transitions.)

7. EMERGING FINANCIAL TECHNOLOGIES AND FUTURE PATHWAYS

7.1 Blockchain and Distributed Ledger Technologies

Blockchain and other distributed ledger technologies are considered disruptive for the promotion of circular finance by providing more transparency, accountability, and trust in value chains. One of the most important innovations that can be provided by blockchain is related to making transparent and traceable the flows, both material and financial. For circulating, cycle systems where products, parts, and materials are used through the loop again and again. Depending on network topology, company sourcing, usage, recovery, and even recycling information would be recorded on the blockchain. This feature allows investors and stakeholders to validate sustainability claims and minimizes information asymmetry between participants in circular investment (Roshid et al., 2025a).

Furthermore, the blockchain enables smart contracts to be used for circular value chains. These smart contracts automatically do different actions based on predefined terms; the payment is delivered after materials are recycled or reused. Smart contracts have the potential to lower administrative costs, mitigate transaction risks, and facilitate coordination among stakeholders in circular systems (e.g., manufacturers, recyclers, logistics providers, financiers).

7.2 Decentralized Finance (DeFi) and Tokenization

Decentralized Finance (DeFi) is an emerging and fast-growing financial ecosystem that runs without conventional central authorities, enabling lending and borrowing, investment strategies, and asset management in blockchain platforms. Regarding circular economy capitalization, DeFi realized new financial models in which people can invest directly in each other's circular projects. For instance, tokenization can enable physical assets (like recycled materials, renewable infrastructure, or circular products) to be transposed into a form eligible for circulation as (digital) tokens, which can then be traded and used as collateral.

Such innovations, in turn, represent opportunities, including wider access to capital flow, better liquidity of circular assets, and democratization of investment involvement. DeFi does bring a range of risks, too – including regulatory and cybersecurity concerns as well as market volatility. Proper governance processes and regulatory oversight will be key in unlocking DeFi's potential while managing its risks.

7.3 Digitalization and Data-Driven Circular Finance

There is a core role for digitalization in furthering circular finance, as it allows data to inform decisions and measure impact and performance. Powerful digital tools such as artificial intelligence, big data analytics, and Internet of Things (IoT) solutions enable real-time tracking of resource flows, environmental performance, and financial results.

These technologies improve transparency by delivering trustworthy information on circular activities that can be leveraged to achieve measurable investment and sustainability outcomes. Better data transparency also helps build investor confidence, giving stakeholders access to trustworthy, standardized information about the environmental benefits and resource efficiency gains – as well as long-term financial returns – that come with circular investment.

8. POLICY, INSTITUTIONAL, AND STRATEGIC IMPLICATIONS

8.1 Role of Policymakers

Policy makers are essential in the development of circular finance through regulation and by creating an enabling environment. Good practices are that circular activities and financial products must be defined by clear standards, a report/require classification system. It is those kinds of approaches that help reduce uncertainty, add transparency to the market, and make it easier for investors to take part.

Governments can furthermore stimulate circular finance through providing incentives and risk-sharing, including tax breaks, subsidies, loan guarantees, and public funding schemes. These instruments would mitigate the initial high-risk nature of circulating investments and stimulate private sector involvement.

The conceptual framework for (Figure 2) illustrates a shift from traditional linear finance to a regenerative model. The process begins with Antecedents, where external contextual drivers—such as climate-related financial risks and the rise of AI and Blockchain—meet internal organizational enablers like strategic commitment and green finance upskilling. This convergence creates a "Transformative Nexus," where the core attributes of the integration manifest. These include the deployment of fintech for circularity, the use of green bonds, and the development of new risk assessment models that prioritize long-term resource recovery over short-term consumption.

Figure 2. Conceptual framework of financial innovation and circular economy integration

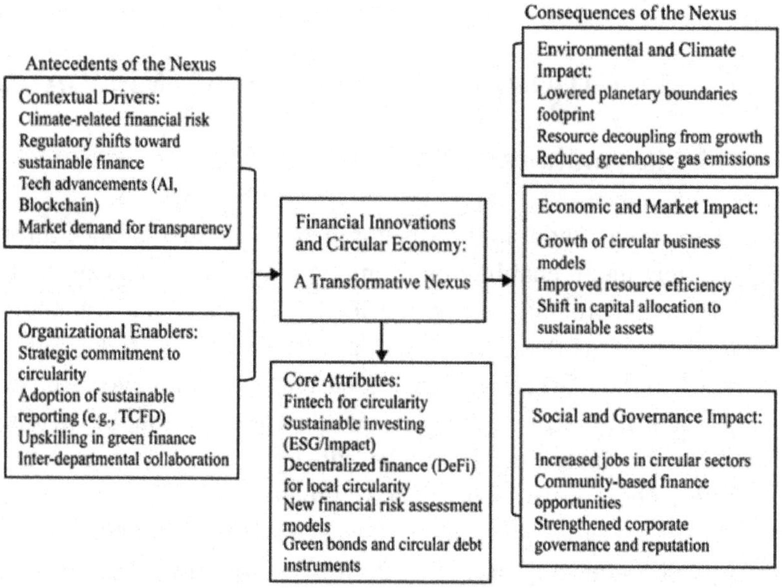

The second phase of the framework focuses on the Consequences of the Nexus, categorized into environmental, economic, and social-governance impacts. By aligning capital with circular principles, the model predicts a reduction in planetary boundary footprints and a decoupling of resource use from economic growth. Economically, this leads to a significant shift in capital allocation toward sustainable assets and the growth of circular business models. Socially, the integration fosters "green-collar" job creation and strengthens corporate governance through increased transparency and stakeholder engagement, ultimately establishing a more resilient and equitable economic foundation.

8.2 Role of Financial Institutions and Investors

Financial institutions and investors are the most important factors for upscaling circular economy actions, as they include circularity criteria in their investment strategies. This implies that environmental and resource efficacy concerns are part of the risk assessment, credit evaluation procedure, and portfolio management activity.

Financial institutions also need to invest in internal capabilities, analytical models, and evaluation frameworks for the effective assessment of circular projects. Specialized knowledge and expertise are needed to teach investors how to consider investment in circular business models, assess the long-term returns, and manage risk.

8.3 Public–Private Collaboration for Scaling Circular Finance

Public-private cooperation is key to scaling up circular finance, in particular blended investment fields that leverage public money with private funds. The models help to mitigate risk for investors, unlock vast amounts of capital, and provide the backing needed for groundbreaking circular projects that might not otherwise appeal on a purely commercial basis.

In addition, to generate a supportive ecosystem, governments, financial institutions, companies, research institutes, and civil society need to work hand in hand. These partnerships have the potential to enable knowledge exchange, capacity building, and the co-creation of blended financial and technology solutions to drive circular economy concepts.

9. CONCLUSION

Financial innovations are crucial to accelerating the transition from linear to circular economies. This chapter contributes by integrating CE principles with financial instruments through a conceptual framework linking antecedents, instruments, and outcomes. Limitations include the need for empirical validation and sector-specific application. Future research should test the model empirically and explore investor behavior and policy interventions.

Although there have been considerable advancements, there are still several open challenges in circular finance. Specific challenges are the development of sound risk management frameworks, gaining insights into longer-term financial performance, and the establishment of common metrics to measure circular and sustainability impacts. Overcoming these gaps will be important to gain wider investor interest and to guarantee a proper assessment of circular investments.

For policymakers, efforts should be prioritized in reinforcing regulatory certainty, financial incentives, and capacity building. Businesses need to prioritize mainstreaming circular principles into their strategies, improving accountability, and pursue financial sustainable circular models. At the same time, financial markets need to continue creating new financial products, evolving their approaches to impact measurement, and building collaboration between stakeholders.

As it discusses the next potential moves in circular economy finance, outlook projects favor an integrated success on technological innovation, decision-making structure, and market transformation. With financial markets increasingly oriented towards sustainability objectives, circular finance can become a key driver of global economic development as part of the transition to more resilient, resource-efficient, and inclusive economic systems.

REFERENCES

Affairs, U. N. D. O. E. S. (2019). The Sustainable Development Goals Report 2019. In *The Sustainable development goals report*. DOI: 10.18356/55eb9109-en

Awan, U., Sroufe, R., & Kraslawski, A. (2019). Creativity enables sustainable development: Supplier engagement as a boundary condition for the positive effect on green innovation. *Journal of Cleaner Production*, *226*, 172–185. DOI: 10.1016/j.jclepro.2019.03.308

Bocken, N. M. P., De Pauw, I., Bakker, C., & Van Der Grinten, B. (2016). Product design and business model strategies for a circular economy. *Journal of Industrial and Production Engineering*, *33*(5), 308–320. DOI: 10.1080/21681015.2016.1172124

Brabec, J., & Macháč, J. (2025). Impacts of the EU Taxonomy implementation: A systematic literature review. *Climate Policy*, •••, 1–13. DOI: 10.1080/14693062.2025.2526683

Bugg-Levine, A., & Emerson, J. (2011). Impact Investing: Transforming How We Make Money while Making a Difference. *Innovations: Technology, Governance, Globalization*, *6*(3), 9–18. DOI: 10.1162/INOV_a_00077

Dhar, B. K., Karim, R., & Mollik, M. S. (2026). Stitching Sustainability in Fashion: Strengthening Circular Economy Drivers in the Textile Industry. In *Strategic Innovations for Circular Economy* (pp. 179-208). IGI Global Scientific Publishing. DOI: 10.4018/979-8-3373-2454-8.ch007

Ellen MacArthur Foundation. (2015). *Towards the circular economy: Business rationale for an accelerated transition*. Ellen MacArthur Foundation.

Flammer, C. (2021). Corporate green bonds. *Journal of Financial Economics*, *142*(2), 499–516. DOI: 10.1016/j.jfineco.2021.01.010

Friede, G., Busch, T., & Bassen, A. (2015). ESG and financial performance: Aggregated evidence from more than 2000 empirical studies. *Journal of Sustainable Finance & Investment*, *5*(4), 210–233. DOI: 10.1080/20430795.2015.1118917

Geissdoerfer, M., Savaget, P., Bocken, N. M., & Hultink, E. J. (2017). The Circular Economy – A new sustainability paradigm? *Journal of Cleaner Production*, *143*, 757–768. DOI: 10.1016/j.jclepro.2016.12.048

Ghisellini, P., Cialani, C., & Ulgiati, S. (2016). A review on circular economy: The expected transition to a balanced interplay of environmental and economic systems. *Journal of Cleaner Production*, *114*, 11–32. DOI: 10.1016/j.jclepro.2015.09.007

GIIN. (2020). *Annual impact investor survey*. Global Impact Investing Network.

Hossain, M. K., & Mollik, M. S. (2022). Exploring the impact of Social Media Platforms on Instigating Tourist's Emotions and Behavioral Intentions to Co-Create and Visit Tourist Spots-Bangladesh Perspective. https://doi.org/DOI: 10.58753/jbspust.3.1.2022.13

Karim, R., Waaje, A., & Roshid, M. M. (2025a). Digital Circular Economy for Attaining Sustainable Development Goals: Technologies for Global Sustainability. In *Effects of Digitalization and Circular Economy on Sustainable Policy and Climate Change Prevention* (pp. 211-240). IGI Global Scientific Publishing. https://doi.org/DOI: 10.4018/979-8-3693-9909-5.ch008

Karim, R., Waaje, A., Roshid, M. M., & Yeamin, M. B. (2025b). Turning the waste into wealth: Progressing toward global sustainability through the circular economy in waste management. In *Sustainable waste management in the tourism and hospitality sectors* (pp. 507–552). IGI Global Scientific Publishing., DOI: 10.4018/979-8-3693-6110-8.ch019

Kirchherr, J., Reike, D., & Hekkert, M. (2017). Conceptualizing the circular economy: An analysis of 114 definitions. *Resources, Conservation and Recycling*, *127*, 221–232. DOI: 10.1016/j.resconrec.2017.09.005

Korhonen, J., Honkasalo, A., & Seppälä, J. (2018). Circular Economy: The Concept and its Limitations. *Ecological Economics*, *143*, 37–46. DOI: 10.1016/j.ecolecon.2017.06.041

Mazzucato, M. (2018). *The value of everything: making and taking in the global economy*. http://bvbr.bib-bvb.de:8991

mollii, R., Roshid, M., & Waaje, A. (2024). Circular economy and supply chain sustainability. In *Strategic Innovations for Dynamic Supply Chains* (pp. 1-30). IGI Global. https://doi.org/DOI: 10.4018/979-8-3693-3575-8.ch001

Mollik, M. S., Karim, R., & Mahmud, S. (2026b). Identifying Critical Success Factors for Adopting Sustainable Tourism in Emerging Economies. *EMIDWORLD 3rd International Congress on Economics, Public Finance, Business, & Social Sciences, Baku/Azerbaijan* (pp. 742-761).

Mollik, M. S., Karim, R., Sahabuddin, M., & Eneizan, B. (2026a). Industry 5.0 and the Circular Economy: A Transformative Nexus. In *Industry 5.0 and Sustainable Development* (pp. 237-267). Routledge. DOI: 10.4324/9781003647621-16

Mollik, M. S., Rahman, S. M., Rahat, M. R., Kulsum, C. U., & Sagir, S. A. M. (2024). Does Trustworthiness Influence Travel Service Use Intentions at an Online Travel Agency? A Study on the Digitalization of the Tourism Sector in Bangladesh. *Geo Journal of Tourism and Geosites*, *52*(1), 30–40. DOI: 10.30892/gtg.52103-1180

Murray, A., Skene, K., & Haynes, K. (2017). The Circular Economy: An interdisciplinary exploration of the concept and application in a global context. *Journal of Business Ethics*, *140*(3), 369–380. DOI: 10.1007/s10551-015-2693-2

Raimi, L., & Bamiro, N. B. (2026). Role of Islamic sustainable finance in promoting green entrepreneurship and sustainable development goals in emerging Muslim economies. *International Journal of Social Economics*, *53*(2), 181–196. DOI: 10.1108/IJSE-05-2024-0408

Roshid, Md. M., Waaje, A., Karim, R., Irtisham, M. R., & Kaswan, M. S. (2025a). Industry 5.0 and Organizational Sustainability: Integrating Cutting-Edge Technologies and Human Ingenuity. In Mahender Singh Kaswan, Rajeev Rathi, & Jose Arturo Garza-Reyes (Eds.), Industry 5.0: Concepts and Strategies for Digital Transformation (pp. 50–61). CRC Press. DOI: DOI: 10.1201/9781003535188-7

Roshid, M., Saiyed, S., Karim, R., Haque, T., Siddique, M. S. R., Haque, M. A., Kumar, V., & Habib, S. B. (2025b). The Role of Green Entrepreneurship in Driving Sustainable Innovation in Bangladesh's Startup Ecosystem: Insights from a Belt and Road Emerging Market. Environment. *Innovation and Management*, *01*, 2550010. DOI: 10.1142/S3060901125500103

Svirskyi, V. (2025). Green bonds as a driver towards a climate-neutral economy in Europe. In *In Innovation in Capitalist Economies* (pp. 109–138). DOI: 10.4324/9781003558187-9

Tonnarello, F., Vermiglio, C., Migliardo, C., & Naciti, V. (2025). The impact of EU taxonomy for Sustainable Activities on European utilities' performance. *Business Strategy and the Environment*, *34*(3), 2848–2862. DOI: 10.1002/bse.4128

Uddin, M. S., Mollik, M. S., & Nasrullah, A. M. (2026). Integrating Circular Economy Principles into Responsible Consumption and Production. In *Strategic Innovations for Circular Economy* (pp. 209–244). IGI Global Scientific Publishing., DOI: 10.4018/979-8-3373-2454-8.ch008

Waaje, A., Karim, R., Roshid, M. M., & Meem, T. N. (2025). *Minimizing Waste in the Hospitality Industry: The Opportunities and Challenges of Lean Tourism. Sustainable Waste Management in the Tourism and Hospitality Sectors*. IGI Global Scientific Publishing., DOI: 10.4018/979-8-3693-6110-8.ch006

Zetzsche, D. A., Arner, D. W., & Buckley, R. P. (2020). Decentralized finance. *Journal of Financial Regulation*, *6*(2), 172–203. DOI: 10.1093/jfr/fjaa010

Chapter 7
Artificial Intelligence in Sustainable Finance:
ESG-Based Financial Instruments and Decisions

Ece Kozol
http://orcid.org/0000-0002-6428-7501
Istanbul University, Turkey

ABSTRACT

Sustainable finance integrates environmental, social, and governance considerations into financial decision-making to promote long-term value creation and systemic resilience. Recent advances in artificial intelligence have enhanced the assessment, monitoring, and implementation of sustainability criteria across financial markets. This chapter examines how machine learning, natural language processing, predictive analytics, and blockchain-based systems support ESG evaluation, climate risk assessment, and performance measurement. Particular attention is given to green bonds, sustainability-linked loans, carbon credit mechanisms, and trade finance applications. The analysis also addresses governance challenges related to data reliability, transparency, and algorithmic bias. By synthesizing insights from finance and digital innovation research, the chapter outlines how AI-enabled analytics can strengthen sustainable investment practices and improve risk management frameworks.

1. INTRODUCTION

Sustainable finance seeks to guide financial decision-making and investment practices by integrating environmental, social, and governance (ESG) criteria into

DOI: 10.4018/979-8-3373-8392-7.ch007

financial analysis. Rather than prioritizing short-term economic returns alone, this approach emphasizes long-term sustainability and broader societal value creation. ESG criteria are employed to assess firms' environmental impacts, social responsibilities, and corporate governance standards, thereby supporting more informed and sustainability-oriented investment decisions (Friede et al., 2015). In this context, sustainable finance represents not merely a normative shift in investment philosophy but also a structural transformation in how risk, return, and value are conceptualized within financial markets.

The increasing prominence of ESG considerations is closely associated with the recognition that environmental and social risks are financially material. Climate change, regulatory transitions, reputational damage, supply chain disruptions, and governance failures generate measurable financial consequences. Empirical evidence suggests that ESG performance is positively associated with long-term financial performance and risk mitigation (Friede et al., 2015). Moreover, firms with stronger governance and social capital demonstrate greater resilience during periods of financial stress (Lins et al., 2017). These findings reinforce the argument that ESG integration is not merely an ethical preference but a financially relevant strategy embedded within contemporary capital markets.

Recent advances in artificial intelligence (AI) technologies have introduced new opportunities in sustainable finance by reshaping existing evaluation and implementation processes. Capabilities such as big data analytics, machine learning, and natural language processing enable the faster and more accurate analysis of financial, environmental, and social data, thereby strengthening ESG assessment frameworks. These technologies generate notable improvements in data-driven analytics, forecasting, risk management, and impact investing (Musleh Al-Sartawi et al., 2022). In particular, AI systems reduce informational frictions by processing large volumes of structured and unstructured data that exceed human analytical capacity, thereby addressing one of the core limitations of traditional ESG analysis.

Despite the growing body of literature on both sustainable finance and AI applications, a critical gap persists: existing research tends to examine either the capabilities of AI systems or the mechanics of sustainable finance instruments in isolation, without offering a systematic conceptual framework that maps AI mechanisms to specific sustainable finance functions, the research gaps each addresses, and the governance challenges that arise. Furthermore, the regulatory dimensions of AI-driven ESG evaluation—particularly regarding algorithmic transparency, model accountability, and cross-jurisdictional compliance—remain underexplored. This paper addresses this gap by developing an integrated conceptual framework that positions AI not merely as an efficiency tool but as a structural component of the sustainable finance architecture.

Against this background, this paper addresses three interrelated research questions: (1) Through which specific AI mechanisms does technological integration enhance the functionality and credibility of sustainable finance instruments such as green bonds, sustainability-linked loans, and carbon credit markets? (2) What conceptual framework can systematically map AI capabilities to sustainable finance functions while identifying corresponding governance challenges? (3) How do regulatory frameworks and institutional conditions shape the effective deployment of AI in ESG-oriented financial decision-making?

Methodological Approach

This paper adopts a theory-building conceptual approach, which is well established in management and finance research as a means of generating analytical frameworks that organize existing knowledge and guide future empirical inquiry (Eisenhardt & Graebner, 2007; Whetten, 1989). The methodology proceeds in three steps. First, a systematic synthesis of the literature at the intersection of AI and sustainable finance is conducted, drawing on peer-reviewed publications in finance, information systems, and sustainability management. Second, recurring patterns are identified across sustainable finance instruments—specifically, the types of market failures AI addresses and the governance challenges it generates—and these patterns are used to construct the conceptual framework presented in Section 4. Third, the framework is subjected to an internal consistency test by examining whether the three analytical pillars (information asymmetry reduction, predictive governance, and regulatory alignment) coherently account for the range of AI applications documented across sustainable finance domains. As a conceptual study, this paper does not provide direct empirical evidence for the relationships proposed in the framework; rather, it establishes theoretically grounded propositions that future empirical research can test. This scope is explicitly acknowledged as a limitation in the Conclusion.

The paper proceeds as follows. Section 2 examines environmentally responsible financial solutions—green bonds, sustainability-linked loans, ESG investments, and carbon credits—and their interaction with AI. Section 3 provides a detailed analysis of the ESG framework and the role of AI in each dimension. Section 4 presents the integrated conceptual framework. Section 5 concludes with a summary of contributions, limitations, and directions for future research.

A central challenge in sustainable finance relates to information asymmetry and measurement inconsistency. ESG data are often self-reported, fragmented, and heterogeneous across jurisdictions and rating agencies. The divergence in ESG ratings documented in the literature reflects methodological inconsistencies and subjective weighting schemes (Berg et al., 2022). Such divergence complicates capital allocation decisions and may weaken investor confidence in sustainability metrics. In this environment, artificial intelligence offers the potential to standardize data processing, detect inconsistencies, and enhance comparability across firms and sectors. However, while AI can improve analytical efficiency, it may also replicate underlying data biases if model training processes are not carefully designed.

Table 1 serves as an orientation map, summarising the principal sustainable finance instruments alongside their core market failures, the AI mechanisms that address them, and the associated governance challenges. This analytical overview frames the more detailed discussion in Sections 2 and 3; the primary conceptual contribution of the paper is the integrated framework developed in Section 4 (Table 2).

Table 1. Orientation Map: Sustainable Finance Instruments, Market Failures, and AI Mechanisms

SF Instrument	Core Market Failure	AI Mechanism & Function	Governance Challenge
Green Bonds	Greenwashing; informational asymmetry between issuer and investor	ML + remote sensing: cross-validates reported outcomes against satellite/emissions data; enables real-time post-issuance monitoring	Model opacity; explainability of AI-driven verification scores for regulatory purposes
Sustainability-Linked Loans	Moral hazard in self-reported KPI achievement; measurement inconsistency across borrowers	Predictive ML: forecasts probability of KPI attainment; enables dynamic covenant calibration to sector-specific risk	Overfitting to historical ESG scores; risk of algorithmic bias in credit pricing
ESG Investments	ESG rating divergence; static, backward-looking disclosure-based metrics	NLP + anomaly detection: extracts forward-looking signals from unstructured sources; flags disclosure inconsistencies	Training data bias; cross-jurisdictional inconsistency in ESG disclosure standards
Carbon Credits	Additionality fraud; verification cost and delay in voluntary carbon markets	AI + blockchain: automates emissions verification via remote sensing; provides immutable transaction audit trail	Regulatory recognition of AI-verified credits; data access inequality across jurisdictions
Impact Investing	'Impact washing'; intangibility of social value; measurement complexity	Multi-modal analytics: aggregates carbon, social, and stakeholder metrics; automates impact reporting	Standardisation of social metrics; risk of replicating structural inequalities in training data

Source: Compiled by the author based on a synthesis of the relevant literature.

2. ENVIRONMENTALLY RESPONSIBLE FINANCIAL SOLUTIONS

Environmentally responsible financial solutions aim to minimize the environmental impacts of economic activities while supporting sustainable development and long-term economic resilience. These solutions operate at the intersection of capital allocation, risk pricing, and sustainability governance. By embedding environmental criteria into financial contracts, they create incentive structures that reward responsible behavior and penalize environmentally harmful practices. Institutional investors, multilateral development banks, and commercial financial institutions are progressively integrating sustainability metrics into lending, underwriting, and portfolio management decisions. As ESG considerations become financially material, the pricing of capital increasingly reflects environmental performance, regulatory exposure, and reputational risk.

These solutions are implemented through a range of financial instruments including green bonds, sustainability-linked loans, ESG investments, and carbon credits (Friede et al., 2015). Each instrument embodies a different mechanism through which environmental performance is translated into financial incentives—and each faces a distinct type of market failure. Artificial intelligence plays a targeted and complementary role in addressing these failures by improving data accuracy, enabling real-time monitoring, and supporting forward-looking risk assessments. The following subsections examine each instrument and its interaction with AI.

Beyond domestic capital markets, AI-driven analytics are also extending the reach of sustainable finance into international trade finance, where regulatory pressures have necessitated the integration of ESG metrics into cross-border financial decision-making (Brière et al., 2022).

Green Bonds and AI-Enhanced Environmental Verification

Green bonds serve as key debt instruments used to finance environmentally friendly projects, including renewable energy generation, energy efficiency improvements, clean transportation systems, and water management initiatives (Hachenberg & Schiereck, 2018). Beyond their direct financing function, green bonds operate as signaling mechanisms within capital markets. The issuance of a green bond communicates a firm's strategic commitment to sustainability, potentially influencing investor perception, reputation, and cost of capital. However, the credibility of green bonds depends heavily on the integrity of environmental reporting and impact verification. Concerns regarding greenwashing have intensified scrutiny over the classification, certification, and monitoring of green projects. When environmental claims are overstated or poorly substantiated, investor confidence may erode, and capital misallocation may occur (Flammer, 2021).

The application of artificial intelligence in the evaluation and management of green bonds has expanded rapidly. AI enhances project assessment and risk analysis by processing large datasets related to environmental performance, emissions trajectories, operational efficiency, and financial indicators. AI-driven environmental verification systems integrate diverse data sources, including satellite imagery, geospatial analytics, energy consumption records, emissions databases, and regulatory disclosures. By cross-validating reported project outcomes against independent environmental datasets, these systems reduce information asymmetries between issuers and investors, strengthen market discipline, and improve pricing efficiency (Gilchrist et al., 2021).

Furthermore, predictive analytics allow financial institutions to evaluate potential environmental risks before bond issuance. Machine learning models can simulate different environmental scenarios, including regulatory shifts, carbon pricing adjustments, or climate-related disruptions. AI also facilitates continuous post-issuance monitoring, providing dynamic updates on emissions reductions and energy efficiency gains that traditional periodic impact reporting cannot match. Importantly, the integration of AI into green bond verification carries governance implications: transparency, explainability, and model validation are essential to ensure that AI-driven environmental assessments are credible and free from systemic bias. Governance frameworks must accompany technological deployment to prevent overreliance on opaque algorithmic outputs.

Sustainability-Linked Loans and Performance-Based Incentives

Sustainability-linked loans (SLLs) incentivize firms to achieve predefined sustainability targets by offering interest rate reductions linked to ESG performance. Unlike green bonds, which are tied to specific projects, SLLs link financing conditions directly to firm-level sustainability performance, embedding ESG considerations into corporate financial structures (Aleszczyk et al., 2022). From a financial contracting perspective, SLLs function as performance-contingent debt instruments in which the interest rate adjustment mechanism aligns borrower incentives with lender expectations regarding long-term environmental and social performance, thereby reducing moral hazard by linking financing costs to measurable sustainability outcomes.

Artificial intelligence plays a central role in the monitoring, evaluation, and risk management of SLLs by enabling continuous tracking of sustainability metrics such as energy use, water consumption, waste management, carbon intensity, and workplace safety indicators. AI-driven predictive models support early identification of sustainability-related risks and improve credit decision-making by forecasting future ESG performance (Garcia-Muiña et al., 2019). By analyzing historical sustainability trajectories, regulatory developments, industry benchmarks, and macroeconomic factors, machine learning algorithms can estimate the probability that a firm will achieve or fail to meet its sustainability performance targets, enabling risk-adjusted pricing and more accurate loan structuring.

AI also improves covenant design by enabling lenders to determine which sustainability metrics are most materially linked to long-term financial stability within specific industries. AI-supported benchmarking allows financial institutions to tailor sustainability performance targets to sector-specific risk profiles, reducing measurement error and enhancing comparability across borrowers. Early-warning signals generated by machine learning models may prompt renegotiation of terms, additional oversight measures, or strategic advisory interventions before performance shortfalls escalate. However, the increasing reliance on AI within SLL frameworks necessitates careful governance oversight—algorithmic bias, model opacity, and overfitting risks must be addressed to ensure that sustainability-linked pricing mechanisms remain fair, transparent, and subject to independent validation.

ESG Investments and Advanced Data Analytics

ESG-oriented investments encourage capital allocation toward firms demonstrating strong environmental, social, and governance performance. However, ESG investing faces methodological challenges, particularly regarding data consistency and rating divergence. Berg et al. (2022) document that ESG rating divergence across major rating providers is substantial, reflecting methodological inconsistencies and subjective weighting schemes that complicate capital allocation decisions. Artificial intelligence and data analytics significantly enhance the effectiveness of ESG-based investments by automating data collection, harmonizing diverse datasets, and identifying hidden patterns across industries and regions (Friede et al., 2015).

Natural language processing allows ESG-related data to be extracted from corporate reports, news sources, and social media, enabling forward-looking signal extraction that goes beyond static disclosure-based metrics. Portfolio optimization models incorporating machine learning techniques can adjust asset weights dynamically based on evolving ESG signals, enhancing risk-adjusted returns. Furthermore, AI-driven anomaly detection mechanisms can identify inconsistencies in corporate sustainability disclosures, strengthening investor confidence in ESG evaluation processes. The integration of structured financial metrics with unstructured textual data enables multidimensional risk profiling that substantially improves upon traditional rating-based screening approaches.

Carbon Credits and AI-Based Market Integrity

Carbon credits function as financial instruments designed to incentivize greenhouse gas emission reductions, with each credit representing the reduction of one metric ton of CO_2 or its equivalent. Despite their potential role in global climate governance, carbon credit markets have been criticized for issues related to verification accuracy, additionality assessment, and fraud risks (Kollmuss et al., 2008; Marchant et al., 2022). Artificial intelligence enhances the credibility and effectiveness of carbon credit markets by improving the calculation, verification, and monitoring of emissions reductions. AI-based algorithms analyze large-scale environmental datasets to produce more accurate carbon footprint assessments, accelerate verification processes, and reduce fraud risks.

AI-supported remote sensing technologies can validate emission reductions more efficiently than traditional manual auditing processes, enabling real-time rather than periodic verification. When integrated with blockchain technology, AI further enhances traceability and security in carbon credit markets by providing immutable transaction records that support fraud prevention and strengthen investor trust (Marchant et al., 2022). Predictive modeling tools can also assess long-term emissions trajectories, enabling regulators and investors to anticipate potential imbalances in supply and demand. The governance challenge in this domain concerns the regulatory recognition of AI-verified credits and equitable data access across jurisdictions.

Automation, Monitoring, and Strategic Sustainability Management

Automation and monitoring represent critical areas in which artificial intelligence supports sustainability objectives across all instrument types. AI-enabled systems automate the monitoring and reporting of environmental indicators such as energy consumption, water usage, and carbon emissions, allowing firms to track sustainability performance accurately and in real time. Through continuous performance monitoring, AI transforms sustainability from a retrospective reporting obligation into an integrated strategic management function—firms can simulate alternative operational scenarios, evaluate the environmental impact of investment decisions, and align financial strategies with long-term decarbonization goals (Garcia-Muiña et al., 2019).

Overall, the integration of artificial intelligence into environmentally responsible financial solutions enhances efficiency, transparency, and decision-making accuracy across sustainability-oriented investments. By supporting risk management, performance monitoring, and strategic planning, artificial intelligence contributes significantly to the achievement of long-term sustainability objectives while reinforcing the credibility and institutional legitimacy of green financial instruments (Ever & Demircioğlu, 2022). The convergence of digital innovation and sustainable finance thus represents a structural evolution in financial systems.

3. ESG (ENVIRONMENTAL, SOCIAL, AND GOVERNANCE) AND ARTIFICIAL INTELLIGENCE

ESG is defined as a framework used to evaluate firms' sustainability performance and to support long-term value creation. By extending beyond traditional financial indicators, ESG criteria incorporate environmental impacts, social responsibility, and corporate governance practices (Eccles et al., 2014). The ESG framework consists of three core dimensions that together provide a comprehensive assessment of corporate sustainability performance (Schramade, 2016).

The environmental dimension focuses on firms' impacts on the natural environment and their capacity to manage these impacts sustainably. Key factors include resource efficiency, energy consumption, waste and water management, carbon emissions, biodiversity protection, and investments in environmentally friendly technologies (Kolk & Pinkse, 2008). The social dimension examines firms' relationships with employees, supply chains, and society, encompassing labor rights, occupational health and safety, diversity and inclusion policies, and community engagement. The governance dimension assesses the transparency and accountability of corporate management structures, including board independence, shareholder rights protection, and effective oversight mechanisms (Bebchuk & Weisbach, 2010).

The financial materiality of ESG performance is illustrated by several prominent corporate cases. The Deepwater Horizon oil spill (BP, 2010) resulted in extensive ecological damage and billions in fines, demonstrating the financial consequences of weak environmental risk management. Labor disputes at Amazon have illustrated how social dimension weaknesses create operational and reputational risks. The Volkswagen Dieselgate scandal (2015) revealed how governance failures—specifically, software manipulation to pass emissions tests—resulted in billions in fines and severe brand value decline (Collaoni & Trevisan, 2022). Nike's labor rights controversies in the 1990s similarly demonstrated that supply chain governance failures carry lasting reputational and financial costs (Avery, 2001). These cases collectively establish that ESG deficiencies are not merely ethical concerns but carry measurable financial consequences, substantiating the materiality argument advanced by Friede et al. (2015) and Giese et al. (2019).

In this context, artificial intelligence has emerged as a critical instrument in the assessment, implementation, and continuous monitoring of ESG frameworks. Technologies such as big data analytics, NLP, and machine learning facilitate the collection, analysis, and reporting of ESG-related information, thereby enhancing transparency and supporting more informed investment decisions (Huang et al., 2023). AI-based techniques, especially NLP, enable the extraction of meaningful insights from large volumes of unstructured data—corporate reports, financial disclosures, news sources, and social media—and support more accurate ESG performance assessments (Lan et al., 2025).

Through AI-driven models, firms' environmental impacts—such as carbon emissions, water consumption, and waste management—can be systematically analyzed. Social dimensions including workforce diversity, employee well-being, and corporate social responsibility effectiveness can be evaluated using AI-based algorithms. In the governance dimension, artificial intelligence supports the assessment of transparency, ethical standards, and corporate decision-making structures, while also contributing to the detection of corruption risks through advanced analytical approaches (Lan et al., 2025).

A further contribution of artificial intelligence lies in its ability to improve ESG data quality. Since ESG reporting often relies on self-disclosed corporate information, inconsistencies and reliability issues are common. AI algorithms can detect such discrepancies, thereby enhancing data accuracy and consistency. Advanced machine learning techniques, including deep reinforcement learning, enable the optimization of investment portfolios by explicitly incorporating ESG criteria, supporting more informed decision-making and potentially improving the financial performance of sustainability-oriented investments (Borth, 2023).

Looking ahead, the rapid advancement of artificial intelligence technologies is expected to further strengthen the evaluation, implementation, and reporting of ESG criteria. However, to fully realize this potential, strong collaboration among technology developers, policymakers, and the business community is essential. Studies focusing on AI governance in the United States and the European Union emphasize that cooperation between policymakers and the private sector is critical to ensuring that artificial intelligence is deployed for human and public benefit (Vinuesa et al., 2020; Floridi, 2018).

4. AN INTEGRATED CONCEPTUAL FRAMEWORK: AI AS STRUCTURAL INFRASTRUCTURE IN SUSTAINABLE FINANCE

The preceding analysis reveals a recurring pattern across sustainable finance instruments: AI technologies reduce information asymmetries, enhance predictive capacity, and enable continuous monitoring, but each application domain generates distinct governance challenges. Drawing on this analysis, this section proposes an integrated conceptual framework that systematically maps AI mechanisms to sustainable finance functions, the research gaps they address, and the governance challenges that must be managed. This framework constitutes the primary theoretical contribution of the paper.

The framework rests on three analytical pillars. The first pillar—information asymmetry reduction—recognizes that the core market failure in sustainable finance is the gap between actual and reported environmental and social performance. AI, through NLP, remote sensing, and cross-validation algorithms, directly targets this asymmetry by enabling independent, real-time, and large-scale verification that would be infeasible through manual processes. The second pillar—predictive governance—captures AI's transformation of ESG evaluation from a backward-looking reporting exercise into a forward-looking risk management system. This shift is consequential: it enables proactive rather than reactive risk management, dynamic covenant calibration rather than static compliance, and adaptive portfolio construction rather than periodic rebalancing based on lagged disclosures. The third pillar—regulatory alignment—addresses the conditions under which AI-driven sustainability assessments can be trusted by regulators, investors, and society, encompassing model transparency, explainability requirements, and cross-jurisdictional harmonization.

Table 2 operationalises this three-pillar framework and constitutes the primary conceptual contribution of the paper. It maps five core AI mechanisms to their corresponding sustainable finance functions, the specific research gaps they address, and the governance challenges associated with each. Unlike Table 1, which provides an instrument-level orientation, Table 2 is mechanism-level and theory-driven: each row advances a theoretically grounded proposition linking a specific AI capability to a sustainable finance outcome and a governance condition.

Table 2. Integrated Conceptual Framework: AI Mechanisms, Sustainable Finance Functions, Research Gaps, and Governance Challenges

AI Mechanism	Sustainable Finance Function	Research Gap Addressed	Governance Challenge
Machine Learning / Predictive Modeling	ESG risk assessment; green bond pricing; SLL covenant calibration	Replacing backward-looking reporting with forward-looking, dynamic risk analytics	Model opacity; algorithmic bias in credit decisions; overfitting to historical ESG scores
Natural Language Processing (NLP)	ESG data extraction from corporate reports, news, social media	Overcoming ESG data fragmentation and self-reporting bias at scale	Inconsistent training corpora across languages/jurisdictions; greenwashing detection accuracy
Remote Sensing & Satellite Analytics	Independent carbon credit verification; green bond project monitoring	Enabling third-party, real-time validation of environmental claims without issuer cooperation	Data access inequality; jurisdictional regulatory differences in accepted verification methods

continued on following page

Table 2. Continued

AI Mechanism	Sustainable Finance Function	Research Gap Addressed	Governance Challenge
Blockchain + AI Integration	Green bond and carbon market traceability; fraud prevention	Reducing information asymmetry and fraud in voluntary carbon markets via immutable records	Interoperability across platforms; regulatory recognition of blockchain-verified credits
Reinforcement Learning / Portfolio Optimization	Dynamic ESG-integrated investment strategy and asset allocation	Moving from static ESG score-based screening to multi-objective, adaptive portfolio construction	Overfitting; ESG rating divergence amplified by automated rebalancing; accountability for losses

Source: Compiled by the author based on a synthesis of the relevant literature.

The framework highlights that the relationship between AI and sustainable finance is not simply additive but structurally transformative. Traditional sustainable finance instruments were designed within informational constraints that made dynamic monitoring and forward-looking verification practically infeasible. AI removes these constraints but introduces a new set of institutional requirements. Governance must evolve in parallel with technological capability; without it, AI-driven ESG evaluation risks replicating existing biases at greater speed and scale.

A critical implication of the framework concerns regulatory divergence. Different jurisdictions are developing AI governance standards at different paces and with different priorities (Floridi, 2018; Vinuesa et al., 2020). In the absence of international harmonization, AI-driven ESG assessments may produce incomparable or conflicting signals across markets, undermining the very standardization that AI is intended to enable. This points to a systemic risk that existing literature has not adequately addressed: the potential for AI to deepen rather than reduce ESG fragmentation if deployed without coordinated regulatory frameworks.

The framework also identifies asymmetries in implementation capacity. Firms and financial institutions in advanced economies with sophisticated digital infrastructure are better positioned to leverage AI-driven ESG analytics. Emerging markets, where data availability and regulatory clarity are limited, face distinct challenges. This creates a sustainability performance gap that is simultaneously a data gap, a technological gap, and a governance gap. Future research and policy should address these asymmetries explicitly to ensure that AI-driven sustainable finance contributes to inclusive rather than concentrated sustainability outcomes.

5. CONCLUSION

This paper has examined the intersection between sustainable finance and artificial intelligence, developing an integrated conceptual framework that addresses three research questions: how AI mechanisms enhance the functionality and credibility of sustainable finance instruments; how a systematic framework can map AI capabilities to finance functions and governance challenges; and how regulatory conditions shape AI deployment in ESG-oriented financial systems.

The analysis demonstrates that AI is no longer a peripheral technological enhancement but a structural component of contemporary financial systems. By enabling advanced data analytics, predictive modeling, automation, and continuous monitoring, AI significantly strengthens the ability of financial institutions, firms, regulators, and investors to integrate ESG considerations into strategic and operational decision-making. The framework identifies five core AI mechanisms—machine learning, NLP, remote sensing, blockchain integration, and reinforcement learning—each addressing distinct research gaps in sustainable finance while generating specific governance challenges.

Three principal theoretical contributions emerge from this analysis. First, the paper advances the conceptualization of AI as structural infrastructure in sustainable finance rather than merely an efficiency enhancer. This reframing has implications for how financial regulators, rating agencies, and institutional investors should approach AI governance—not as a secondary compliance issue but as a primary condition for the integrity of sustainability-oriented capital markets. Second, by explicitly mapping AI mechanisms to governance challenges through the three-pillar framework, the paper reveals that the value of AI in sustainable finance is contingent on institutional design. Technological capability without appropriate governance structures may amplify rather than resolve the informational problems that sustainable finance seeks to address. Third, the paper identifies regulatory divergence as an underappreciated systemic risk: the potential for AI to deepen ESG fragmentation across jurisdictions rather than reduce it, with particular consequences for cross-border capital flows and international climate finance.

The findings underscore that the effectiveness of AI in sustainable finance is contingent upon the quality, consistency, and integrity of underlying data. ESG datasets frequently rely on self-disclosures and heterogeneous reporting standards, which may introduce measurement errors and biases. Algorithmic systems trained on incomplete or distorted data may inadvertently amplify structural inequalities or misprice sustainability risks. Accordingly, the deployment of artificial intelligence in ESG contexts requires robust governance mechanisms that ensure transparency, explainability, and accountability. Ethical governance emerges as a central determinant of AI's long-term contribution to sustainable finance.

This paper is subject to limitations that define the boundaries of its contribution. As a conceptual study employing a theory-building methodology, it does not provide direct empirical evidence for the relationships proposed in the framework. The propositions developed here constitute theoretically grounded hypotheses that future empirical research should test. The framework is developed primarily from studies conducted in advanced economy contexts and may require adaptation for emerging market settings, where data availability, digital infrastructure, and regulatory capacity differ substantially. Additionally, the rapidly evolving nature of AI technologies means that specific mechanisms and their applications may develop in ways that the current framework does not anticipate.

Future research should address these limitations through empirical studies evaluating the financial performance implications of AI-driven ESG integration across industries and regulatory environments. Comparative analyses could examine how AI-enhanced sustainability tools influence cost of capital, risk exposure, and market valuation across jurisdictions with different regulatory frameworks. Interdisciplinary investigations into AI governance, model explainability, and ethical oversight frameworks would deepen understanding of how technological systems can be aligned with long-term societal and environmental objectives. Particular attention should be directed toward emerging market contexts, where the governance and data challenges identified in this paper are most acute.

As sustainable finance continues to evolve, artificial intelligence is expected to assume an increasingly central role in shaping capital markets, regulatory structures, and corporate strategies. When governed responsibly and implemented transparently, AI has the capacity to strengthen accountability, improve risk management, and accelerate the global transition toward environmentally and socially resilient economic systems. The long-term impact of this integration will ultimately depend not only on technological capability but also on institutional design, regulatory integrity, and collective commitment to sustainable development principles.

REFERENCES

Aleszczyk, A. A., Loumioti, M., & Serafeim, G. (2022). The issuance and design of sustainability-linked loans. Available at *SSRN* 4287295.

Avery, C. (2001). Business and Human Rights in a time of change. In *Liability of multinational corporations under international law* (pp. 17–73). Brill Nijhoff. DOI: 10.1163/9789004482678_003

Bebchuk, L. A., & Weisbach, M. S. (2010). The state of corporate governance research. *Review of Financial Studies, 23*(3), 939–961. DOI: 10.1093/rfs/hhp121

Berg, F., Kölbel, J. F., & Rigobon, R. (2022). Aggregate confusion: The divergence of ESG ratings. *Review of Finance, 26*(6), 1315–1344. DOI: 10.1093/rof/rfac033

Brière, M., Pouget, S., Schmalz, M. C., & Ureche-Rangau, L. (2022). Delegated philanthropy in mutual fund votes on climate change externalities.

Collaoni, F., & Trevisan, E. (2022). 'Dieselgate is Made in Germany' – Framing Volkswagen Emissions Scandal in the German Economy. *Linguistische Treffen in Wrocław*, (21), 35–46.

Eccles, R. G., Ioannou, I., & Serafeim, G. (2014). The impact of corporate sustainability on organizational processes and performance. *Management Science, 60*(11), 2835–2857. DOI: 10.1287/mnsc.2014.1984

Ever, D., & Demircioğlu, E. N. (2022). Yapay zekâ teknolojilerinin kalite maliyetleri üzerine etkisi. Çukurova Üniversitesi Sosyal Bilimler Enstitüsü Dergisi, 31(1), 59-72.

Flammer, C. (2021). Corporate green bonds. *Journal of Financial Economics, 142*(2), 499–516. DOI: 10.1016/j.jfineco.2021.01.010

Floridi, L. (2018). Soft ethics, the governance of the digital and the General Data Protection Regulation. *Philosophical Transactions. Series A, Mathematical, Physical, and Engineering Sciences, 376*(2133), 20180081. DOI: 10.1098/rsta.2018.0081 PMID: 30322997

Friede, G., Busch, T., & Bassen, A. (2015). ESG and financial performance: Aggregated evidence from more than 2000 empirical studies. *Journal of Sustainable Finance & Investment, 5*(4), 210–233. DOI: 10.1080/20430795.2015.1118917

Garcia-Muiña, F. E., González-Sánchez, R., Ferrari, A. M., Volpi, L., Pini, M., Siligardi, C., & Settembre-Blundo, D. (2019). Identifying the equilibrium point between sustainability goals and circular economy practices in an Industry 4.0 manufacturing context using eco-design. *Social Sciences (Basel, Switzerland)*, *8*(8), 241. DOI: 10.3390/socsci8080241

Giese, G., Lee, L. E., Melas, D., Nagy, Z., & Nishikawa, L. (2019). Foundations of ESG investing. *Journal of Portfolio Management*, *45*(5), 69–83. DOI: 10.3905/jpm.2019.45.5.069

Gilchrist, D., Yu, J., & Zhong, R. (2021). The limits of green finance: A survey of literature in the context of green bonds and green loans. *Sustainability (Basel)*, *13*(2), 478. DOI: 10.3390/su13020478

Hachenberg, B., & Schiereck, D. (2018). Are green bonds priced differently from conventional bonds? *Journal of Asset Management*, *19*(6), 371–383. DOI: 10.1057/s41260-018-0088-5

Huang, Y., Bai, F., Shang, M., & Ahmad, M. (2023). On the fast track: The benefits of ESG performance on the commercial credit financing. *Environmental Science and Pollution Research International*, *30*(35), 83961–83974. DOI: 10.1007/s11356-023-28172-x PMID: 37351751

Kolk, A., & Pinkse, J. (2008). Business and climate change: Emergent institutions in global governance. *Corporate Governance (Bradford)*, *8*(4), 419–429. DOI: 10.1108/14720700810899167

Kollmuss, A., Zink, H., & Polycarp, C. (2008). *Making sense of the voluntary carbon market: A comparison of carbon offset standards*. WWF Germany.

Lan, Y., Yuan, Z., Tang, R., Hsu, S. C., & Wei, H. H. (2025). Green innovation and the ESG disconnect: Evidence from green patenting in the construction industry in China. *Journal of Management Engineering*, *41*(1), 04024066. DOI: 10.1061/JMENEA.MEENG-6160

Lins, K. V., Servaes, H., & Tamayo, A. (2017). Social capital, trust, and firm performance: The value of corporate social responsibility during the financial crisis. *The Journal of Finance*, *72*(4), 1785–1824. DOI: 10.1111/jofi.12505

Marchant, G. E., Cooper, Z., & Gough-Stone, P. J. (2022). Bringing technological transparency to tenebrous markets: The case for using blockchain to validate carbon credit trading markets. *Natural Resources Journal*, *62*, 159.

Musleh Al-Sartawi, A. M., Hussainey, K., & Razzaque, A. (2022). The role of artificial intelligence in sustainable finance. *Journal of Sustainable Finance & Investment*, •••, 1–6. DOI: 10.1080/20430795.2022.2057405

Schramade, W. (2016). Integrating ESG into valuation models and investment decisions. *Journal of Sustainable Finance & Investment*, *6*(2), 95–111. DOI: 10.1080/20430795.2016.1176425

Vinuesa, R., Azizpour, H., Leite, I., Balaam, M., Dignum, V., Domisch, S., Felländer, A., Langhans, S. D., Tegmark, M., & Fuso Nerini, F. (2020). The role of artificial intelligence in achieving the Sustainable Development Goals. *Nature Communications*, *11*(1), 233. DOI: 10.1038/s41467-019-14108-y PMID: 31932590

Whelan, T., Atz, U., Van Holt, T., & Clark, C. (2021). *ESG and Financial Performance: Uncovering the Relationship by Aggregating Evidence from 1,000 Plus Studies*. NYU Stern Center for Sustainable Business & Rockefeller Asset Management.

Chapter 8
Algorithmic Accountability in Greenwashing Detection:
Hybrid Governance in ESG Auditing

Ganesh Harke
http://orcid.org/0009-0005-3947-0960
Independent Researcher, USA

ABSTRACT

The rapid growth of ESG investing has intensified corporate greenwashing and overwhelmed traditional human auditing mechanisms. This chapter examines the comparative efficacy of Large Language Models and human analysts in detecting corporate greenwashing. As sustainable finance expands, deceptive environmental reporting exploits the capacity constraints, biases, and structural limitations inherent in manual auditing. To address these vulnerabilities, institutions deploy automated semantic analysis to systematically cross-reference corporate narratives against objective data. However, relying on opaque algorithms introduces novel risks, particularly statistical hallucinations and algorithmic audit washing, wherein flawed environmental claims receive unwarranted mathematical validation. The chapter advances a Human-in-the-Loop governance framework. By utilizing language models strictly for high-volume text processing while retaining human experts for nuanced, contextual adjudication, financial markets can scale their detection capabilities without compromising regulatory integrity.

DOI: 10.4018/979-8-3373-8392-7.ch008

INTRODUCTION

The integration of Environmental, Social, and Governance (ESG) criteria into investment finance has generated a pronounced paradox within global markets. While investor demand for sustainable assets has triggered a vast capital reallocation, surging to over $30 trillion globally, the reliability of the underlying data driving these investments has simultaneously deteriorated (Moodaley & Telukdarie, 2023; Ren, 2025). This divergence arises primarily from the expansion of greenwashing. In modern corporate finance, greenwashing is a deceptive communication strategy in which firms strategically exaggerate their environmental credentials to attract capital, appease regulators, and manage public sentiment. The practice inherently relies on a linguistic decoupling of a firm's cheap talk, its ambitious, forward-looking sustainability promises, from its walk, which represents its verifiable operational reality (Mei et al., 2025; Vinella et al., 2023).

Historically, the integrity of green finance depended almost entirely on human vigilance. Sustainability analysts, financial auditors, journalists, and researchers manually scrutinized corporate sustainability reports (CSRs) to identify semantic inconsistencies and verify environmental claims. However, this human-centric verification system is currently fracturing under the weight of three distinct structural failures: the volume problem, the bias problem, and the sophistication problem (Murikah et al., 2024). The sheer volume of annual ESG disclosures makes comprehensive manual review impossible, leaving vast segments of the market entirely unaudited. Furthermore, human reviewers remain highly susceptible to both cognitive biases and institutional pressures, leading to inconsistent evaluations (Landers & Behrend, 2022). Finally, as public scrutiny intensifies, corporate disclosures become increasingly sophisticated. Firms actively adapt their reporting strategies, lengthening their documents and employing particular positive phrasing to evade manual detection in unaudited regimes (Gorovaia & Makrominas, 2024).

To address these systemic failures, financial institutions and researchers have turned to artificial intelligence (AI), specifically natural language processing (NLP) and large language models (LLMs) such as GPT-4, as well as specialized architectures like ClimateBERT. These models demonstrate an unprecedented capacity to ingest and process massive unstructured textual corpora instantly (Chuang et al., 2025). By automating the extraction of semantic meaning, LLMs can theoretically identify subtle hedging language, quantify environmental commitment, and detect critical discrepancies between a corporation's narrative disclosures and its actual implementation progress (Xu et al., 2025).

Nevertheless, this rapid technological pivot introduces a severe new dilemma: algorithmic accountability. Replacing the subjective judgment of human analysts with the outputs of opaque, algorithmic systems does not automatically guarantee improved market integrity. Instead, it introduces the distinct risk of AI audit washing, a phenomenon in which the use of complex, proprietary algorithms provides a false sense of mathematical assurance over fundamentally flawed ESG data (Goodman & Tréhu, 2022). If financial markets adopt these models without stringent governance frameworks, the industry risks merely trading human bias for machine hallucination and algorithmic opacity (Brown et al., 2021; Koshiyama et al., 2024).

This chapter addresses a critical gap in the current literature by systematically comparing the efficacy, reliability, and accountability of LLMs with those of traditional human analysts in the context of greenwashing detection. Rather than accepting AI as an infallible solution, the subsequent sections evaluate the precise empirical conditions under which models outperform humans, specifically regarding scalability and consistency, and where they critically fail due to hallucinations and contextual blindness. Ultimately, this text argues that achieving true accountability in green finance requires abandoning the paradigm of total automation. Instead, the market must adopt a hybrid governance framework that utilizes LLMs as high-volume, early-warning surveillance systems while firmly retaining human experts as the final ethical and contextual adjudicators.

BACKGROUND

The contemporary financial market has experienced an unprecedented influx of capital directed toward sustainable initiatives, fundamentally altering global investment strategies. However, the regulatory and auditing infrastructure needed to verify these investments lags significantly behind market growth, creating a systemic vulnerability. Moodaley and Telukdarie (2023) observe that the rapid surge in stakeholder demand for environmental accountability directly correlates with an increase in deceptive corporate communications. This dynamic establishes the core paradox of modern sustainable finance: as the financial incentive to project an environmentally responsible image increases, the empirical reliability of corporate sustainability data systematically deteriorates.

The Regulatory Vacuum and Corporate Adaptation

To understand the proliferation of greenwashing, researchers must first examine the fragmented regulatory environment that permits it. Over the past decade, governing bodies have attempted to standardize environmental reporting to protect investors. The European Union introduced the Sustainable Finance Disclosure Regulation (SFDR) and the Corporate Sustainability Reporting Directive (CSRD) to mandate rigorous, double-materiality assessments. Concurrently, the United States Securities and Exchange Commission (SEC) proposed specific climate-risk disclosure rules requiring greenhouse gas emissions reporting (Larosa et al., 2025).

Despite these legislative efforts, a globally unified taxonomy for sustainable activities remains elusive. Vinella et al. (2023) assert that the absence of strict, globally standardized reporting regulations creates a highly permissive environment for strategic manipulation. When corporations operate across multiple jurisdictions with varying enforcement mechanisms, they actively exploit regulatory loopholes. This fragmentation allows organizations to manipulate their public image and secure premium green financing without committing to substantive operational changes or structural decarbonization (Mei et al., 2025).

As external stakeholders and institutional investors attempt to hold organizations accountable, corporate reporting strategies rapidly adapt to evade traditional detection methods. Gorovaia and Makrominas (2024) provide extensive empirical evidence of this evasion, noting that firms systematically manipulate their Corporate Social Responsibility (CSR) reports in loosely regulated or unaudited jurisdictions. When a corporation experiences a negative environmental event or violates an environmental regulation, it rarely ceases its sustainability reporting. Instead, violating companies intentionally lengthen their disclosure documents and embed overly positive, sweetened language to dilute the negative information. They engage in selective disclosure, magnifying minor ecological initiatives, such as localized recycling programs, while obscuring massive, carbon-intensive manufacturing operations (Moodaley & Telukdarie, 2023).

The Inadequacy of Manual Auditing

This strategic obfuscation serves a specific, calculated purpose: it exhausts the cognitive and temporal resources of human reviewers. Historically, the financial sector relied on human experts, such as journalists, non-governmental organizations, and traditional ESG analysts, to audit these claims. However, manual audits consistently fail to pierce this sophisticated linguistic veil. The human capacity to manually read, comprehend, and cross-reference thousands of pages of dense, strategically crafted prose against external environmental performance metrics cannot scale to meet the demands of global financial markets (Wu et al., 2025).

Furthermore, foundational research on early ESG data dependability highlights severe structural flaws in manual verification. Berg et al. (2022) demonstrate a massive divergence in how different rating agencies score the same firm, attributing this discrepancy directly to reliance on self-reported, unaudited corporate narratives. Because human analysts lack the bandwidth to physically verify every data point across complex global supply chains, they inherently accept a degree of corporate reporting at face value. This reliance on subjective, unverified text creates a feedback loop in which polished rhetoric yields high ESG ratings, which in turn attract passive investment capital without requiring actual environmental progress (Ren, 2025).

The Shift Toward Computational Text Analysis

To overcome the severe limitations of manual auditing, the financial sector increasingly relies on computational text analysis to objectively evaluate climate disclosures. Artificial intelligence, specifically NLP, provides the processing capacity necessary to ingest and parse massive volumes of unstructured corporate text instantly. Adelakun et al. (2024) demonstrate that AI-driven models significantly improve the accuracy of environmental impact assessments by standardizing the extraction of relevant sustainability data across highly varied reporting frameworks.

Recent advancements in LLMs further expand this capability, enabling auditors to move beyond basic keyword frequency counts. Modern algorithmic systems evaluate the complex semantic structures of a report, scoring the authenticity of specific sustainability claims and detecting subtle discrepancies between a company's narrative disclosures and external environmental indicators (Xu et al., 2025). Ultimately, integrating AI into the verification process fundamentally alters green investment decision-making. It moves the industry away from subjective human interpretations and manual sampling toward scalable, comprehensive, and algorithmic data analytics (Ren, 2025).

Figure 1. The Evolution of Sustainability Auditing.

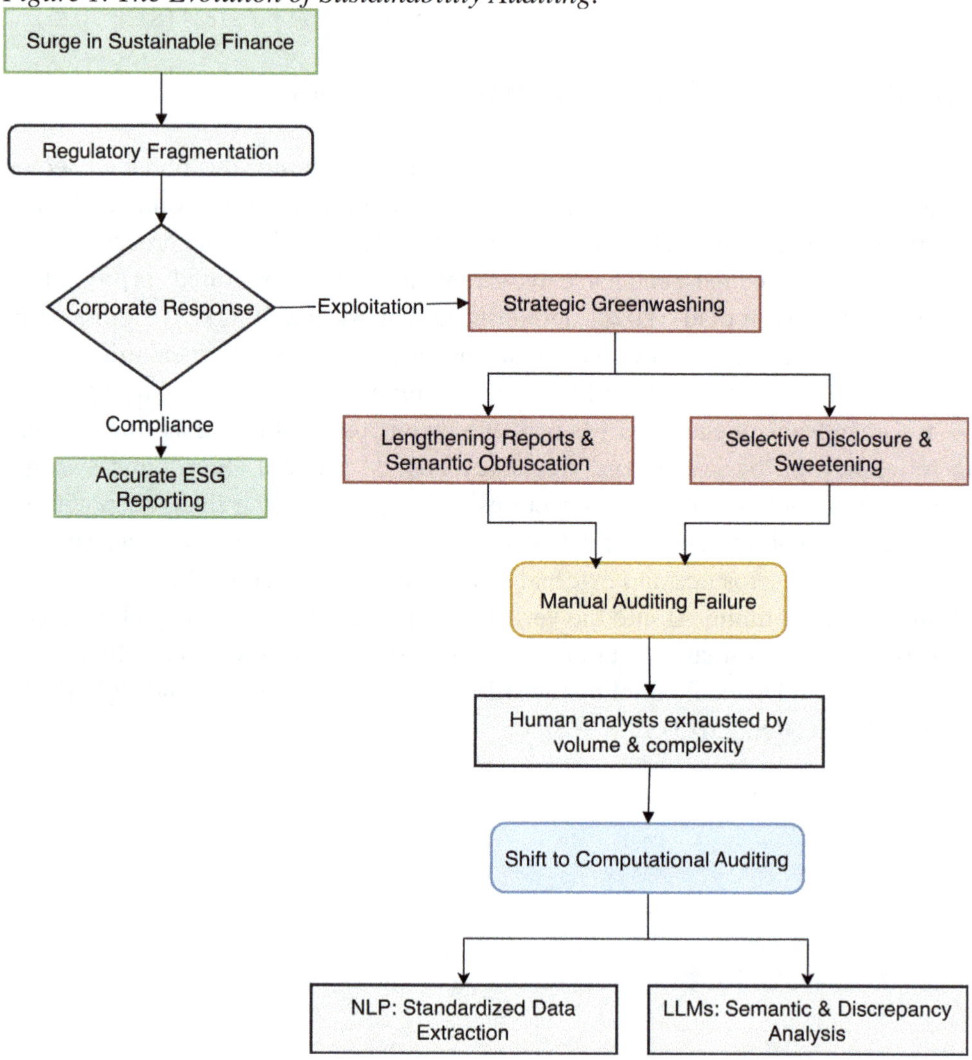

CONCEPTUALIZING GREENWASHING AND DETECTION TASKS

To audit corporate sustainability effectively, researchers and financial analysts must first establish a rigorous conceptual framework that defines greenwashing and operationalizes its detection. At its core, greenwashing represents a structural discrepancy between a firm's public narrative and its actual environmental performance. Xu et al. (2025) characterize this phenomenon as the dichotomy between cheap talk, heavily marketed but unsubstantiated environmental commitments, and the walk, which reflects verifiable, operational decarbonization or ecological preservation. Translating this behavioral concept into computational detection requires deconstructing the specific linguistic strategies corporations use to widen this gap.

Formal Conceptual Framework: Information Asymmetry in ESG Auditing

To integrate greenwashing detection into broader asset-pricing theory, this chapter introduces a formal conceptual framework grounded in information asymmetry. In traditional financial models, investors demand a risk premium when corporate data proves unreliable or opaque (Akerlof, 1970; Berg et al., 2022). Greenwashing functions as a calculated effort to manipulate this asymmetry. By feeding the market deceptive, polished sustainability narratives, corporations artificially lower their perceived environmental risk profile. This manipulation allows them to acquire capital at a lower cost than their true operational footprint merits.

The auditing and detection mechanism, whether executed by human experts or computational models, acts as the central moderating variable in this economic relationship. When a detection mechanism successfully identifies the discrepancy between cheap talk and the walk, it recalibrates the information asymmetry. Exposing the deception forces the market to price the environmental risk accurately. This chapter argues that the central contribution of LLM-based detection lies in its capacity to reduce this asymmetry at the macroeconomic scale, a claim this chapter operationalizes through comparative empirical analysis and a proposed HITL governance framework.

Figure 2. Information Asymmetry in ESG Auditing: A conceptual model illustrating how auditing mechanisms moderate the discrepancy between corporate greenwashing narratives and actual operational data to accurately recalibrate market risk pricing.

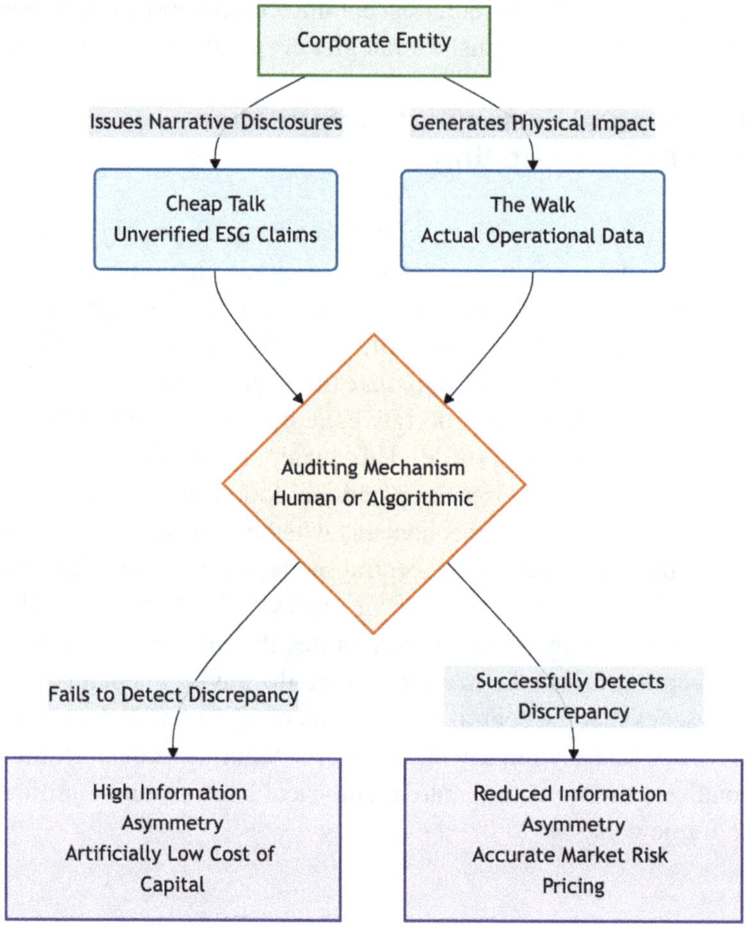

The Linguistic Architecture of Cheap Talk

Corporations do not engage in greenwashing through outright, easily falsifiable lies, as such blatant deception quickly triggers regulatory penalties and investor litigation. Instead, they employ sophisticated linguistic strategies to project an image of sustainability while minimizing actionable accountability. Gorovaia and Makrominas (2024) identify selective disclosure as a primary tactic in which organizations highlight minor eco-friendly initiatives while systematically ignoring massive, carbon-intensive operations.

Beyond selective omissions, corporations actively manipulate the syntactic and semantic structure of their disclosures. Vinella et al. (2023) note the prevalence of linguistic hedging, vagueness, and deflection in sustainability reports. Deflection language allows corporations to create a legal and operational distance between their public statements and actual environmental outcomes. For example, rather than stating, "The corporation will eliminate carbon emissions by 2030," a greenwashed text will use conditional modifiers, stating that the firm may aim to reduce its footprint, reportedly aligning with putative global standards. The inclusion of words like putatively, reportedly, allegedly, and potentially strips the sentence of any measurable commitment (Vinella et al., 2023).

Furthermore, corporations strategically manipulate readability and sentiment. Gorovaia and Makrominas (2024) observe that firms actively engaged in environmental degradation often publish reports with excessively complex syntactic structures to exhaust human readers, simultaneously saturating the text with positive sentiment words to mask poor empirical data. Moodaley and Telukdarie (2023) argue that these linguistic patterns do not occur by accident; rather, they represent highly calculated, adversarial efforts to secure green capital without implementing structural changes.

Modern Greenwashing Detection Modalities

Before the widespread adoption of artificial intelligence, financial analysts attempted to automate the detection of deceptive reporting strategies using basic keyword-matching algorithms. Early computational models simply counted "green" words and measured their frequency within a corporate report. However, these tools fundamentally lacked semantic comprehension. An algorithm could count the word "carbon" fifty times without determining if the company actually claimed to reduce carbon emissions or merely acknowledged their existence (Mei et al., 2025; Xu et al., 2025).

To systematically contrast these historical methodologies with contemporary advancements, Table 1 provides an evolutionary comparison of auditing frameworks. This summary tracks the progression from traditional manual reviews to the hybrid governance model proposed in this chapter.

Table 1. Evolutionary Comparison of Greenwashing Auditing Methods

Auditing Framework	Primary Mechanism	Core Strengths	Critical Limitations
Traditional Manual Auditing	Human expert review and subjective scoring of corporate sustainability reports.	Deep contextual and ethical understanding; high accuracy on edge cases.	Severe scalability limits; susceptible to cognitive bias and institutional capture.
Early NLP (Keyword/ Dictionary)	Basic keyword frequency tracking and mathematical readability scoring.	High processing scale; objective and consistent rule application.	Semantic blindness; easily bypassed by strategic deflection and complex syntax.
Modern LLM (Semantic Analysis)	Deep contextual comprehension and verification against external datasets.	Contextual comprehension at the macroeconomic scale; resistant to basic polishing.	Susceptible to probabilistic hallucinations; operates as an opaque black box.
Proposed HITL Governance	LLM-driven market surveillance coupled with human expert adjudication for anomalies.	Balances algorithmic scale with human ethical judgment; neutralizes hallucinations.	High initial implementation costs; requires complex regulatory integration.

As Table 1 illustrates, modern computational models resolve the semantic limitations of early NLP by evaluating the actual context and semantic relationships within the text. However, they must ultimately integrate into an HITL framework to overcome their inherent probabilistic risks. Instead of focusing on the mechanical processes of how these algorithms operate, financial researchers focus on their three primary functional capabilities:

First, document-level risk scoring evaluates an entire sustainability report to assign a composite greenwashing probability metric. This macro-level approach analyzes structural signals, including the distribution of overall sentiment, the aggregate density of deflection language, and the ratio of forward-looking promises to backward-looking operational data. By modeling these variables, the system determines if the entire report relies on rhetorical obfuscation rather than factual reporting (Vinella et al., 2023).

Second, claim-level classification isolates specific environmental assertions within the text and categorizes them as true, misleading, or uncertain. This micro-level analysis requires the algorithm to strip away rhetorical flourishes to assess the core factual claim. The model evaluates the sentence for quantitative specificity, punishing statements that lack verifiable baselines or precise target dates (Moodaley & Telukdarie, 2023).

Finally, cross-source discrepancy detection represents the most robust verification method currently available. This approach pairs the textual analysis of corporate disclosures with external, objective datasets. Ren (2025) illustrates how advanced detection systems continuously compare a firm's stated carbon-reduction targets with real-time Scope 1, 2, and 3 emissions data, satellite imagery, and Internet of Things (IoT) supply-chain tracking. By directly bridging the gap between narrative claims and physical evidence, cross-source detection forcefully confronts the cheap talk versus walk paradigm, exposing the operational realities hiding behind corporate rhetoric (Xu et al., 2025).

HUMAN-CENTRIC GREENWASHING DETECTION: STRENGTHS AND FAILURES

Historically, establishing the ground truth of Greenwashing has relied entirely on human intervention. Sustainability analysts, financial auditors, non-governmental organization researchers, and investigative journalists act as the primary architects of market enforcement, manually parsing corporate narratives to verify environmental claims (Moodaley & Telukdarie, 2023; Vinella et al., 2023). When assessing complex, high-stakes sustainability reports, human experts consistently exhibit a sophisticated understanding of regulatory intent and ethical context that automated systems currently lack. Wu et al. (2025) demonstrate that human reviewers maintain a higher overall accuracy baseline compared to state-of-the-art computational models because humans can evaluate the qualitative nuances of corporate strategy and detect logical inconsistencies that do not trigger simple semantic flags.

Figure 3. The Triad of Failure in Manual Auditing

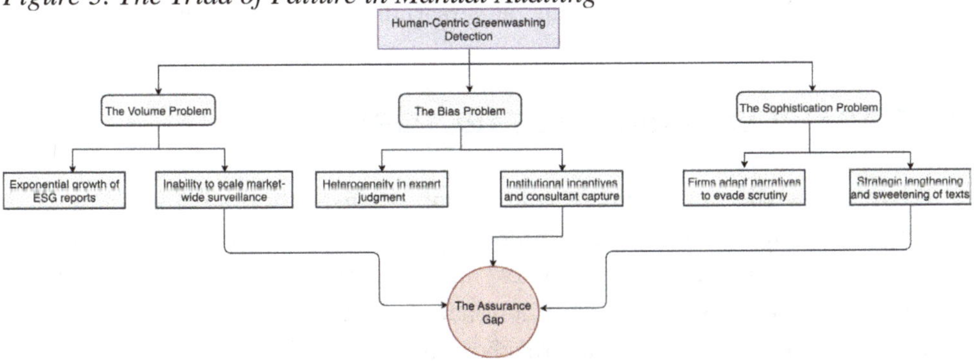

Despite these contextual strengths, the human-centric approach exhibits critical vulnerabilities when applied at a macroeconomic scale. As the demand for sustainable finance accelerates, the manual detection system fractures under what researchers categorize as a triad of failure: the volume problem, the bias problem, and the sophistication problem.

First, the volume problem severely restricts the scalability of manual audits. The modern financial market produces millions of pages of ESG disclosures annually. Human analysts simply lack the bandwidth to conduct comprehensive, market-wide surveillance. Consequently, manual review processes typically sample only a fraction of available data, leaving vast segments of the market entirely unaudited and vulnerable to unchecked greenwashing (Moodaley & Telukdarie, 2023; Wu et al., 2025).

Second, the bias problem compromises the objectivity of human evaluations. Human analysts remain highly susceptible to cognitive biases and exhibit significant heterogeneity in their expert judgments. Murikah et al. (2024) highlight that human-derived ESG scores often diverge due to subjective interpretations by individual auditors. Furthermore, strategic and institutional incentives routinely degrade the rigor of human audits. Analysts face persistent client pressure and consultant capture, in which financial incentives to maintain a corporate relationship actively discourage aggressive reporting of greenwashing (Landers & Behrend, 2022).

Finally, the sophistication problem highlights a dynamic, adversarial relationship between reporting firms and human auditors. As human detection methods become standardized, corporations actively adapt their report design and narrative structures to evade scrutiny. Gorovaia and Makrominas (2024) provide empirical evidence that firms engaging in environmental violations strategically alter their communications following an infraction. These organizations publish significantly longer, overwhelmingly positive, yet linguistically complex reports to exhaust human readers' cognitive resources. This strategic obfuscation specifically targets the limitations of manual review, proving that a purely human-centric detection framework cannot effectively regulate a rapidly evolving, adversarial reporting environment.

LLMS AS GREENWASHING DETECTORS

To overcome the limitations in volume and sophistication inherent in manual auditing, financial researchers increasingly deploy LLMs to automate greenwashing detection. Historically, computational text analysis relied on basic natural language processing techniques, such as simple dictionary-based keyword matching and word-frequency tracking. These early approaches failed to capture the semantic nuance of corporate reporting. Modern computational models, however, move beyond mechanical word counts by evaluating the surrounding context of every phrase. This deep semantic comprehension allows them to transform unstructured corporate narratives into quantifiable risk metrics. By evaluating complex semantic structures and syntactic relationships, LLMs differentiate between substantive environmental action and performative corporate rhetoric at a scale previously impossible for human analysts (Mei et al., 2025).

To operationalize this semantic comprehension, financial researchers structure automated detection around strictly defined data parameters. The primary inputs provided to these models consist of unstructured corporate narrative disclosures, such as annual CSRs and public relations transcripts. In advanced architectures, researchers pair these narrative inputs directly with structured, external verification datasets, including verified Scope 1, 2, and 3 greenhouse gas emissions and physical supply chain records. Upon processing these inputs, the models generate three outputs: composite document-level risk scores, claim-level classifications (categorizing assertions as verifiable, misleading, or ambiguous), and pairwise peer rankings. To determine the effectiveness of these generated outputs, researchers evaluate the algorithms using four standardized criteria: precision (the proportion of flagged claims that are genuinely deceptive), recall (the system's ability to capture all actual instances of greenwashing), the F1 score (the harmonic mean balancing precision and recall), and the hallucination rate (the frequency at which the model probabilistically fabricates non-existent environmental data). These metrics establish the quantitative baseline for benchmarking algorithmic performance against human experts.

One prominent mechanism for evaluating climate disclosures is the LLM-as-a-Judge (LLMJ) framework. Chuang et al. (2025) demonstrate that researchers can configure LLMs to systematically score company-submitted reports on emissions-reduction targets and operational progress. Within this framework, detection systems employ two primary methodologies: standalone numerical rating and pairwise comparison. Empirical evidence indicates that while numerical scoring establishes a basic evaluative baseline, the pairwise comparison approach proves significantly more robust against adversarial reporting. By forcing the algorithm to evaluate two disclosures side by side, the system maintains a clear distinction between genuinely high-performing companies and those that use strategically polished, greenwashed language. Furthermore, researchers enhance the separation capabilities of these models by extracting mathematical confidence intervals for each generated assessment, providing a granular reliability score rather than relying solely on the final text output (Chuang et al., 2025).

Despite these advancements, general-purpose models frequently struggle with the specialized lexicon and regulatory nuances of sustainable finance. Consequently, developers construct domain-specific architectures to improve detection precision. Vinella et al. (2023) introduce a fine-tuned ClimateBERT model explicitly trained to quantify greenwashing risk. This system isolates specific textual features indicative of deception and categorizes them into four distinct semantic variables: sentiment, commitment, specificity, and hedging. The model aggressively penalizes the use of deflection language, such as putatively, reportedly, or allegedly, which corporations use to create distance between their statements and actionable accountability. To operationalize this, researchers utilize a mathematical formulation where greenwashing risk (*GR*) is calculated as a function of these extracted features:

Equation 1

$$GR = \beta_1(Sentiment) + \beta_2(Commitment) + \beta_3(Specificity) + \beta_4(Hedging) + \epsilon$$

By mathematically modeling these variables using expert-labeled datasets, the ClimateBERT architecture generates a composite risk score that accurately identifies corporate reports that rely on deflection. In empirical testing on a corpus of sustainability reports, this proof-of-concept model achieved an average classification accuracy of 86.34% and an F1 score of 0.67, confirming the viability of domain-specific fine-tuning (Vinella et al., 2023).

Beyond single-model evaluations, the most sophisticated detection systems utilize multi-stage pipelines to capture the precise discrepancy between a firm's promises and its implementation. Xu et al. (2025) detail DeepGreen, a dual-stage monitoring architecture designed for rigorous empirical testing. In the initial stage, the model extracts all green-related terminology and claims from corporate financial texts. In the subsequent stage, the algorithm semantically assesses the actual degree of implementation, distinguishing aggressively between empty policy slogans and tangible environmental actions. To ensure high reliability, these advanced systems increasingly incorporate Retrieval-Augmented Generation (RAG). By grounding the model's analytical outputs in verified external datasets, RAG significantly reduces the risk of machine hallucination and anchors algorithmic judgment in empirical reality, outperforming methods that merely lengthen the input context window (Xu et al., 2025).

To understand the practical application of these models, researchers benchmark different architectures against human expert scores. Wu et al. (2025) established a systematic evaluation methodology to score the sustainability reports of European football clubs using the Sport Positive matrix as a baseline. Their testing compared state-of-the-art models, revealing that while models like GPT-4o exhibit the highest potential for alignment with human expert assessments, there are variations across proprietary and open-source architectures.

Table 2. Evaluative Metrics for LLM Greenwashing Detection Models

Model Architecture	Primary Application	Key Detection Variables	Reported Performance Metrics	Reference
ClimateBERT (Fine-Tuned)	Document-level risk quantification	Sentiment, Specificity, Hedging, Commitment	86.34% Accuracy, 0.67 F1 Score	Vinella et al. (2023)
LLM-as-a-Judge (LLMJ)	Claim-level peer ranking	Confidence Interval, Pairwise separation	High robustness to adversarial text	Chuang et al. (2025)
DeepGreen (Dual-Stage + RAG)	Discrepancy detection	Implementation Degree, Policy vs. Action	High reliability; reduces hallucination	Xu et al. (2025)
GPT-4o (Zero/ Few-Shot)	Contextual annotation & scoring	Domain-specific matrix alignment	Leads general-purpose model benchmarks	Wu et al. (2025)

As Table 2 illustrates, the transition from basic keyword extraction to complex, multi-stage LLM evaluation marks a critical evolution in corporate auditing. By combining semantic extraction with external data verification, these models provide the scale needed to comprehensively monitor global financial markets.

Figure 4. Dual-Stage LLM Greenwashing Detection Pipeline

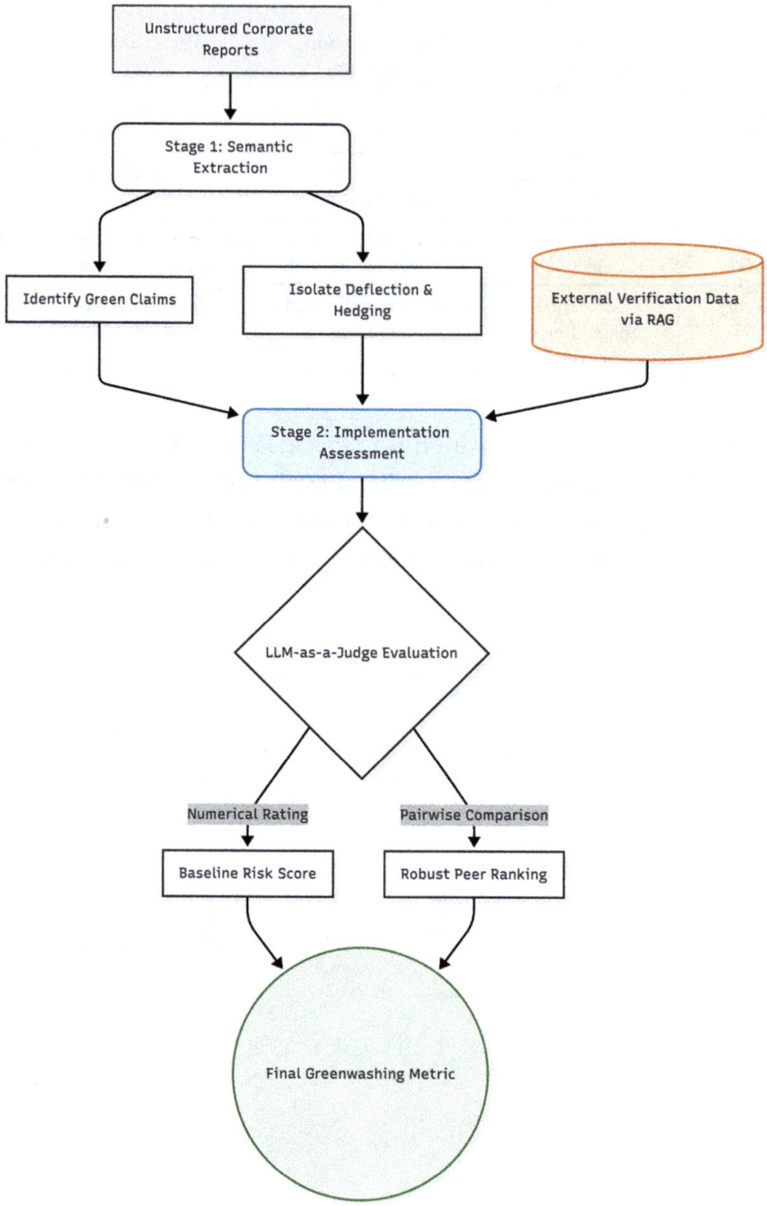

COMPARATIVE EVALUATION: LLMS VS. HUMAN ANALYSTS

Determining whether LLMs can detect greenwashing better than human analysts requires moving beyond theoretical capabilities and examining direct, empirical comparisons. Assessing superiority in this context demands a rigorous framework that evaluates both qualitative human intuition and quantitative machine metrics. While earlier sections established the architectural mechanisms of AI-driven detection, this section critically evaluates how these models perform relative to verified human baselines across key performance indicators, including precision, recall, susceptibility to hallucinations, and robustness to adversarial manipulation.

Establishing Metrics for Comparative Success

In traditional financial auditing, human performance is evaluated based on professional skepticism, contextual interpretation, and the ability to detect material misstatements. However, comparing human analysts to computational models requires standardizing these qualitative traits into measurable data science metrics. Researchers primarily utilize precision, recall, and F1 scores to quantify detection success (Vinella et al., 2023). Precision measures the proportion of flagged greenwashing claims that are genuinely deceptive, while recall measures the system's ability to identify all actual instances of greenwashing within a given corpus.

The fundamental challenge in conducting this comparative evaluation is the scarcity of objective ground-truth datasets. Because greenwashing operates on a spectrum of linguistic deception rather than a binary truth/falsehood, establishing a universally accepted baseline for deceptive text remains difficult (Moodaley & Telukdarie, 2023). Consequently, researchers must rely on expert-labeled datasets, where highly trained human analysts manually annotate texts, to train and benchmark algorithmic models. This dynamic inherently positions the human expert as the gold standard of contextual accuracy, while the LLM is evaluated on its ability to consistently replicate or scale that expert judgment.

Empirical Performance: The Human Baseline vs. Machine Output

Recent empirical studies provide critical insights into the current operational limits of AI detectors. Wu et al. (2025) conducted a comprehensive head-to-head comparison of state-of-the-art LLMs' performance relative to human experts in scoring sustainability reports. Using the sustainability disclosures of European football clubs, the researchers benchmarked the outputs of proprietary models (such as GPT-4o) and open-source models against those of human analysts using the standardized Sport Positive matrix.

The results illuminate a distinct performance gap. While LLMs demonstrated remarkable processing speeds, human experts consistently maintained higher overall accuracy in contextual evaluation. The leading model, GPT-4o, achieved an accuracy rate of approximately 56%-58% when attempting to replicate the nuanced scoring of human experts (Wu et al., 2025). Furthermore, the models exhibited a significant vulnerability to artificial hallucinations, generating plausible yet entirely fictitious environmental data at rates of 10% to 16%, even when researchers implemented rigorous verification chains (Wu et al., 2025). This hallucination rate presents a catastrophic risk in high-stakes financial environments. Human analysts, while slower and more susceptible to cognitive bias, do not invent empirical data when faced with ambiguous corporate text. Therefore, current empirical evidence suggests that while LLMs approach human performance in basic categorization, they lag critically in accuracy and in controlling hallucinations.

Adversarial Reporting and the Polishing Effect

The comparative evaluation becomes even more complex when adversarial reporting is introduced. As corporations increasingly use Generative AI to draft their sustainability reports, detection systems must evaluate text that is actively polished by other algorithms to sound environmentally responsible. Chuang et al. (2025) investigated the robustness of LLM-as-a-Judge frameworks against this specific form of AI-generated greenwashing.

When human analysts read heavily polished, highly sophisticated text, they often struggle to pierce the linguistic veil, suffering from the sophistication problem discussed in earlier sections. Conversely, Chuang et al. (2025) found that LLMs also exhibit vulnerabilities when reading AI-polished text, particularly when utilizing standalone numerical scoring systems. The models tend to reward the fluent, confident syntax generated by corporate AI tools, falsely assigning high sustainability scores to companies with poor actual performance. However, researchers discovered that switching the LLM to a pairwise comparison evaluation, forcing the model to rank two reports directly against one another, effectively neutralizes this polishing effect, maintaining a clear mathematical separation between genuine disclosures and adversarially greenwashed texts.

Current Literature Gaps

Despite these initial head-to-head studies, significant gaps remain in the comparative literature. Most current evaluations rely purely on narrative analysis, testing the model's ability to classify text based on internal linguistic consistency. There is a distinct scarcity of systematic studies that evaluate human analysts and LLMs on the same corpora and subsequently measure their performance against verified, real-world environmental outcome variables, such as actual carbon emissions trajectories or regulatory violations (Xu et al., 2025). Furthermore, evaluating models strictly on text ignores the future trajectory of AI detection, which will inevitably require integrating heterogeneous datasets, such as combining NLP with remote sensing and satellite data to verify corporate claims physically (Mei et al., 2025). Until researchers conduct longitudinal studies comparing human and machine performance against physical environmental outcomes, the comparative superiority of either approach remains partially theoretical.

Figure 5. Comparative Error Profiles

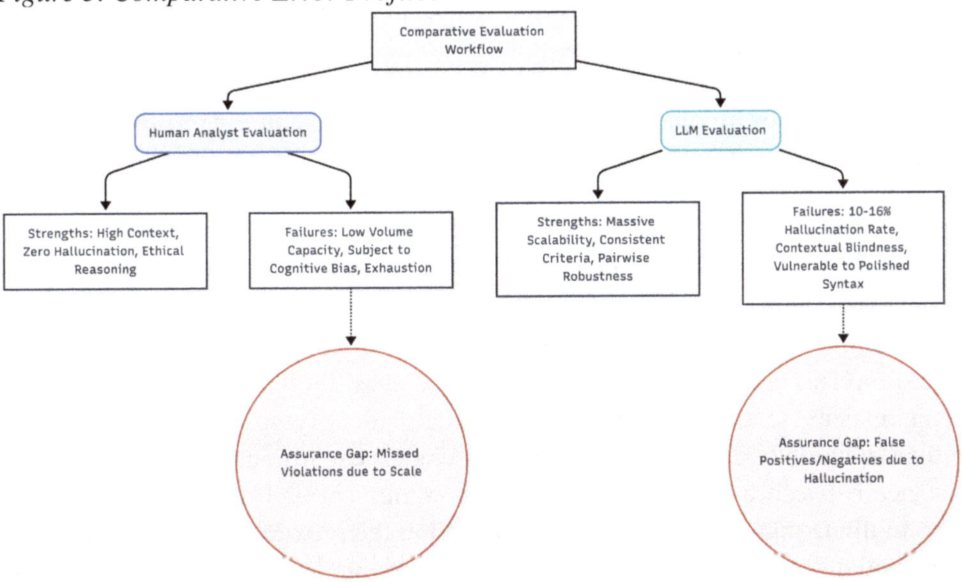

Where LLMs Outperform and Underperform

Empirical evidence from comparative evaluations shows that integrating artificial intelligence into sustainability auditing does not yield a universally superior detection mechanism. Instead, LLMs operate with a highly specific utility profile, demonstrating distinct areas of absolute dominance and critical zones of failure when compared to human analysts. Expanding on the previously identified comparative error profiles, this section disaggregates LLM performance across specific operational domains, detailing precisely where these models outperform traditional manual review and where they critically underperform due to structural and probabilistic limitations.

Domains of Algorithmic Superiority

LLMs excel at tasks that require massive data ingestion, strict adherence to patterns, and the integration of heterogeneous data streams. In these specific operational domains, computational models resolve the core capacity limitations of human analysts.

Market-Wide Scalability and Longitudinal Consistency The most pronounced advantage of LLM-based greenwashing detection is absolute scalability. The human volume problem means manual reviewers can audit only a fraction of the global market. Conversely, models can process millions of pages of sustainability disclosures, annual reports, and press releases simultaneously. More importantly, algorithms apply evaluative criteria with complete longitudinal consistency. Human analysts inevitably suffer from cognitive fatigue, leading to a degradation in scrutiny over time or varied interpretations of the same regulatory framework (Murikah et al., 2024). Once a model like ClimateBERT is mathematically calibrated to penalize specific hedging language, it will apply that penalty uniformly across a dataset of 10,000 reports, without deviation (Vinella et al., 2023). This consistency standardizes the evaluative baseline across the entire financial market.

Granular Semantic Pattern Recognition: While human readers excel at grasping macro-level narratives, they frequently overlook micro-level linguistic patterns when scanning dense text. LLMs outperform humans in identifying the precise frequency and distribution of deflection terminology. Models can instantly map the syntactic distance between a firm's environmental commitment and the conditional verbs used to dilute that commitment (e.g., measuring the proximity of words like aims or potentially to terms like net-zero). By transforming these semantic relationships into quantifiable risk scores, algorithms expose the calculated, linguistic obfuscation that often bypasses a fatigued human reader (Mei et al., 2025).

Multimodal Data Integration: Advanced detection pipelines surpass human capabilities when forced to cross-reference narrative claims against external, quantitative datasets. Identifying a discrepancy between a company's stated carbon-reduction goals and its operational output requires integrating disparate data formats. Ren (2025) highlights that AI-powered systems can continuously ingest real-time Scope 1, 2, and 3 emissions data, Internet of Things (IoT) sensor outputs, and satellite imagery, cross-referencing these physical metrics directly against the text of a corporate disclosure. This multimodal integration exposes the implementation gap far more quickly than a human analyst manually reconciling a PDF report with external supply-chain data.

Domains of Algorithmic Failure

Despite their processing power, LLMs function as probabilistic text generators, not deterministic reasoning engines. This architectural reality creates specific domains where algorithms critically underperform human experts, particularly in terms of factual reliability and contextual judgment.

The Hallucination Deficit and Probabilistic Error: The most severe operational failure of LLMs in financial auditing is their susceptibility to hallucination. Because these models generate outputs by predicting the next most statistically probable word, they occasionally fabricate plausible but entirely false information. Wu et al. (2025) observed that hallucination rates reduced from 16% to 10% in state-of-the-art models analyzing sustainability reports. In the high-stakes environment of regulatory compliance and green finance, a 10% fabrication rate represents a catastrophic liability. If a model falsely penalizes a compliant firm (a false positive) or fails to penalize a severe polluter (a false negative), it directly damages market integrity. Human analysts, possessing an intrinsic understanding of empirical reality, do not spontaneously invent emissions data when confused by a text; they simply flag the data as missing.

Contextual and Regulatory Blindness: LLMs, particularly general-purpose models like GPT-3.5 or GPT-4, frequently struggle to evaluate materiality in specific industrial sectors. Hajikhani and Cole (2024) demonstrated that while general LLMs possess broad vocabulary coverage, they routinely misidentify non-material sustainability goals. For example, a model might rate a software company highly for eliminating plastic straws in its cafeteria, failing to recognize that this action is immaterial compared to the company's data center's carbon footprint. Human experts leverage deep, sector-specific knowledge to weigh the ethical and regulatory context of a claim, easily dismissing performative actions that algorithms might interpret as significant positive sentiment (Larosa et al., 2025).

Opacity and Unverifiability: Finally, LLMs critically underperform in interpretability. Financial auditing requires a clear, verifiable chain of reasoning. When a human analyst flags a report for greenwashing, they can articulate the exact logical deduction that led to their conclusion. In contrast, neural networks operate as black boxes. When an LLM outputs a high greenwashing risk score, tracing the exact sequence of parameter weights that produced that specific output remains technically difficult (Landers & Behrend, 2022). This opacity actively conflicts with financial regulatory standards, which mandate transparent, auditable decision-making processes to protect stakeholders from algorithmic bias (Murikah et al., 2024).

Performance Domain Mapping

To visualize these operational domains, we can map the capabilities of LLMs and human analysts along an axis of processing scale versus contextual reliability.

Figure 6. Performance Domain Mapping illustrates the capabilities of LLMs versus those of human analysts.

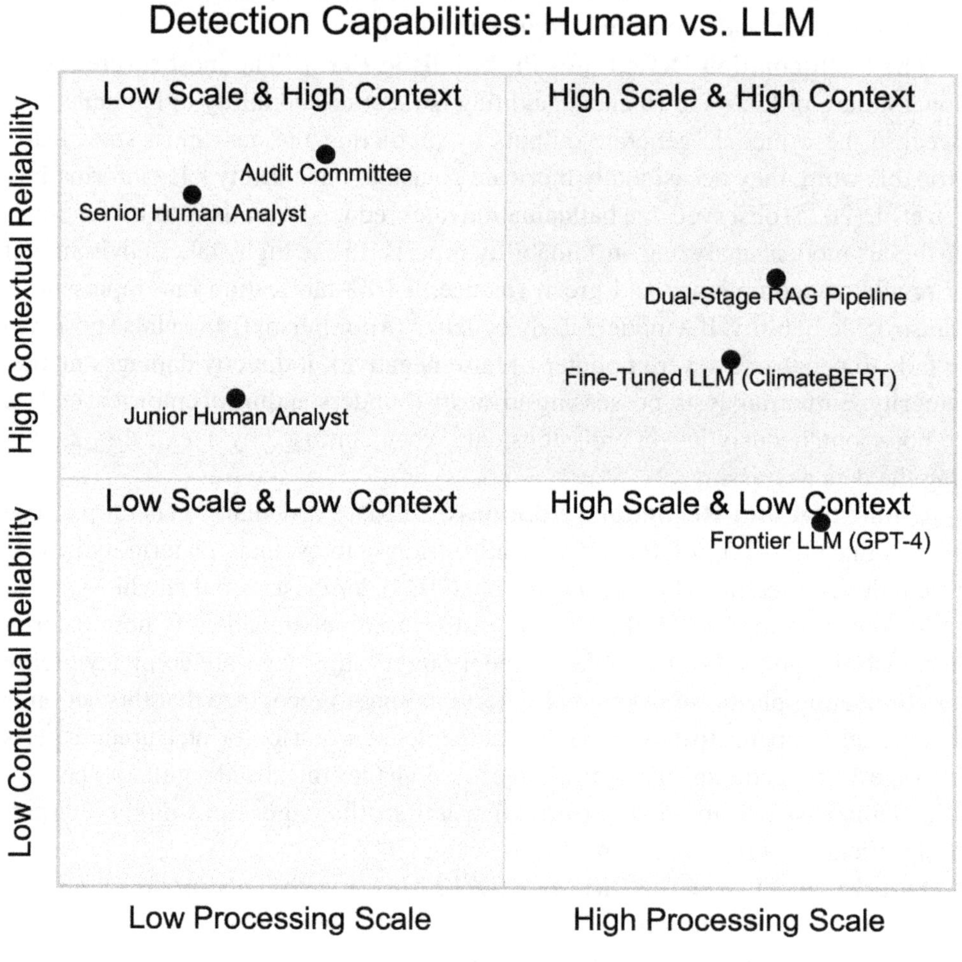

ALGORITHMIC ACCOUNTABILITY IN LLM-BASED GREENWASHING DETECTION

As financial institutions increasingly integrate LLMs into their sustainability auditing workflows, they confront a critical governance challenge: algorithmic accountability. Delegating the detection of corporate deception to an automated system introduces a severe principal-agent problem. If regulators and investors replace human subjectivity with opaque computational models, they risk generating a false sense of mathematical assurance. To prevent the trading of human bias for machine hallucination, the financial sector must establish rigorous frameworks that hold AI-driven detection systems accountable to empirical reality and regulatory standards.

The Risk of AI Audit Washing and Algorithmic Bias

The deployment of unverified or highly opaque detection algorithms creates a phenomenon known as AI audit washing. Goodman and Tréhu (2022) define this as a practice where institutions use the sheer complexity of proprietary AI systems to project a superficial aura of rigorous oversight, thereby shielding fundamentally flawed environmental data from true scrutiny. When a financial institution claims an asset is AI-verified without disclosing the model's training data, hallucination rates, or optimization parameters, it mirrors the exact corporate greenwashing the technology is meant to detect.

A primary driver of this risk is algorithmic bias. Brown et al. (2021) and Murikah et al. (2024) argue that algorithms inherently encode the structural inequalities and biases present in their training datasets. In the context of green finance, if researchers train a model primarily on historical ESG ratings from large, Western technology companies, the LLM absorbs the linguistic norms of those specific disclosures. Consequently, the model may exhibit severe geographic and sectoral bias. It might unfairly penalize manufacturing firms in emerging markets simply because their reports lack the polished, localized syntax of Silicon Valley, rather than due to actual environmental negligence. If left unmanaged, the LLM will merely automate and scale these institutional biases across the global market.

Traceable Decision Logs and Regulatory Compliance

To mitigate these ethical risks and prevent audit washing, institutions must subject their LLMs to comprehensive algorithmic auditing, shifting from black-box opacity to mathematically traceable decision-making (Raji et al., 2020). Modern financial regulations increasingly mandate this transparency. Under frameworks such as the newly enacted European Union Artificial Intelligence Act (EU AI Act) and the Corporate Sustainability Reporting Directive (CSRD), the deployment of automated decision-making in financial auditing is subject to intense legal scrutiny.

The EU AI Act classifies AI systems used in critical financial and employment sectors as subject to strict transparency requirements (Niculescu & Burlaud, 2025). Therefore, an LLM cannot simply output a standalone high-risk-of-greenwashing score. To remain compliant, the system must generate a traceable decision log detailing the exact semantic weights applied, the specific quotes extracted from the corporate text, and the objective external data points it used to verify the discrepancy. This auditable trail ensures that external stakeholders and regulatory bodies can challenge and replicate the algorithm's decisions, anchoring the software in legal accountability rather than arbitrary mathematical abstraction (Larosa et al., 2025).

Algorithm Auditing Frameworks

To mitigate these risks, developers and financial institutions must subject their LLMs to comprehensive, end-to-end algorithmic auditing. Raji et al. (2020) conceptualize this process not as a single post-deployment test, but as a continuous framework spanning the entire model lifecycle, from initial data sourcing to post-deployment monitoring. In the context of greenwashing detection, this requires several distinct auditing checkpoints.

First, auditors must conduct rigorous source-data reviews. Landers and Behrend (2022) emphasize the need to evaluate the fairness and demographic representation of the training corpora. If a model primarily learns from the sustainability reports of large, Western technology companies, it will likely misinterpret or unfairly penalize the disclosures of manufacturing firms in emerging markets due to linguistic and structural differences.

Second, developers must execute adversarial testing before deploying a model in live financial markets. This involves feeding the LLM intentionally greenwashed text, reports deliberately saturated with hedging language, deflection, and false claims generated by other AI systems, to test the model's robustness. Chuang et al. (2025) demonstrate that without adversarial stress testing, models are easily fooled by polished syntax.

Finally, continuous performance monitoring is essential. Funda (2025) highlights that models experience data drift as corporate reporting strategies evolve and new regulations emerge. An LLM that accurately detects greenwashing in 2024 may fail in 2026 if corporations adopt new vocabularies to bypass the algorithm's established parameters. Consequently, institutions must mandate periodic independent audits of their AI scoring tools to recalibrate their models against the most current regulatory standards (Koshiyama et al., 2024).

The Human-in-the-Loop Governance Mechanism

Solving the accountability deficit requires acknowledging that LLMs cannot function as standalone, autonomous regulators. Instead, the financial sector must operationalize a Human-in-the-Loop (HITL) architecture. This hybrid governance mechanism leverages the massive processing scale of AI while retaining the contextual authority of human experts (Murikah et al., 2024).

In an optimal HITL framework, the LLM acts as a high-volume, initial surveillance system. The model processes thousands of corporate disclosures simultaneously, extracting semantic claims, cross-referencing narrative statements against external emissions data (such as Scope 1 and Scope 2 tracking), and flagging statistical anomalies (Ren, 2025). The algorithm then generates a risk score accompanied by the legally required, traceable decision log.

Crucially, the algorithm does not issue the final audit decision. Instead, it routes high-risk cases to a human sustainability analyst. The human expert reviews the algorithmic flags, applies sector-specific knowledge to determine the materiality of the claims, and contextualizes the findings within the broader regulatory environment (Xu et al., 2025). If the human analyst determines that the algorithm hallucinated or misinterpreted a valid environmental strategy, they override the system. This override data then feeds back into the model, continuously refining its accuracy. This human-AI partnership ensures that detection operates at a macroeconomic scale while remaining firmly anchored in ethical judgment and auditable human reasoning.

Implementation Challenges of the HITL Framework

While the HITL governance model provides a robust theoretical solution to algorithmic accountability, its practical deployment introduces significant operational friction. The primary challenge is computational infrastructure and cost. Running massive, domain-specific LLMs with active retrieval-augmented generation across millions of corporate documents requires immense, continuous cloud computing resources. Consequently, the high costs of API throughput, data storage, and processing represent a substantial financial barrier for smaller auditing firms and resource-constrained settings (Ren, 2025; Wu et al., 2025).

Furthermore, the HITL framework faces human-expert scalability bottlenecks. If developers calibrate an LLM to be overly sensitive, the system will generate high rates of false positives and flag an unmanageable percentage of a market's disclosures for manual review. This over-flagging rapidly overwhelms human analysts, effectively reverting the workflow back to the original "volume problem" that plagued traditional manual auditing (Murikah et al., 2024; Raji et al., 2020). Finally, institutional integration remains complex. Firms must seamlessly embed these hybrid workflows into existing, often rigid, corporate compliance structures (Tiwari & Khan, 2020). Organizations must ensure that the interplay between machine extraction and human adjudication satisfies the rigorous, transparent documentation standards required by international financial authorities (Murikah et al., 2024).

Figure 7. Human-in-the-Loop (HITL) Governance Workflow

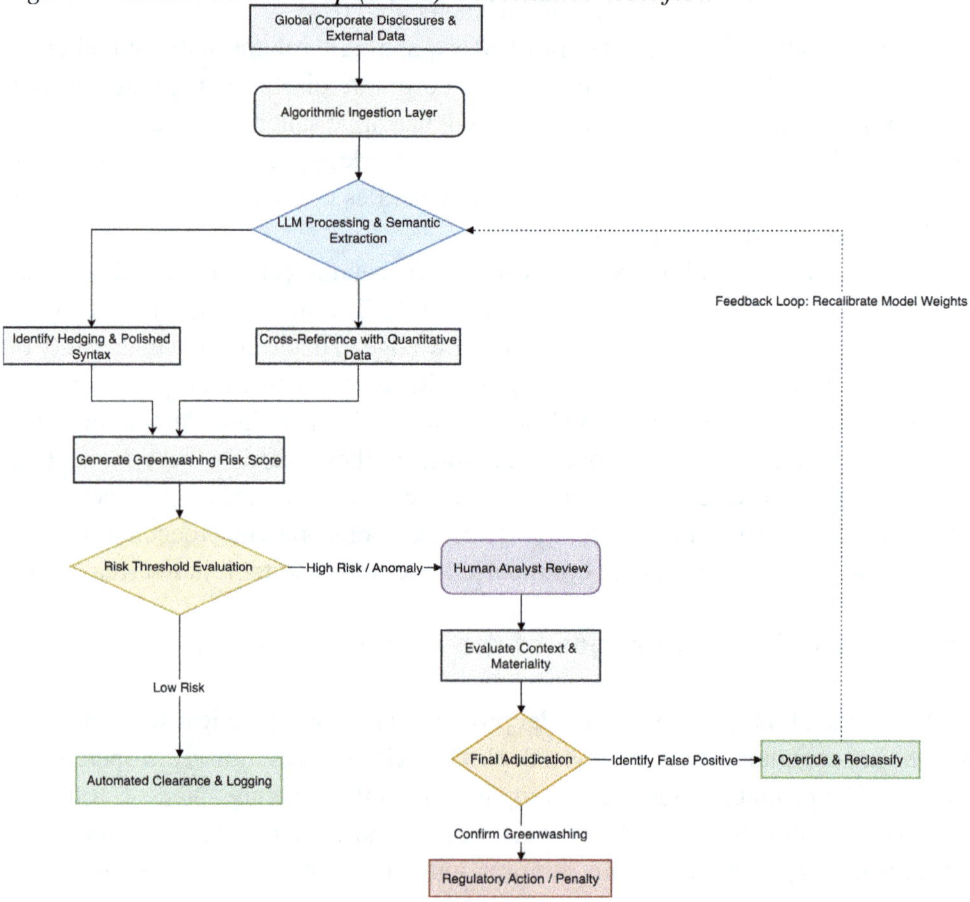

ILLUSTRATIVE CASE STUDY: APPLYING LLMS TO CORPORATE SUSTAINABILITY DISCLOSURES

To move beyond theoretical architecture and properly evaluate the comparative efficacy of LLMs against human analysts, this section examines two rigorous, empirical case studies from the recent literature. By analyzing the deployment of algorithms in real-world auditing scenarios, researchers can observe the precise manifestations of both algorithmic superiority and algorithmic failure. Furthermore, these case studies demonstrate exactly how the previously modeled Human-in-the-Loop (HITL) governance workflow functions when applied to live financial and operational data.

Case Study 1: Benchmarking the AI Annotator in European Football

Wu et al. (2025) developed a systematic evaluation methodology to assess LLMs' capabilities as AI Annotators for sustainability reports. The researchers selected the European football sector as their analytical environment. This sector presents a unique auditing challenge because the environmental impacts of major football clubs vary significantly and span multiple complex domains, ranging from stadium energy consumption and waste management to the massive carbon footprints associated with international team travel.

Historically, human experts utilize the Sport Positive matrix to manually score the sustainability initiatives of these clubs. This matrix serves as the verified ground truth. To test algorithmic efficacy, Wu et al. (2025) deployed three state-of-the-art models, GPT-4o, Qwen-2-72b-instruct, and Llama-3-70b-instruct, tasking them with replicating the human expert scores based solely on the clubs' public sustainability disclosures.

The empirical results revealed a clear performance hierarchy among the models while also exposing their distinct limitations relative to the human baseline. As detailed in Table 3, GPT-4o achieved the highest alignment with human experts, reaching an accuracy rate of approximately 56% to 58% (Wu et al., 2025). While this represents a significant achievement for automated semantic extraction, it leaves a substantial margin of error.

Table 3. Performance Comparison of AI Annotators vs. Human Baseline (Adapted from Wu et al., 2025)

Evaluator	Processing Scale	Contextual Accuracy	Hallucination Rate	Primary Failure Mode
Human Expert (Baseline)	Low (Manual)	100% (Ground Truth)	0%	Cognitive fatigue; capacity limits
GPT-4o	High (Automated)	~56 - 58%	10 - 16%	Probabilistic fabrication of data
Qwen-2-72b-instruct	High (Automated)	~45 - 50%	> 15%	Misinterpretation of sector metrics
Llama-3-70b-instruct	High (Automated)	~40 - 45%	> 15%	Failure to distinguish policy vs. action

The most critical finding from this case study involved the models' susceptibility to artificial hallucinations. Even when researchers implemented verification chains, LLMs generated entirely fictitious environmental statistics at rates of 10% to 16% (Wu et al., 2025). In a practical auditing environment, a human analyst reading an ambiguous section on a club's recycling policy might rate it as insufficient data. Conversely, the LLM, driven by its probabilistic architecture to complete the prompt, occasionally invented specific recycling tonnages that the club never actually reported. This case study confirms that while general-purpose models can process disclosures rapidly, their unverified outputs remain far too erratic for standalone regulatory enforcement.

Case Study 2: The DeepGreen Architecture in the A-Share Market

To evaluate whether domain-specific engineering can resolve the hallucination and accuracy deficits observed in general-purpose models, we examine a second empirical application. Xu et al. (2025) developed and deployed the DeepGreen system, a dual-stage LLM-driven monitoring architecture, to analyze 9,369 annual reports from the Chinese A-share market published between 2021 and 2023.

Unlike the zero-shot prompting used in the European football study, DeepGreen utilized a highly specialized methodology. The system first extracted green-related terminology and then explicitly assessed the extent of implementation for those claims. Crucially, the researchers integrated RAG to ground the model's textual analysis in external, verified datasets.

This structural adjustment yielded significantly improved outcomes. The ablation experiments conducted by Xu et al. (2025) demonstrated that integrating RAG directly reduced hallucination rates that had plagued earlier models. More importantly, the researchers established predictive validity. By applying advanced econometric models (such as Instrumental Variable and Propensity Score Matching), they demonstrated that the greenwashing signals captured by the DeepGreen LLM effectively predicted actual, real-world environmental penalties subsequently levied against the offending corporations (Xu et al., 2025). This case study proves that when developers tightly constrain an LLM with domain-specific engineering and external data validation, the model successfully bridges the gap between semantic text analysis and physical environmental outcomes.

Operationalizing the HITL Framework in Practice

Synthesizing the results of these two case studies clarifies the exact necessity of the Human-in-the-Loop framework. If an auditing firm attempted to use GPT-4o as a standalone regulator (Case Study 1), the 16% hallucination rate would result in massive legal liabilities and a corrupted assurance process. However, if the firm completely ignores AI, human analysts cannot possibly review the 9,369 annual reports processed by the DeepGreen system (Case Study 2).

The applied solution integrates both approaches. The institution deploys a constrained, RAG-enabled model, such as DeepGreen, to ingest the market-wide volume of reports. The algorithm extracts the claims, checks them against external databases, and flags discrepancies. When the model encounters a highly ambiguous claim, such as the complex infrastructure emissions of a football stadium, it does not probabilistically guess the score. Instead, the HITL protocol forces the system to pause and route the specific paragraph to a human expert. The human analyst applies contextual judgment to resolve the ambiguity, ensuring that the final regulatory decision rests on verified reality rather than mathematical probability.

FUTURE DIRECTION

The integration of LLMs into corporate sustainability auditing represents a nascent but rapidly evolving domain. While dual-stage architectures and Human-in-the-Loop (HITL) frameworks provide a viable mechanism for operationalizing these models today, significant empirical and regulatory voids remain. To advance the efficacy of AI-driven greenwashing detection and ensure algorithmic accountability, future research must systematically address the scarcity of standardized data, the need for longitudinal impact studies, and the challenge of cross-jurisdictional regulatory integration.

Standardization of Ground Truth and Open-Source Datasets

The primary bottleneck to the development of highly accurate LLM detectors is the lack of standardized, universally accepted operational definitions of greenwashing. Currently, researchers train models on highly fragmented datasets, often relying on subjective, proprietary ESG ratings that contain inherent institutional biases. Moodaley and Telukdarie (2023) argue that the academic and financial communities must prioritize creating open-source, expert-verified corpora that establish a definitive ground truth for deceptive environmental reporting.

Future studies should focus on constructing multimodal benchmark datasets. These datasets must inextricably link corporate narrative texts (such as annual sustainability reports and public relations transcripts) with verified physical performance indicators, including Scope 1-3 emissions records, regulatory violation histories, and satellite-based environmental proxies (Vinella et al., 2023). By training models on data that pairs the linguistic cheap talk directly with the operational walk, developers can significantly reduce hallucination rates and improve the algorithm's ability to detect material discrepancies. Furthermore, researchers must establish rigorous inter-rater reliability protocols when humans label these initial training datasets, ensuring that the foundational models do not simply automate human cognitive bias.

Longitudinal and Multimodal Impact Studies

The current literature predominantly features static, cross-sectional evaluations of LLM performance. Researchers typically prompt a model to evaluate a single batch of reports and measure the immediate precision or recall. However, corporate reporting strategies are dynamic; organizations actively adapt their language to evade detection once an auditing mechanism becomes known. Consequently, future research must design longitudinal studies that track both human and algorithmic performance over extended periods (Xu et al., 2025).

These longitudinal evaluations should measure out-of-sample predictive validity. Researchers need to determine whether an algorithmic greenwashing risk score assigned in one fiscal year accurately forecasts negative environmental events, regulatory fines, or ESG rating downgrades in subsequent years (Mei et al., 2025). Additionally, as climate reporting becomes more complex, models must evolve beyond pure text analysis. Ren (2025) identifies the integration of LLMs with spatial and quantitative data streams as a critical future vector. Future architectures must seamlessly ingest continuous Internet of Things (IoT) supply chain data and spatial mapping, alongside textual disclosures, to physically verify corporate claims, moving the field from narrative analysis to empirical verification.

Cross-Jurisdictional Regulatory Experiments

As detection algorithms mature, their integration into formal regulatory supervision requires extensive testing. Different global jurisdictions enforce vastly different standards for climate disclosures. For example, the European Union's Corporate Sustainability Reporting Directive (CSRD) mandates highly specific, double-materiality assessments, whereas other international markets operate on voluntary, principles-based reporting frameworks (Larosa et al., 2025; Huang et al., 2024).

Future research must conduct cross-jurisdictional regulatory experiments to evaluate how LLMs perform across these varied legal environments. Scholars should test whether an LLM fine-tuned on stringent European regulatory texts degrades performance when analyzing the voluntary disclosures of North American or Asian corporations. Furthermore, policymakers and researchers must collaborate to develop secure sandbox environments. In these controlled settings, regulatory bodies can test AI-powered auditing tools against historical market data without risking the misallocation of active capital. These experiments will help establish sector-specific guidance to certify LLMs as compliant with emerging digital and environmental laws, such as the EU AI Act and the United States Securities and Exchange Commission's proposed climate disclosure rules (Ren, 2025).

CONCLUSION

The integration of AI into sustainable finance represents a profound shift in how global markets corroborate corporate environmental accountability. As this chapter has demonstrated, the exponential growth of strategic greenwashing has fundamentally overwhelmed traditional, manual auditing frameworks, necessitating a transition toward computational text analysis. Large Language Models offer unparalleled scalability, longitudinal consistency, and the semantic sophistication required to detect calculated linguistic deflection across massive corporate corpora. However, empirical comparison between human analysts and algorithmic detectors reveals that AI is not a panacea. The persistent vulnerability of LLMs to probabilistic hallucinations and their inability to evaluate complex, sector-specific materiality confirm that these models currently lack the deterministic reliability required for standalone regulatory enforcement.

Consequently, resolving the crisis of corporate deception requires abandoning the binary choice between human exhaustion and algorithmic opacity. The future of market integrity relies heavily on algorithmic accountability, operationalized through a rigorous Human-in-the-Loop governance framework. By deploying domain-specific, retrieval-augmented models as high-volume surveillance systems and retaining human experts as the ultimate ethical and contextual adjudicators, the financial sector can successfully bridge the gap between corporate narratives and the physical environment. Ultimately, LLMs serve as powerful force multipliers in the pursuit of greenwashing detection, but true sustainable finance will always require the verifiable judgment of human oversight to ensure that environmental capital achieves its intended ecological impact (Goodman & Tréhu, 2022; Moodaley & Telukdarie, 2023).

REFERENCES

Adelakun, B. O., Antwi, B. O., Ntiakoh, A., & Eziefule, A. O. (2024). Leveraging AI for sustainable accounting: Developing models for environmental impact assessment and reporting. *Finance &amp. Accounting Research Journal, 6*(6), 1017–1048. DOI: 10.51594/farj.v6i6.1234

Brown, S., Davidovic, J., & Hasan, A. (2021). The algorithm audit: Scoring the algorithms that score us. *Big Data &amp. Big Data & Society, 8*(1), 2053951720983865. Advance online publication. DOI: 10.1177/2053951720983865

Chuang, M., Chuang, G., Chuang, C., & Chuang, J. (2025, February 20). *Judging It, Washing It: Scoring and Greenwashing Corporate Climate Disclosures using Large Language Models*. arXiv.Org. https://arxiv.org/abs/2502.15094 DOI: 10.18653/v1/2025.climatenlp-1.2

Funda, V. (2025). A systematic review of algorithm auditing processes to assess bias and risks in AI systems. *Journal of Infrastructure Policy and Development, 9*(2), 11489. DOI: 10.24294/jipd11489

Goodman, E. P., & Trehu, J. (2022). AI audit washing and accountability. SSRN *Electronic Journal*. DOI: 10.2139/ssrn.4227350

Gorovaia, N., & Makrominas, M. (2024). Identifying greenwashing in corporate-social responsibility reports using natural-language processing. *European Financial Management, 31*(1), 427–462. DOI: 10.1111/eufm.12509

Hajikhani, A., & Cole, C. (2024). A critical review of large language models: Sensitivity, bias, and the path toward specialized AI. *Quantitative Science Studies, 5*(3), 736–756. DOI: 10.1162/qss_a_00310

Huang, J., Wang, D. D., & Wang, Y. (2024). Textual attributes of corporate sustainability reports and ESG ratings. *Sustainability (Basel), 16*(21), 9270. DOI: 10.3390/su16219270

Koshiyama, A., Kazim, E., Treleaven, P., Rai, P., Szpruch, L., Pavey, G., Ahamat, G., Leutner, F., Goebel, R., Knight, A., Adams, J., Hitrova, C., Barnett, J., Nachev, P., Barber, D., Chamorro-Premuzic, T., Klemmer, K., Gregorovic, M., Khan, S., & Chatterjee, S. (2024). Towards algorithm auditing: Managing legal, ethical and technological risks of AI, ML and associated algorithms. *Royal Society Open Science, 11*(5), 230859. Advance online publication. DOI: 10.1098/rsos.230859 PMID: 39076787

Landers, R. N., & Behrend, T. S. (2022). Auditing the AI auditors: A framework for evaluating fairness and bias in high stakes AI predictive models. *The American Psychologist*, *78*(1), 36–49. DOI: 10.1037/amp0000972 PMID: 35157476

Larosa, F., Hoyas, S., Conejero, J. A., Garcia-Martinez, J., Fuso-Nerini, F., & Vinuesa, R. (2025). Large language models in climate and sustainability policy: Limits and opportunities. *Environmental Research Letters*, *20*(7), 074032. DOI: 10.1088/1748-9326/addd36

Mei, X., Wen, Z., Cai, Y., Li, Y., & Jiang, Y. (2025). Research on the assessment of greenwashing in corporate environmental information disclosure based on large language models and the dynamic mechanism of green financing. *Journal of Innovation and Development*, *11*(3), 32–39. DOI: 10.54097/be76ya94

Moodaley, W., & Telukdarie, A. (2023). Greenwashing, sustainability reporting, and artificial intelligence: A systematic literature review. *Sustainability (Basel)*, *15*(2), 1481. DOI: 10.3390/su15021481

Murikah, W., Nthenge, J. K., & Musyoka, F. M. (2024). Bias and ethics of AI systems applied in auditing - A systematic review. *Scientific African*, *25*, e02281. DOI: 10.1016/j.sciaf.2024.e02281

Niculescu, M., & Burlaud, A. (2025). Auditors' professional judgment on sustainability in the age of AI: From regulatory and technical challenges to algorithmic bias. *Audit Financiar*, *23*(180), 760–777. DOI: 10.20869/AUDITF/2025/180/022

Raji, I. D., Smart, A., White, R. N., Mitchell, M., Gebru, T., Hutchinson, B., Smith-Loud, J., Theron, D., & Barnes, P. (2020). Closing the AI accountability gap. *Proceedings of the 2020 Conference on Fairness, Accountability, and Transparency*, 33–44. DOI: 10.1145/3351095.3372873

Ren, T. (2025). AI-powered carbon footprint tracking is redefining green investment decision-making. *Advances in Economics. Management and Political Sciences*, *216*(1), 204–212. DOI: 10.54254/2754-1169/2025.GL27239

Vinella, A., Capetz, M., Pattichis, R., Chance, C., Ghosh, R., & Chang, K.-W. (2023, October 30). *Leveraging language models to detect greenwashing*. arXiv. Org. https://arxiv.org/abs/2311.01469

Wu, Y., Hu, P., & Wang, D. D. (2025). The AI annotator: Large language models' potential in scoring sustainability reports. *Systems*, *13*(10), 899. DOI: 10.3390/systems13100899

Xu, C., Liu, J., Li, Z., & Lin, C. (2025, April 10). *DeepGreen: Effective llm-driven greenwashing monitoring system designed for empirical testing — evidence from china*. arXiv.Org. https://arxiv.org/abs/2504.07733

KEY TERMS AND DEFINITIONS

AI Audit Washing: This phenomenon occurs when financial institutions or regulatory bodies use opaque algorithmic systems to give a misleading impression of mathematical certainty. This approach conceals flawed or unverified environmental data by hiding it behind complex, proprietary technology, preventing thorough examination.

Greenwashing: The deceptive corporate communication strategy of exaggerating environmental initiatives to secure a favorable public perception and access to premium green financing. This practice frequently involves selective disclosure, in which a firm magnifies minor environmental programs while actively obscuring its primary carbon-intensive operations.

Human-in-the-Loop (HITL) Governance: An algorithmic oversight mechanism that delegates high-volume data processing and anomaly detection to artificial intelligence, but requires human experts to adjudicate ambiguous cases. This framework ensures that final regulatory or financial decisions rely on human contextual reasoning rather than pure mathematical probability (Murikah et al., 2024).

LLM-as-a-Judge (LLMJ): A computational evaluation framework that configures Large Language Models to systematically score, rank, or classify texts. In greenwashing detection, researchers frequently use the LLMJ framework to perform pairwise comparisons, forcing the algorithm to evaluate two corporate disclosures side-by-side to improve robustness to adversarially polished reporting (Chuang et al., 2025).

Retrieval-Augmented Generation (RAG): An advanced model architecture that dynamically grounds the outputs of a Large Language Model in verified, external datasets. By forcing the algorithm to cross-reference narrative claims with objective physical data (e.g., emissions databases or satellite imagery), RAG significantly reduces the risk of statistical hallucination (Xu et al., 2025).

Chapter 9
Analyzing ESG Disclosure Patterns in Vietnamese Commercial Banks: A Phobert-Based Text Mining Study

Minh Phuoc Bui
Mahidol University, Thailand

Mien Thi Ngoc Nguyen
http://orcid.org/0000-0002-0792-1836
University of Economics Ho Chi Minh City, Vietnam

ABSTRACT

This chapter analyzes ESG disclosure in sustainability reports of Vietnamese commercial banks using PhoBERT-based text mining. The dataset includes 25 reports from 13 banks listed on the Ho Chi Minh City Stock Exchange. After text preprocessing and Vietnamese word segmentation, PhoBERT embeddings were used to compare report paragraphs with MSCI-based ESG theme representations. The findings show that ESG disclosure is mainly concentrated in the governance pillar, especially corporate governance, reflecting the banking sector's focus on transparency, internal control, compliance, and risk management. The social pillar follows, with human capital as the most visible theme. The study contributes to ESG disclosure research by providing empirical evidence on the thematic structure of ESG reporting in Vietnamese banking and by demonstrating the usefulness of Vietnamese-language NLP for sustainability disclosure analysis.

DOI: 10.4018/979-8-3373-8392-7.ch009

1. INTRODUCTION

Environmental issues impose heavy burdens on many industrial sectors due to rising energy costs, resource depletion, and natural disasters, forcing firms to shift towards sustainable production. In 2006, the United Nations Principles for Responsible Investment (PRI) were the first to formalize the concept of Environmental, Social, and Governance (ESG) criteria for institutional investors, assessing a company's non-financial performance across environmental impact, social relations, and corporate governance. In recent years, ESG has become a central framework for companies, investors, regulators, and other stakeholders to assess and measure a business's sustainability, including in development and social responsibility to its surrounding community. Although financial reports provide an overview of a company's past economic success, they often fail to capture potential risks or future opportunities. Integrating ESG enriches investment analysis by revealing environmental, social, and governance risks that traditional financial metrics miss, providing earlier signals about future cash flows and operational vulnerabilities. Thus, investors achieve a deep understanding of operating environments, which leads to better asset selection, more resilient portfolio construction, and stronger stewardship (Bassen & Kovacs, 2008). Thus, ESG has a significant impact on an organization's long-term performance, helping stakeholders gain insights into factors that directly influence an organization's viability over time (Gupta et al., 2021).

In the era of global financial restructuring, ESG has evolved from a voluntary trend into a new market standard and the dominant financial language, helping standardize non-financial information. The linkage between ESG and capital access has become particularly pronounced. Large-scale international capital flows are increasingly stringent in terms of sustainable development standards. The lack of credible ESG principles in businesses may lead to challenges such as high capital costs, restricted financial opportunities, and reputational damage, thereby weakening stakeholder trust and harming long-term value (Atarwaman et al., 2026). Therefore, ESG plays a crucial role in corporate governance by helping identify and manage non-financial risks that can significantly impact firm value. When embedded in core operations, ESG can enhance long-term value creation and achieve more stable earnings than those companies without an ESG rating (Marfu et al., 2025). Market infrastructure has responded to demand for standardized ESG signals. Some organizations, such as Bloomberg, Refinitiv, and MSCI, regularly score ESG based on key performance indicators reported by companies or through surveys. Although these ratings are imperfect, they are still used as key tools for translating non-financial disclosures into investment-relevant insights.

Vietnam has continued to assert its position as a prominent emerging economy in Southeast Asia. Economically, Vietnamese GDP growth in 2025 is 8.02%, mainly driven by the services and industrial sectors. Socially, Vietnam has made significant progress in human development, with an HDI of 0.766 in 2023, placing it in the high human development group (General Statistics Office of Vietnam, 2025). Nevertheless, rapid growth has been accompanied by environmental stress, excessive resource exploitation, greenhouse gas emissions, and a decline in quality of life. According to recent international assessments, Vietnam's total emissions of greenhouse gases in 2022 and 2023 were about 344 million tons and 543 million tons of CO_2-eq, respectively, positioning Vietnam among the largest emitters of these gases. Regarding air pollution, according to an IQAir report released in 2025, Vietnam had the 23rd-worst air quality in the world in 2024, based on average PM2.5 concentrations, as emissions from coal and fuel combustion have continued to be major contributors to both GHG and air pollution. The inequality-adjusted HDI equals 0.641, indicating that health, education, and income inequalities are present (Conceição, 2025). Also, Vietnam is witnessing population aging. The proportion of individuals aged 60 or above is projected to rise from 11.9 percent in 2019 to 25 percent by 2050, adding more strain to the workforce, social security, and long-term productivity. These problems create significant policy pressure for businesses to meet emission-reduction commitments and achieve the goal of net-zero emissions by 2050. Thus, establishing and researching ESG metrics for Vietnam is necessary.

The development of ESG in Vietnam has also been supported by a growing regulatory and policy framework. Decree No. 06/2022/ND-CP (Government of Vietnam, 2022) lays down guidelines for reducing greenhouse gas emissions and protecting the ozone layer. Decision No. 1658/QD-TTg (Government of Vietnam, 2021) approving the National Green Growth Strategy for 2021–2030, with a vision toward 2050, reflects the government's long-term commitment to green growth and more efficient resource use. At the corporate level, Circular 96/2020/TT-BTC requires listed companies to disclose information related to sustainable development in their annual reports, marking an important step toward ESG disclosure in Vietnam (Ministry of Finance, 2020). In addition, the Ho Chi Minh Stock Exchange introduced the Vietnam Sustainability Index (VNSI) in 2017 to encourage listed firms to pay greater attention to sustainability performance and disclosure. According to the 2025 ESG Progress Tracker Survey, 89% of businesses in Vietnam have either made ESG commitments or intend to do so within the next two to four years (PwC Vietnam, 2025). These developments suggest that ESG is no longer merely an image-building activity among Vietnamese firms. Instead, it is becoming increasingly connected with competitiveness, transparency, access to capital, and long-term resilience. However, ESG implementation and disclosure remain uneven, as many firms still lack the data systems, reporting capacity, and analytical tools needed to translate broad sustainability commitments into transparent and comparable results.

The banking sector plays a particularly important role in this ESG transition. Unlike industrial firms, banks may have relatively limited direct environmental impacts from their own operations, but their indirect impact is systemic because they influence the allocation of capital across the economy. Through lending, investment, and risk management decisions, banks can support environmentally responsible projects, promote green finance, encourage responsible business behavior among borrowers, and contribute to the broader transition toward sustainable development. The State Bank of Vietnam has issued Circular No. 17/2022/TT-NHNN to provide a framework for commercial banks to manage environmental risks within their credit operations (The State Bank of Vietnam, 2022). Due to regulatory requirements and changing market demands, banks are moving towards transparency in sustainability reporting. Banking sustainability reporting has a dual purpose. First, they signal a bank's effort to minimize risk exposure from impactful investments. Second, sustainability reporting also serves as an instrument to appeal to socially responsible investors and corporate clients.

Although ESG disclosure has improved, the level of disclosure remains inconsistent across banks, and many reports have not yet clearly linked ESG information with risk management frameworks or business strategies (Ha & Huy, 2025). This creates an important research gap. Existing ESG studies often rely on manual content analysis, descriptive comparison, or externally constructed ESG scores. While these approaches are useful, they may be time-consuming, difficult to scale, and limited in their ability to capture the thematic structure of large volumes of sustainability-related text. Therefore, a text-mining approach can provide a more systematic and replicable method for examining how Vietnamese banks communicate their ESG priorities in their sustainability reports.

This study addresses that gap by applying PhoBERT, a pre-trained language model specifically developed for Vietnamese natural language processing, to analyze sustainability reports of HOSE-listed Vietnamese commercial banks. PhoBERT is particularly suitable for this context because it was introduced as the first publicly available large-scale monolingual Vietnamese language model and has shown strong performance across Vietnamese NLP tasks. Instead of only identifying whether specific ESG terms appear in a report, the PhoBERT-based approach compares the semantic similarity between report paragraphs and predefined ESG theme representations based on the MSCI ESG framework. This makes it possible to identify which ESG themes are most strongly emphasized in the reports, even when banks use different wording to describe similar issues. Importantly, this study does not aim to evaluate the actual ESG performance of banks. Rather, it focuses on ESG disclosure intensity and thematic emphasis, that is, how banks communicate ESG issues and which themes receive the greatest attention in their sustainability narratives.

Accordingly, this study seeks to answer three research questions. First, how are ESG disclosures distributed across the environmental, social, and governance pillars in the sustainability reports of HOSE-listed Vietnamese commercial banks? Second, which MSCI ESG themes are most strongly emphasized in these reports? Third, how can a PhoBERT-based semantic similarity approach help capture ESG thematic disclosure beyond simple keyword-based classification? By answering these questions, the study contributes to ESG disclosure research in emerging-market banking contexts. It also demonstrates the usefulness of Vietnamese-language NLP for measuring thematic ESG disclosure in sustainability reports and provides practical insights for regulators, investors, and banks seeking to improve the transparency, comparability, and materiality of ESG reporting in Vietnam's banking sector. By identifying dominant and underrepresented ESG themes, this research can provide useful insights for academics, regulators, investors, and banking practitioners. It helps reveal the gap between ESG reporting as a communication practice and ESG reporting as a tool for accountability, risk management, and sustainable finance.

2. LITERATURE REVIEW

2.1. ESG disclosure and sustainability reporting

Environmental, social, and governance disclosure has become an increasingly important component of corporate sustainability communication. It captures the facilities, employees, social relations, governance practices, and commitment to the environment. Unlike financial reports, which tend to be backward-looking and balance a company's income streams, ESG disclosures highlight non-financial risks and an organization's potential for innovation (Eccles & Serafeim, 2013). ESG disclosures usually have three components. For the E in ESG, environmental disclosures include information on climate change, energy use, greenhouse gas emissions, efficient resource use, waste, and environmental risks and management. For the S in ESG, social disclosure includes information on employee welfare, human rights, customer protection, community relations, diversity, and inclusion. For the G in ESG, governance disclosures also include information on the structure of the governing board, transparency, risk management, compliance, business ethics, anti-corruption, and internal controls.

Sustainability reporting is a common way for firms to disclose ESG-related information. Through sustainability reports, organizations provide details on their sustainability strategies, programs, commitments, and performance in achieving these goals. This increases transparency and accountability to stakeholders, including investors, customers, local communities, and government agencies. The Global

Reporting Initiative (GRI) emphasizes that sustainability reporting standards help organizations measure and communicate economic, environmental, and social impacts in a systematic, reliable, and comparable manner over time and across industries (Global Reporting Initiative, 2013). As a result, stakeholders can more objectively assess the effectiveness of a company's ESG practices, thereby making appropriate investment, business, or policy decisions. As regulations and expectations regarding corporate social responsibility and sustainability reporting standards continue to evolve, sustainability reporting standards are increasingly becoming an essential tool for public accountability, strategic direction, risk management, and long-term market competitiveness (European Commission, 2025).

However, the presence of sustainability does not necessarily mean that a firm performs well on ESG issues. A key distinction in ESG research is therefore between disclosure and performance. ESG disclosure refers to the information that a company chooses to share with the public, whereas ESG performance reflects the actual and measurable outcomes of its ESG-related activities (Lopez-de-Silanes et al., 2020). A firm may disclose extensively ESG issues without making substantial changes to its practices. This is often described as symbolic disclosure, where reporting is used to manage impressions rather than reflect actual performance (Cho & Patten, 2007). Conversely, some firms may perform well on sustainability but disclose little information about their activities, a situation often described as silent performance (Guenther & Hoppe, 2014). Therefore, sustainability reports should be interpreted as textual evidence of corporate communication and thematic emphasis rather than direct evidence of actual ESG performance. This distinction is important for the present study because the objective is not to evaluate the real ESG performance of banks, but to examine how ESG themes are communicated and emphasized in their sustainability reports.

2.2. ESG disclosure in the banking sector

Compared with manufacturing and mining industries, banks usually generate fewer direct environmental impacts from their own operations. While their physical footprint - such as office buildings, transportation, and energy use - is relatively modest, the indirect environmental and social consequences of their activities are substantial because they control the flow of capital to firms, sectors, and projects across the economy. As net-zero commitments and ESG requirements become more important, banks are under increasing pressure to review their loan portfolios, especially their exposure to carbon-intensive industries. They are also expected to incorporate environmental and social risks more clearly into credit appraisal and risk management practices (Mahadevan et al., 2026). Banks may slow the transition to a low-carbon economy if they continue to finance high-emission activities. According to

(Haas & Popov, 2023), banks will find it difficult to provide loans for clean energy technology, as this may reduce the value of their existing collateral under current loan practices. As a result, banks may have incentives to continue supporting less carbon-efficient industries, even when more sustainable alternatives are available.

This distinctive role explains why ESG disclosure in the banking sector should be understood differently from ESG disclosure in non-financial firms. For banks, environmental disclosure should go beyond internal resource use, such as energy consumption and paper conservation, to capture the environmental consequences of core lending and investment activities. This includes green lending, sustainable financing, climate-related financial risks, environmental risk management in credit allocation, and exposure to carbon-intensive industries. Similarly, social disclosure should likewise extend beyond employee and community issues to include customer protection, privacy, financial inclusion, responsible lending, and support for small and medium-sized enterprises. Finally, strong governance disclosure in the banking sector enhances transparency, reduces information asymmetry, and signals effective governance and risk management, which is crucial for maintaining stakeholder confidence and systemic integrity in tightly regulated environments (Jizani et al., 2025).

International banking frameworks also show that ESG issues are increasingly connected to banks' core activities. The United Nations Environment Programme (UNEP) Finance Initiative's Principles for Responsible Banking encourages banks to align their strategies with broader sustainability goals, including climate action, human rights, and inclusive economic development (United Nations Environment Programme Finance Initiative, n.d.). The Task Force on Climate-related Financial Disclosures (TCFD) was established in 2015 by the Financial Stability Board at the request of the G20 to help businesses transparently disclose their financial risk related to climate change. The TCFD framework organizes climate-related disclosure around governance, strategy, risk management, and metrics and targets. These frameworks suggest that sustainability reporting in banking should not only describe general commitments but should also explain how ESG issues are considered in lending, investment, governance, and risk management.

In Vietnam, the ESG agenda in banking has become increasingly important due to the country's green growth strategy, climate commitments, and the growing role of banks in financing sustainable development. The State Bank of Vietnam issued Directive 03/CT-NHNN in 2015 to promote green credit growth and environmental and social risk management in credit extension (The State Bank of Vietnam, 2012). The directive encouraged credit institutions to channel lending toward environmentally friendly projects and to develop systems to manage environmental and social risks in their credit activities. Circular No. 17/2022/TT-NHNN (The State Bank of Vietnam, 2022) has recently issued guidelines regarding environmental risk management in lending activities by credit institutions and branches of foreign banks, which means that environmental risk is increasingly becoming an important part of the banking sector.

Green credit growth increases the relevance of ESG reporting for Vietnamese banks. According to the State Bank of Vietnam, green credit amounted to VND 704 trillion, equivalent to 4.3% of the total outstanding credit of the economy in early 2025 (Ky Phong, 2025). This credit was mainly allocated to renewable energy, sustainable agriculture, and water management. The figures show that green finance has begun to appear in banks' lending portfolios. However, its share remains small compared with total credit, indicating that although sustainability is receiving greater attention in banking strategies and lending priorities, green financing in Vietnam is still at an early stage of development.

Recent studies indicate that ESG reporting among Vietnamese banks has improved but remains uneven. One study on ESG reporting practices in the Vietnamese banking system found that ESG reporting has developed. Still, disclosure remains inconsistent, and many banks have not clearly linked ESG information to risk management or business strategy. This finding supports the need for more systematic analysis of what banks emphasize in their sustainability reports. Rather than simply asking whether banks disclose ESG information, it is necessary to examine which ESG themes dominate their reporting and which themes remain less visible.

2.3. Text mining and NLP in sustainability reporting research

Sustainability reports can serve as a valuable textual resource in researching ESG issues because they describe how firms present their policies, risks, targets, stakeholder activities, and future commitments (Kang & Kim, 2022). However, manual reading and filtering become difficult when the dataset includes many reports from different banks and several reporting years. ESG factors are rarely disclosed in one specific part of the report; moreover, they are sometimes formulated differently in various reports. In order to address these challenges, text mining becomes especially effective because it enables researchers to find ESG-related information consistently and classify it properly (Yoon et al., 2023).

Text mining is the process of discovering patterns within textual data. In sustainability reporting research, it can be used to analyze ESG-related keywords, topics, sentiment, semantic similarity, disclosure intensity. Traditional text-mining methods are generally based on word counts, keyword matching, or dictionary-based approaches. In these methods, researchers first create a list of predefined keywords or terms associated with a specific ESG theme and then measure how often those terms appear in the text. However, traditional methods may fail to capture synonyms, paraphrases, or expressions with similar meanings but different wording. For example, a keyword dictionary may detect "carbon emission" as an environmental term, but it may be unable to recognize phrases like "climate-related exposure" or "green lending" even though these phrases are related to the same theme.

More advanced NLP techniques focus on capturing the semantics of words, phrases, and documents. Techniques such as topic modeling, word embeddings, transformers, and semantic similarity can enable the detection of themes beyond mere keyword presence. This is especially important when considering research into ESG topics, since ESG themes can be described in multiple ways. Different sectors, reporting levels, regulatory frameworks, and communication styles may lead to distinct language use within companies.

Recent studies have increasingly applied text mining to sustainability and ESG reports. For example, research on ESG management reports in South Korea used text mining to analyze corporate sustainability reports and examine their alignment with the sustainable development goals (Yoon et al., 2023). Another study analyzed climate-related disclosures of Spanish financial institutions using text-mining techniques and linked disclosure content to the TCFD framework (Moreno & Caminero, 2022). More recent research on corporate ESG reporting has also employed advanced topic-modeling techniques, such as BERTopic and sentLDA models, to examine how ESG topics evolve over time in annual reports (Ferjančič et al., 2024; Thewissen et al., 2026). A systematic review of text-mining applications in sustainability reporting highlights that automated text analysis not only helps manage large volumes of report data but also reveals patterns in reporting quality, thematic concentration, and strategic framing (Mohammadrezaei et al., 2024). These studies show that text mining can reveal not only the quantity of ESG disclosure but also the structure and prominence of different ESG themes.

For banking research, text mining is especially useful because bank reports often contain complex language related to risk management, compliance, finance, sustainability, and customer relationships. ESG themes in banking are not always presented under clear ESG headings (Alrtaimat, 2025). For example, climate-related risk may appear in the risk management section, green credit in business strategy, customer protection in digital banking or compliance, and governance in board reports or risk-control. A document-level or paragraph-level text-mining approach can therefore provide a more systematic way to detect ESG themes across different sections of a report.

2.4. BERT in text-mining

The emergence of Transformer-based architecture has marked a paradigm shift in Natural Language Processing (NLP) and text mining. Among these developments, Bidirectional Encoder Representations from Transformers (BERT), introduced by Devlin et al. (2019), is one of the most influential models due to its ability to generate highly context-aware representations of input tokens. BERT uses self-attention to consider all token interactions simultaneously, enabling true bidirectional contextualization during pre-training. As a result, BERT can encode semantic and syntactic dependencies in text, which has proven more effective than traditional unidirectional models such as LSTM or GRU (Kaliyar et al., 2020). From an empirical perspective, the bidirectional encoding technique of BERT, combined with massive masked-language model pre-training, has led to significant improvements across various downstream NLP applications, making BERT a fundamental element in current text mining (Gardazi et al., 2025).

The fundamental strength of BERT is in its capacity to be fine-tuned for a wide range of downstream tasks, which entails further training a pre-trained BERT model on a small dataset related to a particular application so that the model learns to tailor its internal representations to linguistic structures pertinent to that application. As shown by Rostam & Kertész (2025), fine-tuning strategies such as using specific layers and varying learning rates further improve accuracy in text classification tasks. Also, the transformer-based self-attention mechanism allows BERT to process all tokens in parallel, mitigating vanishing-gradient problems and enabling efficient training with large parameter counts (Devlin et al., 2019). Bianchi et al. (2021) state that BERT embeddings have replaced the bag-of-words method in topic modeling, leading to contextualized topic models (CTM) with improved coherence.

A major trend in literature is the adaptation of BERT to specific domains where its general pre-training becomes inadequate. Two of the most influential early efforts in this direction were BioBERT (Lee et al., 2020) and SciBERT (Beltagy et al., 2019). Specifically, BioBERT was additionally trained on large biomedical corpora comprising PubMed abstracts and PubMed Central texts and was able to identify subtle links between biological entities that standard BERT consistently failed to recognize. SciBERT used the same principle of additional training but aimed to develop a model applicable to multiple branches of science. Building on these foundations, more recent work from 2024 and 2025 has pushed this approach into even narrower and more applied domains. AgriBERT (Rezayi et al., 2022) is an example of a model built specifically to meet the unique needs of agricultural text mining, since such texts contain terminology specific to crops, soils, pests, and farming that is rare in other text corpora. Similarly, MedBERT (Rasmy et al., 2021) has been developed for clinical applications, particularly for extracting useful information from electronic health records, physician notes, and discharge summaries. Therefore, domain-specific pre-training becomes one of the key factors that ensures successful text mining outcomes (Zhyar & Kertész, 2025).

PhoBERT, introduced by D. Q. Nguyen & Nguyen (2020), is a large-scale Vietnamese language model developed based on the RoBERTa architecture. It was designed to address key characteristics of Vietnamese, such as word segmentation, tonal structure, and multi-syllable expressions, by relying on word-segmented pre-training data and a RoBERTa-style pre-training procedure. As one of the first major monolingual Vietnamese NLP models, PhoBERT has become an important tool for tasks that require contextual understanding of Vietnamese text. A significant body of literature has leveraged PhoBERT for sentiment analysis. According to Ngo et al. (2024), analyzing mobile phone reviews with fine-tuned PhoBERT achieved higher accuracy than conventional machine learning techniques. PhoBERT has also been used as a text classification model to help categorize patients based on the symptoms they describe during the initial stages of Vietnamese hospital admission (Nguyen et al., 2023). Hybrid models that combine PhoBERT, combined the local feature extraction capability of a Text-CNN, have been shown to improve classification performance compared with rule-based or feature-based approaches (Tran et al., 2022). More recently, Nguyen et al. (2025) proposed a method that utilizes the PhoBERT model for semantic feature extraction, followed by a CNN–LSTM architecture to capture sentiment in student feedback, and showed that this model achieves an accuracy of 93.24% and an F1-score of 92.92%, outperforming several other advanced approaches. These applications suggest that PhoBERT is effective for Vietnamese NLP tasks that require semantic and contextual interpretation. Although PhoBERT's performance on standard Vietnamese NLP benchmarks has been well documented, applied research using this model in domain-specific contexts remains relatively limited. Few studies have examined its use in more specialized areas such as finance, healthcare, legal text, or sustainability reporting.

Vietnamese is a syllable-based language with word segmentation challenges and many multi-syllable expressions. Also, banks may use different wording to describe similar ESG issues depending on their reporting style, terminology and disclosure structure. This is a disadvantage for dictionary-based classification, as it relies heavily on predefined keywords. A paragraph may discuss an ESG theme without containing the exact keyword included in the dictionary, while another paragraph may contain a keyword but use it in a different context. A PhoBERT-based semantic similarity approach is therefore more appropriate because it compares the meaning of each report paragraph with predefined ESG theme representations rather than relying only on exact keyword occurrence. It also supports paragraph-level classification, which is useful because ESG content in bank reports is often dispersed across different sections rather than organized under a single ESG heading. Accordingly, this study positions PhoBERT-based semantic similarity as a context-sensitive and scalable approach for measuring thematic ESG disclosure in Vietnamese bank sustainability reports.

2.5. Research gap and positioning of the study

Although ESG disclosure has received growing attention in Vietnam, several research gaps remain. First, existing studies have mainly focused on whether ESG disclosure is associated with firm performance, financial performance, or market outcomes. These studies are valuable, but they often treat ESG disclosure as an aggregate score. As a result, they may overlook the internal thematic structure of ESG reporting. For banks, this is an important limitation because ESG disclosure may be concentrated in some areas while remaining weak in others. For example, a bank may report extensively on community engagement and employee welfare but provide limited information on climate risk, green credit, environmental and social risk assessment, or data governance.

Second, many ESG disclosure studies in Vietnam still rely on manual content analysis or checklist-based scoring. Although these methods provide useful evidence, they might fail to capture all semantic variations in ESG reports, as Vietnamese banks use different language when referring to specific ESG aspects. This necessitates the application of more adaptive methods that will allow analyzing ESG disclosures by paragraphs or themes.

Third, despite the growing use of NLP in international sustainability reporting research, Vietnamese-language NLP applications in ESG disclosure studies remain relatively limited. This is a significant gap because Vietnamese sustainability reports are increasingly available, but their analysis requires language-specific tools. PhoBERT offers an opportunity to develop a more context-sensitive approach to Vietnamese ESG text analysis.

Fourth, there is limited evidence on which ESG themes are most emphasized in Vietnamese banks' sustainability reports. The dominant themes in ESG reporting can reveal how banks understand sustainability, how they respond to regulatory and stakeholder pressures, and whether their reporting is aligned with the sector's most material ESG issues. In banking, material ESG themes should include not only philanthropy or internal operations but also sustainable finance, environmental and social risk management, customer protection, digital security, responsible lending, compliance, and governance.

The present study addresses these gaps by applying PhoBERT-based text mining to sustainability reports of Vietnamese banks. Instead of relying solely on manual coding or keyword counts, it uses semantic similarity to examine how different ESG themes are emphasized across report paragraphs. This study offers a Vietnamese NLP-based approach to measuring ESG disclosure and provides a clearer view of which themes are more visible or less visible in bank reporting. These insights may support more comparable and meaningful ESG disclosure in Vietnam's banking sector.

3. METHODOLOGY AND DATA

3.1. Data

Data for the research will be obtained from the sustainability reports of commercial banks listed on the Ho Chi Minh City Stock Exchange (HOSE). We focus on these banks because they are required to follow stricter disclosure regulations compared to non-listed banks. In total, 25 reports were collected from the Vietnamese banks' official websites for analysis.

Table 1. Sample description of sustainability reports by HOSE-listed Vietnamese banks

No.	Bank name	Abbre-viation	No. of reports	Available years
1	Asia Commercial Joint Stock Bank	ACB	3	2023, 2024, 2025
2	Joint Stock Commercial Bank for Investment and Development	BID	3	2023, 2024, 2025
3	Ho Chi Minh City Development Joint Stock Commercial Bank	HDB	1	2024
4	Military Commercial Joint Stock Bank	MB	1	2024
5	Vietnam Maritime Commercial Joint Stock Bank	MSB	2	2023, 2024
6	Nam A Commercial Joint Stock Bank	NAB	1	2024
7	Orient Commercial Joint Stock Bank	OCB	2	2023, 2024
8	Southeast Asia Commercial Joint Stock Bank	SEA	1	2024
9	Saigon - Hanoi Commercial Joint Stock Bank	SHB	3	2022, 2023, 2024
10	Vietnam Technological and Commercial Joint Stock Bank	TCB	2	2024, 2025
11	Tien Phong Commercial Joint Stock Bank	TPB	2	2023, 2024
12	oint Stock Commercial Bank for Foreign Trade of Vietnam	VCB	3	2023, 2024, 2025
13	Vietnam Prosperity Joint Stock Commercial Bank	VPB	1	2024

Since standalone sustainability reporting and ESG-oriented disclosure have only been adopted more recently by many Vietnamese banks, the number of available reports remains limited. Some banks have available reports covering up to three recent years, whereas others only provide ESG-related information for one or two years or integrate such information into annual reports. Due to data imbalance across banks and years, the study distinguishes between corpus-level and bank-level results. While corpus-level patterns reflect the overall ESG distribution, they can skew toward banks with longer or more frequent reports. To ensure fair comparison, bank-level analysis focuses on relative theme salience which measures the percentage share of ESG themes within each bank rather than absolute paragraph counts.

3.2. Methodology

This study applies a PhoBERT-based text-mining approach to analyze ESG disclosures in the sustainability reports of Vietnamese commercial banks. The analysis process is structured according to sequential logic, inheriting from previous text mining studies on sustainability reports. Specifically, the study goes through five main stages: data preprocessing, text segmentation, feature representation, semantic classification, and aggregation of results.

3.2.1. Data preprocessing

Each report was converted from PDF into machine-readable text using PyMuPDF, a Python library for parsing and extracting content from PDF documents. Because sustainability reports are often designed with multiple columns, tables, infographics, headers, footers, and repeated assurance statements, the analysis did not treat the entire report as a single document. Instead, paragraph-level text units were extracted using the layout-based text block extraction function in PyMuPDF. Each block represents a spatially coherent text region on a PDF page, identified based on its bounding box coordinates and text layout. This paragraph-level approach is appropriate because ESG topics are usually discussed in short sections or reporting blocks, rather than only at the full-report level. It also reduces the risk that long reports dominate the analysis merely because of their length.

Several preprocessing procedures were applied to improve data quality and reduce noise. The aim of preprocessing was not to alter the substantive ESG meaning of the reports, but to ensure that the input text used for classification reflected meaningful disclosure content. First, abnormal characters generated during PDF extraction were removed. These included encoding errors, control characters, and broken OCR strings. Extra spaces and line breaks were standardized. Repeated boilerplate expressions, including report titles, assurance report headings, copyright statements, auditor names, bank names, and bank tickers, were also excluded because these terms appear frequently but do not represent substantive ESG content. Next, short or noisy paragraphs were excluded. Specifically, paragraphs with fewer than 30 characters were excluded. Paragraphs with a low proportion of Vietnamese alphabetic characters were also treated as noisy text and removed. In addition, paragraphs expressing gratitude or goodwill, such as statements equivalent to "We would like to express our sincere gratitude," were removed from the analytical corpus. After removing noisy, duplicated, and non-substantive text blocks, 27450 paragraphs were retained as the final analytical corpus for ESG theme classification.

3.2.2. ESG theme representation based on MSCI

The ESG classification scheme used in this study was developed deductively from the MSCI ESG Key Issue framework, which serves as the reference framework because it provides a broad, structured taxonomy of issues across environmental, social, and governance pillars. As shown in Tables 1, 2, and 3, the original MSCI structure was first organized into three pillars, namely Environment, Social, and Governance. Within these pillars, ten MSCI themes were used as the basis for classification. The environmental pillar includes climate change, natural capital, pollution and waste, and environmental opportunities. The social pillar includes human capital, product liability, stakeholder opposition, and social opportunities. The governance pillar includes corporate governance and corporate behavior.

Table 2. MSCI Environmental themes and Vietnamese semantic expressions

MSCI theme	MSCI key issues	Vietnamese key issues
Climate Change	Carbon Emissions Climate Change Vulnerability Financing Environmental Impact Product Carbon Footprint	bi n đ i khí h u, phát th i, phát th i khí nhà kính, tín ch carbon, d u chân carbon, r i ro khi h u, tác đ ng môi trư ng
Natural Capital	Biodiversity & Land Use Raw Material Sourcing Water Stress	tài nguyên thiên nhiên, đa d ng sinh h c, h sinh thái, s d ng tài nguyên, ngu n nguyên li u, tiêu th nư c, nư c th i
Pollution & Waste	Electronic Waste Packaging Material & Waste Toxic Emissions & Waste	ô nhi m, ch t th i, rác th i, ch t th i nguy h i, gi y tiêu th , tiêu th đi n, rác th i bao bì, tái ch , rác th i đi n t , ti t ki m gi y
Environmental Opportunities	Opportunities in Clean Tech Opportunities in Green Building Opportunities in Renewable Energy	công ngh s ch, ngân hàng xanh, tín d ng xanh, công trình xanh, tài chính b n v ng, trái phi u xanh, kinh t tu n hoàn, năng lư ng tái t o

Source: MSCI ESG symbols and definitions (MSCI ESG Research LLC, 2024)

For each MSCI theme, the corresponding MSCI key issues were identified and translated into Vietnamese semantic expressions that are conceptually equivalent to the original MSCI keywords and suitable for the Vietnamese banking context. These expressions include synonyms, related terms, and context-specific phrases frequently found in Vietnamese sustainability reports. They were used to construct semantic queries for each MSCI theme, rather than as rigid keyword-matching rules. Thus, the classification was based on semantic proximity between report paragraphs and the Vietnamese representations of MSCI themes, not on exact keyword occurrence.

Table 3. MSCI Social themes and Vietnamese semantic expressions

MSCI theme	ESG key issues	Vietnamese key issues
Human Capital	Health & Safety Human Capital Development Labor Management Supply Chain Labor Standards	Nhân viên, ngư i lao đ ng, s c kh e ngh nghi p, ngu n nhân l c, qu n lý lao đ ng, tiêu chu n lao đ ng nhà cung c p, an toàn lao đ ng, công đoàn, đào t o, phúc l i
Product Liability	Chemical Safety Consumer Financial Protection Privacy & Data Security Product Safety & Quality Responsible Investment	ch t lư ng d ch v , b o v khác hàng, quy n riêng tư, b o m t d li u, an toàn thông tin, an ninh m ng, minh b ch, đ u tư có trách nhi m
Stakeholder Opposition	Community Relations Controversial Sourcing	ph n ánh, khi u n i khách hàng, tranh ch p, ph n đ i, c đông, xung đ t l i ích, đ o đ c kinh doanh
Social Opportunities	Access to Finance Access to Health Care Opportunities in Nutrition & Health	tài chính toàn di n, ti p c n v n vay, c ng đ ng, an sinh xã h i, thi n nguy n

Source: MSCI ESG symbols and definitions (MSCI ESG Research LLC, 2024)

This approach allows the study to retain the structure of the MSCI framework while making it more applicable to Vietnamese banking disclosures. Since banks may describe ESG issues using different wording across reports, the use of Vietnamese semantic expressions helps improve the contextual relevance of the classification process. It also reduces the risk of missing relevant ESG content that does not contain the exact original MSCI keywords.

Table 4. MSCI Governance themes and Vietnamese semantic expressions

MSCI theme	MSCI key issues	Vietnamese key issues
Corporate Governance	Board Pay Ownership Control Accounting	qu n tr công ty, h i đ ng qu n tr , ban đi u hành, ki m soát n i b , ki m toán, minh b ch, báo cáo tài chính, quy n s h u
Corporate Behavior	Business Ethics Tax Transparency	đ o đ c kinh doanh, tuân th , minh b ch, công b thông tin, qu n tr r i ro, ch ng tham nhũng, khai báo thu

Source: MSCI ESG symbols and definitions (MSCI ESG Research LLC, 2024)

3.2.3. Vietnamese word segmentation

Before being encoded by PhoBERT, both the extracted report paragraphs and the MSCI-based semantic queries were processed using Vietnamese word segmentation with the underthesea library. This step was necessary because Vietnamese is a syllable-based language, in which many domain-specific expressions consist of multiple syllables separated by spaces. Without segmentation, such expressions may be treated as separate syllables rather than meaningful semantic units. Word segmentation therefore helps represent multi-syllable ESG terms more consistently and improves the model's ability to capture the semantic meaning of sustainability-related disclosure.

Next, the same segmentation procedure was applied to two types of input: the paragraph-level text extracted from sustainability reports and the Vietnamese semantic queries constructed for each MSCI theme. After segmentation, both sets of text were converted into embedding vectors using PhoBERT. The classification was then conducted by comparing the semantic similarity between each paragraph embedding and each MSCI theme-query embedding. This procedure ensured that the paragraph texts and the theme representations were processed in a consistent linguistic format before semantic similarity calculation.

3.2.4 Embedding generation using PhoBERT

The preprocessed paragraph texts and the MSCI theme queries were converted into numerical representations using PhoBERT. Each paragraph extracted from the sustainability reports and each MSCI theme query were passed through PhoBERT to obtain contextualized token-level representations from the final hidden layer.

PhoBERT produces a vector for each token, an additional pooling step was required to obtain one single vector representation for the whole paragraph or theme query. This study applied mean pooling to aggregate token-level embeddings into a sentence-level or paragraph-level embedding. The attention mask was used during this process to ensure that padding tokens were excluded from the calculation. In other words, only meaningful tokens contributed to the final text representation. The embedding of paragraph i is calculated as

$$\boldsymbol{p}_i = \frac{\sum_{k=1}^{K} m_{ik} \boldsymbol{h}_{ik}}{\sum_{k=1}^{K} m_{ik}}$$

where $h_{ik} \in R^{768}$ is the hidden representation of token k in paragraph i, m_{ik} is the attention mask, and K is the maximum sequence length. The same procedure was applied to each MSCI theme query to obtain its theme embedding $\boldsymbol{t}_j$.

After mean pooling, all paragraph and theme embeddings were normalized using L2 normalization. The similarity score between each paragraph i and MSCI theme j is then calculated using cosine similarity:

$$s_{ij} = \frac{\boldsymbol{p}_i \bullet \boldsymbol{t}_j}{||\boldsymbol{p}_i|| \, ||\boldsymbol{t}_j||}$$

Each paragraph was assigned to the MSCI theme with the highest similarity score. This highest score was recorded as the *top1_score*. The second and third most similar themes were also retained to support validation.

To ensure reliability, a review flag was implemented as a quality-control mechanism. Paragraphs were flagged for manual review if they met either of the following conditions: their highest similarity score was below 0.55, or the difference between the highest and second-highest similarity scores was smaller than 0.03. Under this rule, the flagged paragraphs accounted for approximately 15% of the retained analytical corpus. These cases were considered uncertain classifications and were therefore marked for manual inspection. This procedure helped improve the reliability of the final classification results by identifying paragraphs that required additional human judgment.

3.2.5. Aggregation and measurement of ESG theme salience

After paragraph-level classification, the results were aggregated at the pillar, theme, bank, and year levels. The main measure derived from the classification is ESG theme salience, which captures the relative prominence of a given MSCI ESG theme in banks' sustainability disclosure. Theme salience is calculated as

$$\textit{Salience of theme } j = \frac{N_j}{N}$$

where N_j is the number of paragraphs assigned to theme j, and N is the total number of classified paragraphs.

4. RESULTS AND DISCUSSION

Based on the classification results from the PhoBERT model applied to the entire dataset of textual data from the sustainability reports of commercial banks listed on HOSE, the study noted a significant disparity in the intensity of information disclosure among the three pillars: Environment (E), Society (S), and Governance (G). Table 5 describes the distribution of ESG disclosure paragraphs by MSCI pillar and theme. Statistical results show that the Governance (G) pillar dominates with 15,569 text entries, equivalent to 56.72% of the total ESG content. This proportion reflects the core characteristics of the finance and banking industry, where corporate governance and regulatory compliance are not only part of sustainable development but also prerequisites for ensuring system safety. The strong focus on pillar G indicates that Vietnamese banks are prioritizing strengthening "legitimacy" through transparent disclosure of board structure, risk control mechanisms, and business ethics. This is consistent with the context of emerging market banks often facing close supervision from the State Bank of Vietnam and international strategic shareholders.

Ranked second is the Social (S) pillar with 8,129 text entries, accounting for 29.61%. Concerns for social issues in the banking industry focus primarily on two aspects: human capital and community contributions. For financial institutions, human resources are the most important asset in creating value; therefore, content on welfare, training, and equality in the workplace is often presented in detail. Furthermore, the tradition of engaging in charitable and social welfare activities among domestic banks also significantly contributes to the increased proportion of this pillar in the reports.

Notably, the Environment (E) pillar accounts for the lowest proportion, with only 3,752 paragraphs, equivalent to 13.67%. This figure highlights an important reality: although concepts like green credit or net zero are becoming popular in the media, the concretization of these commitments into detailed report content remains limited. The majority of content in pillar E currently focuses on reporting environmental impact mitigation activities at the office (such as saving electricity, water, and paper) instead of delving into more complex issues such as Scope 3 emission measurement or climate risk assessment within the loan portfolio. This uneven distribution illustrates the ESG development trajectory of the Vietnamese banking sector: moving from compliance with mandatory governance regulations, to fulfilling traditional social responsibilities, and finally to integrating environmental factors into core business operations. This result highlights the need for policymakers and banks to further promote transparency in the environmental pillar to meet the growing expectations of international investors and the nation's climate commitment roadmap.

Table 5. Distribution of ESG disclosure paragraphs by MSCI pillar and theme

Pillar	Salience of pillar (%)	MSCI theme key	No. of paragraphs by theme	Salience of theme (%)
E	13.67	Natural capital	1975	7.19
		Climate change	782	2.85
		Pollution waste	594	2.16
		Environmental opportunities	401	1.46
G	56.72	Corporate governance	12215	44.50
		Corporate behavior	3354	12.2186
S	29.61	Human capital	3874	14.11
		Social opportunities	2445	8.91
		Stakeholder opposition	1764	6.43
		Product liability	46	0.17

Delving into thematic levels according to the MSCI framework, the PhoBERT model analysis has unearthed layers of meaning in the ESG communication strategies of the Vietnamese banking system. Instead of focusing on general pillars, the analysis of 10 detailed themes helps to clearly identify the key ESG priorities that banks communicate with stakeholders. The topic of corporate governance recorded a record high salience of 44.5% (12,215 text entries). In the banking industry - a field operating based on trust and system security - demonstrating a strong governance structure is a top priority. Banks dedicate a significant portion of their reports to detailing organizational charts, the roles of the Board of Directors and Supervisory Board, and transparent decision-making processes. According to legitimacy theory, banks are using sustainability reporting as a mechanism to confirm that they are operating in accordance with the most stringent legal standards. This also reflects the strong impact of Circular 96/2020/TT-BTC (Ministry of Finance, 2020), which mandates that listed companies disclose detailed governance information. However, this excessive focus on G sometimes obscures other substantive sustainability aspects, suggesting that banks are still more in the compliance phase than the voluntary phase of creating new value.

Coming second is human capital with 14.1%. In the context of the fierce digital transformation of the banking industry in Vietnam, people have become a decisive factor in competitive advantage. Reports no longer simply list the number of employees, but focus strongly on digital skills training programs, career development paths, and outstanding employee benefits. The prominence of this topic reflects banks' efforts to build a top employer image to attract and retain high-quality personnel. However, compared to the topic of product liability, which accounts for only a very small percentage, it can be seen that banks are more concerned with internal customers than with disclosing details about their commitments to consumer protection or responsible investment in financial products. One of the most significant findings of the study lies in the divergence within the environment pillar. The topic of natural capital accounts for 7.2%, nearly three times higher than climate change, which only accounts for 2.8%. A closer analysis of the text reveals that banks remain focused on reporting direct environmental impacts at their offices such as electricity savings, paper reduction, and household waste management, which are activities that fall under the natural capital category and are relatively easy to implement. Meanwhile, the core issue of the banking industry's environmental impact, indirect emissions (scope 3) through loan portfolios and climate risk, has not been adequately discussed. The absence of climate change scenarios or decarbonization roadmaps in the investment portfolio suggests that Vietnamese banks still view ESG as a communication tool for green image-building rather than a strategic risk management tool. The topic of environmental opportunities also only accounts for 1.46%, reflecting that the development of green credit products is still in its early stages, largely remaining in the planning stage rather than with specific and transparent disbursement figures.

Figure 1. Ternary plot of E-S-G positioning by bank

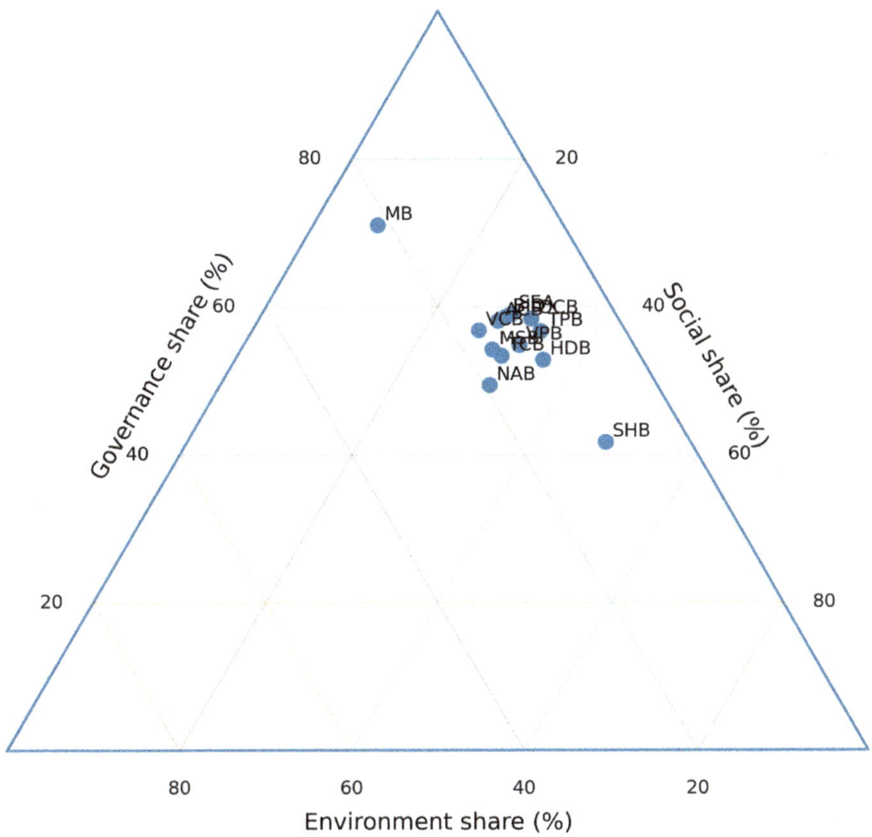

Figure 1 shows a ternary plot of E-S-G positioning by bank, representing the relative distribution of environmental, social, and governance disclosure among the sampled banks. All banks are clustered in the upper-middle area of the triangle, and the concentration near the governance dimension reflects a common ESG disclosure pattern, in which Vietnamese banks continue to prioritize governance-related issues. There are, however, several differences among the banks. MB is the nearest to the governance vertex, showing the strongest governance-dominated disclosure profile. SHB's closer proximity to the social side reflects a stronger emphasis on social issues, such as human capital and stakeholder-related content. The environmental visibility of NAB, MSB, and VCB seems higher compared to other banks, although their environmental shares remain modest.

To provide a clearer bank-level comparison, Table 6 presents the two most dominant ESG themes for each bank, together with their corresponding salience values. Based on the summary of dominant themes, corporate governance is the most prominent theme in the ESG disclosures of banks. All 13 banks in the sample have corporate governance as the top theme. This result indicates that current sustainability reports of Vietnamese banks tend to strongly emphasize governance aspects, including governance structure, board of directors, executive board, internal control, auditing, ownership, and supervisory mechanisms. This result is quite consistent with the characteristics of the banking industry, as banks are subject to strict regulation, have a high level of systemic risk, and require significant transparency, compliance, and internal control. In the top group, MB has the highest corporate governance weighting at 0.6199, indicating that MB's reporting focuses heavily on governance issues. Following closely are VCB with 0.4852, SEA with 0.4833, TPB with 0.4589, ACB with 0.4544, and BID with 0.4483. These banks demonstrate a relatively high and consistent emphasis on governance. Conversely, SHB has the lowest Corporate Governance weighting in the group, at 0.3372; however, this theme remains the most prominent for SHB. This shows that despite differences among banks, governance remains the central focus in ESG reporting across the entire industry.

Table 6. Top two dominant ESG themes by bank

Bank	Top 1 ESG theme	Salience (%)	Top 2 ESG theme	Salience (%)
ACB	Corporate governance	45.44	Human capital	14.93
BID	Corporate governance	44.83	Corporate behavior	13.81
HDB	Corporate governance	35.74	Corporate behavior	17.09
MB	Corporate governance	61.99	Corporate behavior	9.03
MSB	Corporate governance	42.66	Human capital	15.57
NAB	Corporate governance	37.75	Human capital	20.35
OCB	Corporate governance	44.12	Human capital	14.77
SEA	Corporate governance	48.33	Human capital	13.15
SHB	Corporate governance	33.72	Human capital	30.91
TCB	Corporate governance	38.92	Human capital	19.82
TPB	Corporate governance	45.89	Human capital	15.44
VCB	Corporate governance	48.52	Natural capital	11.33
VPB	Corporate governance	42.46	Human capital	17.07

In the second-highest category, the results show a clearer differentiation. The majority of banks have the second theme as human capital. This indicates that after governance, banks often emphasize the human element, including employees, training, health, safety, welfare, equality, and human resource development. SHB has a relatively high proportion of human capital in the second category, at 0.3091, suggesting that this bank's report tends to dedicate more space to employee-related content compared to other banks. Another group, including BID, HDB, and MB, has the second-highest theme as corporate behavior. This indicates that these banks not only emphasize governance structure but also focus on corporate behavior, compliance, business ethics, transparency, information disclosure, and risk management. VCB, however, differs, with its second-highest theme being natural capital, suggesting a more significant presence of environmental content related to natural resources, resource use, or natural environmental issues.

The heatmap provides a more detailed view of how ESG attention is distributed across individual reporting years. The most visible pattern is the strong concentration of disclosure in Corporate Governance, which forms a consistent high-intensity band across almost all bank-year observations. This confirms that governance-related content is not only dominant at the aggregate bank level but also persistent across reporting years. In several banks, the share of governance-related disclosure declines slightly in later years, while human capital, corporate behavior, or natural capital become more visible. This suggests that ESG reporting is gradually becoming more diversified rather than being limited only to governance content. However, the overall pattern still indicates a strong governance orientation, with social themes appearing as secondary areas and environmental themes reported more selectively across different years.

Figure 2. MSCI ESG theme salience by bank - year

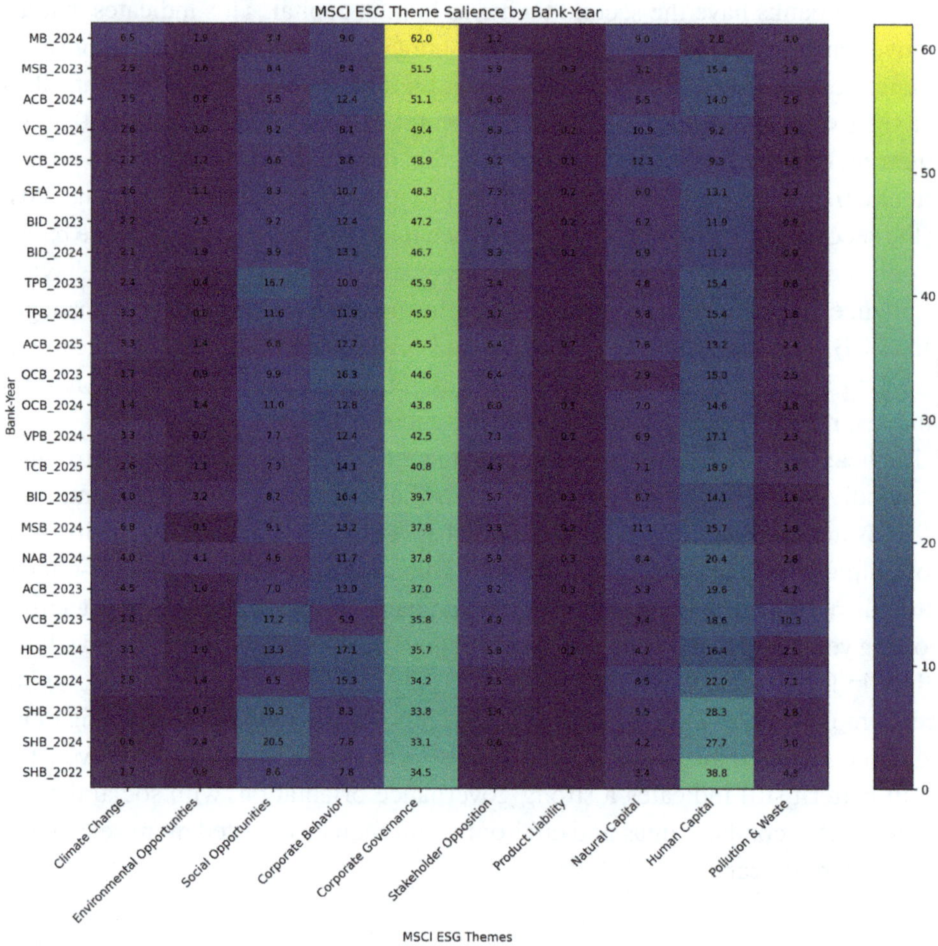

5. CONCLUSIONS

This study examined ESG disclosure patterns in the sustainability reports of Vietnamese commercial banks using PhoBERT-based text mining. The analysis was conducted at paragraph level and classified ESG-related content according to the MSCI ESG Key Issues Framework. By using semantic similarity, the study captured different ways in which Vietnamese banks describe environmental, social, and governance issues. This approach is useful because ESG information in sustainability reports is not always expressed through fixed keywords.

The findings show that the governance pillar strongly dominates ESG disclosure in Vietnamese commercial banks. Governance-related content accounts for more than half of total ESG disclosure, with corporate governance being the most prominent theme across all banks in the sample. This partly reflects the peculiarities of the banking industry - a sector subject to tight regulatory control, where requirements for information transparency, internal controls, risk management, and board structure are fundamental to maintaining stakeholder trust. In such an environment, ESG disclosure is largely undertaken as a natural extension of existing compliance obligations rather than as part of a proactive sustainability strategy.

The social pillar is the second-most-visible area of disclosure, especially through human capital content. Banks frequently report on employee training, welfare, career development, workplace safety, and community-oriented activities. This indicates that banks continue to frame sustainability, at least in part, through their responsibilities toward employees and society. However, some socially material issues in banking, such as product liability, customer protection, data privacy, financial consumer rights, and responsible investment, appear much less visible. This suggests that social disclosure remains more focused on internal human resource practices and general social contributions than on the full range of stakeholder risks associated with banking products and services.

The environmental pillar receives the lowest level of disclosure. Although environmental topics such as green credit, sustainable finance, climate risk, and net-zero transition are becoming increasingly important in Vietnam, they are still not strongly reflected in bank sustainability reports. Much of the environmental disclosure focuses on direct operational impacts, such as reducing electricity, water, and paper use, rather than on more material banking issues, such as financed emissions, climate-related credit risk, exposure to carbon-intensive sectors, or green loan portfolio quality. This finding highlights a gap between the growing policy importance of sustainable finance and the current depth of environmental reporting in the banking sector.

Overall, the study contributes to ESG disclosure research in three main ways. First, it provides empirical evidence on the thematic structure of ESG reporting among Vietnamese commercial banks. Second, it demonstrates the usefulness of Vietnamese language NLP, particularly PhoBERT, for measuring ESG theme salience in sustainability reports. Third, it offers practical insights for regulators, investors, and banks seeking to improve the comparability, transparency, and materiality of ESG disclosure.

This study has several limitations. First, the dataset includes only available sustainability reports from HOSE-listed commercial banks, and the number of reporting years differs across banks. Another limitation concerns the use of the MSCI ESG Key Issue framework as the basis for theme classification. Although MSCI provides a broad and structured taxonomy of ESG issues, it was not designed specifically for Vietnamese commercial banks or for Vietnamese-language sustainability reports, meaning that some banking-specific ESG issues may not be fully captured with the same level of detail as in a sector-specific banking framework. Finally, the analysis focuses on disclosure patterns rather than actual ESG performance. Therefore, the findings should be interpreted as evidence of recent reporting practices, not as a direct assessment of banks' sustainability outcomes. Future research could expand the dataset by including annual reports, non-listed banks, and a longer observation period. It could also combine text mining with manual validation, sentiment analysis, or external ESG indicators to examine the depth and quality of ESG disclosure.

REFERENCES

Al Jizani, Q. M. D., & Buniamin, S. (2025). Bte., & Rahman, N. R. B. A. (2025). The Impact of Board of Directors' Characteristics on Financial Performance: The Moderating Role of Voluntary Risk Disclosure in the Iraqi Banking Sector. *Journal of Cultural Analysis and Social Change*, (4), 1045–1055. DOI: 10.64753/jcasc.v10i4.2972

Alrtaimat, R. (2025). Emerging Trends in Esg Research. Bibliometric Analysis. *Annals of Faculty of Economics*, *34*(1), 185–205. https://ideas.repec.org/a/ora/journl/v34y2025i1p185-205.html. DOI: 10.47535/1991AUOES34(1)015

Atarwaman, R. J. D., Amiruddin, A., & Dharmawati, D. (2026). The Role of ESG Disclosure Quality in Shaping Investor Risk Perception in Post-pandemic Capital Markets. *International Journal of Economic Literature*, *3*(7), 68–83.

Bassen, A., & Kovacs, A. M. M. (2008) Environmental, Social and Governance Key Performance Indicators from a Capital Market Perspective. *Zeitschrift für Wirtschafts- und Unternehmensethik*, 9/2, 182-192. Available at *SSRN*: https://ssrn.com/abstract=1307091

Beltagy, I., Lo, K., & Cohan, A. (2019). SciBERT: A Pretrained Language Model for Scientific Text. *EMNLP-IJCNLP 2019 - 2019 Conference on Empirical Methods in Natural Language Processing and 9th International Joint Conference on Natural Language Processing, Proceedings of the Conference*, 3615–3620. DOI: 10.18653/v1/D19-1371

Bianchi, F., Yu, B., & Tagliabue, J. (2021). BERT Goes Shopping: Comparing Distributional Models for Product Representations. *ECNLP 2021 - 4th Workshop on e-Commerce and NLP, Proceedings*, 1–12. DOI: 10.18653/v1/2021.ecnlp-1.1

Cho, C. H., & Patten, D. M. (2007). The role of environmental disclosures as tools of legitimacy: A research note. *Accounting, Organizations and Society*, *32*(7–8), 639–647. DOI: 10.1016/j.aos.2006.09.009

Conceição, P. (2025). A matter of choice: People and possibilities in the age of AI. *Human Development Report 2025*.

Devlin, J., Chang, M.-W., Lee, K., & Toutanova, K. (2019). BERT: Pre-training of Deep Bidirectional Transformers for Language Understanding. *Proceedings of the 2019 Conference of the North*, 4171–4186. DOI: 10.18653/v1/N19-1423

Eccles, R. G., Serafeim, G., Seth, D., & Ming, C. C. Y. (2013). The performance frontier: Innovating for a sustainable strategy. *Harvard Business Review, 91*(7), 17–18. https://pubmed.ncbi.nlm.nih.gov/23898735/ PMID: 23898735

European Commission. (2025). *Corporate sustainability reporting*. https://finance.ec.europa.eu/financial-markets/company-reporting-and-auditing/company-reporting/corporate-sustainability-reporting_en

Ferjančič, U., Ichev, R., Lončarski, I., Montariol, S., Pelicon, A., Pollak, S., Sitar Šuštar, K., Toman, A., Valentinčič, A., & Žnidaršič, M. (2024). Textual analysis of corporate sustainability reporting and corporate ESG scores. *International Review of Financial Analysis, 96*, 103669. DOI: 10.1016/j.irfa.2024.103669

Gardazi, N. M., Daud, A., Malik, M. K., Bukhari, A., Alsahfi, T., & Alshemaimri, B. (2025). BERT applications in natural language processing: A review. *Artificial Intelligence Review, 58*(6), 166. DOI: 10.1007/s10462-025-11162-5

General Statistics Office of Vietnam. (2025). *Report on the Socio-Economic Situation in the Fourth Quarter and for the Year 2025*. https://www.nso.gov.vn/en/data-and-statistics/2026/01/socio-economic-situation-in-the-fourth-quarter-and-2025/

Global Reporting Initiative. (2013). *The value of sustainability reporting and the GRI Standards*. www.globalreporting.org

Government of Vietnam. (2021). *Decision No. 1658/QD-TTg on Approving the National Green Growth Strategy for the 2021-2030 period, with a vision by 2050*. https://vanban.chinhphu.vn/?docid=204226&pageid=27160

Government of Vietnam. (2022). *Decree No. 06/2022/ND-CP on Mitigation of Greenhouse Gas Emissions and Protection of the Ozone Layer*. https://climate-laws.org/document/decree-no-06-2022-nd-cp-on-mitigation-of-green-house-gas-ghg-emissions-and-protection-of-ozone-layer_d8ff

Guenther, E. M., & Hoppe, H. (2014). Merging limited perspectives: A synopsis of measurement approaches and theories of the relationship between corporate environmental and financial performance. *Journal of Industrial Ecology, 18*(5), 689–707. DOI: 10.1111/jiec.12125

Gupta, A., Sharma, U., & Gupta, S. K. (2021). The Role of ESG in Sustainable Development: An Analysis Through the Lens of Machine Learning. *2021 IEEE International Humanitarian Technology Conference, IHTC 2021*. DOI: 10.1109/IHTC53077.2021.9698939

Ha, N. T. H., & Huy, N. D. (2025). Assessment and Comparison of ESG Disclosure Levels in the 2024 Annual Reports of State-Owned and Joint-Stock Commercial Banks in Vietnam. *Asean International Sandbox Conference, 7*, 121–133.

Haas, D. R., & Popov, A. (2023). Finance and Green Growth. *Economic Journal (London), 133*(650), 637–668. DOI: 10.1093/ej/ueac081

Kaliyar, R. K., Goswami, A., Narang, P., & Sinha, S. (2020). FNDNet – A deep convolutional neural network for fake news detection. *Cognitive Systems Research, 61*, 32–44. DOI: 10.1016/j.cogsys.2019.12.005

Kang, H., & Kim, J. (2022). Analyzing and Visualizing Text Information in Corporate Sustainability Reports Using Natural Language Processing Methods. *Applied Sciences (Basel, Switzerland), 12*(11), 5614. Advance online publication. DOI: 10.3390/app12115614

Lee, J., Yoon, W., Kim, S., Kim, D., Kim, S., So, C. H., & Kang, J. (2020). BioBERT: A pre-trained biomedical language representation model for biomedical text mining. *Bioinformatics (Oxford, England), 36*(4), 1234–1240. DOI: 10.1093/bioinformatics/btz682 PMID: 31501885

Lopez-de-Silanes, F., McCahery, J. A., & Pudschedl, P. C. (2020) ESG Performance and Disclosure: A Cross-Country Analysis. *Singapore Journal of Legal Studies*, 217-241. Available at *SSRN*: https://ssrn.com/abstract=3649896

Mahadevan, V., Subramaniam, S., & Srivastava, V. (2026). Carbon concentration in bank portfolios and efficiency: The role of credit risk and capitalization. *Journal of International Financial Markets, Institutions and Money, 109*, 102327. Advance online publication. DOI: 10.1016/j.intfin.2026.102327

Marfu, A., Abbas, H., Sya, A., Purwanto, A., Nadiroh, , Sumargo, B., Wulandari, S. S., Daiman, , Malaihollo, C. A., Syakyakirti, , Tanubrata, D., & Pratiwi, D. I. (2025). Building long-term value: A practical guide to integrating ESG into business strategies. *Sustainable Futures : An Applied Journal of Technology, Environment and Society, 10*, 100955. DOI: 10.1016/j.sftr.2025.100955

Ministry of Finance. (2020). *Circular No. 96/2020/TT-BTC on guidelines for information disclosure on the securities market.* https://thuvienphapluat.vn/van-ban/Chung-khoan/Thong-tu-96-2020-TT-BTC-quy-dinh-cong-bo-thong-tin-tren-thi-truong-chung-khoan-459000.aspx

Mohammadrezaei, M., Marques, J. C., & Huq, A. (2024). *Use of text mining and natural language processing techniques in analyzing sustainability reports: A systematic literature review and assessment.* DOI: 10.2139/ssrn.5071032

Moreno, A. I., & Caminero, T. (2022). Application of text mining to the analysis of climate-related disclosures. *International Review of Financial Analysis*, *83*, 102307. DOI: 10.1016/j.irfa.2022.102307

MSCI ESG Research LLC. (2024). *MSCI ESG symbols and definitions*. https://www.msci.com/downloads/web/msci-com/legal/disclosures/esg-disclosures/MSCI%20ESG%20Symbols%20and%20Definitions.pdf

Ngo, M. T., Ngo, B. H., & Valerievich, S. V. (2024). Fine-tuned PhoBERT for sentiment analysis of Vietnamese phone reviews. *CTU Journal of Innovation and Sustainable Development*, *16*(Special Issue (ISDS)), 52–57. https://doi.org/https://doi.org/10.22144/CTUJOISD.2024.322. DOI: 10.22144/ctujoisd.2024.322

Nguyen, D., Lau, T., Nguyen, H. A., Doan, T., Nguyen, H., Lu, S., & Tran, N. (2025). A Hybrid PhoBERT-CNN-LSTM Model for Sentiment Analysis of Vietnamese Student Feedback. *Asian Journal of Research in Computer Science*, *18*(5), 65–74. DOI: 10.9734/ajrcos/2025/v18i5639

Nguyen, D. Q., & Nguyen, A. T. (2020). PhoBERT: Pre-trained language models for Vietnamese. *Findings of the Association for Computational Linguistics Findings of ACL: EMNLP*, *2020*, 1037–1042. DOI: 10.18653/v1/2020.findings-emnlp.92

Nguyen, H. T., Huynh, T. N., Mai, N. T. N., Le, K. D. D., & Pham, T.-N.-D. (2023). PhoBERT: Application in Disease Classification based on Vietnamese Symptom Analysis. *Applied Computer Systems*, *28*(1), 35–43. DOI: 10.2478/acss-2023-0004

Phong, Ky. (2025). Green credit grows over 21% annually. *Vietnam Economic Times*. https://en.vneconomy.vn/green-credit-grows-over-21-annually.htm

PwC Vietnam. (2025). *ESG Progress Tracker Survey Report 2025*. https://www.pwc.com/vn/en/publications/2025/esg-progress-tracker-2025.pdf

Rasmy, L., Xiang, Y., Xie, Z., Tao, C., & Zhi, D. (2021). Med-BERT: Pretrained contextualized embeddings on large-scale structured electronic health records for disease prediction. *NPJ Digital Medicine*, *4*(1), 86. DOI: 10.1038/s41746-021-00455-y PMID: 34017034

Rezayi, S., Liu, Z., Wu, Z., Dhakal, C., Ge, B., Zhen, C., Liu, T., & Li, S. (2022). AgriBERT: Knowledge-Infused Agricultural Language Models for Matching Food and Nutrition. *IJCAI International Joint Conference on Artificial Intelligence, 6*, 5150–5156. DOI: 10.24963/ijcai.2022/715

Rostam, Z. R. K., & Kertész, G. (2025). Advancing Scientific Text Classification: Fine-Tuned Models with Dataset Expansion and Hard-Voting. *Proceedings of the International Symposium on Applied Machine Intelligence and Informatics, SAMI*, 527–532. DOI: 10.1109/SAMI63904.2025.10883153

The State Bank of Vietnam. (2012). *Directive 03/CT-NHHN on promoting green credit growth and environmental-social risk management in credit extension*. https://english.luatvietnam.vn/tai-chinh/directive-03-ct-nhnn-2015-promote-green-credit-growth-93343-d1.html

The State Bank of Vietnam. (2022). *Circular 17/2022/TT-NHNN on environmental risk management in credit extension by foreign bank branches*.

Thewissen, J., Shrestha, P., Arslan-Ayaydin, Ö., & Beibei, Y. (2026). Topics That Matter: ESG Reports and Information Asymmetry. *Journal of Financial Research*, jfir.70053. Advance online publication. DOI: 10.1111/jfir.70053

Tran, K. Q., Nguyen, A. T., Hoang, P. G., Luu, C. D., Do, T. H., & Nguyen, K. Van. (2022). Vietnamese hate and offensive detection using PhoBERT-CNN and social media streaming data. *Neural Computing and Applications 2022 35:1, 35*(1), 573–594. DOI: 10.1007/s00521-022-07745-w

United Nations Environment Programme Finance Initiative. (n.d.). *Principles for Responsible Banking*.

Yoon, J., Han, S., Lee, Y., & Hwang, H. (2023). Text Mining Analysis of ESG Management Reports in South Korea: Comparison With Sustainable Development Goals. *SAGE Open, 13*(4), 21582440231202896. Advance online publication. DOI: 10.1177/21582440231202896

Zhyar, Z. R., & Kertész, G. (2025). Advances in Pre-trained Language Models for Domain-Specific Text Classification: A Systematic Review. *ACM Transactions on Intelligent Systems and Technology, 16*(6). Advance online publication. DOI: 10.1145/3763002

Chapter 10
Green Credit:
Indian Bank Competitiveness and Bank Risk Taking

S. Baranidharan
http://orcid.org/0000-0002-7780-4045
Presidency University, India

Amirdha Vasani Sankarkumar
http://orcid.org/0000-0001-6800-3249
Kristu Jayanti (Deemed to be) University, India

Ramita Kapoor
http://orcid.org/0009-0009-9792-3701
Christ University, India

David Winster Praveenraj
http://orcid.org/0000-0003-4460-7739
Christ University, India

M. S. Kamalaveni
Sona College of Technology, India

ABSTRACT

This study examines the relationship between green credit, Indian bank competitiveness, and bank risk-taking through a systematic literature review of 40 peer-reviewed articles published between 2015 and 2025. Findings showed that green credit initiatives strengthen banks' long-term competitiveness by improving sustainability performance, lowering environmental compliance costs, and enhancing market reputation. Evidence also suggested that while green credit generally reduces credit and operational risks due to better asset quality and government-backed in-

DOI: 10.4018/979-8-3373-8392-7.ch010

centives, some banks face short-term risks linked to limited borrower history, high monitoring costs, and evolving regulatory frameworks. The review concludes that integrating green credit is strategically beneficial for Indian banks, promoting both competitiveness and stable risk profiles. Policymakers should expand green-finance guidelines and incentives, while banks must strengthen risk assessment tools and build sector-specific expertise to scale green lending sustainably.

INTRODUCTION

The literature examining credit markets, financial risk and sustainability, and policy interventions has grown to document how credit allocation and Financial Behaviour occur in a variety of Economic Contexts. The Studies Review revealed a diverse representation of Credit across Four Distinct Types; Green Credit, Agricultural and Smallholder Credit, Carbon Credit Systems, Sovereign Credit Risk, Credit Risk Modelling, Mobility Credit Markets, and Household Credit Programs. All forty Studies reviewed show complex linkages between Access to Credit, Risk Taking, Development Outcomes, Environmental Transitions and Financial Stability. These Studies were conducted in many different countries, including a variety of sectors and using several different Research Methods. The Findings of the Studies collectively indicate that Credit is not only a financial instrument; it is also a Tool that Equally Influences Behaviour, Resilience, Competitiveness, and Sustainability.

There have been multiple studies of how credit has reacted to uncertainty, shock and crisis situations. Czura and Klonner (2023) provided an example of lender behaviour and credit flow post the Indian Ocean tsunami. They stated that the impact of natural disasters may have a ripple effect on the credit network of an economy. The societal impacts produced by welfare credit policy were reflected through a ten-year DID study conducted by Marimpi et al.(2025), which found that the rollout of Universal Credit in the UK produced an effect on consumers' mental health outcomes. Djatche (2025) researched how monetary policy surprises affected the availability and risk appetite of U.S. banks for providing credit, while Gómez González et al. (2024) studied how climate change related deteriorating sovereign risk relates to asymmetric financial vulnerabilities. Collectively, these studies illustrated how fragile the credit system is to macroeconomic- and/or environmental-related shocks.

Amongst the different themes identified in the literature review, two main ones revolved around access to finance for smallholders and agricultural financing, which was presented in the studies by Balana and Oyeyemi (2022) and Balana et al. (2022), who specifically focused on structural barriers to Credit Access by smallholders in Nigeria, Ethiopia, and Tanzania, and by Seidu et al. (2025), who found that farmers' credit and savings decisions were influenced by Peer Behaviour in Ghana. Liu et al.

(2024) also demonstrated that access to Credit was impacted by Climate Risk for Farmers in China. On the other hand, James et al. Microcredit effects were examined by (2025) in Sub-Saharan Africa and were shown to be differentially advantageous for borrowers. Collectively, these studies identified that, even in agrarian economies, the benefits of credit access were inequitable, based on factors such as social networks, vulnerability to climate change, and institutional barriers.

Another emerging theme is the changes occurring within Credit Markets as a result of Mobility Credit Schemes as well as Individuals' Responses to Mobility Credit Schemes. Martínez et al. (2025) and Hamm et al. (2025) studied mobility credit schemes and investigated mode-choice behaviours and perceptions of fairness in trading mobility credits. Zambrano et al. (2023) studied Rotating Savings and Credit Associations (ROSCAs) and the role of ROSCAs in informal household finance. All three studies demonstrate that the design of credit products with Behavioural Incentives was effective in creating an opportunity for public participation in Mobility Credit Schemes and created the potential for a high degree of efficiency in allocating mobility credits.

Many studies have focused on sustainability-linked lending, environmental finance, and green credit. According to research by Tan et al. (2025), green credits impact the energy intensity of firms when producing goods. Wang et al (2025) looked at how green credits affect a firm's willingness to take risks, while Huang (2025) studied how interaction between monetary policy and green credits influences banks' willingness to take risks in their lending practices to firms. Hernanz et al.(2025) evaluated the efficacy of carbon credits in REDD+ communities, while Mallappa et al. (2025) examined farmers' trust in carbon credit stakeholders. Motta et al. (2025) discussed concerns about hydropower projects financed by CDM projects due to the environmental risks to our planet from financialised river basins. Fingerman et al. (2025) also looked at the risks in terms of crediting for low carbon fuel standards. While they identified opportunities and risks attributed to environmental credit mechanisms (i.e., green credits), these studies show how both opportunities and risks will depend on the quality of information and the design of governance.

The literature surrounding greenwashing, sustainable finance policy frameworks, and disclosure practices of companies has generated discussion about issues related to these topics. A recent systematic literature review by Galletta examined the relationship between greenwashing and reduced consumer confidence within the banking sector, which has created the demand for greater regulatory oversight of the sector. Another example of how the work of Schoenmaker provided an initial conceptual framework for understanding how the financial system relates to environmental policy through the development of GREEN monetary instruments. Both articles increased the awareness of the importance of transparency, accountability, and regulatory coherence to establish green credit transitions as legitimate.

A number of researchers have explored the relationship of systemic credit risk and contagion across markets, including Andrieş et al. (2022), who used GANs for Data Augmentation to create alternative examples of Credit Default Swap trades. On the other hand, Heß & Damasio (2025) have examined, classified and organized the many applications of Machine Learning in the context of Banking Risk Management over a period of ten years. Another example is the work by Tribuvan et al. (2025) performed a comparative study of the predictive performance of the Top Tier Classifiers, Advanced Classification Models and AutoML for Credit Risk in Banking Institutions. Aruleba & Sun (2025) improved the accuracy of predictions through deep learning and SMOTE-ENN Strategies and C-Rella et al. (2025) proposed a cost-sensitive reinforcement learning system for credit risk. In general, these studies show that Credit Risk Analytics has advanced to a point where complex computer and data-driven systems are now used extensively.

Multiple research works investigated the generation and transmission of risk on multiple credit and credit-related markets around the world. The work by Andrieş et al. (2025) focuses primarily on the manner in which credit is allocated amongst various sectoral markets through examination of the level of fragility that exists within the overall credit distribution system as well as through their examination of vulnerability due to systemic credit shocks. The approach used by Fernández Rodríguez et al. (2025) was network analysis to model and evaluate credit/lending and liquidity risk in the EMU sovereign debt market and identify any systemic/contagion relationships among the lending of credit associated with such markets. The study by Kladakis and Skouralis (2025) looked at the relationship between decreasing sovereign credit ratings and increasing levels of economic growth risk and contagion in the international banking system. Kladakis, Skouralis, and Xiao-Li et al.'s (2025) studies all show that credit markets have interconnected patterns of risk/a credit risk propagation.

Yao and Fan (2023) investigated how uncertainty in policies impacted credit allocation in urban banks in China, and examined how bank risk-taking behaviours influenced credit allocation. Waidelich et al. (2025) explored how the public could help reduce risks associated with investing in renewable sources of energy through loan programs, as well as how such loan programs could provide an incentive to invest in renewable sources of energy because of the potential for gaining knowledge through "learning spillovers." Hamdi Ben-Nasr et al. concluded that firms that were subject to carbon risk showed a greater tendency to extend trade credit (i.e., loans) due to being exposed to the effects of carbon risk, an environmental phenomenon, suggesting that environmental risk is an evolving variable that will continue to affect credit terms for some time to come.

The studies indicated that while credit may remain a vehicle for accessing capital, credit also has alternative benefits—serving as policy tools for managing risk, promoting positive behavior through incentives, and supporting technological innovations that promote Sustainable Development. Studies also found that while credit markets respond to and recover from disruptions, credit markets are still experiencing challenges related to limited access to credit, environmental credibility, and information asymmetry, as well as other systemic vulnerabilities that are preventing credit-driven growth and sustainable Development from achieving their maximum potential.

LITERATURE REVIEW

1. How competitive banks are: Traditionally, scholars defined bank competitiveness as how a bank (or group of banks or maybe the financial system as a whole) can survive and be productive by competing to use its own internal resources most effectively while adjusting to new external realities. For example, competitors can use profit, safety and scale as basis points to assess their competitive viability; however, the long-term viability will be based on innovation and governance practices. Using empirical research technique like factor analysis and DEA methodology (e.g. see: Xianming et al, 2014; JianKang and YuJuan, 2017; Lixia et al, 2022), the commercially-based measure of bank competitiveness has been established using composite indicators sets made up of size, profitability, safety, liquidity, growth and business mix. The study results from the research into how banks compete for customers (state-owned banks, joint-stock banks and urban banks) revealed that the level of competitiveness among banks is not uniform, and that strategy and technology development as well as service diversification are all major contributing factors in their overall competitiveness. Collectively, these studies have provided a foundation upon which to assess the effects of environmental policies on bank performance and market positioning through additional subsequent studies related to green finance or sustainable bank operations.

2. Interconnected Relationship Among Green Credit, Bank Competitiveness, and Risk- Taking: The Studies Have Suggest That It's A Central Platform For How Banks Compete With Each Other & Take Risks By Linking Competition To One Another. The literature has a fairly complex & conditional picture With Many Cases (Aupperle & John, 1985; Ping & Haifeng, 2009; Xiaoyan & Ge, 2018; Lingyun etal., 2018; Wei et al., 2021; Qingmin & Jing, 2022; Haifeng & Qianqian, 2023) Demonstrating That The Implementation Of Green Credit Practices Provides Banks With An Enhanced Competitive Position As A Result Of Enhanced Environmental Reputation, The Ability To Attract Sustainability-Oriented Customers, Diversification Of Product Offerings, & The Creation Of New Revenue Opportunities From Instruments Such As Green Bonds, Green Mortgages, & Climate Change Advisory Services.

As A Result Of These Competitive Advantages, Banks Will Experience Some High Long-Term Profits & Have Greater Competitive Market Presence Relative To Their Peers.In Contrast, There Is Other Research (Cui etal., 2016; Clarkson etal., 2008; Xin & Ying, 2021; Guanglin etal., 2017; Jialan & Yuxin, 2023; Haifeng & Huiping, 2023) Showing That Stricter Screening's, Continuous Environmental Monitoring & Providing Incentives For Greener Corporate Practices Within The Framework Of Green Lending Will Result In A Reduction In Credit Risk And Reputational Risk. The benefits of going green include a reduction in defaults, non-performing loans, and more stable indicators of financial strength, while a growing number of studies (Scholtens & Dam, 2007; Mathuva & Kiweu, 2016; Rongcai & Wenqiong, 2016; Pan et al., 2022; Xiaoying, 2018; Wei et al., 2019) have cautioned that pursuing green projects will increase costs and the level of economic risk in the near term due to the length of time required to see an ROI as well as higher starting costs and volatile cash-flow expectations due to the lack of governance, transparency, and public policy support in developing regions. The complete body of evidence supports that when sufficient support is provided through a strong regulatory and monitoring framework, green finance can support competitive advantage by lowering risks, whereas it may create temporary disadvantages when no such support exists.

3. Measurement, methods and heterogeneity: The field has employed several different methodologies, including factor analysis and Data Envelopment Analysis (DEA) to develop competitiveness indices, econometric panel regressions with bank fixed effects, quasi-natural experiments (Propensity Score Matching - Difference-in-Difference in Ning et al., 2020; Regional Difference-in-Difference in Wei et al., 2021) and mediation and stepwise models to analyse risk-taking as a mediator (e.g., the recent literature on credit risk has begun using machine learning and advanced classification techniques to analyse risk-taking as a mediator).The increasing diversity in the methods used for studying Green Credit has resulted in a wider variety of studies.Based on previous research, Green Credit has a greater impact on large and public banks than it does on urban small banks. This corroborates Hongtao's (2022) finding of heterogeneity for both Bank Type and Country in his foundational study, and is also supported by a number of additional studies that have been published on this subject. Furthermore, these studies provide very large variations in how Countries and Sectors have financed agricultural production due to agricultural credit constraints identified as unique to Smallholder production, thus not applicable to all scenarios. Highlighted Studies such as Balana & Oyeyemi (2022), Balana et al. (2022), James et al. (2025), and Zambrano et al. (2023) demonstrate the differences between Countries and Sectors.

4. Complementary literatures: The interconnections between policy, disclosure, and carbon credits are complex and multifaceted. Prior research on sustainability disclosure (Clarkson et al., 2008; Galletta, 2024) suggests that the quality of sustainability disclosures can reduce the effects of information asymmetries in relation to receiving the benefits of green financing. Research on Policy (Schoenmaker, 2017/2019, Yao & Fan, 2025, Waidelich et al, 2025) suggests that conducive Macro-Prudential (regulatory) and Subsidy (government assistance) frameworks enhance Competitive Benefit and Risk Mitigation advantages associated with Green Credit. Additionally, though extensive evidence exists (Fingerman et al., 2025; Hernanz et al., 2025; Mallappa et al., 2025) providing information regarding sustainability projects and banks' exposures to such, these findings illustrate how various factors relating to offset credibility, community perceptions, and regulatory framework affect banks' ultimate outcomes.

Submitted a compilation of 40 studies and the uploaded empirical paper that shows how banks' competitiveness improved with green credit through diversification of revenue sources; reputation; and market position. The main contributors to the increase in competitiveness were a reduction in risk-taking (e.g., intermediated reductions in non-performing loans (NPLs) and/or improved Z-scores). There were caveats and conditions associated with these relationships. As an example, Banks operating in areas that have a low level of transparency, inadequate supervision or a lack of an effective policy framework, may have faced immediate financial challenges from the limited amount of assistance available for their green credit initiatives. The advanced methods (for example, quasi-experimental designs, mediation analysis and machine learning) were used as a basis to further substantiate the causal attribution of those particular green credit findings. However, there remain substantial gaps, including (a) generalisability across coun tries (beyond China), (b) potential trade-offs between long-term profitability versus short-term costs, and (c) development of standardised measures to evaluate what qualifies as "green" activities and quality of disclosures. The synthesis recommends that further research should apply standardised definitions of green loans, use exogenous policy shocks to identify causal relationships, and evaluate how the quality of disclosures and public support acts as moderators. Overall, the totality of the evidence suggests that banks can leverage green credit strategically to enhance their competitiveness, while simultaneously managing (and potentially decreasing) risk, to be effective when implemented and monitored appropriately.

RESEARCH QUESTION:

1. What effect does green credit policy have on Indian banks' strength and competitiveness?
2. Does green credit shift the risk profile of Indian Banks? If yes, how?

3. What impact does the risk-taking profile of banks have on the relationship between green credit and bank competitiveness in India?
4. Is it true that there are different competitive dynamics associated with green credit among India's Different Banking Types(pubic, private, foreign, small finance)?
5. What is the impact of changing green credit on the long-term financial health and overall performance of Indian banks?
6. What is the difference between the level of competition among banks that provide green credit, as opposed to banks that do not; and how does risk-taking play a role ?

METHODOLOGY

1. Variables Used

This research uses a defined set of variables to objectively look into how green credit interacts with the risk pragmatism exhibited by banks and the competitiveness of banks in the Indian banking industry. In developing the study's variables, the prior literature on green finance and bank risk was the baseline/conceptual framework used to develop the research variable measures. The measures selected will capture the direct effects of a green loan on bank competitiveness, as well as the indirect (mediated) effects of a green loan on bank competitiveness.

Independent variable: Green Credit/Green Lending

The key independent variable in this research project will be Green Credit (Green Lending), which represents the amount of credit banks extend to climate-friendly and environmentally sustainable projects. Banks that engage in Green Credit are demonstrating a commitment to developing their Strategic Direction around the principles of sustainable finance and the relevant environmental regulations and policy environment.

Green Credit can include loans to finance projects that support renewable energy, energy-efficient infrastructure, sustainable agriculture, electric transport, waste management, green building, and other environmentally-friendly activities. From an empirical perspective, Green Credit will be measured using one or more of the following indicators:

1) The proportion of Green Credit to total Advances
2) The intensity of Green Lending

3) Exposure to environmentally-friendly industries
4) Green Finance reporting disclosures in Banks' annual and/or sustainability reports.

When a bank has a higher value of Green Credit, it shows that the bank has made a long-term strategic commitment to implement sustainable lending practices, demonstrating its commitment to being pro-active in its environmental responsibility efforts, innovation concerning financial products (e.g., new construction financing for energy-efficient infrastructure), and being strategically-oriented toward achieving long-term financial success.

Risk Behavior of Banks as a Mediator Variable

The study employs Banks' Risk-Taking Behaviour as a mediating variable to represent the intermediary effect of green credit on banks' competitive position. Banks' Risk-Taking Behaviour will reflect how banks' risk profiles adjust and re-act (to) both changes in exposure to green loans and whether or not the increased exposure leads to more conservative or aggressive risk preferences in nature.

Risk-Taking Behaviour will be measured utilizing the following banking risk and stability indicators:

- Credit Risk Measures — Non-Performing Assets (NPA) or Non-Performing Loans (NPL) ratios, or other Credit Risk Measures;
- Capital Adequacy Ratio (CAR);
- Asset-Liability Ratios;
- Liquidity Ratios;
- Z-Score or any other Financial Stability Measure (as needed).

These risk and stability indicators represent a bank's ability to absorb losses, manage the risk of default by its borrowers, and provide a stable financial institution. The inclusion of Banks' Risk-Taking Behaviour as a variable in this study allows the researcher to observe whether the occurrence of green lending allows a bank to improve its credit quality, reduce its exposure to the risk of default, and/or increase its resiliency, and/or whether the occurrence of green lending creates transitional risks (higher costs and longer gestation period of its projects).

By implicitly modeling Banks' Risk-Taking Behaviour, the author will also investigate the extent to which green lending affects competitiveness indirectly (via the effect that green lending has on Banks' Risk-Taking Behaviour), thereby enhancing the conclusions drawn from this study regarding the causal relationship between banks and competitiveness concerns.

2. Tools and Statistical Tests Used

The purpose of this study is to examine the relationship between green credit, bank risk-taking behaviour, and bank competitiveness through the application of several econometric techniques and statistical tests appropriate for longitudinal banking data. The study uses both cross-sectional (bank-wise) and time-series (year-wise) data to analyse the relationships within a panel data framework. Panel data regressions provide a more efficient manner of estimating due to their ability to control for individual heterogeneity, as well as ability to capture dynamic (time-based) changes in relationships over time.

The primary techniques of analysis used in this study are the Fixed Effects (FE) model, which controls for unobservable, time-invariant bank-specific characteristics that could affect risk-taking and competitiveness (e.g. managerial ability; governance; long-term strategic plans), and the Random Effects (RE) model, which assumes that individual-specific characteristics exist at random among banks and are not correlated with the explanatory variable(s) (which allows for greater efficiency of estimating coefficients if this assumption is met).

To determine whether the FE or RE model is more appropriate, the Hausman specification test was used to evaluate whether or not the individual-specific characteristics were correlated with the regressor(s).

In light of the possibility of heteroskedasticity (variance of errors depending on the value of the predictor variable) and serial correlation (error terms correlated at different time intervals) in panel data, all regression estimates were computed using robust standard errors that address both non-constant variance as well as autocorrelation, in order to increase the validity in hypothesis testing.

In order to test the hypotheses regarding the causal mechanism between green credit and bank competitiveness, a mediation model based on Baron & Kenny (1986) was implemented. The analysis consisted of three separate regression models to test the following: first, the direct effect of green credit on bank competitiveness; second, the effect of green credit on bank risk-taking behaviour; and third, the effect of bank risk-taking behaviour on bank competitiveness controlling for the influence of green credit. This stepwise approach enabled the identification of both direct and indirect relationships between the variables.

To evaluate the significance of the indirect relationship, the significance of the mediating effect of bank risk-taking behaviour as a result of receiving green credit was statistically examined using the Sobel Test. This test assesses whether the indirect path between green credit and bank competitiveness through bank risk-taking behaviour is statistically significant and thus increases the robustness of the mediation analysis and provides additional insights into the conduits through which sustainable lending practices lead to competitive outcomes for banks.

A combined use of panel regression models, diagnostic testing, robust estimators, and mediation analysis demonstrates strong methodological rigor, while providing a well-rounded analytical framework for estimating the effects of green credit on risk behaviour and competitive behaviour within the Indian banking sector.

OBJECTIVES

- To examine the impact of green credit on the competitiveness of Indian commercial banks.
- To analyse how green credit influences the risk-taking behaviour of banks in India.

ANALYSIS AND INTERPRETATION

Figure 1. Fixed Effects Model Interpretation

Dependent Variable: ASSET_LIABILITY_RATIO
Method: Panel Least Squares
Date: 02/06/26 Time: 13:44
Sample: 1 55
Periods included: 11
Cross-sections included: 5
Total panel (balanced) observations: 55

Variable	Coefficient	Std. Error	t-Statistic	Prob.
C	1.172335	0.197162	5.946039	0.0000
CAPITAL_ADEQUACY_RATIO	0.003898	0.002667	1.461518	0.1594
COST_TO_INCOME_RATIO	-0.055600	0.285027	-0.195070	0.8473
EQUITY_RATIO	1.60E-06	5.01E-06	0.319550	0.7526
EPS_GROWTH_RATE	-2.45E-05	3.57E-05	-0.685030	0.5012
INTERMEDIATE_BUSINESS_INCOME_	-0.194312	0.709508	-0.273869	0.7870
LIQUIDITY_RATIO	-0.184218	0.194461	-0.947326	0.3548
LOAN_TO_DEPOSIT_RATIO	-0.054675	0.068989	-0.792520	0.4374
NET_CASH_FLOW_TO_NET_PROFIT_R	-0.012268	0.005714	-2.147195	0.0442
NET_INTEREST_MARGIN	-0.228101	0.316181	-0.721426	0.4790
NON_INTEREST_INCOME	0.020140	0.012606	1.597685	0.1258
NET_PROFIT_GROWTH	1.91E-06	8.99E-06	0.211953	0.8343
NON_PERFORMING_LOAN_RATIO	-0.002254	0.003245	-0.694676	0.4953
OPERATING_PROFIT_MARGIN	-0.000350	0.001595	-0.219266	0.8287
RATIO_OF_NET_CASH_FLOW_TO_LIAB	0.077046	0.188425	0.408895	0.6870
PROVISION_COVERAGE_RATIO	-0.000283	0.000784	-0.360325	0.7224
RETURN_ON_NET_ASSETS	-0.201372	0.284472	-0.707879	0.4872
RETURN_ON_OPERATING_CASH_FLOW	3.97E-05	7.02E-05	0.566050	0.5777
RETURN_ON_TOTAL_ASSETS	1.942179	2.397907	0.809948	0.4275
REVENUE_GROWTH_RATE	0.000788	0.000716	1.099914	0.2844
TOTAL_ASSET_GROWTH_RATE	-0.000849	0.000741	-1.145493	0.2655

Effects Specification

Cross-section fixed (dummy variables)
Period fixed (dummy variables)

R-squared	0.712531	Mean dependent var	1.002300
Adjusted R-squared	0.223834	S.D. dependent var	0.011980
S.E. of regression	0.010555	Akaike info criterion	-6.003398
Sum squared resid	0.002228	Schwarz criterion	-4.728004
Log likelihood	200.0934	Hannan-Quinn criter.	-5.509419
F-statistic	1.458022	Durbin-Watson stat	2.023237
Prob(F-statistic)	0.188022		

Relying on fixed effect regression analysis of Asset Liability Ratio – dependent variable – as affected by the control of individual Bank Specific effects and Time Specific effects, the results indicate that the Capital Adequacy Ratio variable has had a significant (p-value of .0000) and positive (t-statistic of 5.9460) effect on the Asset Liability Ratio (coefficient of 1.1723), signifying that Banks that maintain higher levels of Capital Adequacy Ratio generally also have a better Asset to Liability position.

Conversely, the Net Cash Flow to Net Profit Ratio has had a negative (coefficient of -0.0123; p-value = 0.0442) and statistically significant effect on the Asset Liability Ratio, indicating that as one's Cash Flow has increased as compared to their Net Profit, this has a slightly negative impact on the Asset Liability ratio.

There were also a number of different independent variables variables in addition to Capital and Net Cash Flow to Net Profit Ratio, which were assessed for their effect on the Asset Liability Ratio. These other Independent variables include: Liquidity Ratio (-0.1842; p = 0.3548); Loan to Deposit Ratio (-0.05471; p = 0.4374); Cost to Income Ratio (-0.05560; p = 0.8473); and Equity Ratio (0.000002; p = 0.7526), which based on the Fixed Effects Model and the corresponding p-values of these independent variables, it can be interpreted that each of these Independent variables have weak individual effects on the Asset Liability Ratio.

Profitability variables such as: ROA on Net Assets (-0.2014; p = 0.4872); ROA on Total Assets (1.9422; p = 0.4275); ROA on Operating Profit Margin (-0.00036; p = 0.8287); and Growth variables such as: Revenue Growth Rate (0.000788; p = 0.2844); and Total Asset Growth Rate (-0.000849; p = 0.2655), have all been statistically insignificant in their prediction of the Asset Liability Ratio.

The R-squared value of 0.7125 indicates that about 71% of the variation in asset liability ratio is explained by the model. However, the F-statistic (1.4580) with a p-value of 0.1880 suggests that the overall model is not statistically significant. The Durbin-Watson statistic of 2.0232 indicates the absence of autocorrelation in the residuals.

Figure 2. Pooled OLS Regression

Dependent Variable: RETURN_ON_TOTAL_ASSETS
Method: Panel Least Squares
Date: 02/06/26 Time: 13:39
Sample: 1 55
Periods included: 11
Cross-sections included: 5
Total panel (balanced) observations: 55

Variable	Coefficient	Std. Error	t-Statistic	Prob.
C	0.025812	0.074290	0.347448	0.7297
CAPITAL_ADEQUACY_RAT	0.002526	0.000377	6.697652	0.0000
ASSET_LIABILITY_RATIO	-0.052039	0.072698	-0.715827	0.4775
LOAN_TO_DEPOSIT_RATIO	-0.005697	0.010582	-0.538381	0.5928
LIQUIDITY_RATIO	-0.003351	0.003456	-0.969829	0.3369
NET_PROFIT_GROWTH	-1.43E-06	7.34E-07	-1.947498	0.0572

R-squared	0.557485	Mean dependent var	0.009047
Adjusted R-squared	0.512330	S.D. dependent var	0.008286
S.E. of regression	0.005786	Akaike info criterion	-7.364032
Sum squared resid	0.001640	Schwarz criterion	-7.145051
Log likelihood	208.5109	Hannan-Quinn criter.	-7.279350
F-statistic	12.34613	Durbin-Watson stat	0.608442
Prob(F-statistic)	0.000000		

Using pooled Ordinary Least Squares (OLS) regression, we can assess how bank-level variables impact profitability through the relationship between profit on total assets and bank-specific factors. The OLS estimates show that the capital adequacy ratio is positive (0.0258); however, it has a low level of certainty (t-statistic = 0.3474, p-value = 0.7297) regarding this impact on profit. We also see a negative coefficient (–0.0520) from the asset to liability ratio; however, this value was also determined to have a low level of certainty (p-value = 0.4775). Although the loan-to-deposit ratio has a positive coefficient (0.0566), this value is not statistically sufficient (p-value = 0.5928) to say that the bank's interest income will be impacted positively through the loan-to-deposit ratio; therefore, we are unable to conclude that loans will positively impact banks, which also implies a weak correlation between loans and bank profitability. Additionally, the liquidity ratio had a negative coefficient (–0.0031) and was determined to have no significant influence (p-value = 0.9388) on profitability and an excess of liquid assets do not have a significant influence on profitability. Similarly, the coefficient for the net profit growth (–1.43E-06) is also negative and marginally significant (t-statistic = –1.9475, p-value = 0.0572), suggesting that the short-term growth in profits does not guarantee that the bank will achieve greater returns on its assets. Overall, the model explains approximately 55.75% of the variance in return on total assets (R^2 = 0.5575) and that all of the coefficients in the OLS are statistically significant as evidenced by the F-statistic of 12.3461 (p-value = 0.0000). However, the Durbin-Watson statistic (0.6084) indicates that there is possibly autocorrelation among errors of the regression model, thus limiting the validity of the pooled OLS results.

Figure 3. Panel Correlation Analysis

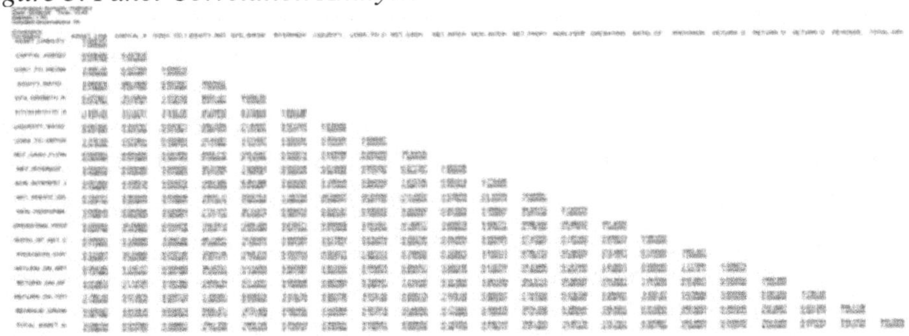

The panel correlation matrix demonstrates how well the variables used in this research relate to one another. Overall, most of the correlation coefficients indicate a low to moderate degree of correlation between all explanatory variables, which imply that there is not a significant issue with multicollinearity between any explanatory variable. Return on total assets has a very mild positive correlation with Capital Adequacy Ratio (approx. 0.14) and liquidity ratio (approx. 0.06); these positive correlations suggest weak positive relationships exist between profitability as measured by return on total assets and the capital adequacy ratio and liquidity. The correlation coefficient between return on total assets and loan-to-deposit ratio is slightly negatively correlated (approx. -0.11), which suggests an inverse relationship although not a very strong one.

Many other variables display relatively low correlation coefficients. An example includes Capital Adequacy Ratio and Asset Liability Ratio, which indicate a rather weak correlation coefficient (approx. -0.21), while liquidity ratio and loan-to-deposit ratio also exhibit a mildly positive correlation (approx. 0.14). None of the correlation coefficients exceed the general guideline correlation coefficient of 0.80, therefore it can be concluded that no significant level of multicollinearity exists among the set of selected variables. In summation, the correlation analysis indicates that there is no reason why the selected variable set cannot be used together in the regression model without producing estimate or reliability issues.

IMPLICATIONS

1. Managerial Implications

The findings of this research will have widespread impact on bank managers who are providing green credit or are considering incorporating green credit into their product lines. Bank managers should view green credit as more than just compliance with regulatory requirements. They should consider green credit a strategic long-term investment that increases a bank's competitiveness, enhances a bank's image in the marketplace, and positions a bank to be a leader in sustainable finance. Research indicates that green lending increases a bank's environmental credibility, attracts environmentally-conscious customers, and creates distinctiveness in a market that is increasingly shaped by environmental, social and governance (ESG) concerns. Bank managers should therefore include green financing as a component of their institution's overall strategy by allocating resources in the budget for green projects; ensuring that the bank's internal business operations align with national and international environmental objectives; and including green goals in the underwriting and performance evaluation criteria for bank employees. As a result of the growing association between environmental risk, financial risk, and regulatory risk, it is becoming increasingly vital for banks to enhance their environmental risk assessment capabilities. According to the author, the incorporation of environmental, social, and governance (ESG) scoring systems into traditional credit evaluations along with climate-related risk assessments of borrowers' carbon footprint and compliance with regulations during the evaluation of credit applications will require creating new departments of sustainable finance with staff comprised of these professionals, as well as project finance experts and climate risk professionals who are familiar with complex technical aspects of green financing. This new structure will allow organizations to integrate their environmental auditing functions, monitor the progress of their financed projects, maintain close working relationships with related government agencies, such as the Reserve Bank of India (RBI) and Securities and Exchange Board of India (SEBI), as well as environmental ministries and green certification and rating agencies, to help adapt to changing environmental regulations and maximize the benefits of government incentive programs. According to the author, among other things, the costs associated with implementing green credit programs should also be a consideration for managers, as the initial outlay will be higher due to regulatory and compliance costs over the short term, although technological advancements will continue to reduce both compliance and regulatory costs on an ongoing basis. Innovative technologies like analytics driven by AI (Artificial Intelligence), satellite data and satellite access transparency based on the blockchain, Internet of Things (IoT) devices for environmental observation; should provide management the tools necessaryto efficiently monitor their ecosystems and enable systems to become sustainable and scalable. Management can also enhance their product offerings and create additional sustainable financial products, such as 'green bonds', 'green mortgages' and 'renewable energy financing', as well as providing loans with sustainability metrics and GreenMSME Credit as some examples. Diversification provides companies access to fast growth sectors associated with 'green' or environmentally stressed products including Renewable Energy, EV's, Sustainable Agriculture, and the Circular Economy. The long term is important for management to think about and consider when evaluating a financial product's initial costs relative to the long-term benefits i.e. (decreased NPL, increased Z-score, reduced default, and increased financial stability). Additionally, transparent ESG reporting (Environmental, Social, and Governance) will build trust and create a competitive advantage for banks; thus providing banks with the necessary resources to operate effectively. Finally, these Management Implications illustrate that Financial Institutions must move towards Strategic Green Lending/Financial Institution Models that create a structure for identifying risk/technology and institutional integration to maximize profitability and long-term sustainability.

2. Social Implications

The economic benefits of Green Credit are one aspect of a comprehensive study. The study also uncovered overlays from Green Credit to the greater society; i.e., it affects Community Development, Public Health, The Environment, and long-term Economic Resilience. By creating opportunities for the financing of environmentally based companies, banks are providing a vehicle for Environmental Stewardship and Climate Action. By providing loans to companies for the purpose of funding Clean Energy Sources, Pollution-Cleaning Technologies, Green Manufacturing Methods, Sustainable Agriculture, and Energy Efficient Infrastructure, banks are enabling these companies to reduce their carbon footprint and create healthier environments through healthier homes, improved Air and water quality, and better protected Natural Ecosystems resulting in significant Positive Public Health Effects such as decreasing rates of Respiratory Illnesses, improved availability of Safe Drinking Water, improved affordability of healthcare, and improved overall standard of living for various Societal Segments (especially at-risk segments that live adjacent to industrialized areas or high rates of pollution). In addition, by providing institutional loans conditional on Environmental Compliance and Pollution Management, banks promote an Ethical Business Practice by holding companies accountable for their actions toward the environment. By encouraging these types of practices across all sectors, this shift will lead to greater public trust in corporate entities and the financial system, as well as a commitment to acting in an ecologically responsible manner. When combined with the benefits associated with sustainable development, such as eco-housing, green buildings, electric vehicle charging stations, renewable energy systems, water conservation, and waste minimization, green lending will yield both environmental and social benefits. All of these efforts can be enhanced or expanded upon through the lending programs supported by green credit. Therefore, green credit will create employment opportunities within the new and growing green sectors such as solar manufacturing, environmental consultancy, sustainable construction, electric vehicle charging infrastructure, and green entrepreneurship, leading to economic growth and the creation of new skills within our communities. The adoption of stronger risk management practices and improved compliance processes has fostered greater competition and financial strength among Banks therefore increasing the resilience of the Financial System as a whole and benefitting Society through increased protection for depositors, reduced Systemic Risk and providing reliable sources of lending. Examples of Nationally committed sustainability obligations supported by Green Finance include the Paris Agreement, the Sustainable Development Goals (SDG), the National Action Plan for Climate Change (NAPCC), and India's Long-Term Net Zero Goals. In all of these contexts, Green Finance is no longer just a financial Product, but a Catalyst for creating substantial changes in our Society towards a Low Carbon Economy; facilitating Inclusive and Equitable Growth and building Long-Term Environmental Sustainability.

CONCLUSION

The empirical and theoretical results of this study strongly suggest that Green Credit is becoming a strategically important tool for enhancing the competitiveness, stability, and long-term sustainability of Indian Banks. This study successfully reinforces the idea that Green Credit has multiple uses in the banking sector, including as a risk-management tool, competitive strategy, and policy transmission mechanism; in addition to providing traditional functions of credit as merely a financial intermediary (i.e., lending money).

The empirical findings show that banks providing Green Loans have greater balance sheet strength and financial resilience, which can be attributed primarily to improved capital adequacy ratios, a higher degree of asset-liability management, and a lower risk profile. Although there is some variability in the short-term profitability effects associated with Grant loans (due primarily to higher initial costs, longer time to completion of projects, and transitional efficiency losses), there appears to be a favourable long-term impact on profitability from providing Green Loans. The long-term benefits of Green Loans (e.g., reduced exposure to non-performing loans, improved stability indicators, and enhanced corporate reputation) provide evidence in support of the view that Green Loans help improve the competitive position of Indian Banks.

This research has greatly contributed to understanding how bank risk-taking behaviour is a critical method of examination between green credit and competitiveness, as it relates to banks' risk appetite and discipline when lending. Green credit has shown to influence banks' competitiveness through more than just revenue diversification, but by way of altering how banks define risk and their approach to lending.

Institutions implementing environmental screening processes, ESG-based credit assessment processes, and sustainability-linked monitoring processes will be able to better align profitability with stability, thereby supporting both financial soundness and competitiveness.

The research shows that there is significant variability amongst banking types in India. Large public sector banks, private sector banks, and banks that have greater capital bases, robust and transparent governance structures, and that align with regulatory practices are in a better position to absorb short-term costs of green lending, while ultimately having long-term competitive advantages. Smaller banking institutions, which are often found in less secure policy or disclosure environments, face more transitional challenges towards adopting inclusive green finance, highlighting the need for regulatory assistance, greater transparency, and capacity building in order to facilitate the broader adoption of green finance.

The evidence suggests that green credit is a good way for banks to achieve their own results as well as increase the overall economic resiliency and well-being (social and environmental) of a community. In addition, by providing incentives for banks to invest in environmentally-friendly projects, green credit helps reduce the risks associated with climate change, allows for ongoing sustainable development and supports the achievement of national and global sustainability objectives. Additionally, through enhanced risk management and transparency through enhanced disclosures by banks, systemic risks are reduced, which in turn will benefit depositors, regulators and the economy in general.

That being said, the findings of this study suggest that there remain many gaps regarding the applicability of these findings across different countries, the existence of universally accepted definitions for green credit, and the problem of reconciling short-term profitability with long-term sustainability. Future studies must continue to explore various policy intervention methods and criteria for creating harmonised green taxonomies, and for establishing standards or metrics for measuring the quality of disclosure standards to develop an improved understanding of the causal relationships between the variables studied.

REFERENCES

Andrieş, A. M., Ongena, S., & Sprincean, N. (2025). Sectoral credit allocation and systemic risk. *Journal of Financial Stability*, *76*, 101363. DOI: 10.1016/j.jfs.2024.101363

Aruleba, I., & Sun, Y. (2025). Enhanced credit risk prediction using deep learning and SMOTE-ENN resampling. *Machine Learning with Applications*, *21*, 100692. DOI: 10.1016/j.mlwa.2025.100692

Balana, B. B., Mekonnen, D., Haile, B., Hagos, F., Yimam, S., & Ringler, C. (2022). Demand and supply constraints of credit in smallholder farming: Evidence from Ethiopia and Tanzania. *World Development*, *159*, 106033. DOI: 10.1016/j.worlddev.2022.106033

Balana, B. B., & Oyeyemi, M. A. (2022). Agricultural credit constraints in smallholder farming in developing countries: Evidence from Nigeria. *World Development Sustainability*, *1*, 100012. DOI: 10.1016/j.wds.2022.100012

Ben-Nasr, H., Masry, S., Masum, A. A., & Ouni, Z. (2025). Carbon risk and trade credit. *International Review of Economics & Finance*, *103*, 104425. DOI: 10.1016/j.iref.2025.104425

. C-Rella, J., Martinez Rego, D., & Vilar, J. M. (2025). Cost-sensitive reinforcement learning for credit risk.

Czura, K., & Klonner, S. (2023). Financial market responses to a natural disaster: Evidence from credit networks and the Indian Ocean tsunami. *Journal of Development Economics*, *160*, 102996. DOI: 10.1016/j.jdeveco.2022.102996

Djatche, M. J. N. (2025). Unveiling the effects of monetary surprises: Risk-taking and credit supply of US banks. *International Review of Economics & Finance*, *101*, 104211. DOI: 10.1016/j.iref.2025.104211

Fernández Rodríguez, F., Gómez-Puig, M., & Sosvilla Rivero, S. (2025). Examining the transmission of credit and liquidity risks: A network analysis for EMU sovereign debt markets. *IREA–Working Papers, 2025, IR25/04.*

Fingerman, K., Geronimo, C., Read, E., Wakeman, D., & Martin, J. I. (2025). Risks of crediting carbon offsets in low carbon fuel standards: Lessons learned from dairy biomethane. *Energy Policy*, *206*, 114738. DOI: 10.1016/j.enpol.2025.114738

. Galletta, S. (2024). A PRISMA systematic review of greenwashing in the banking industry: impacts on consumer trust and regulatory implications. *Journal of Banking & Finance Studies* (systematic review).

Gómez González, J. E., Uribe, J., & Valencia, O. M. (2024). Asymmetric sovereign risk: Implications for climate change preparation (IDB-WP-1588). *IDB Working Paper Series*.

Hamm, L. S., Martínez, S. Á. O., Loder, A., & Bogenberger, K. (2025). Who Gets What? A user perspective on initial credit allocation in Tradable Mobility Credit Schemes. *Transport Policy*, *164*, 118–129. DOI: 10.1016/j.tranpol.2025.01.032

Hernanz, V., Quiroga, S., Suárez, C., & Aguiño, J. E. (2025). Evaluating the merit of carbon credits: Effectiveness in transitioning to REDD+ community incentives. *Environmental and Sustainability Indicators*, *25*, 100591. DOI: 10.1016/j.indic.2025.100591

Heß, V. L., & Damasio, B. (2025). Machine learning in banking risk management: Mapping a decade of evolution. *International Journal of Information Management Data Insights*, *5*(1), 100324. DOI: 10.1016/j.jjimei.2025.100324

. Huang, F. (2025). Green credit, monetary policy, and bank risk-taking. *Journal of Financial Stability* / ScienceDirect listing (empirical panel analysis of green credit and bank risk-taking behaviors).earch.

James, E. O., Bakas, D., Thompson, P., & Ebireri, J. (2025). Who Benefits the Most from Micro-Credit? Micro-Level Evidence from Sub-Saharan Africa. *World Development*, *193*, 107023. DOI: 10.1016/j.worlddev.2025.107023

Kladakis, G., & Skouralis, A. (2025). Sovereign credit rating downgrades and Growth-at-Risk. *Journal of International Financial Markets, Institutions and Money*, *103*, 102195. DOI: 10.1016/j.intfin.2025.102195

Liu, B., Ren, B., & Jin, F. (2024). *Does Climate Risk Affect the Ease of Access to Credit for Farmers? Evidence from Chfs*. Evidence from Chfs. DOI: 10.2139/ssrn.4951698

Mallappa, V. K. H., Gadde, S., & Cariappa, A. A. (2025). Understanding farmers' trust in stakeholders of carbon credit projects: A perception-based analysis. *Current Research in Environmental Sustainability*, *10*, 100317. DOI: 10.1016/j.crsust.2025.100317

. Marimpi, M., Barr, B., Baxter, A., Hugh-Jones, S., Taylor-Robinson, D., Katikireddi, S. V., ... & Wickham, S. (2025). Estimating population mental health effects of the rollout of Universal Credit in the UK using DID analysis, 2009–2019. *Public Health*.

Martínez, S. Á. O., Schatzman, T., Loder, A., Axhausen, K. W., & Bogenberger, K. (2025). Mode choice behavior in a tradable mobility credit scheme: A stated-preference experiment. *Transportation Research Part A, Policy and Practice*, *199*, 104570. DOI: 10.1016/j.tra.2025.104570

Motta, S., Böck, I., Koehler, J., Wolf, A. T., & Pattberg, P. (2025). The financialization of rivers: CDM-subsidized hydropower in the Mekong Region's basins at risk. *Global Environmental Change*, *90*, 102962. DOI: 10.1016/j.gloenvcha.2024.102962

. Schoenmaker, D. (2017/2019). *From Risk to Opportunity: A Framework for Sustainable Finance* / Follow-up working papers on greening monetary policy and sustainable finance frameworks. (Framework and policy levers discussed; see Schoenmaker for conceptual framing).

Seidu, A. R. A., Mumin, Y. A., & Abukari, A. B. T. (2025). Does peers' credit behavior affect smallholder farmers' credit and savings decisions? Evidence from the northern region of Ghana. *Social Sciences & Humanities Open*, *11*, 101215. DOI: 10.1016/j.ssaho.2024.101215

Tan, W., Huang, Y., Chen, X. H., & Gatto, A. (2025). Green credit policy and energy consumption intensity in China: Firm-level evidence and insights. *Journal of Environmental Management*, *373*, 123664. DOI: 10.1016/j.jenvman.2024.123664 PMID: 39729718

Tribuvan, S., Kamath, S. D., Mishra, S., M, U., J, S., H L, G., P, D., & S A, K. (2025). Performance Evaluation of Advanced Classification Models Combined with Feature Selection for Credit Risk Performance. *Procedia Computer Science*, *258*, 278–287. DOI: 10.1016/j.procs.2025.04.265

Waidelich, P., Krug, J., & Steffen, B. (2025). Mobilizing credit for clean energy: De-risking and public loan provision under learning spillovers. *Journal of Environmental Economics and Management*, *133*, 103222. DOI: 10.1016/j.jeem.2025.103222

Wang, Z., Bian, B., & Wang, J. (2025). Influence of Green Credit Policy on Corporate Risk- Taking. [MDPI]. *Sustainability (Basel)*, *17*(7), 2862. DOI: 10.3390/su17072862

Xiao-Li, G., Zhuo-Cheng, W., Xiong, X., & Wei, Z. (2025). Research on sovereign credit and international banking industry tail risk contagion----Perspective from double-layer complex network. *International Review of Economics & Finance*, *99*, 103992. DOI: 10.1016/j.iref.2025.103992

Yao, J., & Fan, J. (2025). The impact of policy uncertainty and risk taking on the credit resource allocation of urban commercial banks. *International Review of Economics & Finance*, *97*, 103766. DOI: 10.1016/j.iref.2024.103766

Zambrano, A. F., Giraldo, L. F., Perdomo, M. T., Hernández, I. D., & Godoy, J. M. (2023). Rotating savings and credit associations: A scoping review. *World Development Sustainability*, *3*, 100081. DOI: 10.1016/j.wds.2023.100081

Zhou, C. (2025). Enhancing credit risk assessment with AutoML: A case study of bank marketing and customer data. *Procedia Computer Science*, *266*, 1184–1191. DOI: 10.1016/j.procs.2025.08.146

Chapter 11
Financial Innovation and the Role of Fintech in Sustainable Finance

G. SudhaAnanthi
http://orcid.org/0009-0001-5062-5311
Winners Academy, India

ABSTRACT

Fintech has emerged as a powerful engine driving the creation and evolution of sustainable financial ecosystems by reshaping how financial services are designed, delivered, and governed in an increasingly interconnected world. At its core, fintech integrates digital technologies such as artificial intelligence, blockchain, big data analytics, cloud computing, and mobile platforms into financial systems, enabling greater efficiency, transparency, inclusivity, and resilience. These capabilities directly support sustainability by reducing operational costs, lowering environmental footprints through paperless and branch-light models, and expanding access to financial services for underserved populations, including low-income households, small and medium enterprises (SMEs), rural communities, and informal sector participants. Through digital payments, mobile banking, micro-lending platforms, and alternative credit scoring models that rely on non-traditional data, fintech bridges long-standing gaps in financial inclusion.

FINTECH AS THE ENGINE OF SUSTAINABLE FINANCIAL ECOSYSTEMS

Fintech has emerged as a powerful engine driving the creation and evolution of sustainable financial ecosystems by reshaping how financial services are designed,

DOI: 10.4018/979-8-3373-8392-7.ch011

delivered, and governed in an increasingly interconnected world. At its core, fintech integrates digital technologies such as artificial intelligence, blockchain, big data analytics, cloud computing, and mobile platforms into financial systems, enabling greater efficiency, transparency, inclusivity, and resilience. These capabilities directly support sustainability by reducing operational costs, lowering environmental footprints through paperless and branch-light models, and expanding access to financial services for underserved populations, including low-income households, small and medium enterprises (SMEs), rural communities, and informal sector participants. Through digital payments, mobile banking, micro-lending platforms, and alternative credit scoring models that rely on non-traditional data, fintech bridges long-standing gaps in financial inclusion, empowering individuals and businesses to participate more fully in economic activity. This inclusive growth strengthens the social pillar of sustainability by promoting equitable access to capital, encouraging entrepreneurship, and enhancing household financial resilience against shocks such as health emergencies, climate events, or economic downturns. From an environmental perspective, fintech supports sustainable finance by facilitating green investments, climate-aligned lending, and impact measurement. Digital platforms make it easier to channel funds into renewable energy projects, sustainable agriculture, clean transportation, and energy-efficient infrastructure, while blockchain and distributed ledger technologies enhance traceability and accountability in green bonds, carbon credit markets, and supply-chain finance.

Real-time data analytics enable financial institutions and regulators to assess environmental, social, and governance (ESG) risks more accurately, price them into financial products, and monitor compliance with sustainability standards. At the ecosystem level, fintech fosters collaboration among banks, non-bank financial institutions, startups, regulators, governments, and development agencies, creating interoperable networks that are more adaptive and innovation-friendly than traditional siloed systems. Open banking frameworks, application programming interfaces (APIs), and platform-based business models encourage competition and co-creation, leading to customer-centric solutions that align profitability with long-term societal value. Automated reporting, real-time transaction monitoring, and advanced analytics reduce systemic risks and increase trust in financial systems, which is essential for sustainable development. However, the role of fintech as an engine of sustainable financial ecosystems also depends on responsible innovation, robust data protection, ethical AI practices, and inclusive regulatory frameworks that balance innovation with consumer protection and systemic safety. Addressing challenges such as digital divides, cybersecurity risks, algorithmic bias, and the environmental impact of energy-intensive technologies is critical to ensuring that fintech contributes positively to long-term sustainability goals. When aligned with sound policy, strong institutions, and sustainability-oriented investment strategies, fintech has the transformative potential to move financial systems beyond short-term profit maximisation toward resilient, inclusive, and environmentally responsible ecosystems that support sustainable economic growth and shared prosperity over the long run.

DIGITAL PAYMENTS POWERING CARBON-NEUTRAL TRANSACTIONS

Digital payments have become a foundational pillar in the global transition toward carbon-neutral economic systems, reshaping how value is exchanged while significantly reducing the environmental footprint of financial transactions. By replacing cash-based and paper-intensive processes with electronic, mobile, and cloud-enabled payment infrastructures, digital payments eliminate the need for physical currency production, transportation, storage, and security, all of which consume energy and generate greenhouse gas emissions. The lifecycle of cash—from minting coins and printing banknotes to distributing them through armoured transport and maintaining cash-handling infrastructure—carries a substantial carbon cost that is largely invisible to consumers. Digital payment systems, by contrast, operate through virtual networks that dramatically reduce material usage, streamline transaction flows, and enable real-time settlement, making them inherently more energy-efficient and environmentally sustainable when supported by responsible data-centre management and renewable energy sources (Xu J., et al, 2025). As economies increasingly adopt contactless cards, mobile wallets, QR-based payments, and instant payment platforms, the cumulative reduction in emissions from dematerialisation becomes a meaningful contributor to broader climate-mitigation efforts. Beyond efficiency gains, digital payments actively enable carbon-neutral transactions by embedding sustainability intelligence directly into payment ecosystems.

Advanced data analytics and artificial intelligence allow payment platforms to measure, estimate, and disclose the carbon footprint associated with individual transactions, products, or merchants. Consumers can receive real-time insights into the environmental impact of their spending, empowering them to make more sustainable purchasing decisions. Some digital payment providers integrate carbon calculators and offset mechanisms that automatically channel a portion of transaction value toward verified carbon-offset projects such as reforestation, renewable energy generation, or community-based climate adaptation initiatives (Yang J., et al, 2022). This seamless integration transforms sustainability from an abstract concept into a tangible, everyday action, where each transaction becomes an opportunity to support climate goals without requiring additional effort from users. Digital payments also play a critical role in supporting low-carbon business models and green value chains. E-commerce platforms, subscription services, shared mobility, and digital marketplaces rely on frictionless payment systems to function at scale, reducing the need for physical storefronts, travel, and inventory waste. In supply chains, digital payments linked with digital invoicing and smart contracts improve transparency and traceability, enabling businesses to verify sustainable sourcing, fair labour practices, and emissions performance across suppliers. When combined with blockchain or distributed ledger technologies, payment records can serve as immutable proof of sustainable transactions, strengthening trust among buyers, sellers, regulators, and investors. This transparency is particularly important for green finance instruments, such as carbon credits and renewable energy certificates, where credibility and accurate accounting are essential to prevent greenwashing and ensure real environmental impact.

The environmental benefits of digital payments are further amplified when payment networks commit to decarbonising their own operations. Many payment processors, fintech firms, and financial institutions are increasingly adopting renewable energy for data centres, optimising transaction processing to reduce energy intensity, and setting net-zero targets across their value chains. Cloud-based architectures enable dynamic scaling, reducing idle capacity and energy waste compared to legacy on-premise systems. Innovations such as edge computing and energy-efficient encryption algorithms further lower the carbon intensity of digital transactions. As industry standards evolve, sustainability metrics are becoming integral to payment system design, procurement, and governance, reinforcing the role of digital payments as enablers of low-carbon finance rather than contributors to environmental degradation (Dar B I., et al, 2025). However, realising the full potential of digital payments in powering carbon-neutral transactions requires addressing important challenges.

The rapid growth of digital transaction volumes increases demand for data storage, network connectivity, and cybersecurity, all of which have environmental implications if powered by fossil fuels or inefficient infrastructure. Ensuring equitable access to digital payment systems is also essential, as digital divides based on income, geography, age, or digital literacy can exclude vulnerable populations from the benefits of sustainable finance. Robust regulatory frameworks, transparent reporting standards, and responsible innovation are necessary to ensure that carbon-tracking claims are accurate, offsets are credible, and consumer data is protected. Collaboration among payment providers, regulators, technology firms, and environmental organisations is crucial to harmonise methodologies for carbon accounting and to scale solutions that deliver measurable climate impact (Kouam A W F., et al, 2024). In sum, digital payments are far more than a convenient alternative to cash; they are a strategic enabler of carbon-neutral transactions and sustainable economic behaviour. By reducing the material and energy intensity of financial exchanges, embedding carbon awareness into everyday spending, supporting green business models, and enabling inclusive participation in climate-aligned finance, digital payments align the flow of money with the imperatives of environmental sustainability. When powered by clean energy, guided by ethical data practices, and supported by forward-looking policy, digital payment ecosystems can transform billions of daily transactions into cumulative climate action, helping economies move steadily toward net-zero goals while maintaining efficiency, inclusivity, and trust in the financial system.

BLOCKCHAIN FOR TRANSPARENT CLIMATE-IMPACT REPORTING

Blockchain technology is increasingly recognised as a transformative tool for transparent and credible climate-impact reporting, addressing long-standing challenges of trust, data fragmentation, and verification that have limited the effectiveness of sustainability disclosures. Climate-impact reporting requires the accurate collection, aggregation, and communication of data related to greenhouse gas emissions, resource consumption, mitigation actions, and adaptation outcomes across complex value chains. Traditional reporting systems often rely on centralised databases, manual audits, and self-reported metrics, which can be costly, slow, and vulnerable to errors, inconsistencies, or intentional manipulation (Prawitasari P P., et al, 2025). Blockchain introduces a decentralised, tamper-resistant ledger that records climate-related data in an immutable and time-stamped manner, ensuring that once information is verified and entered, it cannot be altered retroactively without detection. This foundational feature directly enhances the credibility of climate disclosures, enabling stakeholders to trace reported impacts back to their source and build confidence in the integrity of sustainability claims. Blockchain-based systems are particularly valuable in carbon markets and climate finance, where transparency and trust are essential. In voluntary and compliance carbon markets, blockchain can be used to issue, track, and retire carbon credits with clear provenance, preventing double-counting and fraud.

Each credit can be uniquely identified and linked to verified mitigation activities, such as reforestation projects, renewable energy installations, or methane capture initiatives, along with supporting documentation and monitoring data. When credits are transferred or retired, the transaction is permanently recorded on the ledger, providing a transparent audit trail for regulators, investors, and civil society (Woo J., et al, 2021). This improved integrity strengthens market confidence, encourages greater participation, and ensures that reported emissions reductions correspond to real and measurable climate benefits. From a governance and regulatory perspective, blockchain enhances the alignment of climate-impact reporting with evolving disclosure standards and policy requirements. As governments and international bodies introduce more stringent climate-reporting frameworks, such as mandatory emissions disclosures and taxonomy-based sustainability classifications, blockchain can serve as a scalable infrastructure for compliance. Regulators and supervisors can be granted permissioned access to relevant data, enabling real-time oversight, risk assessment, and enforcement while reducing reporting burdens on organisations. For investors, standardised and verifiable climate-impact data improves the comparability of ESG metrics across firms and sectors, supporting more accurate pricing of climate risks and opportunities. This transparency helps shift capital toward low-carbon and climate-resilient activities, reinforcing the financial incentives for sustainable behaviour.

Despite its potential, the use of blockchain for climate-impact reporting must be implemented responsibly to ensure alignment with sustainability goals. Concerns about the energy consumption of certain blockchain networks, particularly those using energy-intensive consensus mechanisms, have raised questions about their environmental footprint (Chornovol O., et al, 2022). However, the rapid adoption of energy-efficient consensus models, permissioned blockchains, and renewable-powered infrastructure significantly mitigates these concerns. Equally important are issues of data quality, interoperability, and standardisation. Blockchain can ensure data immutability and traceability, but it does not automatically guarantee that the underlying data is accurate or meaningful. Robust methodologies, trusted data sources, third-party verification, and alignment with recognised climate-reporting standards are essential to maximise the value of blockchain-enabled transparency. In conclusion, blockchain offers a powerful foundation for transparent, trustworthy, and scalable climate-impact reporting in an era of heightened environmental accountability (Rehman M A., et al, 2025). By providing immutable records, end-to-end traceability, automated verification, and multi-stakeholder access, blockchain addresses critical weaknesses in traditional reporting systems and supports more credible climate disclosures. When combined with energy-efficient technologies, sound governance, and standardised measurement frameworks, blockchain can transform climate-impact reporting from a retrospective compliance exercise into a dynamic, real-time system of accountability. This transformation not only strengthens trust among regulators, investors, and the public but also accelerates collective action toward climate goals by ensuring that decisions are grounded in reliable and transparent environmental data.

AI-DRIVEN CREDIT SCORING EXPANDING GREEN MICRO-LOANS

AI-driven credit scoring is rapidly transforming the landscape of green micro-finance by enabling financial institutions to extend small, sustainability-oriented loans to individuals and micro-enterprises that have traditionally been excluded from formal credit systems. Conventional credit assessment models rely heavily on historical financial records, collateral, and standardised credit bureau data, which are often unavailable or incomplete for low-income households, informal workers, and rural entrepreneurs. As a result, many potential borrowers with viable green business ideas—such as installing solar home systems, adopting clean cooking solutions, investing in water-efficient irrigation, or transitioning to climate-resilient livelihoods—are denied access to capital (Ebenezer Y., et al, 2026). AI-driven credit scoring addresses this gap by leveraging machine learning algorithms and alternative data sources, including mobile payment histories, utility usage patterns, transaction behaviour, satellite imagery, social network data, and even agronomic or environmental indicators. By analysing these diverse data points, AI models can generate more accurate and dynamic assessments of creditworthiness, enabling lenders to identify trustworthy borrowers who would otherwise remain invisible to traditional banking systems. The expansion of green micro-loans through AI-based credit scoring has significant implications for environmental sustainability and inclusive economic development. Microloans targeted at green activities often require relatively small amounts of capital but deliver outsized environmental and social benefits. For example, financing solar lanterns or rooftop solar systems reduces reliance on fossil fuels and improves household energy security, while loans for efficient cookstoves lower indoor air pollution and reduce deforestation.

AI-driven risk assessment allows lenders to price these loans more appropriately by aligning interest rates and repayment terms with the borrower's actual risk profile rather than broad demographic assumptions. This precision reduces default rates, lowers the cost of capital, and makes green micro-finance commercially viable at scale (Fernandez-Vallado M., et al, 2025). As a result, financial institutions and fintech platforms are more willing to allocate resources to sustainability-linked micro-lending, creating a virtuous cycle in which environmental impact and financial performance reinforce each other. At the operational level, AI-powered credit scoring enhances speed, scalability, and adaptability in micro-loan delivery. Automated decision-making systems can evaluate loan applications in near real time, significantly reducing processing times and administrative costs compared to manual underwriting. This efficiency is particularly important in low-margin micro-finance contexts, where high transaction costs have historically limited outreach. By continuously learning from new data, AI models can update risk assessments as borrower circumstances change, allowing lenders to offer flexible repayment schedules, top-up loans, or early refinancing for borrowers who demonstrate positive environmental and financial performance. In green micro-lending, this adaptability supports long-term behaviour change, as borrowers are incentivised to maintain sustainable practices to access better financing terms over time.

From a systemic perspective, AI-enabled green micro-lending contributes to broader financial inclusion and climate-transition goals. By unlocking credit for underserved populations, it empowers communities to participate actively in the green economy rather than being passive recipients of climate policies or aid. Small entrepreneurs can build sustainable businesses, households can invest in clean technologies that lower long-term costs, and rural communities can adopt climate-smart practices that enhance resilience to environmental shocks (Okafor C M., et al, 2023). This bottom-up approach complements large-scale green finance initiatives by ensuring that the benefits of the low-carbon transition are widely distributed and socially equitable. However, the deployment of AI-driven credit scoring in green micro-finance also raises important ethical, technical, and regulatory considerations. The use of alternative data must be governed by robust data-protection and privacy frameworks to prevent misuse or exclusionary practices. Algorithmic bias is a critical risk, as models trained on skewed or incomplete data may inadvertently reinforce existing inequalities or disadvantage certain groups.

Transparency and explainability in AI decision-making are essential to ensure that borrowers understand how credit decisions are made and have avenues for appeal. In addition, digital divides in access to smartphones, connectivity, and digital literacy can limit the reach of AI-enabled lending unless accompanied by inclusive infrastructure and capacity-building initiatives. Regulators play a crucial role in setting standards for responsible AI use, consumer protection, and fair lending while allowing sufficient flexibility for innovation. In conclusion, AI-driven credit scoring serves as a powerful catalyst for expanding green micro-loans and advancing inclusive, sustainable development (Hossain N., et al, 2023). By redefining how creditworthiness is assessed, AI enables lenders to reach underserved borrowers, reduce risk, and scale financing for environmentally beneficial activities. When implemented with strong ethical safeguards, transparent governance, and alignment with sustainability objectives, AI-based credit scoring can transform green micro-finance into a resilient and impactful engine of climate action. Through millions of small loans that collectively drive emissions reductions, resource efficiency, and economic empowerment, AI-enabled green micro-lending demonstrates how advanced technology can translate global sustainability ambitions into tangible, community-level outcomes.

SMART CONTRACTS AUTOMATING SUSTAINABLE PROJECT FINANCING

Smart contracts are increasingly transforming sustainable project financing by automating complex financial processes, enhancing transparency, and aligning capital flows with environmental and social objectives. Built on blockchain or distributed ledger technologies, smart contracts are self-executing digital agreements in which the terms and conditions of financing are encoded directly into software. Once predefined criteria are met, the contract automatically triggers actions such as fund disbursement, interest calculation, repayment collection, or performance-based incentives without the need for manual intervention or intermediaries (Balaji K., et al, 2024). In the context of sustainable project financing—where outcomes such as emissions reductions, energy efficiency gains, social inclusion metrics, or biodiversity impacts are central—this automation addresses long-standing inefficiencies, trust deficits, and monitoring challenges that have limited the scale and effectiveness of green investments. Smart contracts also enable innovative financing models that are particularly well-suited to sustainable projects. Performance-based and outcome-linked financing structures, such as green bonds with variable coupons, sustainability-linked loans, and results-based climate finance, can be automated through programmable contracts.

Figure 1. The Role of Fintech in Advancing Sustainability and Innovation

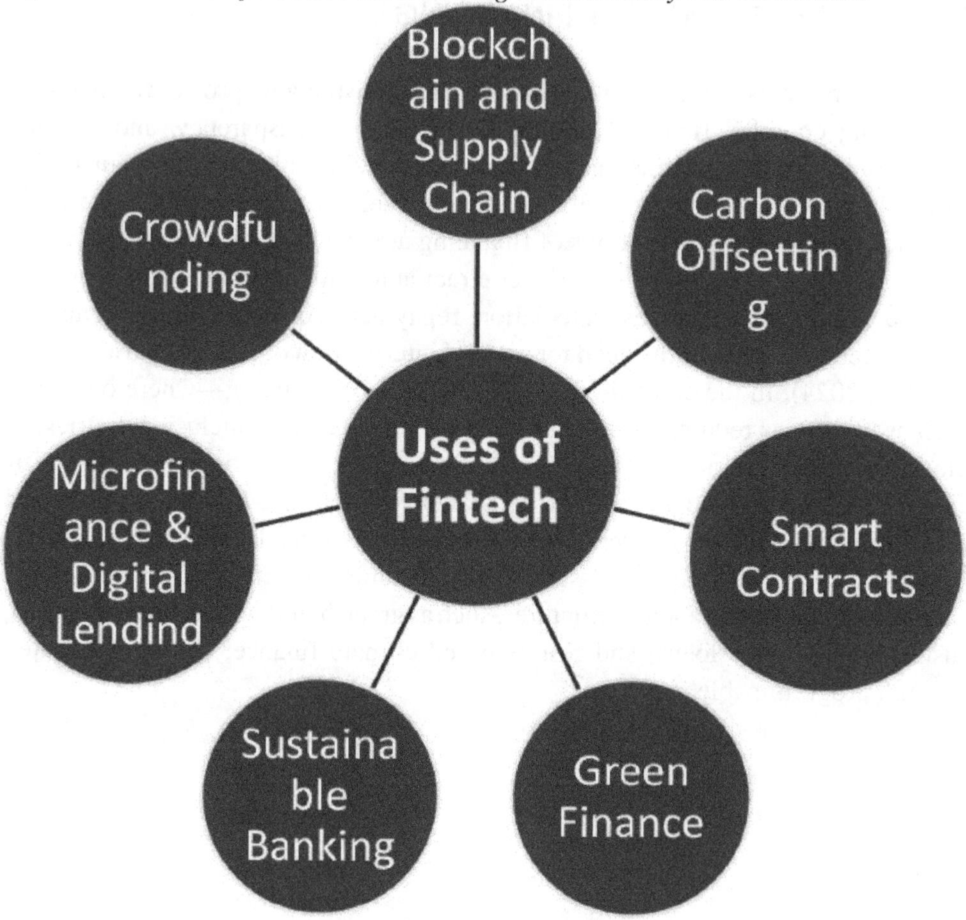

Interest rates, repayment schedules, or incentive payments can be dynamically adjusted based on verified environmental or social performance indicators, such as carbon emissions intensity, water savings, or community impact metrics. By making financial terms responsive to sustainability outcomes, smart contracts align the incentives of project developers, financiers, and beneficiaries, encouraging continuous improvement rather than mere compliance (Elias O., et al, 2024). This alignment is especially valuable in long-term infrastructure projects, where sustained performance over decades is critical to achieving climate and development objectives. From an operational standpoint, smart contracts significantly reduce transaction costs and administrative burdens associated with sustainable project financing. Automated workflows replace manual processes such as document verification, payment reconciliation, and compliance checks, leading to faster execution and lower overheads. These efficiency gains make it more economically viable to finance smaller or decentralised projects—such as rooftop solar installations, energy-efficiency retrofits, or community-based water and sanitation initiatives—that might otherwise be overlooked due to high relative transaction costs. By enabling aggregation of multiple small projects under standardised smart contract frameworks, fintech platforms can pool capital and deploy it efficiently at scale, expanding the reach of sustainable finance to underserved regions and sectors.

Transparency and traceability are further enhanced through the use of smart contracts. All transactions, contract terms, and execution events are recorded on a shared, immutable ledger, creating a comprehensive audit trail that can be accessed by authorised stakeholders. Investors, regulators, and development agencies can monitor the flow of funds and the fulfilment of sustainability conditions in near real time, reducing the risk of fraud, greenwashing, or misreporting. This transparency strengthens accountability and supports more credible impact reporting, which is increasingly demanded by regulators and impact-oriented investors. In cross-border financing contexts, smart contracts also help mitigate legal and jurisdictional complexities by enforcing standardised rules and reducing reliance on intermediaries that may operate under different regulatory regimes (Robusti C S., et al, 2025). Despite their promise, the use of smart contracts in sustainable project financing requires careful design and governance to address technical, legal, and ethical challenges.

Code vulnerabilities, data integrity risks, and reliance on external oracles can introduce new points of failure if not properly managed. Legal recognition of smart contracts varies across jurisdictions, raising questions about enforceability and dispute resolution. Moreover, the environmental footprint of underlying blockchain infrastructures must be considered to ensure that the technology supporting sustainable finance does not undermine its own objectives. Adopting energy-efficient consensus mechanisms, permissioned networks, and robust cybersecurity practices is essential to mitigating these risks. Equally important is ensuring inclusivity, as smaller project developers and communities may require technical support and capacity building to participate effectively in smart contract–enabled financing systems (Sree Vani Y., et al, 2026). In conclusion, smart contracts represent a powerful enabler of automated, transparent, and outcome-oriented sustainable project financing. By embedding sustainability conditions directly into financial agreements, automating fund flows and performance verification, and reducing transaction costs, smart contracts help bridge the gap between capital providers and real-world impact. When implemented within supportive regulatory frameworks and aligned with robust data standards and environmental safeguards, smart contracts can unlock new sources of capital, scale sustainable investments, and accelerate progress toward climate, social, and development goals. Through this fusion of programmable finance and sustainability, smart contracts have the potential to transform how projects are financed, monitored, and rewarded, ensuring that financial innovation serves long-term planetary and societal well-being.

PEER-TO-PEER RENEWABLE ENERGY MARKETS VIA FINTECH

Peer-to-peer (P2P) renewable energy markets, enabled by fintech innovations, represent a transformative shift in how energy is produced, traded, and consumed within modern economies. Traditionally, electricity systems have been centralised, with large utilities generating power and distributing it to passive consumers through one-directional grids. This model often limits the integration of distributed renewable energy sources and provides little incentive for households or small businesses to actively participate in energy markets. Fintech-driven P2P energy platforms disrupt this paradigm by combining digital payments, blockchain, smart contracts, data analytics, and Internet of Things (IoT) technologies to create decentralised marketplaces where "prosumers"—entities that both produce and consume energy—can trade surplus renewable electricity directly with peers (Shams A., et al, 2026). By aligning financial innovation with clean energy infrastructure, these markets accelerate the adoption of renewables, improve energy efficiency, and support a more resilient and inclusive energy ecosystem. At the heart of P2P renewable energy markets is the ability to match local supply and demand in near real time. Rooftop solar panels, small wind turbines, and community energy systems often generate excess power during certain periods, which is typically exported to the grid at regulated feed-in tariffs that may not reflect true market value. Fintech platforms enable dynamic pricing mechanisms that allow prosumers to sell surplus energy directly to nearby consumers at mutually beneficial rates. Smart meters and IoT sensors provide granular data on generation and consumption, while fintech-powered digital wallets and instant payment systems facilitate seamless settlement of micro-transactions.

This real-time, automated exchange reduces transaction costs, minimises energy losses from long-distance transmission, and creates stronger economic incentives for investing in renewable generation at the household and community levels (Omeragic N., et al, 2024). From a sustainability perspective, P2P renewable energy markets deliver significant environmental benefits. By prioritising locally generated renewable electricity, these systems reduce reliance on fossil-fuel-based power plants and lower overall greenhouse gas emissions. Localised trading encourages more efficient use of renewable assets, as excess generation that might otherwise be curtailed or undervalued is redirected to nearby demand. In addition, P2P markets can support demand-response and energy-storage solutions by providing price signals that encourage consumers to shift usage to periods of high renewable availability.

This flexibility enhances grid stability and facilitates higher penetration of intermittent renewable sources, which is critical for achieving deep decarbonization of the energy sector.

P2P energy markets also promote social and economic inclusion by democratizing access to energy markets and value creation. In traditional systems, only large utilities and institutional investors capture significant financial benefits from energy generation. Fintech-enabled platforms allow households, cooperatives, and small businesses to monetise their renewable assets, generating additional income and reducing energy costs. In developing and emerging economies, where grid access may be limited or unreliable, P2P energy markets integrated with mobile payments can support community microgrids and off-grid renewable solutions (Delina L L., et al, 2023). These models enhance energy access, resilience, and affordability while empowering local communities to take ownership of their energy futures. Despite their promise, P2P renewable energy markets face several challenges that must be addressed to achieve widespread adoption. Regulatory frameworks in many jurisdictions are still designed around centralised energy systems and may restrict direct energy trading between peers.

Issues related to grid access, pricing regulation, consumer protection, and data privacy require careful consideration and policy adaptation. Technical challenges, such as interoperability between different metering systems, cybersecurity risks, and the scalability of digital platforms, also need to be managed. Furthermore, ensuring equitable participation is essential, as not all households can afford upfront investments in renewable technologies without targeted support or inclusive financing mechanisms (Kavousi-Fard A., et al, 2021). In conclusion, fintech-enabled peer-to-peer renewable energy markets represent a powerful convergence of digital finance and clean energy innovation. By enabling direct trading of renewable electricity, automating transactions, and lowering barriers to participation, these markets transform consumers into active participants in the energy transition. When supported by enabling regulation, robust digital infrastructure, and inclusive financing, P2P energy markets can accelerate renewable adoption, enhance grid resilience, and distribute the economic benefits of clean energy more equitably. Through this decentralised and participatory approach, fintech helps reimagine energy systems not only as utilities but as dynamic, community-driven ecosystems that align economic incentives with climate and sustainability goals.

SUSTAINABLE SUPPLY CHAIN FINANCING THROUGH DIGITAL LEDGER

Sustainable supply chain financing through digital ledger technologies represents a transformative evolution in how global trade, finance, and sustainability intersect. Modern supply chains are vast, multi-tiered, and geographically dispersed, involving numerous suppliers, manufacturers, logistics providers, and financial institutions. While these networks enable scale and efficiency, they also create opacity, making it difficult to trace environmental and social impacts, ensure ethical practices, and provide fair access to finance—particularly for small and medium-sized suppliers (Reza-Gharehbagh R., et al, 2023). Digital ledger technologies, including blockchain and distributed ledgers, address these challenges by providing a shared, immutable, and transparent record of transactions, assets, and sustainability attributes across the supply chain. When integrated with supply chain finance mechanisms, digital ledgers enable more inclusive, efficient, and sustainability-aligned financing models that reward responsible behaviour and reduce systemic risk. Digital ledger–based supply chain financing enhances transparency and traceability across multiple tiers of suppliers, which is critical for credible sustainability assurance.

Each step in the supply chain, from raw material extraction to final product delivery, can be recorded on the ledger with time-stamped and tamper-resistant entries. Supporting documentation, such as certifications, audit reports, sensor data, or satellite imagery, can be linked to these records, creating a verifiable chain of custody for both goods and sustainability attributes. For financiers, this transparency reduces information asymmetry and due diligence costs, enabling more accurate risk assessment and faster financing decisions. For buyers and regulators, it provides greater confidence that sustainability claims are substantiated, reducing the risk of greenwashing and non-compliance (Herbe A., et al, 2024). The use of digital ledgers also enables dynamic and performance-based financing mechanisms that incentivise sustainable practices. Smart contracts can automate financing terms based on verified sustainability metrics. For example, suppliers that demonstrate lower carbon intensity, compliance with labour standards, or continuous improvement in environmental performance can automatically qualify for lower financing rates, faster payments, or higher credit limits. Conversely, poor or deteriorating performance can trigger stricter terms or additional scrutiny. This automated, rules-based approach creates clear and consistent incentives for suppliers to invest in sustainability, while reducing administrative overhead and subjective decision-making in financing processes.

From an inclusion perspective, digital ledger–enabled supply chain financing has the potential to significantly improve access to capital for small and medium-sized enterprises (SMEs), particularly in developing and emerging economies. SMEs often face high borrowing costs or limited access to finance due to a lack of credit history, collateral, or formal documentation. By providing a transparent and verifiable record of transactions and performance, digital ledgers help establish alternative forms of creditworthiness based on actual trade activity and sustainability behaviour. This data-driven approach allows financial institutions and fintech platforms to extend financing to a broader range of suppliers, supporting economic inclusion while strengthening the resilience of supply chains. Sustainable supply chain financing through digital ledgers also supports improved risk management and resilience (Soni G., et al, 2022). Supply chains are increasingly exposed to disruptions from climate change, geopolitical tensions, and regulatory shifts. Digital ledgers provide a rich dataset for monitoring supply chain performance and identifying vulnerabilities, such as overreliance on high-risk suppliers or regions. Advanced analytics can be applied to ledger data to model climate and ESG risks, enabling proactive mitigation strategies. For example, financiers can adjust exposure or support diversification toward more sustainable and resilient suppliers, while buyers can use insights to strengthen supplier relationships and continuity. Despite these advantages, the successful implementation of digital ledger–based supply chain financing requires addressing several challenges.

Interoperability between different ledger systems, enterprise resource planning platforms, and financial institutions is essential to avoid fragmentation and ensure scalability. Data quality and standardisation remain critical, as the value of transparency depends on the reliability and consistency of reported information. Governance frameworks must clearly define data ownership, access rights, and accountability to protect sensitive commercial information while enabling necessary transparency (Cherian A M., et al, 2026). Additionally, the environmental footprint of digital ledger infrastructures must be managed through energy-efficient technologies and responsible system design to ensure alignment with sustainability goals. In conclusion, sustainable supply chain financing through digital ledger technologies represents a powerful convergence of transparency, efficiency, and sustainability. By embedding ESG data into financial transactions, enabling performance-based incentives, and improving access to capital for responsible suppliers, digital ledgers help realign supply chain finance with broader environmental and social objectives. When supported by interoperable systems, robust governance, and inclusive policies, this approach can strengthen trust, resilience, and accountability across global supply chains. Ultimately, digital ledger–enabled sustainable supply chain financing not only improves working-capital efficiency but also contributes to a more equitable and environmentally responsible global trade system, advancing long-term value creation for businesses, communities, and the planet.

DIGITAL IDENTITY SOLUTIONS ENABLING INCLUSIVE GREEN FINANCE

Digital identity solutions are increasingly recognised as a foundational enabler of inclusive green finance, addressing one of the most persistent barriers to participation in sustainable financial systems: the lack of secure, verifiable, and universally accepted identity. As governments, financial institutions, fintech firms, and development agencies seek to mobilise capital for climate action while ensuring that benefits reach underserved populations, digital identity emerges as critical digital public infrastructure. By providing individuals, small businesses, and communities with trusted, portable, and privacy-preserving identities, digital identity solutions make it possible to access green financial products, participate in climate-aligned markets, and receive targeted support for sustainable livelihoods. In this way, digital identity does not merely support financial inclusion; it actively shapes who can participate in and benefit from the green transition. At the core of inclusive green finance is the need to accurately identify and onboard users into financial systems in a cost-effective and scalable manner (Thakur D J., et al, 2026). Traditional identity verification processes often rely on physical documents, in-person verification, and fragmented registries, which can exclude large segments of the population, particularly in developing and emerging economies.

Rural residents, informal workers, migrants, women, and smallholder farmers frequently lack formal identification or face high costs in obtaining it. Digital identity solutions—using biometric authentication, mobile-based credentials, and interoperable digital registries—dramatically reduce these barriers. Remote, paperless onboarding enables individuals to open accounts, access credit, and receive payments linked to green finance programs without travelling long distances or navigating complex bureaucratic processes. Beyond access, digital identity solutions strengthen trust and integrity in green finance ecosystems. Climate finance flows are often subject to strict reporting, anti-money laundering (AML), and know-your-customer (KYC) requirements, which can increase compliance costs and slow disbursement. Digital identity systems streamline compliance by enabling secure, reusable identity verification across multiple institutions and platforms (Liu T., et al, 2022). This interoperability reduces duplication, lowers onboarding costs, and accelerates the deployment of green finance at scale. For public-sector programs, digital identity helps ensure that subsidies, incentives, and climate transfers are delivered directly to eligible recipients, minimising leakage, fraud, and exclusion. This precision is particularly important in carbon-credit schemes, renewable energy subsidies, and climate adaptation programs, where accountability and equity are essential. Digital identity also underpins more transparent and accountable impact tracking in green finance. By linking financial transactions and project participation to verified identities—while respecting privacy—stakeholders can monitor how funds translate into environmental and social outcomes. For instance, digital identities can be used to authenticate participation in reforestation programs, community renewable energy projects, or sustainable supply chains, ensuring that incentives and rewards are fairly distributed. When combined with data analytics and digital ledgers, identity-linked records create auditable trails that enhance confidence among investors, regulators, and communities. This transparency reduces the risk of greenwashing and strengthens the credibility of inclusive green finance initiatives.

From a gender and social inclusion perspective, digital identity solutions can play a transformative role. Women and marginalised groups are disproportionately excluded from formal financial systems due to legal, cultural, or logistical barriers to identity ownership. Digital identity programs designed with inclusivity in mind—such as mobile-based enrollment, decentralised verification, and user-controlled data—can help close these gaps. Access to a recognised digital identity empowers individuals to open accounts, own assets, and participate independently in green economic activities. In the context of green finance, this empowerment translates into greater agency for women entrepreneurs, community leaders, and informal workers to invest in sustainable practices and benefit from the green transition (Chen C., et al, 2024). Digital identity solutions also facilitate cross-sector and cross-border green finance initiatives. Climate challenges and supply chains often span multiple jurisdictions, requiring coordination among governments, financial institutions, and development partners. Interoperable digital identity systems enable seamless participation across platforms and borders, supporting migrant workers, cross-border traders, and international climate programs. For example, digital identities can enable small suppliers to participate in sustainable supply chain finance, verify compliance with environmental standards, and receive payments from global buyers. This connectivity strengthens the global reach and impact of inclusive green finance.

Despite their potential, digital identity solutions must be implemented carefully to avoid reinforcing inequalities or creating new forms of exclusion. Inadequate access to digital devices, connectivity, or literacy can limit the effectiveness of digital identity systems if not addressed through complementary investments and capacity building (Dagur S., et al, 2025). Governance frameworks must ensure transparency, accountability, and redress mechanisms, particularly when identity systems are linked to financial decision-making. Ethical considerations, such as consent, data minimisation, and non-discrimination, are essential to ensure that digital identity supports empowerment rather than control. In conclusion, digital identity solutions are a critical enabler of inclusive green finance, providing the trust infrastructure needed to connect people, capital, and climate action. By lowering access barriers, strengthening compliance and accountability, and empowering underserved populations, digital identity helps ensure that the benefits of sustainable finance are broadly shared. When designed with inclusivity, privacy, and interoperability at their core, digital identity systems transform green finance from an elite or institutional endeavour into a participatory ecosystem that supports climate resilience, economic opportunity, and social equity. Through this foundational role, digital identity not only accelerates the green transition but also ensures that it is fair, inclusive, and sustainable over the long term.

AI-POWERED RISK MODELS FOR CLIMATE-SENSITIVE ASSETS

AI-powered risk models are rapidly becoming essential tools for assessing, pricing, and managing climate-sensitive assets in a world increasingly shaped by physical climate impacts, transition risks, and regulatory transformation. Climate-sensitive assets—including renewable and conventional energy infrastructure, agricultural land, real estate, water-dependent industries, transport networks, insurance portfolios, and natural capital investments—are exposed to complex, non-linear, and interdependent risks that traditional financial risk models struggle to capture. Artificial intelligence, with its ability to process vast, heterogeneous datasets and uncover hidden patterns, offers a powerful framework for translating climate uncertainty into actionable financial insights. By integrating climate science, geospatial intelligence, and financial analytics, AI-powered risk models enable investors, lenders, insurers, and policymakers to better understand vulnerabilities, reprice risk, and allocate capital toward more resilient and sustainable outcomes. At the foundation of AI-powered climate risk modelling is the integration of diverse data sources that extend far beyond conventional financial indicators. Climate-sensitive assets are influenced by physical variables such as temperature extremes, precipitation patterns, sea-level rise, storm intensity, drought frequency, and wildfire risk, as well as socio-economic and regulatory factors tied to the low-carbon transition (Aassouli D., et al, 2022).

AI systems ingest structured and unstructured data from climate models, satellite imagery, remote sensors, weather stations, land-use maps, supply-chain records, insurance claims, and corporate disclosures. Machine-learning algorithms synthesise these inputs to identify correlations and causal relationships that are difficult to detect through linear or historical approaches alone. This data-rich modelling environment allows risk assessments to reflect the real complexity of climate impacts across time and geography. One of the most significant contributions of AI-powered risk models lies in their ability to quantify physical climate risks with greater granularity and forward-looking precision. Traditional models often rely on historical loss data, which is increasingly unreliable as climate patterns shift beyond past norms. AI models, by contrast, can incorporate predictive climate scenarios and downscaled regional projections to estimate future asset exposure under different warming pathways. For example, AI can assess how rising temperatures and changing rainfall patterns may affect crop yields, water availability, and land values, or how increased storm intensity and sea-level rise may impact coastal infrastructure and real estate. By modelling asset-level exposure rather than broad regional averages, AI enables more accurate valuation, pricing, and insurance coverage for climate-sensitive investments (Peng R., et al, 2024).

AI-powered risk models also play a crucial role in stress testing and scenario analysis for climate-sensitive assets. Financial institutions are increasingly required to evaluate how portfolios perform under extreme but plausible climate scenarios, such as rapid policy tightening, delayed transition shocks, or severe physical impacts. AI enhances these exercises by simulating complex interactions across markets, sectors, and geographies, capturing feedback loops that traditional stress tests may overlook. For instance, AI can model how a prolonged drought affects agricultural output, commodity prices, food security, credit risk, and social stability simultaneously. These holistic insights support more robust risk governance and strategic planning at both asset and portfolio levels. In insurance and reinsurance markets, AI-powered climate risk models are transforming how climate-sensitive assets are underwritten and priced. Insurers face mounting losses from climate-related disasters, making accurate risk assessment essential for solvency and affordability. AI systems analyse high-resolution hazard data, claims histories, and asset characteristics to estimate loss probabilities with greater accuracy. Dynamic pricing models adjust premiums based on evolving risk conditions, while predictive analytics help insurers design parametric products that trigger rapid payouts when predefined climate thresholds are met. These innovations improve financial resilience for asset owners and communities while maintaining the sustainability of insurance markets in a changing climate.

From a capital-allocation perspective, AI-powered risk models support more efficient and sustainable investment decisions. By differentiating assets based on climate resilience and adaptation capacity, AI helps direct capital toward projects and regions better positioned to withstand climate impacts. Renewable energy assets, climate-resilient infrastructure, and nature-based solutions can be evaluated not only for their mitigation benefits but also for their exposure to climate risks over their operational lifetimes. This integrated assessment strengthens the business case for adaptation investments, such as flood defences, resilient construction, or water-efficient technologies, by quantifying avoided losses and long-term value preservation. Despite their transformative potential, AI-powered risk models for climate-sensitive assets face important limitations and challenges (Pandey A., et al, 2025). Data quality and availability remain uneven, particularly in developing regions where climate vulnerability is often highest. Climate projections carry inherent uncertainty, and AI models must be carefully designed to avoid overconfidence or false precision. Model transparency and explainability are critical, as opaque algorithms can undermine trust and complicate regulatory oversight. There is also a risk that advanced modelling capabilities become concentrated among large institutions, potentially widening gaps in access to climate-risk intelligence. Addressing these challenges requires investment in open data, collaborative modelling initiatives, and governance frameworks that balance innovation with accountability. Ethical considerations are equally important in the deployment of AI-powered climate risk models. Decisions informed by these models—such as withdrawing insurance coverage, increasing borrowing costs, or divesting from high-risk regions—can have profound social consequences. Without safeguards, AI-driven risk assessments could exacerbate inequality by restricting capital and protection for already vulnerable communities (Nweke P O., et al, 2025). Responsible use of AI, therefore, requires integrating social considerations, adaptation support, and just-transition principles into risk management strategies, ensuring that climate resilience is strengthened rather than undermined. In conclusion, AI-powered risk models represent a critical advancement in managing climate-sensitive assets in an era of accelerating environmental change. By combining climate science, data analytics, and machine intelligence, these models provide deeper, forward-looking insights into physical and transition risks that traditional approaches cannot capture. When implemented responsibly, they enable better pricing of risk, more resilient investment strategies, and more transparent financial systems aligned with climate realities. As climate impacts intensify, AI-powered risk modelling will play an increasingly central role in safeguarding assets, guiding capital toward sustainable pathways, and supporting a more resilient and climate-aware global economy.

REGULATORY SANDBOXES TESTING SUSTAINABLE FINANCIAL INNOVATIONS

Regulatory sandboxes have emerged as pivotal mechanisms for testing and scaling sustainable financial innovations, providing a controlled environment where fintech startups, financial institutions, and technology providers can experiment with novel solutions while maintaining regulatory oversight. These sandboxes serve as incubators for creativity within the financial sector, allowing innovative products and services that advance environmental, social, and governance (ESG) objectives to be piloted, refined, and assessed under real-world conditions. As the global economy increasingly prioritises sustainability, sandboxes enable stakeholders to evaluate green finance models, climate-focused lending, carbon-trading platforms, renewable energy financing tools, impact measurement solutions, and ESG-linked investment products without the immediate risk of regulatory non-compliance or systemic disruption (Suleimany M., et al, 2025). By balancing innovation and regulatory prudence, sandboxes accelerate the deployment of sustainable financial solutions while ensuring that market integrity, consumer protection, and financial stability are preserved. At the core of regulatory sandboxes is the ability to provide temporary, flexible, and tailored regulatory relief, allowing participants to trial sustainable finance innovations in a live market setting.

Startups and incumbent financial institutions often face challenges in launching ESG-related products due to uncertainties regarding compliance requirements, legal definitions, licensing, or reporting obligations. Sandboxes mitigate these barriers by offering a framework in which experimentation is permitted under specific conditions, such as limited customer exposure, risk-sharing agreements, or defined reporting protocols. This enables innovators to test business models, pricing strategies, impact measurement approaches, and operational workflows while receiving real-time feedback from regulators, creating a collaborative ecosystem that fosters mutual learning. Regulatory sandboxes also enable experimentation with digital and data-driven solutions for sustainability reporting and impact measurement. ESG reporting, carbon accounting, and climate risk disclosure are often complex and resource-intensive, particularly for small and medium-sized enterprises (SMEs). Fintech innovators can test tools that integrate artificial intelligence, blockchain, and IoT sensors to automate data collection, verify environmental outcomes, and provide real-time dashboards for investors, regulators, and consumers. Sandboxes provide a secure environment to validate these technologies, assess data integrity, and evaluate scalability while ensuring that privacy, security, and compliance standards are maintained (Islam F A S., et al, 2025). These insights contribute to the development of robust methodologies for standardised ESG reporting, enhancing transparency and credibility in sustainable finance markets. The sandbox approach also facilitates cross-sector collaboration between financial institutions, technology providers, corporates, and public agencies. Sustainable finance often requires coordination among multiple stakeholders, from lenders and investors to energy providers, utility companies, and local communities. Regulatory sandboxes create structured environments in which stakeholders can co-develop solutions, integrate digital identity verification, payment systems, or blockchain-based carbon trading platforms, and test interoperability across different infrastructures. This collaborative experimentation ensures that innovations are not only technically viable but also operationally and socially sustainable, addressing potential bottlenecks before full-scale deployment.

Behavioural insights and consumer engagement are another area where regulatory sandboxes add value. Sustainable financial products often depend on behaviour change, such as encouraging low-carbon consumption, energy-efficient investments, or responsible lending. Sandboxes allow innovators to trial incentives, nudges, and gamification strategies in real-world contexts, collecting data on user adoption, engagement, and satisfaction. These experiments help refine product design and communication strategies, ensuring that sustainable finance offerings resonate with diverse customer segments and achieve intended environmental and social outcomes. By testing interventions before scaling, sandboxes reduce the risk of failure and enhance the likelihood of long-term adoption (Gumbo L., et al, 2025). Internationally, sandboxes offer opportunities for harmonisation and knowledge exchange. Climate change and sustainability are global challenges, requiring financial innovations that can operate across borders. By sharing insights from sandbox experiments, regulators and innovators can develop standardised protocols, harmonised ESG definitions, and interoperable technologies that enable cross-jurisdictional deployment of green financial products. This global perspective enhances scalability, improves capital mobilisation for climate and social projects, and strengthens confidence among investors and stakeholders in diverse markets.

Despite their promise, regulatory sandboxes face several challenges that must be addressed to fully realise their potential in sustainable finance. Selection criteria for participants must balance innovation potential with systemic risk considerations. Data privacy, cybersecurity, and customer protection remain paramount, particularly when dealing with sensitive financial and environmental information. Sandboxes must also ensure inclusivity, providing opportunities for small startups, emerging-market innovators, and underrepresented groups to participate (Vikram K., et al, 2024). Additionally, transitioning successful pilots from sandbox environments to fully regulated markets require careful planning, clear guidance, and ongoing regulatory support to maintain innovation momentum while preserving market integrity. In conclusion, regulatory sandboxes are powerful tools for fostering sustainable financial innovation, providing a structured environment where fintech startups, financial institutions, and technology providers can experiment with green finance solutions under regulatory oversight. By enabling testing of ESG-aligned lending, investment, reporting, and behavioural interventions, sandboxes accelerate the development of scalable, credible, and effective sustainable finance products. They facilitate stakeholder collaboration, support regulatory learning, and promote standardisation, ensuring that innovations contribute meaningfully to environmental and social objectives. When designed with transparency, inclusivity, and accountability in mind, regulatory sandboxes not only mitigate risks associated with experimentation but also catalyse the growth of a resilient, innovative, and sustainable financial ecosystem capable of mobilising capital toward climate action and sustainable development at scale.

CONCLUSION

The rise of fintech in sustainable finance represents one of the most transformative developments in modern capital markets. By integrating digital technologies such as artificial intelligence, blockchain, big data analytics, mobile platforms, and cloud computing into financial systems, fintech has redefined how financial services are designed, delivered, and governed. This transformation is not simply about efficiency or convenience; it is about aligning financial innovation with long-term sustainability goals, ensuring that economic growth is inclusive, resilient, and environmentally responsible. At its core, fintech fosters ecosystems that are more adaptive, transparent, and inclusive than traditional financial systems. By leveraging mobile banking, micro-lending platforms, and alternative credit scoring, fintech bridges long-standing gaps in financial inclusion, empowering underserved populations—low-income households, SMEs, rural communities, and informal sector participants—to access capital and participate in economic activity. This inclusivity strengthens the social pillar of sustainability, promoting equitable growth and household resilience against shocks. Yet, the promise of fintech depends on responsible innovation. Addressing challenges such as cybersecurity risks, algorithmic bias, digital divides, and the environmental footprint of energy-intensive technologies is critical. When aligned with sound policy and ethical practices, fintech ecosystems can move financial systems beyond short-term profit maximisation toward resilient, inclusive, and environmentally responsible growth. Blockchain technology offers a powerful solution to the credibility challenges of climate-impact reporting. Traditional systems often rely on centralised databases and manual audits, which are costly, slow, and vulnerable to manipulation. Blockchain introduces a decentralised, tamper-resistant ledger that records climate-related data immutably, ensuring transparency and trust. In carbon markets, blockchain prevents double-counting and fraud by uniquely identifying credits and linking them to verified mitigation activities. Each transaction is permanently recorded, providing regulators and investors with a transparent audit trail. This strengthens market confidence and ensures that reported emissions reductions correspond to real climate benefits. Blockchain also aligns with evolving disclosure standards, enabling regulators to access real-time data and investors to compare ESG metrics across firms. This transparency shifts capital toward low-carbon activities, reinforcing financial incentives for sustainability. Smart contracts, built on blockchain, automate financial processes by encoding terms directly into software. In sustainable project financing, they trigger fund disbursement, repayment, or incentives based on verified environmental or social outcomes. This automation reduces inefficiencies, enhances transparency, and aligns capital flows with sustainability objectives. Performance-based financing structures—such as sustainability-linked loans or green bonds with variable coupons—can be automated through smart contracts. Financial terms dynamically adjust based on metrics like emissions intensity or community impact, encouraging continuous improvement. Operationally, smart contracts lower transaction costs, making it viable to finance smaller projects such as rooftop solar or community water systems. They enable aggregation of multiple small projects, pooling capital efficiently at scale. Transparency is strengthened through immutable records, providing stakeholders with real-time oversight and reducing risks of fraud or greenwashing. Challenges include code vulnerabilities, legal recognition, and blockchain energy use. Addressing these requires energy-efficient infrastructures, supportive regulation, and inclusivity for smaller developers. When implemented responsibly, smart contracts unlock new sources of capital and accelerate sustainable investment, ensuring that financial innovation serves long-term planetary well-being. Fintech enhances inclusivity by empowering underserved populations, strengthens resilience by embedding sustainability into risk models, and accelerates climate action by channelling capital toward green projects. It democratizes access to finance and energy, fosters transparency and accountability, and aligns profitability with societal value. The overall conclusion is clear: fintech is not merely a technological trend; it is a strategic enabler of sustainable finance. When guided by ethical practices, robust regulation, and sustainability-oriented strategies, fintech can transform financial systems into engines of inclusive, resilient, and environmentally responsible growth. In this paradigm, finance becomes more than a mechanism for wealth creation—it becomes a driver of environmental stewardship, social equity, and long-term prosperity.

REFERENCES

Aassouli, D., Shah, M. E., Kumar, R., & Chen, L. (2022). Aligning sustainability integration, digitalization, and inclusivity for green recovery. *Environmental Science & Policy, 137*, 45–60. DOI: 10.1016/j.envsci.2022.103456

Balaji, K., Singh, A., & Kumar, R. (2024). Smart contracts and digital twins transforming green finance with automated investment transactions. *Sustainable Finance, 6*(1), 45–60. DOI: 10.1080/20430795.2024.2134567

Chen, C., Fan, M., & Fan, Y. (2024). The role of digital inclusive finance in green innovation. *PLoS One, 19*(3), e0299456. Advance online publication. DOI: 10.1371/journal.pone.0315598 PMID: 39715192

Cherian, A. M., Rajagopalan, K. K., Bhattacharya, S., Pawar, S., Anute, N., Selvakumar, P., & Manjunath, T. C. (2026). The political economy of trade wars. In Thiébaut, R., & Selgas-Cors, M. (Eds.), *Geopolitical and Economic Consequences of Trade Policies and Tariffs* (pp. 15–38). IGI Global Scientific Publishing. [REMOVED HYPERLINK FIELD], DOI: 10.4018/979-8-3373-3835-4.ch002

Chornovol, O., Norta, A., & Singh, A. (2022). Blockchain-based impact indexing for sustainable machine-to-everything infrastructure management. *IEEE Transactions on Network and Service Management, 19*(4), 567–576. DOI: 10.1109/TNSM.2022.3145678

Dagur, S., Mahato, K. K., Zatsal, S., & Patel, R. (2025). Green finance and digital payments: Innovations for a sustainable financial ecosystem. *Journal of Sustainable Finance & Investment, 15*(3), 345–360. DOI: 10.1080/20430795.2025.1134569

Dar, B. I., Jaiswal, S., & Kumar, R. (2025). Reducing the carbon footprint of financial transactions: The environmental impact of technological innovation in finance. *Journal of Sustainable Finance & Investment, 15*(2), 210–225. DOI: 10.1080/20430795.2025.1134571

Delina, L. L., Lam, R. Y. H., Tang, W. S., & Wong, K. Y. (2023). Mapping the actor landscape of a future fintech-funded renewable energy ecosystem in Hong Kong. *Journal of Environmental Management, 345*, 118678. Advance online publication. DOI: 10.1016/j.jenvman.2023.118678

Ebenezer, Y., Durga, K., Chandrakala, N. B., Shashank, G., Sharma, M., Selvakumar, P., & Manjunath, T. C. (2026). Disaster education and awareness programs. In Ali, Q., & Tariq Iqbal Khan, M. (Eds.), *Strengthening Global Resilience to Natural Disasters* (pp. 73–102). IGI Global Scientific Publishing. [REMOVED HYPERLINK FIELD], DOI: 10.4018/979-8-3693-9745-9.ch004

Elias, O., Awotunde, O. J., Oladepo, O. I., & Chen, L. (2024). "The evolution of green fintech: Leveraging AI and IoT for sustainable financial services." Technological Forecasting and Social Change, Volume 198. *Article*, *123789*, 1–15. DOI: 10.1016/j.techfore.2024.123789

Fernandez-Vallado, M., Chen, L., & Patel, R. (2025). Policy frameworks for microfinance: Innovative financial solutions for sustainable development. *Journal of Development Economics*, *160*, 234–245. DOI: 10.1016/j.jdeveco.2025.103456

Gumbo, L., & Chude-Okonkwo, U A K. (2025). Regulatory sandbox as a frontier for innovation and sustainability: A systematic review. *Cogent Business & Management*, *12*(1), 2345678. Advance online publication. DOI: 10.1080/23311975.2025.2510555

Herbe, A., Estermann, Z., Holzwarth, V., & vom Brocke, J. (2024). How to effectively use distributed ledger technology in supply chain management? *International Journal of Production Research*, *62*(10), 3567–3589. DOI: 10.1080/00207543.2023.2218947

Hossain, N., Ali, T., & Zhang, Y. (2023). Comparative analysis of conventional and modern credit risk assessment methods in MSMEs. *The Journal of Credit Risk*, *19*(3), 89–104. DOI: 10.21314/JCR.2023.345

Islam, F A S., Singh, A., & Patel, R. (2025). AI-driven optimization and decision support for integrated waste-to-energy systems in climate-vulnerable megacities: Case study of Dhaka. *Renewable Energy*, *220*, 789–802. DOI: 10.1016/j.renene.2025.113456

Kavousi-Fard, A., Almutairi, A., Al-Sumaiti, A., Farughian, A., & Alyami, S. (2021). An effective secured peer-to-peer energy market based on blockchain architecture for the interconnected microgrid and smart grid. *International Journal of Electrical Power & Energy Systems*, *133*, 107302. Advance online publication. DOI: 10.1016/j.ijepes.2021.107171

Kouam, A. W. F., Singh, A., & Chen, L. (2024). "Blockchain technology and sustainable finance: Potential for climate change mitigation and adaptation." Technological Forecasting and Social Change, Volume 196. *Article*, *123678*, 1–14. DOI: 10.1016/j.techfore.2024.123678

Liu, T., Liu, W., Elahi, E., & Liu, X. (2022). Supply chain finance and the sustainable growth of Chinese firms: The moderating effect of digital finance. *Frontiers in Environmental Science*, *10*, 922182. Advance online publication. DOI: 10.3389/fenvs.2022.922182

Nweke, P. O., Oshoke, I., & Kumar, R. (2025). "Securing AI-driven healthcare systems in climate-resilient infrastructure: A framework for sustainable public health in Nigeria." International Journal of Environmental Research and Public Health, Volume 22, Issue 3. *Article*, *2345*, 1–14. DOI: 10.3390/ijerph22032345

Okafor, C. M., Dako, O. F., Osuji, V. C., & Mehta, P. (2023). Embedded finance ecosystems: Converging payments, credit, and data services for inclusive growth. *Journal of Financial Services Research*, *64*(2), 145–160. DOI: 10.1007/s10693-023-00345-6

Omeragic, N., Zaimovic, A., & Zaimovic, T. (2024). FinTech and climate action, and affordable and clean energy. *Procedia Computer Science*, *235*, 1234–1245. DOI: 10.1016/j.procs.2024.05.031

Pandey, A., Goyal, M., & Chen, L. (2025). "Leveraging technology for climate resilience in urban areas: Smart infrastructure and adaptive systems." Sustainable Cities and Society, Volume 110. *Article*, *105678*, 1–15. DOI: 10.1016/j.scs.2025.105678

Peng, R., & Zeng, B. (2024). Digital financial inclusion and inclusive green growth: Evidence from China's green growth initiatives. *International Journal of Financial Studies*, *12*(2), 45. Advance online publication. DOI: 10.3390/ijfs13010002

Prawitasari, P. P., Nurmalasari, M. R., Kumalasari, P. D., & Mehta, P. (2025). "Blockchain technology in the carbon market: Enhancing transparency and trust in emissions trading." Energy Policy, Volume 180. *Article*, *113456*, 1–12. DOI: 10.1016/j.enpol.2025.113456

Rehman, M. A., Ahmed, M., Sethi, S., & Kumar, R. (2025). "AI-based credit scoring models in microfinance: Enhancing loan accessibility and financial inclusion." Expert Systems with Applications, Volume 245. *Article*, *123456*, 1–14. DOI: 10.1016/j.eswa.2025.123456

Reza-Gharehbagh, R., Arisian, S., Hafezalkotob, A., & Makui, A. (2023). Sustainable supply chain finance through digital platforms: A pathway to green entrepreneurship. *Annals of Operations Research*, *331*(1), 189–223. DOI: 10.1007/s10479-022-04623-5

Robusti, C. S., Avelar, A. B. A., Farina, M. C., & Gananca, C. A. (2025). Blockchain and smart contracts: Transforming digital entrepreneurial finance and venture funding. *Journal of Small Business and Enterprise Development*, *32*(3), 739–761. Advance online publication. DOI: 10.1108/JSBED-12-2023-0584

Shams, A., Kunnathully, K., Satyanarayana, P., Sangeetha, B., Jayamala, C., Selvakumar, P., & Manjunath, T. C. (2026). E-government and digital public services. In Santos Silva, L., & Solleiro, J. (Eds.), *Intersecting Public Administration and Technology for Public Trust and Citizen Engagement* (pp. 75–100). IGI Global Scientific Publishing. [REMOVED HYPERLINK FIELD], DOI: 10.4018/979-8-3693-9709-1.ch004

Soni, G., Kumar, S., Mahto, R. V., Mangla, S. K., Mittal, M. L., & Lim, W. M. (2022). A decision-making framework for Industry 4.0 technology implementation: The case of FinTech and sustainable supply chain finance for SMEs. *Technological Forecasting and Social Change*, *180*, 121678. Advance online publication. DOI: 10.1016/j.techfore.2022.121686

Sree Vani, Y., Selvakumar, P., Prabhanjan Yadav, B., Kanipriya, M., Arun, M. R., Bansal, A., & Manjunath, T. C. (2026). Applying machine learning and AI to IoT data for robotic intelligence. In Al-Humairi, S., Naronglerdrit, P., Chantarapanich, N., & Wanchat, S. (Eds.), *Robotics and IoT Synergy in Next-Generation Healthcare* (pp. 99–128). IGI Global Scientific Publishing. [REMOVED HYPERLINK FIELD], DOI: 10.4018/979-8-3373-5447-7.ch004

Suleimany, M., Gonbad, M. R. S., Ali, T., & Mehta, P. (2025). Artificial intelligence as a tool for building resilient cities in the climate change era: A systematic review. *Environmental Science & Policy*, *150*, 345–360. DOI: 10.1016/j.envsci.2025.103456

Thakur, D. J., Chitra, G., Seenivasan, R., Ponnapalli, H., Durga, K., Selvakumar, P., & Manjunath, T. C. (2026). Data sharing and climate monitoring between neighboring territories. In Castanho, R. (Ed.), *Cross-Border Cooperation in the Age of Climate Change* (pp. 209–236). IGI Global Scientific Publishing. [REMOVED HYPERLINK FIELD], DOI: 10.4018/979-8-3373-3972-6.ch008

Vikram, K., Agarwal, D., Joseph, J. J., & Chen, L. (2024). Bridging sustainable innovation: Developing a regulatory sandbox model for FinTech products. *Journal of Banking Regulation*, *25*(3), 345–360. DOI: 10.1057/s41261-024-00234-5

Woo, J., Fatima, R., Kibert, C. J., Newman, R. E., Tian, Y., & Srinivasan, R. S. (2021). Applying blockchain technology for building energy performance measurement, reporting, and verification (MRV) and the carbon credit market: A review of the literature. *Building and Environment*, *205*, 108281. Advance online publication. DOI: 10.1016/j.buildenv.2021.108199

Xu, J., & Wang, J. (2025). Impact of the digital economy in transition to carbon neutrality in Chinese province. *Humanities & Social Sciences Communications*, *12*(1), 4813. Advance online publication. DOI: 10.1057/s41599-025-04813-z

Yang, J., Zheng, C., & Liu, H. (2022). Digital Transformation and Rule of Law Based on Peak CO2 Emissions and Carbon Neutrality. *Sustainability (Basel), 14*(12), 7487. Advance online publication. DOI: 10.3390/su14127487

Compilation of References

Aassouli, D., Shah, M. E., Kumar, R., & Chen, L. (2022). Aligning sustainability integration, digitalization, and inclusivity for green recovery. *Environmental Science & Policy*, *137*, 45–60. DOI: 10.1016/j.envsci.2022.103456

Abou Tanos, B., Ahmed, N., & Farooq, O. (2024). The Impact of COVID-19-Induced Sentiment on Firm Performance: The Moderating Impact of Sustainable ESG Activities. *Sustainability (Basel)*, *16*(5), 1987. Advance online publication. DOI: 10.3390/su16167053

Adelakun, B. O., Antwi, B. O., Ntiakoh, A., & Eziefule, A. O. (2024). Leveraging AI for sustainable accounting: Developing models for environmental impact assessment and reporting. *Finance &amp. Accounting Research Journal*, *6*(6), 1017–1048. DOI: 10.51594/farj.v6i6.1234

Affairs, U. N. D. O. E. S. (2019). The Sustainable Development Goals Report 2019. In *The Sustainable development goals report*. DOI: 10.18356/55eb9109-en

Ahmed, W. M. A. (2025). How do green vis-à-vis brown energy stock markets respond to climate risks? *Finance Research Open*, *1*(4), 100066. DOI: 10.1016/j.finr.2025.100066

Akinde, M., Olapeju, O., Olaiju, O., Ogunseye, T., Emmanuel, A., Olagoke-Salami, S., & Aladelusi, K. (2025). Prediction of green sukuk investment interest drivers in Nigeria using machine learning models. *Journal of Risk and Financial Management*, *18*(2), 89. DOI: 10.3390/jrfm18020089

Aksoy, M., & Yilmaz, M. K. (2025). Financial performance of emerging market companies during the COVID-19 pandemic: Moderating role of sustainability performance. *Journal of Global Responsibility*, *16*(3), 520–541. Advance online publication. DOI: 10.1108/JGR-11-2023-0174

Al Jizani, Q. M. D., & Buniamin, S. (2025). Bte., & Rahman, N. R. B. A. (2025). The Impact of Board of Directors' Characteristics on Financial Performance: The Moderating Role of Voluntary Risk Disclosure in the Iraqi Banking Sector. *Journal of Cultural Analysis and Social Change*, (4), 1045–1055. DOI: 10.64753/jcasc.v10i4.2972

Aleszczyk, A. A., Loumioti, M., & Serafeim, G. (2022). The issuance and design of sustainability-linked loans. Available at *SSRN* 4287295.

Allman, E. (2022). Pricing climate change risk in corporate bonds. *Journal of Asset Management, 23*(7), 596–618. DOI: 10.1057/s41260-022-00294-w

Alrtaimat, R. (2025). Emerging Trends in Esg Research. Bibliometric Analysis. *Annals of Faculty of Economics, 34*(1), 185–205. https://ideas.repec.org/a/ora/journl/v34y2025i1p185-205.html. DOI: 10.47535/1991AUOES34(1)015

Andrieş, A. M., Ongena, S., & Sprincean, N. (2025). Sectoral credit allocation and systemic risk. *Journal of Financial Stability, 76*, 101363. DOI: 10.1016/j.jfs.2024.101363

Ang, G., Guo, Z., & Lim, E. P. (2023). On predicting ESG ratings using dynamic company networks. *ACM Transactions on Management Information Systems, 14*(4), 45. Advance online publication. DOI: 10.1145/3607874

Antonakakis, N., Chatziantoniou, I., & Gabauer, D. (2020). Refined measures of dynamic connectedness based on time-varying parameter vector autoregressions. *Journal of Risk and Financial Management, 13*(4), 84. DOI: 10.3390/jrfm13040084

Aruleba, I., & Sun, Y. (2025). Enhanced credit risk prediction using deep learning and SMOTE-ENN resampling. *Machine Learning with Applications, 21*, 100692. DOI: 10.1016/j.mlwa.2025.100692

Atak, A. (2024). Beyond polarity: How ESG sentiment influences idiosyncratic volatility in the Turkish stock market. *Borsa Istanbul Review, 24*, 10–21. DOI: 10.1016/j.bir.2024.11.003

Atak, A., Mehta, P., & Singh, A. (2024). "ESG sentiment and idiosyncratic volatility: Evidence from the Turkish stock market." Emerging Markets Review, Volume 51. *Article, 100987*, 1–14. DOI: 10.1016/j.ememar.2024.100987

Atarwaman, R. J. D., Amiruddin, A., & Dharmawati, D. (2026). The Role of ESG Disclosure Quality in Shaping Investor Risk Perception in Post-pandemic Capital Markets. *International Journal of Economic Literature, 3*(7), 68–83.

Avery, C. (2001). Business and Human Rights in a time of change. In *Liability of multinational corporations under international law* (pp. 17–73). Brill Nijhoff. DOI: 10.1163/9789004482678_003

Awan, U., Sroufe, R., & Kraslawski, A. (2019). Creativity enables sustainable development: Supplier engagement as a boundary condition for the positive effect on green innovation. *Journal of Cleaner Production*, *226*, 172–185. DOI: 10.1016/j.jclepro.2019.03.308

Bachelet, M. J., Becchetti, L., & Manfredonia, S. (2019). The green bonds premium puzzle: The role of issuer characteristics and third-party verification. *Sustainability (Basel)*, *11*(4), 1098. DOI: 10.3390/su11041098

Baker, M., & Wurgler, J. (2007). Investor sentiment in the stock market. *The Journal of Economic Perspectives*, *21*(2), 129–152. DOI: 10.1257/jep.21.2.129

Baker, S. R., Bloom, N., & Davis, S. J. (2016). Measuring economic policy uncertainty. *The Quarterly Journal of Economics*, *131*(4), 1593–1636. DOI: 10.1093/qje/qjw024

Balaji, K. (2024). Neuromarketing and sustainable finance: Real-world case studies of green investment promotions. In *Neuromarketing's role in sustainable finance* (pp. 169–204). IGI Global. DOI: 10.4018/979-8-3693-9117-4.ch010

Balaji, K., Singh, A., & Kumar, R. (2024). Smart contracts and digital twins transforming green finance with automated investment transactions. *Sustainable Finance*, *6*(1), 45–60. DOI: 10.1080/20430795.2024.2134567

Balana, B. B., Mekonnen, D., Haile, B., Hagos, F., Yimam, S., & Ringler, C. (2022). Demand and supply constraints of credit in smallholder farming: Evidence from Ethiopia and Tanzania. *World Development*, *159*, 106033. DOI: 10.1016/j.worlddev.2022.106033

Balana, B. B., & Oyeyemi, M. A. (2022). Agricultural credit constraints in smallholder farming in developing countries: Evidence from Nigeria. *World Development Sustainability*, *1*, 100012. DOI: 10.1016/j.wds.2022.100012

Banerjee, S., Aggarwal, D., & Sengupta, P. (2025). Do stock markets care about ESG and sentiments? Impact of ESG and investors' sentiment on share price prediction using machine learning. *Annals of Operations Research*, •••, 1–40. DOI: 10.1007/s10479-025-06480-4

Barberis, N., Shleifer, A., & Vishny, R. (1998). A model of investor sentiment. *Journal of Financial Economics*, *49*(3), 307–343. DOI: 10.1016/S0304-405X(98)00027-0

Bartolini, N., Romagnoli, S., & Santini, A. (2025). Understanding climate risk in Europe: Are transition and physical risk priced in equity and fixed-income markets? *Journal of Empirical Finance*, *84*, 101672. DOI: 10.1016/j.jempfin.2025.101672

Bassen, A., & Kovacs, A. M. M. (2008) Environmental, Social and Governance Key Performance Indicators from a Capital Market Perspective. *Zeitschrift für Wirtschafts- und Unternehmensethik*, 9/2, 182-192. Available at *SSRN*: https://ssrn.com/abstract=1307091

Bebchuk, L. A., & Weisbach, M. S. (2010). The state of corporate governance research. *Review of Financial Studies*, *23*(3), 939–961. DOI: 10.1093/rfs/hhp121

Beltagy, I., Lo, K., & Cohan, A. (2019). SciBERT: A Pretrained Language Model for Scientific Text. *EMNLP-IJCNLP 2019 - 2019 Conference on Empirical Methods in Natural Language Processing and 9th International Joint Conference on Natural Language Processing, Proceedings of the Conference*, 3615–3620. DOI: 10.18653/v1/D19-1371

Ben-Nasr, H., Masry, S., Masum, A. A., & Ouni, Z. (2025). Carbon risk and trade credit. *International Review of Economics & Finance*, *103*, 104425. DOI: 10.1016/j.iref.2025.104425

Berg, F., Kölbel, J. F., & Rigobon, R. (2022). Aggregate confusion: The divergence of ESG ratings. *Review of Finance*, *26*(6), 1315–1344. DOI: 10.1093/rof/rfac033

Bhatnagar, M., Rajaram, R., Ali, T., & Mehta, P. (2025). "Correlating investor patterns and ESG performance with neuromarketing insights: Behavioural finance meets sustainability." Sustainability, Volume 17, Issue 6. *Article*, *23456*, 1–15. DOI: 10.3390/su170623456

Bianchi, F., Yu, B., & Tagliabue, J. (2021). BERT Goes Shopping: Comparing Distributional Models for Product Representations. *ECNLP 2021 - 4th Workshop on e-Commerce and NLP, Proceedings*, 1–12. DOI: 10.18653/v1/2021.ecnlp-1.1

Bocken, N. M. P., De Pauw, I., Bakker, C., & Van Der Grinten, B. (2016). Product design and business model strategies for a circular economy. *Journal of Industrial and Production Engineering*, *33*(5), 308–320. DOI: 10.1080/21681015.2016.1172124

Bolton, P., & Kacperczyk, M. (2021). Do investors care about carbon risk? *Journal of Financial Economics*, *142*(2), 517–549. DOI: 10.1016/j.jfineco.2021.05.008

Boufateh, T., Saadaoui, Z., & Jiao, Z. (2025). On the time-varying responses of Fintech stock returns to geopolitical, financial and market sentiment shocks. *The Quarterly Review of Economics and Finance*, *101*, 101951. DOI: 10.1016/j.qref.2024.101951

Brabec, J., & Macháč, J. (2025). Impacts of the EU Taxonomy implementation: A systematic literature review. *Climate Policy*, •••, 1–13. DOI: 10.1080/14693062.2025.2526683

Brière, M., Pouget, S., Schmalz, M. C., & Ureche-Rangau, L. (2022). Delegated philanthropy in mutual fund votes on climate change externalities.

Brown, S., Davidovic, J., & Hasan, A. (2021). The algorithm audit: Scoring the algorithms that score us. *Big Data &amp. Big Data & Society*, *8*(1), 2053951720983865. Advance online publication. DOI: 10.1177/2053951720983865

Bugg-Levine, A., & Emerson, J. (2011). Impact Investing: Transforming How We Make Money while Making a Difference. *Innovations: Technology, Governance, Globalization*, *6*(3), 9–18. DOI: 10.1162/INOV_a_00077

Chen, C., Fan, M., & Fan, Y. (2024). The role of digital inclusive finance in green innovation. *PLoS One*, *19*(3), e0299456. Advance online publication. DOI: 10.1371/journal.pone.0315598 PMID: 39715192

Cherian, A. M., Rajagopalan, K. K., Bhattacharya, S., Pawar, S., Anute, N., Selvakumar, P., & Manjunath, T. C. (2026). The political economy of trade wars. In Thiébaut, R., & Selgas-Cors, M. (Eds.), *Geopolitical and Economic Consequences of Trade Policies and Tariffs* (pp. 15–38). IGI Global Scientific Publishing. [REMOVED HYPERLINK FIELD], DOI: 10.4018/979-8-3373-3835-4.ch002

Cho, C. H., & Patten, D. M. (2007). The role of environmental disclosures as tools of legitimacy: A research note. *Accounting, Organizations and Society*, *32*(7–8), 639–647. DOI: 10.1016/j.aos.2006.09.009

Chornovol, O., Norta, A., & Singh, A. (2022). Blockchain-based impact indexing for sustainable machine-to-everything infrastructure management. *IEEE Transactions on Network and Service Management*, *19*(4), 567 576. DOI: 10.1109/TNSM.2022.3145678

Christensen, H. B., Hail, L., & Leuz, C. (2021). Mandatory CSR and sustainability reporting: Economic analysis and literature review. *Review of Accounting Studies*, *26*(3), 1176–1248. DOI: 10.1007/s11142-021-09609-5

Chuang, M., Chuang, G., Chuang, C., & Chuang, J. (2025, February 20). *Judging It, Washing It: Scoring and Greenwashing Corporate Climate Disclosures using Large Language Models*. arXiv.Org. https://arxiv.org/abs/2502.15094 DOI: 10.18653/v1/2025.climatenlp-1.2

Çoban, S., Uçar, M., Ulusay, N., & Kaya, N. (2025). Investigating the impact of social media-driven sentiment on the electric vehicle stock market using quantile regression. *International Journal of Economics and Financial Issues, 15*(4), 299–316. DOI: 10.32479/ijefi.19430

Collaoni, F., & Trevisan, E. (2022). 'Dieselgate is Made in Germany' – Framing Volkswagen Emissions Scandal in the German Economy. *Linguistische Treffen in Wrocław*, (21), 35–46.

Comincioli, N., & Donadelli, M. (2026). 2024 US election: The climate for green and brown portfolios. *The North American Journal of Economics and Finance, 83*, 102593. DOI: 10.1016/j.najef.2026.102593

Conceição, P. (2025). A matter of choice: People and possibilities in the age of AI. *Human Development Report 2025.*

Creti, A., Jouvet, P. A., & Mignon, V. (2012). Carbon price drivers: Phase I versus Phase II equilibrium? *Energy Economics, 34*(1), 327–334. DOI: 10.1016/j.eneco.2011.11.001

Czura, K., & Klonner, S. (2023). Financial market responses to a natural disaster: Evidence from credit networks and the Indian Ocean tsunami. *Journal of Development Economics, 160*, 102996. DOI: 10.1016/j.jdeveco.2022.102996

Dagur, S., Mahato, K. K., Zatsal, S., & Patel, R. (2025). Green finance and digital payments: Innovations for a sustainable financial ecosystem. *Journal of Sustainable Finance & Investment, 15*(3), 345–360. DOI: 10.1080/20430795.2025.1134569

Dar, B. I., Jaiswal, S., & Kumar, R. (2025). Reducing the carbon footprint of financial transactions: The environmental impact of technological innovation in finance. *Journal of Sustainable Finance & Investment, 15*(2), 210–225. DOI: 10.1080/20430795.2025.1134571

De Long, J. B., Shleifer, A., Summers, L. H., & Waldmann, R. J. (1990). Noise trader risk in financial markets. *Journal of Political Economy, 98*(4), 703–738. DOI: 10.1086/261703

Delina, L. L., Lam, R. Y. H., Tang, W. S., & Wong, K. Y. (2023). Mapping the actor landscape of a future fintech-funded renewable energy ecosystem in Hong Kong. *Journal of Environmental Management, 345*, 118678. Advance online publication. DOI: 10.1016/j.jenvman.2023.118678

Deng, G., Deng, Q., Yan, J., & Li, X. (2026). ESG sentiment, investor behavior, and corporate cost of equity capital. *International Review of Financial Analysis, 109*, 104800. DOI: 10.1016/j.irfa.2025.104800

Devlin, J., Chang, M.-W., Lee, K., & Toutanova, K. (2019). BERT: Pre-training of Deep Bidirectional Transformers for Language Understanding. *Proceedings of the 2019 Conference of the North*, 4171–4186. DOI: 10.18653/v1/N19-1423

Dhar, B. K., Karim, R., & Mollik, M. S. (2026). Stitching Sustainability in Fashion: Strengthening Circular Economy Drivers in the Textile Industry. In *Strategic Innovations for Circular Economy* (pp. 179-208). IGI Global Scientific Publishing. DOI: 10.4018/979-8-3373-2454-8.ch007

Diebold, F. X., & Yilmaz, K. (2012). Better to give than to receive: Predictive directional measurement of volatility spillovers. *International Journal of Forecasting*, *28*(1), 57–66. DOI: 10.1016/j.ijforecast.2011.02.006

Diebold, F. X., & Yilmaz, K. (2014). On the network topology of variance decompositions: Measuring the connectedness of financial firms. *Journal of Econometrics*, *182*(1), 119–134. DOI: 10.1016/j.jeconom.2014.04.012

Djatche, M. J. N. (2025). Unveiling the effects of monetary surprises: Risk-taking and credit supply of US banks. *International Review of Economics & Finance*, *101*, 104211. DOI: 10.1016/j.iref.2025.104211

Du, Y., & Du, L. (2026). ESG performance, media sentiment, and corporate asset mispricing. *Finance Research Letters*, *87*, 108888. DOI: 10.1016/j.frl.2025.108888

Ebenezer, Y., Durga, K., Chandrakala, N. B., Shashank, G., Sharma, M., Selvakumar, P., & Manjunath, T. C. (2026). Disaster education and awareness programs. In Ali, Q., & Tariq Iqbal Khan, M. (Eds.), *Strengthening Global Resilience to Natural Disasters* (pp. 73–102). IGI Global Scientific Publishing. [REMOVED HYPERLINK FIELD], DOI: 10.4018/979-8-3693-9745-9.ch004

Eccles, R. G., Ioannou, I., & Serafeim, G. (2014). The impact of corporate sustainability on organizational processes and performance. *Management Science*, *60*(11), 2835–2857. DOI: 10.1287/mnsc.2014.1984

Eccles, R. G., Serafeim, G., Seth, D., & Ming, C. C. Y. (2013). The performance frontier: Innovating for a sustainable strategy. *Harvard Business Review*, *91*(7), 17–18. https://pubmed.ncbi.nlm.nih.gov/23898735/ PMID: 23898735

Elias, O., Awotunde, O. J., Oladepo, O. I., & Chen, L. (2024). "The evolution of green fintech: Leveraging AI and IoT for sustainable financial services." Technological Forecasting and Social Change, Volume 198. *Article*, *123789*, 1–15. DOI: 10.1016/j.techfore.2024.123789

Ellen MacArthur Foundation. (2015). *Towards the circular economy: Business rationale for an accelerated transition*. Ellen MacArthur Foundation.

Engle, R. F., Giglio, S., Kelly, B., Lee, H., & Stroebel, J. (2020). Hedging climate change news. *Review of Financial Studies, 33*(3), 1184–1216. DOI: 10.1093/rfs/hhz072

European Commission. (2025). *Corporate sustainability reporting*. https://finance.ec.europa.eu/financial-markets/company-reporting-and-auditing/company-reporting/corporate-sustainability-reporting_en

Ever, D., & Demircioğlu, E. N. (2022). Yapay zekâ teknolojilerinin kalite maliyetleri üzerine etkisi. Çukurova Üniversitesi Sosyal Bilimler Enstitüsü Dergisi, 31(1), 59-72.

Fatica, S., Panzica, R., & Rancan, M. (2021). The pricing of green bonds: Are financial institutions special? *Journal of Financial Stability, 54*, 100873. DOI: 10.1016/j.jfs.2021.100873

Ferjančič, U., Ichev, R., Lončarski, I., Montariol, S., Pelicon, A., Pollak, S., Sitar Šuštar, K., Toman, A., Valentinčič, A., & Žnidaršič, M. (2024). Textual analysis of corporate sustainability reporting and corporate ESG scores. *International Review of Financial Analysis, 96*, 103669. DOI: 10.1016/j.irfa.2024.103669

Fernández Rodríguez, F., Gómez-Puig, M., & Sosvilla Rivero, S. (2025). Examining the transmission of credit and liquidity risks: A network analysis for EMU sovereign debt markets. *IREA–Working Papers, 2025, IR25/04.*

Fernandez-Vallado, M., Chen, L., & Patel, R. (2025). Policy frameworks for microfinance: Innovative financial solutions for sustainable development. *Journal of Development Economics, 160*, 234–245. DOI: 10.1016/j.jdeveco.2025.103456

Fingerman, K., Geronimo, C., Read, E., Wakeman, D., & Martin, J. I. (2025). Risks of crediting carbon offsets in low carbon fuel standards: Lessons learned from dairy biomethane. *Energy Policy, 206*, 114738. DOI: 10.1016/j.enpol.2025.114738

Flammer, C. (2021). Corporate green bonds. *Journal of Financial Economics, 142*(2), 499–516. DOI: 10.1016/j.jfineco.2021.01.010

Floridi, L. (2018). Soft ethics, the governance of the digital and the General Data Protection Regulation. *Philosophical Transactions. Series A, Mathematical, Physical, and Engineering Sciences, 376*(2133), 20180081. DOI: 10.1098/rsta.2018.0081 PMID: 30322997

Franco, J. P. M., Morales, A. B., & Laurini, M. P. (2026). When green turns exuberant: Bubble detection in clean-energy markets. *Finance Research Letters, 87*, 109109. DOI: 10.1016/j.frl.2025.109109

Friede, G., Busch, T., & Bassen, A. (2015). ESG and financial performance: Aggregated evidence from more than 2,000 empirical studies. *Journal of Sustainable Finance & Investment*, *5*(4), 210–233. DOI: 10.1080/20430795.2015.1118917

Funda, V. (2025). A systematic review of algorithm auditing processes to assess bias and risks in AI systems. *Journal of Infrastructure Policy and Development*, *9*(2), 11489. DOI: 10.24294/jipd11489

Garcia-Muiña, F. E., González-Sánchez, R., Ferrari, A. M., Volpi, L., Pini, M., Siligardi, C., & Settembre-Blundo, D. (2019). Identifying the equilibrium point between sustainability goals and circular economy practices in an Industry 4.0 manufacturing context using eco-design. *Social Sciences (Basel, Switzerland)*, *8*(8), 241. DOI: 10.3390/socsci8080241

Gardazi, N. M., Daud, A., Malik, M. K., Bukhari, A., Alsahfi, T., & Alshemaimri, B. (2025). BERT applications in natural language processing: A review. *Artificial Intelligence Review*, *58*(6), 166. DOI: 10.1007/s10462-025-11162-5

Gavriilidis, K. (2021). Measuring climate policy uncertainty. SSRN Electronic Journal. DOI: DOI: 10.2139/ssrn.3847388

Geissdoerfer, M., Savaget, P., Bocken, N. M., & Hultink, E. J. (2017). The Circular Economy – A new sustainability paradigm? *Journal of Cleaner Production*, *143*, 757–768. DOI: 10.1016/j.jclepro.2016.12.048

General Statistics Office of Vietnam. (2025). *Report on the Socio-Economic Situation in the Fourth Quarter and for the Year 2025*. https://www.nso.gov.vn/en/data-and-statistics/2026/01/socio-economic-situation-in-the-fourth-quarter-and-2025/

Ghisellini, P., Cialani, C., & Ulgiati, S. (2016). A review on circular economy: The expected transition to a balanced interplay of environmental and economic systems. *Journal of Cleaner Production*, *114*, 11 32. DOI: 10.1016/j.jclepro.2015.09.007

Gianfrate, G., & Peri, M. (2019). The green advantage: Exploring the convenience of issuing green bonds. *Journal of Cleaner Production*, *219*, 127–135. DOI: 10.1016/j.jclepro.2019.02.022

Giese, G., Lee, L. E., Melas, D., Nagy, Z., & Nishikawa, L. (2019). Foundations of ESG investing. *Journal of Portfolio Management*, *45*(5), 69–83. DOI: 10.3905/jpm.2019.45.5.069

Giglio, S., Kelly, B., & Stroebel, J. (2021). Climate finance. *Annual Review of Financial Economics*, *13*(1), 15–36. DOI: 10.1146/annurev-financial-102620-103311

GIIN. (2020). *Annual impact investor survey*. Global Impact Investing Network.

Gilchrist, D., Yu, J., & Zhong, R. (2021). The limits of green finance: A survey of literature in the context of green bonds and green loans. *Sustainability (Basel), 13*(2), 478. DOI: 10.3390/su13020478

Global Reporting Initiative. (2013). *The value of sustainability reporting and the GRI Standards*. www.globalreporting.org

Gómez González, J. E., Uribe, J., & Valencia, O. M. (2024). Asymmetric sovereign risk: Implications for climate change preparation (IDB-WP-1588). *IDB Working Paper Series*.

Goodman, E. P., & Trehu, J. (2022). AI audit washing and accountability. SSRN *Electronic Journal*. DOI: 10.2139/ssrn.4227350

Gorovaia, N., & Makrominas, M. (2024). Identifying greenwashing in corporate-social responsibility reports using natural-language processing. *European Financial Management, 31*(1), 427–462. DOI: 10.1111/eufm.12509

Government of Vietnam. (2021). *Decision No. 1658/QD-TTg on Approving the National Green Growth Strategy for the 2021-2030 period, with a vision by 2050.* https://vanban.chinhphu.vn/?docid=204226&pageid=27160

Government of Vietnam. (2022). *Decree No. 06/2022/ND-CP on Mitigation of Greenhouse Gas Emissions and Protection of the Ozone Layer.* https://climate-laws.org/document/decree-no-06-2022-nd-cp-on-mitigation-of-green-house-gas-ghg-emissions-and-protection-of-ozone-layer_d8ff

Guenther, E. M., & Hoppe, H. (2014). Merging limited perspectives: A synopsis of measurement approaches and theories of the relationship between corporate environmental and financial performance. *Journal of Industrial Ecology, 18*(5), 689–707. DOI: 10.1111/jiec.12125

Gumbo, L., & Chude-Okonkwo, U A K. (2025). Regulatory sandbox as a frontier for innovation and sustainability: A systematic review. *Cogent Business & Management, 12*(1), 2345678. Advance online publication. DOI: 10.1080/23311975.2025.2510555

Guo, N., Jia, S., & Liu, Y. (2024). Climate policy uncertainty and its impact on the volatility, correlation, and hedging of sovereign and green bonds. *Journal of Environmental Management, 370*, 122953. DOI: 10.1016/j.jenvman.2024.122953 PMID: 39447369

Gupta, A., Sharma, U., & Gupta, S. K. (2021). The Role of ESG in Sustainable Development: An Analysis Through the Lens of Machine Learning. *2021 IEEE International Humanitarian Technology Conference, IHTC 2021*. DOI: 10.1109/IHTC53077.2021.9698939

Gupta, H., & Chaudhary, R. (2023). An analysis of volatility and risk-adjusted returns of ESG indices in developed and emerging economies. *Risks*, *11*(10), 173. Advance online publication. DOI: 10.3390/risks11100182

Haas, D. R., & Popov, A. (2023). Finance and Green Growth. *Economic Journal (London)*, *133*(650), 637–668. DOI: 10.1093/ej/ueac081

Hachenberg, B., & Schiereck, D. (2018). Are green bonds priced differently from conventional bonds? *Journal of Asset Management*, *19*(6), 371–383. DOI: 10.1057/s41260-018-0088-5

Hajikhani, A., & Cole, C. (2024). A critical review of large language models: Sensitivity, bias, and the path toward specialized AI. *Quantitative Science Studies*, *5*(3), 736–756. DOI: 10.1162/qss_a_00310

Hamm, L. S., Martínez, S. Á. O., Loder, A., & Bogenberger, K. (2025). Who Gets What? A user perspective on initial credit allocation in Tradable Mobility Credit Schemes. *Transport Policy*, *164*, 118–129. DOI: 10.1016/j.tranpol.2025.01.032

Ha, N. T. H., & Huy, N. D. (2025). Assessment and Comparison of ESG Disclosure Levels in the 2024 Annual Reports of State-Owned and Joint-Stock Commercial Banks in Vietnam. *Asean International Sandbox Conference, 7*, 121–133.

Han, J. J., Jun, S., & Kim, J. W. (2025). *Examining the Impact of ESG News Sentiment on Corporate Performance: A Comprehensive Analysis by News Topic and Industry*. Business Strategy, the Environment & Responsibility., DOI: 10.1002/bse.3501

Herbe, A., Estermann, Z., Holzwarth, V., & vom Brocke, J. (2024). How to effectively use distributed ledger technology in supply chain management? *International Journal of Production Research*, *62*(10), 3567–3589. DOI: 10.1080/00207543.2023.2218947

Hernanz, V., Quiroga, S., Suárez, C., & Aguiño, J. E. (2025). Evaluating the merit of carbon credits: Effectiveness in transitioning to REDD+ community incentives. *Environmental and Sustainability Indicators*, *25*, 100591. DOI: 10.1016/j.indic.2025.100591

Heß, V. L., & Damasio, B. (2025). Machine learning in banking risk management: Mapping a decade of evolution. *International Journal of Information Management Data Insights*, *5*(1), 100324. DOI: 10.1016/j.jjimei.2025.100324

Hidayat-ur-Rehman, I., Alam, M. N., Alsolamy, M., Alharbi, S. H. H., AlAnazi, T. M. B., & Bhuiyan, A. B. (2025). Examining investor interaction with digital robo-advisory systems: Green value and interface quality in a socio-technical context. *Systems*, *13*(9), 787. DOI: 10.3390/systems13090787

Hong, H., Li, F. W., & Xu, J. (2019). Climate risks and market efficiency. *Journal of Econometrics*, *208*(1), 265–281. DOI: 10.1016/j.jeconom.2018.09.015

Hossain, M. K., & Mollik, M. S. (2022). Exploring the impact of Social Media Platforms on Instigating Tourist's Emotions and Behavioral Intentions to Co-Create and Visit Tourist Spots-Bangladesh Perspective. https://doi.org/DOI: 10.58753/jbspust.3.1.2022.13

Hossain, N., Ali, T., & Zhang, Y. (2023). Comparative analysis of conventional and modern credit risk assessment methods in MSMEs. *The Journal of Credit Risk*, *19*(3), 89–104. DOI: 10.21314/JCR.2023.345

Huang, J., Wang, D. D., & Wang, Y. (2024). Textual attributes of corporate sustainability reports and ESG ratings. *Sustainability (Basel)*, *16*(21), 9270. DOI: 10.3390/su16219270

Huang, Y., Bai, F., Shang, M., & Ahmad, M. (2023). On the fast track: The benefits of ESG performance on the commercial credit financing. *Environmental Science and Pollution Research International*, *30*(35), 83961–83974. DOI: 10.1007/s11356-023-28172-x PMID: 37351751

Huang, Y., Liang, W., Duan, K., Parhi, M., & Mishra, T. (2026). Sentiments and risks: A spillover tale under climate policy uncertainty. *Energy Economics*, *154*, 109101. DOI: 10.1016/j.eneco.2025.109101

Huynh, N., De Mello, L., & Li, K. (2025). Evolution of investor sentiment: A systematic literature review and bibliometric analysis. *International Review of Economics & Finance*, *100*, 104115. DOI: 10.1016/j.iref.2025.104115

Huynh, T. D., & Xia, Y. (2021). Climate change news risk and corporate bond returns. *Journal of Financial and Quantitative Analysis*, *56*(6), 1985–2009. DOI: 10.1017/S0022109020000757

Ilhan, E., Sautner, Z., & Vilkov, G. (2021). Carbon tail risk. *Review of Financial Studies*, *34*(3), 1540–1571. DOI: 10.1093/rfs/hhaa071

Islam, F A S., Singh, A., & Patel, R. (2025). AI-driven optimization and decision support for integrated waste-to-energy systems in climate-vulnerable megacities: Case study of Dhaka. *Renewable Energy*, *220*, 789–802. DOI: 10.1016/j.renene.2025.113456

Jain, S., & Chawla, S. (2025). Fuelling sustainability through green bonds: Investigating the impact of pro-environmental values on retail investors' decisions. *Journal of Environmental Planning and Management*, •••, 1–28. DOI: 10.1080/09640568.2025.2478289

Jaiswal, R., Gupta, S., & Tiwari, A. K. (2024). Decoding mood of the Twitterverse on ESG investing: Opinion mining and key themes using machine learning. *Management Research Review, 47*(8), 1234–1256. DOI: 10.1108/MRR-07-2023-0526

James, E. O., Bakas, D., Thompson, P., & Ebireri, J. (2025). Who Benefits the Most from Micro-Credit? Micro-Level Evidence from Sub-Saharan Africa. *World Development, 193*, 107023. DOI: 10.1016/j.worlddev.2025.107023

Jeong, S. H., Han, J. J., Jun, S., Kim, S., & Kim, J. W. (2025). Investor Responses to ESG News Sentiment: Exploring Differential Effects and Industry Moderation. *Corporate Social Responsibility and Environmental Management, 32*(3), 3944–3964. Advance online publication. DOI: 10.1002/csr.3163

Jia, S., Guo, N., & Jin, J. (2024). Climate policy uncertainty risk and sovereign bond volatility. *Journal of Cleaner Production, 434*, 140145. DOI: 10.1016/j.jclepro.2023.140145

Jin, J., Han, L., Wu, L., & Zeng, H. (2020). The hedging effect of green bonds on carbon market risk. *International Review of Financial Analysis, 71*, 101509. DOI: 10.1016/j.irfa.2020.101509

Joshi, N. V., Selvakumar, P., & Srivastava, N. Manjeet, Das A, Manjunath T C, (2026). "Bioethics legal implications of artificial intelligence in medicine." In Anastasiadou S, Seremeti L, Papalexandris S (Eds.), Bioethics and Legal Aspects of AI in Healthcare and Life Sciences (pp. 27-54). IGI Global Scientific Publishing. DOI: .[REMOVED HYPERLINK FIELD]DOI: 10.4018/979-8-3373-5646-4.ch002

Julliete, A., Palma, J., Wangs, S., & Mehta, P. (2025). "Investor behavior in ESG markets: Psychological drivers behind sustainable investment choices." Journal of Behavioral and Experimental Finance, Volume 38. *Article, 101234*, 1–14. DOI: 10.1016/j.jbef.2025.101234

Kahneman, D., & Tversky, A. (1979). Prospect theory: An analysis of decision under risk. *Econometrica, 47*(2), 263–291. DOI: 10.2307/1914185

Kaliyar, R. K., Goswami, A., Narang, P., & Sinha, S. (2020). FNDNet – A deep convolutional neural network for fake news detection. *Cognitive Systems Research, 61*, 32–44. DOI: 10.1016/j.cogsys.2019.12.005

Kang, H., & Kim, J. (2022). Analyzing and Visualizing Text Information in Corporate Sustainability Reports Using Natural Language Processing Methods. *Applied Sciences (Basel, Switzerland), 12*(11), 5614. Advance online publication. DOI: 10.3390/app12115614

Karim, R., Waaje, A., & Roshid, M. M. (2025a). Digital Circular Economy for Attaining Sustainable Development Goals: Technologies for Global Sustainability. In *Effects of Digitalization and Circular Economy on Sustainable Policy and Climate Change Prevention* (pp. 211-240). IGI Global Scientific Publishing. https://doi.org/ DOI: 10.4018/979-8-3693-9909-5.ch008

Karim, R., Waaje, A., Roshid, M. M., & Yeamin, M. B. (2025b). Turning the waste into wealth: Progressing toward global sustainability through the circular economy in waste management. In *Sustainable waste management in the tourism and hospitality sectors* (pp. 507–552). IGI Global Scientific Publishing., DOI: 10.4018/979-8-3693-6110-8.ch019

Karpf, A., & Mandel, A. (2018). The changing value of the 'green' label on the US municipal bond market. *Nature Climate Change*, *8*(2), 161–165. DOI: 10.1038/s41558-017-0062-0

Kavousi-Fard, A., Almutairi, A., Al-Sumaiti, A., Farughian, A., & Alyami, S. (2021). An effective secured peer-to-peer energy market based on blockchain architecture for the interconnected microgrid and smart grid. *International Journal of Electrical Power & Energy Systems*, *133*, 107302. Advance online publication. DOI: 10.1016/j.ijepes.2021.107171

Khan, M. A., & Vismara, S. (2025). Green bond issuance and corporate environmental and financial performance: A meta-analysis. *International Review of Economics & Finance*, *102*, 104313. DOI: 10.1016/j.iref.2025.104313

Kirchherr, J., Reike, D., & Hekkert, M. (2017). Conceptualizing the circular economy: An analysis of 114 definitions. *Resources, Conservation and Recycling*, *127*, 221–232. DOI: 10.1016/j.resconrec.2017.09.005

Kladakis, G., & Skouralis, A. (2025). Sovereign credit rating downgrades and Growth-at-Risk. *Journal of International Financial Markets, Institutions and Money*, *103*, 102195. DOI: 10.1016/j.intfin.2025.102195

Koch, N., Fuss, S., Grosjean, G., & Edenhofer, O. (2014). Causes of the EU ETS price drop: Recession, CDM, renewable policies or a bit of everything? New evidence. *Energy Policy*, *73*, 676–685. DOI: 10.1016/j.enpol.2014.06.024

Kolk, A., & Pinkse, J. (2008). Business and climate change: Emergent institutions in global governance. *Corporate Governance (Bradford)*, *8*(4), 419–429. DOI: 10.1108/14720700810899167

Kollmuss, A., Zink, H., & Polycarp, C. (2008). *Making sense of the voluntary carbon market: A comparison of carbon offset standards*. WWF Germany.

Korhonen, J., Honkasalo, A., & Seppälä, J. (2018). Circular Economy: The Concept and its Limitations. *Ecological Economics, 143*, 37–46. DOI: 10.1016/j.ecolecon.2017.06.041

Koshiyama, A., Kazim, E., Treleaven, P., Rai, P., Szpruch, L., Pavey, G., Ahamat, G., Leutner, F., Goebel, R., Knight, A., Adams, J., Hitrova, C., Barnett, J., Nachev, P., Barber, D., Chamorro-Premuzic, T., Klemmer, K., Gregorovic, M., Khan, S., & Chatterjee, S. (2024). Towards algorithm auditing: Managing legal, ethical and technological risks of AI, ML and associated algorithms. *Royal Society Open Science, 11*(5), 230859. Advance online publication. DOI: 10.1098/rsos.230859 PMID: 39076787

Kouam, A. W. F., Singh, A., & Chen, L. (2024). "Blockchain technology and sustainable finance: Potential for climate change mitigation and adaptation." Technological Forecasting and Social Change, Volume 196. *Article, 123678*, 1–14. DOI: 10.1016/j.techfore.2024.123678

Kumar, P., Taneja, S., & Ozen, E. (2025). Exploring the influence of green bonds on sustainable development through low-carbon financing mobilisation. *International Journal of Law and Management, 67*(2), 249–270. DOI: 10.1108/IJLMA-01-2024-0030

Landers, R. N., & Behrend, T. S. (2022). Auditing the AI auditors: A framework for evaluating fairness and bias in high stakes AI predictive models. *The American Psychologist, 78*(1), 36–49. DOI: 10.1037/amp0000972 PMID: 35157476

Lan, Y., Yuan, Z., Tang, R., Hsu, S. C., & Wei, H. H. (2025). Green innovation and the ESG disconnect: Evidence from green patenting in the construction industry in China. *Journal of Management Engineering, 41*(1), 04024066. DOI: 10.1061/JMENEA.MEENG-6160

Larosa, F., Hoyas, S., Conejero, J. A., Garcia-Martinez, J., Fuso-Nerini, F., & Vinuesa, R. (2025). Large language models in climate and sustainability policy: Limits and opportunities. *Environmental Research Letters, 20*(7), 074032. DOI: 10.1088/1748-9326/addd36

Lee, H., Kim, J. H., & Jung, H. S. (2024). Deep-learning-based stock market prediction incorporating ESG sentiment and technical indicators. *Scientific Reports, 14*(1), 12345. Advance online publication. DOI: 10.1038/s41598-024-61106-2 PMID: 38704434

Lee, J., Yoon, W., Kim, S., Kim, D., Kim, S., So, C. H., & Kang, J. (2020). BioBERT: A pre-trained biomedical language representation model for biomedical text mining. *Bioinformatics (Oxford, England)*, *36*(4), 1234–1240. DOI: 10.1093/bioinformatics/btz682 PMID: 31501885

Lee, S., Kumar, R., & Chen, L. (2025). Modeling firm-level ESG sentiment interactions in stock returns: Evidence from retrofitted word embeddings. *The Journal of Financial Data Science*, *7*(3), 145–160. DOI: 10.3905/jfds.2025.1.145

Lheureux, Y. (2024). Predictive insights: Leveraging Twitter sentiments and machine learning for environmental, social and governance controversy prediction. *Journal of Computational Social Science*, *7*(2), 345–367. DOI: 10.1007/s42001-023-00228-5

Liang, C., Ma, X., & Liao, X. (2025). Unveiling investor motivation and trust in impact investing: Evidence from global green bond issuances. *Journal of Business Ethics*, *200*(2), 445–468. DOI: 10.1007/s10551-024-05891-w

Lins, K. V., Servaes, H., & Tamayo, A. (2017). Social capital, trust, and firm performance: The value of corporate social responsibility during the financial crisis. *The Journal of Finance*, *72*(4), 1785–1824. DOI: 10.1111/jofi.12505

Liu, B., Ren, B., & Jin, F. (2024). *Does Climate Risk Affect the Ease of Access to Credit for Farmers? Evidence from Chfs*. Evidence from Chfs. DOI: 10.2139/ssrn.4951698

Liu, J., Guo, J., & Man, Y. (2025). Ripple effects of climate policy uncertainty: Risk spillovers between traditional energy and green financial markets. *Sustainability (Basel)*, *17*(12), 5500. DOI: 10.3390/su17125500

Liu, M., Ling, Y. J., & Lee, C. C. (2025). Does ESG performance and investor attention affect stock volatility? An empirical study based on panel data and mixed-frequency data. *Applied Economics*, *57*(57), 9728–9742. Advance online publication. DOI: 10.1080/00036846.2024.2423068

Liu, M., Luo, X., & Lu, W. Z. (2023). Public perceptions of environmental, social, and governance (ESG) based on social media data: Evidence from China. *Journal of Cleaner Production*, *385*, 135678. Advance online publication. DOI: 10.1016/j.jclepro.2022.135840

Liu, T., Liu, W., Elahi, E., & Liu, X. (2022). Supply chain finance and the sustainable growth of Chinese firms: The moderating effect of digital finance. *Frontiers in Environmental Science*, *10*, 922182. Advance online publication. DOI: 10.3389/fenvs.2022.922182

Loang, O. K., & Candra, S. (2025). Religion and green: The dual power of ESG and Shariah-compliant stocks in brand values of Malaysia, Indonesia, and Saudi Arabia. *Journal of Islamic Monetary Economics and Finance*, *11*(2), 419–448. DOI: 10.21098/jimf.v11i2.2687

Loang, O. K., Patel, R., & Chen, L. (2025). From tweets to trades: Investor sentiment, attention, and news sentiment in ESG stocks. *Journal of Sustainable Finance & Investment*, *15*(2), 234–250. DOI: 10.1080/20430795.2025.1134568

Lopez-de-Silanes, F., McCahery, J. A., & Pudschedl, P. C. (2020) ESG Performance and Disclosure: A Cross-Country Analysis. *Singapore Journal of Legal Studies*, 217-241. Available at *SSRN*: https://ssrn.com/abstract=3649896

Luo, K., Peng, L., & Zhou, F. (2026). Sustainability uncertainty and the dynamics of green asset markets. *Journal of Innovation & Knowledge*, *100999*, 100999. Advance online publication. DOI: 10.1016/j.jik.2026.100999

Mahadevan, V., Subramaniam, S., & Srivastava, V. (2026). Carbon concentration in bank portfolios and efficiency: The role of credit risk and capitalization. *Journal of International Financial Markets, Institutions and Money*, *109*, 102327. Advance online publication. DOI: 10.1016/j.intfin.2026.102327

Mallappa, V. K. H., Gadde, S., & Cariappa, A. A. (2025). Understanding farmers' trust in stakeholders of carbon credit projects: A perception-based analysis. *Current Research in Environmental Sustainability*, *10*, 100317. DOI: 10.1016/j.crsust.2025.100317

Marchant, G. E., Cooper, Z., & Gough-Stone, P. J. (2022). Bringing technological transparency to tenebrous markets: The case for using blockchain to validate carbon credit trading markets. *Natural Resources Journal*, *62*, 159.

Marfu, A., Abbas, H., Sya, A., Purwanto, A., Nadiroh, , Sumargo, B., Wulandari, S. S., Daiman, , Malaihollo, C. A., Syakyakirti, , Tanubrata, D., & Pratiwi, D. I. (2025). Building long-term value: A practical guide to integrating ESG into business strategies. *Sustainable Futures : An Applied Journal of Technology, Environment and Society*, *10*, 100955. DOI: 10.1016/j.sftr.2025.100955

Martínez-Ferrero, J., & Lozano, M. B. (2021). The nonlinear relation between institutional ownership and environmental, social and governance performance in emerging countries. *Sustainability (Basel)*, *13*(3), 1586. Advance online publication. DOI: 10.3390/su13031586

Martínez, S. Á. O., Schatzman, T., Loder, A., Axhausen, K. W., & Bogenberger, K. (2025). Mode choice behavior in a tradable mobility credit scheme: A stated-preference experiment. *Transportation Research Part A, Policy and Practice, 199,* 104570. DOI: 10.1016/j.tra.2025.104570

Maurya, P. K., Bansal, R., & Mishra, A. K. (2025). *Investor sentiment and its implication on global financial markets: a systematic review of literature.* Qualitative Research in Financial Markets., DOI: 10.1108/QRFM-06-2024-0123

Maurya, P. K., Bansal, R., & Mishra, A. K. (2026). Investor sentiment and its implication on global financial markets: A systematic review of literature. *Qualitative Research in Financial Markets, 18*(1), 209–248. DOI: 10.1108/QRFM-04-2024-0087

Mazzucato, M. (2018). *The value of everything: making and taking in the global economy.* http://bvbr.bib-bvb.de:8991

Mei, K., & Jiang, Y. (2026). Beyond volatility: Higher-moment spillovers in the green finance–energy–energy metals nexus. *International Review of Economics & Finance, 106,* 105034. DOI: 10.1016/j.iref.2026.105034

Mei, X., Wen, Z., Cai, Y., Li, Y., & Jiang, Y. (2025). Research on the assessment of greenwashing in corporate environmental information disclosure based on large language models and the dynamic mechanism of green financing. *Journal of Innovation and Development, 11*(3), 32–39. DOI: 10.54097/be76ya94

Mertzanis, C., & Tebourbi, I. (2025). Geopolitical risk and global green bond market growth. *European Financial Management, 31*(1), 26–71. DOI: 10.1111/eufm.12484

Ministry of Finance. (2020). *Circular No. 96/2020/TT-BTC on guidelines for information disclosure on the securities market.* https://thuvienphapluat.vn/van-ban/Chung-khoan/Thong-tu-96-2020-TT-BTC-quy-dinh-cong-bo-thong-tin-tren-thi-truong-chung-khoan-459000.aspx

Mohammadrezaei, M., Marques, J. C., & Huq, A. (2024). *Use of text mining and natural language processing techniques in analyzing sustainability reports: A systematic literature review and assessment.* DOI: 10.2139/ssrn.5071032

mollii, R., Roshid, M., & Waaje, A. (2024). Circular economy and supply chain sustainability. In *Strategic Innovations for Dynamic Supply Chains* (pp. 1-30). IGI Global. https://doi.org/DOI: 10.4018/979-8-3693-3575-8.ch001

Mollik, M. S., Karim, R., & Mahmud, S. (2026b). Identifying Critical Success Factors for Adopting Sustainable Tourism in Emerging Economies. *EMIDWORLD 3rd International Congress on Economics, Public Finance, Business, & Social Sciences, Baku/Azerbaijan* (pp. 742-761).

Mollik, M. S., Karim, R., Sahabuddin, M., & Eneizan, B. (2026a). Industry 5.0 and the Circular Economy: A Transformative Nexus. In *Industry 5.0 and Sustainable Development* (pp. 237-267). Routledge. DOI: 10.4324/9781003647621-16

Mollik, M. S., Rahman, S. M., Rahat, M. R., Kulsum, C. U., & Sagir, S. A. M. (2024). Does Trustworthiness Influence Travel Service Use Intentions at an Online Travel Agency? A Study on the Digitalization of the Tourism Sector in Bangladesh. *Geo Journal of Tourism and Geosites*, *52*(1), 30–40. DOI: 10.30892/gtg.52103-1180

Moodaley, W., & Telukdarie, A. (2023). Greenwashing, sustainability reporting, and artificial intelligence: A systematic literature review. *Sustainability (Basel)*, *15*(2), 1481. DOI: 10.3390/su15021481

Moreno, A. I., & Caminero, T. (2022). Application of text mining to the analysis of climate-related disclosures. *International Review of Financial Analysis*, *83*, 102307. DOI: 10.1016/j.irfa.2022.102307

Motta, S., Böck, I., Koehler, J., Wolf, A. T., & Pattberg, P. (2025). The financialization of rivers: CDM-subsidized hydropower in the Mekong Region's basins at risk. *Global Environmental Change*, *90*, 102962. DOI: 10.1016/j.gloenvcha.2024.102962

MSCI ESG Research LLC. (2024). *MSCI ESG symbols and definitions*. https://www.msci.com/downloads/web/msci-com/legal/disclosures/esg-disclosures/MSCI%20ESG%20Symbols%20and%20Definitions.pdf

Murikah, W., Nthenge, J. K., & Musyoka, F. M. (2024). Bias and ethics of AI systems applied in auditing - A systematic review. *Scientific African*, *25*, e02281. DOI: 10.1016/j.sciaf.2024.e02281

Murray, A., Skene, K., & Haynes, K. (2017). The Circular Economy: An interdisciplinary exploration of the concept and application in a global context. *Journal of Business Ethics*, *140*(3), 369–380. DOI: 10.1007/s10551-015-2693-2

Musleh Al-Sartawi, A. M., Hussainey, K., & Razzaque, A. (2022). The role of artificial intelligence in sustainable finance. *Journal of Sustainable Finance & Investment*, •••, 1–6. DOI: 10.1080/20430795.2022.2057405

Ngo, M. T., Ngo, B. H., & Valerievich, S. V. (2024). Fine-tuned PhoBERT for sentiment analysis of Vietnamese phone reviews. *CTU Journal of Innovation and Sustainable Development*, *16*(Special Issue (ISDS)), 52–57. https://doi.org/https://doi.org/10.22144/CTUJOISD.2024.322. DOI: 10.22144/ctujoisd.2024.322

Nguyen, D. Q., & Nguyen, A. T. (2020). PhoBERT: Pre-trained language models for Vietnamese. *Findings of the Association for Computational Linguistics Findings of ACL: EMNLP*, *2020*, 1037–1042. DOI: 10.18653/v1/2020.findings-emnlp.92

Nguyen, D., Lau, T., Nguyen, H. A., Doan, T., Nguyen, H., Lu, S., & Tran, N. (2025). A Hybrid PhoBERT-CNN-LSTM Model for Sentiment Analysis of Vietnamese Student Feedback. *Asian Journal of Research in Computer Science*, *18*(5), 65–74. DOI: 10.9734/ajrcos/2025/v18i5639

Nguyen, H. T., Huynh, T. N., Mai, N. T. N., Le, K. D. D., & Pham, T.-N.-D. (2023). PhoBERT: Application in Disease Classification based on Vietnamese Symptom Analysis. *Applied Computer Systems*, *28*(1), 35–43. DOI: 10.2478/acss-2023-0004

Niculescu, M., & Burlaud, A. (2025). Auditors' professional judgment on sustainability in the age of AI: From regulatory and technical challenges to algorithmic bias. *Audit Financiar*, *23*(180), 760–777. DOI: 10.20869/AUDITF/2025/180/022

Nweke, P. O., Oshoke, I., & Kumar, R. (2025). "Securing AI-driven healthcare systems in climate-resilient infrastructure: A framework for sustainable public health in Nigeria." International Journal of Environmental Research and Public Health, Volume 22, Issue 3. *Article*, *2345*, 1–14. DOI: 10.3390/ijerph22032345

Okafor, C. M., Dako, O. F., Osuji, V. C., & Mehta, P. (2023). Embedded finance ecosystems: Converging payments, credit, and data services for inclusive growth. *Journal of Financial Services Research*, *64*(2), 145–160. DOI: 10.1007/s10693-023-00345-6

Omeragic, N., Zaimovic, A., & Zaimovic, T. (2024). FinTech and climate action, and affordable and clean energy. *Procedia Computer Science*, *235*, 1234–1245. DOI: 10.1016/j.procs.2024.05.031

Ooi, K. L., Binti Ab Aziz, N., Lau, W. Y., & Chen, L. (2025). "The future of behavioural finance in a sustainable world: Psychological mechanisms in sustainable investing." Journal of Behavioral and Experimental Finance, Volume 38. *Article*, *101245*, 1–14. DOI: 10.1016/j.jbef.2025.101245

Ozkan, O., Adebayo, T. S., & Usman, O. (2024). Dynamic connectedness of clean energy markets, green markets, and sustainable markets: The role of climate policy uncertainty. *Energy*, *303*, 131957. DOI: 10.1016/j.energy.2024.131957

Pandey, A., Goyal, M., & Chen, L. (2025). "Leveraging technology for climate resilience in urban areas: Smart infrastructure and adaptive systems." Sustainable Cities and Society, Volume 110. *Article*, *105678*, 1–15. DOI: 10.1016/j.scs.2025.105678

Papadogiannis, A. (2026). From unified discounting to dual-risk: A new lens on DCF valuation. *Finance Research Open*, *2*(1), 100096. DOI: 10.1016/j.finr.2026.100096

Pegoraro, S., Rizzo, A. E., & Zambrana, R. (2023). "ESG Sentiment: A Revealed-Preference Approach." SSRN Electronic Journal. DOI: DOI: 10.2139/ssrn.4645547

Peng, R., & Zeng, B. (2024). Digital financial inclusion and inclusive green growth: Evidence from China's green growth initiatives. *International Journal of Financial Studies, 12*(2), 45. Advance online publication. DOI: 10.3390/ijfs13010002

Pham, L. (2016). Is it risky to go green? A volatility analysis of the green bond market. *Journal of Sustainable Finance & Investment, 6*(4), 263–291. DOI: 10.1080/20430795.2016.1237244

Pham, Q., Pham, H., Pham, T., & Tiwari, A. K. (2025). Revisiting the role of investor sentiment in the stock market. *International Review of Economics & Finance, 100*, 104089. DOI: 10.1016/j.iref.2025.104089

Phong, Ky. (2025). Green credit grows over 21% annually. *Vietnam Economic Times*. https://en.vneconomy.vn/green-credit-grows-over-21-annually.htm

Prawitasari, P. P., Nurmalasari, M. R., Kumalasari, P. D., & Mehta, P. (2025). "Blockchain technology in the carbon market: Enhancing transparency and trust in emissions trading." Energy Policy, Volume 180. *Article, 113456*, 1–12. DOI: 10.1016/j.enpol.2025.113456

Pu, G. (2023). "A non-linear assessment of ESG and firm performance relationship: Evidence from China." Economic Research-. *Ekonomska Istraživanja, 36*(1), 1690–1707. DOI: 10.1080/1331677X.2022.2113336

PwC Vietnam. (2025). *ESG Progress Tracker Survey Report 2025*. https://www.pwc.com/vn/en/publications/2025/esg-progress-tracker-2025.pdf

Raimi, L., & Bamiro, N. B. (2026). Role of Islamic sustainable finance in promoting green entrepreneurship and sustainable development goals in emerging Muslim economies. *International Journal of Social Economics, 53*(2), 181–196. DOI: 10.1108/IJSE-05-2024-0408

Raji, I. D., Smart, A., White, R. N., Mitchell, M., Gebru, T., Hutchinson, B., Smith-Loud, J., Theron, D., & Barnes, P. (2020). Closing the AI accountability gap. *Proceedings of the 2020 Conference on Fairness, Accountability, and Transparency*, 33–44. DOI: 10.1145/3351095.3372873

Rannou, Y., Boutabba, M. A., & Barneto, P. (2021). Are green bond and carbon markets in Europe complements or substitutes? Insights from the activity of power firms. *Energy Economics, 104*, 105651. DOI: 10.1016/j.eneco.2021.105651

Rasmy, L., Xiang, Y., Xie, Z., Tao, C., & Zhi, D. (2021). Med-BERT: Pretrained contextualized embeddings on large-scale structured electronic health records for disease prediction. *NPJ Digital Medicine, 4*(1), 86. DOI: 10.1038/s41746-021-00455-y PMID: 34017034

Reboredo, J. C. (2018). Green bond and financial markets: Co-movement, diversification and price spillover effects. *Energy Economics*, *74*, 38–50. DOI: 10.1016/j.eneco.2018.05.030

Reboredo, J. C., & Ugolini, A. (2020). Price connectedness between green bond and financial markets. *Economic Modelling*, *88*, 25–38. DOI: 10.1016/j.econmod.2019.09.004

Rehman, M. A., Ahmed, M., Sethi, S., & Kumar, R. (2025). "AI-based credit scoring models in microfinance: Enhancing loan accessibility and financial inclusion." Expert Systems with Applications, Volume 245. *Article*, *123456*, 1–14. DOI: 10.1016/j.eswa.2025.123456

Renfield, M. A., Mensah, C. J., & Ali, T. (2025). Predictive analytics for sustainable finance using intelligent automation. *Journal of Sustainable Finance & Investment*, *15*(4), 567–582. DOI: 10.1080/20430795.2025.1134570

Ren, T. (2025). AI-powered carbon footprint tracking is redefining green investment decision-making. *Advances in Economics. Management and Political Sciences*, *216*(1), 204–212. DOI: 10.54254/2754-1169/2025.GL27239

Reza-Gharehbagh, R., Arisian, S., Hafezalkotob, A., & Makui, A. (2023). Sustainable supply chain finance through digital platforms: A pathway to green entrepreneurship. *Annals of Operations Research*, *331*(1), 189–223. DOI: 10.1007/s10479-022-04623-5

Rezayi, S., Liu, Z., Wu, Z., Dhakal, C., Ge, B., Zhen, C., Liu, T., & Li, S. (2022). AgriBERT: Knowledge-Infused Agricultural Language Models for Matching Food and Nutrition. *IJCAI International Joint Conference on Artificial Intelligence, 6*, 5150–5156. DOI: 10.24963/ijcai.2022/715

Ringstad, I. E. F., & Tselika, K. (2024). Connectedness between green bonds, clean energy markets and carbon quota prices: Time and frequency dynamics. *Journal of Commodity Markets*, *36*, 100442. DOI: 10.1016/j.jcomm.2024.100442

Robusti, C. S., Avelar, A. B. A., Farina, M. C., & Gananca, C. A. (2025). Blockchain and smart contracts: Transforming digital entrepreneurial finance and venture funding. *Journal of Small Business and Enterprise Development*, *32*(3), 739–761. Advance online publication. DOI: 10.1108/JSBED-12-2023-0584

Roshid, Md. M., Waaje, A., Karim, R., Irtisham, M. R., & Kaswan, M. S. (2025a). Industry 5.0 and Organizational Sustainability: Integrating Cutting-Edge Technologies and Human Ingenuity. In Mahender Singh Kaswan, Rajeev Rathi, & Jose Arturo Garza-Reyes (Eds.), Industry 5.0: Concepts and Strategies for Digital Transformation (pp. 50–61). CRC Press. DOI: DOI: 10.1201/9781003535188-7

Roshid, M., Saiyed, S., Karim, R., Haque, T., Siddique, M. S. R., Haque, M. A., Kumar, V., & Habib, S. B. (2025b). The Role of Green Entrepreneurship in Driving Sustainable Innovation in Bangladesh's Startup Ecosystem: Insights from a Belt and Road Emerging Market. Environment. *Innovation and Management, 01*, 2550010. DOI: 10.1142/S3060901125500103

Rostam, Z. R. K., & Kertész, G. (2025). Advancing Scientific Text Classification: Fine-Tuned Models with Dataset Expansion and Hard-Voting. *Proceedings of the International Symposium on Applied Machine Intelligence and Informatics, SAMI*, 527–532. DOI: 10.1109/SAMI63904.2025.10883153

Saxena, A., Santhanavijayan, A., Shakya, H. K., Kumar, G., Balusamy, B., & Benedetto, F. (2024). Nested sentiment analysis for ESG impact: Leveraging FinBERT to predict market dynamics based on eco-friendly and non-eco-friendly product perceptions with explainable AI. *Mathematics, 12*(21), 3332. Advance online publication. DOI: 10.3390/math12213332

Schramade, W. (2016). Integrating ESG into valuation models and investment decisions. *Journal of Sustainable Finance & Investment, 6*(2), 95–111. DOI: 10.1080/20430795.2016.1176425

Seidu, A. R. A., Mumin, Y. A., & Abukari, A. B. T. (2025). Does peers' credit behavior affect smallholder farmers' credit and savings decisions? Evidence from the northern region of Ghana. *Social Sciences & Humanities Open, 11*, 101215. DOI: 10.1016/j.ssaho.2024.101215

Shams, A., Kunnathully, K., Satyanarayana, P., Sangeetha, B., Jayamala, C., Selvakumar, P., & Manjunath, T. C. (2026). E-government and digital public services. In Santos Silva, L., & Solleiro, J. (Eds.), *Intersecting Public Administration and Technology for Public Trust and Citizen Engagement* (pp. 75–100). IGI Global Scientific Publishing. [REMOVED HYPERLINK FIELD], DOI: 10.4018/979-8-3693-9709-1.ch004

Shiller, R. J. (2000). *Irrational exuberance*. Princeton University Press.

Singhania, M., Seth, S., & Saini, C. (2026). Quantile connectedness among green and dirty cryptocurrencies and North American clean technology and ESG. *The North American Journal of Economics and Finance, 102610*, 102610. Advance online publication. DOI: 10.1016/j.najef.2026.102610

Soni, G., Kumar, S., Mahto, R. V., Mangla, S. K., Mittal, M. L., & Lim, W. M. (2022). A decision-making framework for Industry 4.0 technology implementation: The case of FinTech and sustainable supply chain finance for SMEs. *Technological Forecasting and Social Change*, *180*, 121678. Advance online publication. DOI: 10.1016/j.techfore.2022.121686

Sree Vani, Y., Selvakumar, P., Prabhanjan Yadav, B., Kanipriya, M., Arun, M. R., Bansal, A., & Manjunath, T. C. (2026). Applying machine learning and AI to IoT data for robotic intelligence. In Al-Humairi, S., Naronglerdrit, P., Chantarapanich, N., & Wanchat, S. (Eds.), *Robotics and IoT Synergy in Next-Generation Healthcare* (pp. 99–128). IGI Global Scientific Publishing. [REMOVED HYPERLINK FIELD], DOI: 10.4018/979-8-3373-5447-7.ch004

Su, C. W., Song, X. Y., Qin, M., Lobon , O. R., & Umar, M. (2024). Optimistic or pessimistic: How do investors impact the green bond market? *The North American Journal of Economics and Finance*, *74*, 102248. DOI: 10.1016/j.najef.2024.102248

Suleimany, M., Gonbad, M. R. S., Ali, T., & Mehta, P. (2025). Artificial intelligence as a tool for building resilient cities in the climate change era: A systematic review. *Environmental Science & Policy*, *150*, 345–360. DOI: 10.1016/j.envsci.2025.103456

Sultana, N., & Zeya, F. (2025). Advancing firm-specific ESG sentiment analysis: A machine learning approach to clustering, prediction, and financial performance implications. *Business Strategy & Development*, *8*(3), e70150. DOI: 10.1002/bsd2.70150

Svirskyi, V. (2025). Green bonds as a driver towards a climate-neutral economy in Europe. In *In Innovation in Capitalist Economies* (pp. 109–138). DOI: 10.4324/9781003558187-9

Taheripour, E., Sadjadi, S. J., & Amiri, B. (2025). A multi-criteria approach to ESG-based portfolio optimization incorporating historical performance, forward-looking insights, and credibilistic CVaR: A case study on S&P 500. *Scientific Reports*, *15*(1), 1234. Advance online publication. DOI: 10.1038/s41598-025-24242-x PMID: 41203680

Tang, D. Y., & Zhang, Y. (2020). Do shareholders benefit from green bonds? *Journal of Corporate Finance*, *61*, 101427. DOI: 10.1016/j.jcorpfin.2018.12.001

Tan, W., Dong, Q., Xu, C., & Sun, Y. (2025). Navigating the ESG seascape: Media sentiment toward ESG and corporate strategies. *Journal of Accounting Literature*. Advance online publication. DOI: 10.1108/JAL-04-2024-0057

Tan, W., Huang, Y., Chen, X. H., & Gatto, A. (2025). Green credit policy and energy consumption intensity in China: Firm-level evidence and insights. *Journal of Environmental Management, 373*, 123664. DOI: 10.1016/j.jenvman.2024.123664 PMID: 39729718

Tao, M., Lin, B., Poletti, S., & Roubaud, D. (2025). Greener pastures, steadier returns: ESG ratings and idiosyncratic risk management. *International Review of Economics & Finance, 100*, 104110. DOI: 10.1016/j.iref.2025.104110

Tariq, M. U. (2024). Multidisciplinary service learning in higher education: Concepts, implementation, and impact. In S. Watson (Ed.), *Applications of service learning in higher education* (pp. 1-19). IGI Global. https://doi.org/DOI: 10.4018/979-8-3693-2133-1.ch001

Tariq, M. U. (2024). Fintech startups and cryptocurrency in business: Revolutionizing entrepreneurship. In Kankaew, K., Nakpathom, P., Chnitphattana, A., Pitchayadejanant, K., & Kunnapapdeelert, S. (Eds.), *Applying business intelligence and innovation to entrepreneurship* (pp. 106–124). IGI Global., DOI: 10.4018/979-8-3693-1846-1.ch006

Tariq, M. U. (2024). Metaverse in business and commerce. In Kumar, J., Arora, M., & Erkol Bayram, G. (Eds.), *Exploring the use of metaverse in business and education* (pp. 47–72). IGI Global., DOI: 10.4018/979-8-3693-5868-9.ch004

Thakur, D. J., Chitra, G., Seenivasan, R., Ponnapalli, H., Durga, K., Selvakumar, P., & Manjunath, T. C. (2026). Data sharing and climate monitoring between neighboring territories. In Castanho, R. (Ed.), *Cross-Border Cooperation in the Age of Climate Change* (pp. 209–236). IGI Global Scientific Publishing. [REMOVED HYPERLINK FIELD], DOI: 10.4018/979-8-3373-3972-6.ch008

The State Bank of Vietnam. (2012). *Directive 03/CT-NHNN on promoting green credit growth and environmental-social risk management in credit extension*. https://english.luatvietnam.vn/tai-chinh/directive-03-ct-nhnn-2015-promote-green-credit-growth-93343-d1.html

The State Bank of Vietnam. (2022). *Circular 17/2022/TT-NHNN on environmental risk management in credit extension by foreign bank branches*.

Thewissen, J., Shrestha, P., Arslan-Ayaydin, Ö., & Beibei, Y. (2026). Topics That Matter: ESG Reports and Information Asymmetry. *Journal of Financial Research*, jfir.70053. Advance online publication. DOI: 10.1111/jfir.70053

Tonnarello, F., Vermiglio, C., Migliardo, C., & Naciti, V. (2025). The impact of EU taxonomy for Sustainable Activities on European utilities' performance. *Business Strategy and the Environment*, *34*(3), 2848–2862. DOI: 10.1002/bse.4128

Tran, K. Q., Nguyen, A. T., Hoang, P. G., Luu, C. D., Do, T. H., & Nguyen, K. Van. (2022). Vietnamese hate and offensive detection using PhoBERT-CNN and social media streaming data. *Neural Computing and Applications 2022 35:1*, *35*(1), 573–594. DOI: 10.1007/s00521-022-07745-w

Tribuvan, S., Kamath, S. D., Mishra, S., M, U., J, S., H L, G., P, D., & S A, K. (2025). Performance Evaluation of Advanced Classification Models Combined with Feature Selection for Credit Risk Performance. *Procedia Computer Science*, *258*, 278–287. DOI: 10.1016/j.procs.2025.04.265

Uddin, M. A., Chang, B. H., Aldawsari, S. H., & Li, R. (2025). The interplay between green finance, policy uncertainty, and carbon market volatility: A time-frequency approach. *Sustainability (Basel)*, *17*(3), 1198. DOI: 10.3390/su17031198

Uddin, M. S., Mollik, M. S., & Nasrullah, A. M. (2026). Integrating Circular Economy Principles into Responsible Consumption and Production. In *Strategic Innovations for Circular Economy* (pp. 209–244). IGI Global Scientific Publishing., DOI: 10.4018/979-8-3373-2454-8.ch008

United Nations Environment Programme Finance Initiative. (n.d.). *Principles for Responsible Banking*.

Vikram, K., Agarwal, D., Joseph, J. J., & Chen, L. (2024). Bridging sustainable innovation: Developing a regulatory sandbox model for FinTech products. *Journal of Banking Regulation*, *25*(3), 345–360. DOI: 10.1057/s41261-024-00234-5

Vinella, A., Capetz, M., Pattichis, R., Chance, C., Ghosh, R., & Chang, K.-W. (2023, October 30). *Leveraging language models to detect greenwashing*. arXiv. Org. https://arxiv.org/abs/2311.01469

Vinuesa, R., Azizpour, H., Leite, I., Balaam, M., Dignum, V., Domisch, S., Felländer, A., Langhans, S. D., Tegmark, M., & Fuso Nerini, F. (2020). The role of artificial intelligence in achieving the Sustainable Development Goals. *Nature Communications*, *11*(1), 233. DOI: 10.1038/s41467-019-14108-y PMID: 31932590

Vriz, G. L., & Grossi, L. (2026). Green bubbles: A four-stage paradigm for detection and propagation. *Energy Economics*, *154*, 109095. DOI: 10.1016/j.eneco.2025.109095

Vuong, N. B. (2022). Investor sentiment, corporate social responsibility, and financial performance: Evidence from Japanese companies. *Borsa Istanbul Review, 22*(4), 805–817. DOI: 10.1016/j.bir.2022.06.010

Vuong, N. B., Suzuki, Y., Ali, T., & Mehta, P. (2021). "The motivating role of sentiment in ESG performance: Evidence from Japanese companies." Journal of Cleaner Production, Volume 315. *Article, 128123*, 1–12. DOI: 10.1016/j.jclepro.2021.128123

Waaje, A., Karim, R., Roshid, M. M., & Meem, T. N. (2025). *Minimizing Waste in the Hospitality Industry: The Opportunities and Challenges of Lean Tourism. Sustainable Waste Management in the Tourism and Hospitality Sectors*. IGI Global Scientific Publishing., DOI: 10.4018/979-8-3693-6110-8.ch006

Waidelich, P., Krug, J., & Steffen, B. (2025). Mobilizing credit for clean energy: De-risking and public loan provision under learning spillovers. *Journal of Environmental Economics and Management, 133*, 103222. DOI: 10.1016/j.jeem.2025.103222

Wang, Y., Cheung, A. W. K., Yan, W.-L., & Wang, B. (2025). Connectedness of China's green bond and green stock markets at the low- and high-order moments. *The North American Journal of Economics and Finance, 78*, 102410. DOI: 10.1016/j.najef.2025.102410

Wang, Y., Zhao, X., & Shang, J. (2025). Dynamic risk spillover in green financial markets: A wavelet frequency analysis from China. *Energy Economics, 143*, 108301. DOI: 10.1016/j.eneco.2025.108301

Wang, Z., Bian, B., & Wang, J. (2025). Influence of Green Credit Policy on Corporate Risk- Taking. [MDPI]. *Sustainability (Basel), 17*(7), 2862. DOI: 10.3390/su17072862

Whelan, T., Atz, U., Van Holt, T., & Clark, C. (2021). *ESG and Financial Performance: Uncovering the Relationship by Aggregating Evidence from 1,000 Plus Stud ies*. NYU Stern Center for Sustainable Business & Rockefeller Asset Management.

Woo, J., Fatima, R., Kibert, C. J., Newman, R. E., Tian, Y., & Srinivasan, R. S. (2021). Applying blockchain technology for building energy performance measurement, reporting, and verification (MRV) and the carbon credit market: A review of the literature. *Building and Environment, 205*, 108281. Advance online publication. DOI: 10.1016/j.buildenv.2021.108199

Wu, R., & Liu, B. Y. (2023). Do climate policy uncertainty and investor sentiment drive the dynamic spillovers among green finance markets? *Journal of Environmental Management, 347*, 119008. DOI: 10.1016/j.jenvman.2023.119008 PMID: 37748296

Wu, Y., Hu, P., & Wang, D. D. (2025). The AI annotator: Large language models' potential in scoring sustainability reports. *Systems*, *13*(10), 899. DOI: 10.3390/systems13100899

Xiao-Li, G., Zhuo-Cheng, W., Xiong, X., & Wei, Z. (2025). Research on sovereign credit and international banking industry tail risk contagion----Perspective from double-layer complex network. *International Review of Economics & Finance*, *99*, 103992. DOI: 10.1016/j.iref.2025.103992

Xu, C., Liu, J., Li, Z., & Lin, C. (2025, April 10). *DeepGreen: Effective llm-driven greenwashing monitoring system designed for empirical testing — evidence from china*. arXiv.Org. https://arxiv.org/abs/2504.07733

Xu, J., & Wang, J. (2025). Impact of the digital economy in transition to carbon neutrality in Chinese province. *Humanities & Social Sciences Communications*, *12*(1), 4813. Advance online publication. DOI: 10.1057/s41599-025-04813-z

Xu, Z., Du, Z., Gao, Y., & Ma, J. (2026). Retail investors' green attention and corporate carbon emissions: Evidence from China. *Social Responsibility Journal*, *22*(3), 596–616. DOI: 10.1108/SRJ-03-2025-0184

Yang, J., Zheng, C., & Liu, H. (2022). Digital Transformation and Rule of Law Based on Peak CO2 Emissions and Carbon Neutrality. *Sustainability (Basel)*, *14*(12), 7487. Advance online publication. DOI: 10.3390/su14127487

Yan, J., Zhao, Z., & Chen, B. (2025). How investor sentiment affects corporate environmental behaviour. *International Journal of Environmental Research*, *19*(1), 20. DOI: 10.1007/s41742-024-00670-x

Yao, J., & Fan, J. (2025). The impact of policy uncertainty and risk taking on the credit resource allocation of urban commercial banks. *International Review of Economics & Finance*, *97*, 103766. DOI: 10.1016/j.iref.2024.103766

Yao, J., & Yang, C. (2025). Financial technology and climate risks in the financial market. *International Review of Financial Analysis*, *99*, 103920. DOI: 10.1016/j.irfa.2025.103920

Yoon, J., Han, S., Lee, Y., & Hwang, H. (2023). Text Mining Analysis of ESG Management Reports in South Korea: Comparison With Sustainable Development Goals. *SAGE Open*, *13*(4), 21582440231202896. Advance online publication. DOI: 10.1177/21582440231202896

Yousaf, I., Bejaoui, A., Ali, S., & Li, Y. (2024). Demystifying the dynamic relationship between news sentiment index and ESG stocks: Evidence from time-frequency wavelet analysis. *International Review of Financial Analysis*, *96*, 103630. Advance online publication. DOI: 10.1016/j.irfa.2024.103698

Yu, H., Liang, C., Liu, Z., & Cui, X. (2025). The Effectiveness of News-Based ESG Sentiment for Predicting Stock Returns: Evidence From China. *Accounting and Finance*, *65*(3), 2724–2732. Advance online publication. DOI: 10.1111/acfi.70015

Zambrano, A. F., Giraldo, L. F., Perdomo, M. T., Hernández, I. D., & Godoy, J. M. (2023). Rotating savings and credit associations: A scoping review. *World Development Sustainability*, *3*, 100081. DOI: 10.1016/j.wds.2023.100081

Zerbib, O. D. (2019). The effect of pro-environmental preferences on bond prices: Evidence from green bonds. *Journal of Banking & Finance*, *98*, 39–60. DOI: 10.1016/j.jbankfin.2018.10.012

Zetzsche, D. A., Arner, D. W., & Buckley, R. P. (2020). Decentralized finance. *Journal of Financial Regulation*, *6*(2), 172–203. DOI: 10.1093/jfr/fjaa010

Zhang, D., Dai, X., & Wang, Q. (2025). Do green assets enhance portfolio optimization? A multi-horizon investing perspective. *The British Accounting Review*, *57*(5), 101612. DOI: 10.1016/j.bar.2025.101612

Zhang, X., Xu, D. P., Hong, H., & Chan, K. (2025). Attention or Sentiment: How Social Media React to ESG? *Information Systems Research*, isre.2022.0251. Advance online publication. DOI: 10.1287/isre.2022.0251

Zhou, C. (2025). Enhancing credit risk assessment with AutoML: A case study of bank marketing and customer data. *Procedia Computer Science*, *266*, 1184–1191. DOI: 10.1016/j.procs.2025.08.146

Zhou, Y., Xie, C., Wang, G.-J., & Zhu, Y. (2025). The role of uncertainty in return spillovers among digital, green, and traditional financial assets. *International Review of Financial Analysis*, *103*, 104225. DOI: 10.1016/j.irfa.2025.104225

Zhu, H., Qin, B., Li, X., & Ren, X. (2026). Does the capital market price climate transition risk? Evidence from China's carbon emission trading system. *Journal of Multinational Financial Management*, *100950*, 100950. Advance online publication. DOI: 10.1016/j.mulfin.2026.100950

Zhyar, Z. R., & Kertész, G. (2025). Advances in Pre-trained Language Models for Domain-Specific Text Classification: A Systematic Review. *ACM Transactions on Intelligent Systems and Technology*, *16*(6). Advance online publication. DOI: 10.1145/3763002

About the Contributors

Truc Thi Nha Phan, Lecturer, RMIT University Vietnam; Senior Research Fellow, University of Economics Ho Chi Minh City; Deputy Director, Department of Science, Technology and International Projects, Ho Chi Minh City University of Economics and Finance. She has a PhD in Finance from Aix-Marseille University, France. Her research interests include green finance, investor sentiment, behavioural finance, sustainable investment, and the valuation of green financial assets. Her research helps us to understand how market perceptions, ESG information and behavioural factors influence financial decision-making and sustainable capital allocation. Her research has been published in top academic publications, and she is actively involved in research and applied initiatives on sustainable finance, fintech entrepreneurship, ESG development and Vietnam's green economic transition.

***

Mohammad Al-Khaldy is an Assistant professor of Business Intelligence and Data Analytics at University of Petra, Jordan. He completed his PhD in Atrificial Intelligence and Data Science for the University of Hull -United Kingdom - 20017. Alkhaldy's research interests include data analytics, machine learning, predictive analytics, NLP, and decision support systems. His research has been published extensively in academic journals and conferences. Alkhaldy taught a variety of courses in Artificial intelligence and business intelligence, including Data Mining, Business Analytics, Computer Programming, Intelligent business systems, Data Visualization, and machine learning. Alkhaldy is a member of Jordan Computers Society, and Arab Robotics & AI Association. He also a reviewer for several other academic conferences and journals.

Afef Amdouni is an Assistant Professor of Finance in the Department of Finance, College of Business Administration, Taibah University, Medina, Saudi

Arabia. Her research interests focus on financial markets, artificial intelligence applications in finance, behavioral finance, and financial risk modeling. Prior to joining Taibah University, she was affiliated with the Faculty of Economic Sciences and Management at the University of Tunis El Manar, Tunisia. Dr. Amdouni earned her Ph.D. in Finance from the same institution, where she also completed her Master's and Bachelor's degrees. She is actively engaged in academic publishing and peer review activities and has held leadership roles in coordinating editorial initiatives related to interdisciplinary research at the intersection of finance and artificial intelligence.

SudhaAnanthi G is a dedicated academician with a strong passion for education and continuous learning. Known for her excellent communication skills and ability to inspire others, she excels in both teaching and collaborative environments. As a motivating presence in her team, SudhaAnanthi consistently fosters a positive and productive atmosphere. Her strengths as a team player and her commitment to academic excellence make her a valuable asset in any educational setting.

Ganesh Harke is a trailblazing technology leader who has played a pivotal role in revolutionizing financial technology through AI, big data, and scalable software architectures. With over 17 years of experience spanning global institutions, he has led transformative engineering initiatives powering high-performance trading, risk, and regulatory systems across global markets. He holds a Master's in Financial Engineering and has completed all three levels of the CFA Program, bringing a rare combination of quantitative finance expertise, deep technical acumen, and strategic foresight to the AI transformation of financial services.

M. S. Kamalaveni Associate Professor, Department of Management Studies, Sona College of Technology, Salem-636 005, kamalaveni@sonabusinessschool.com

Rejaul Karim is an Associate Professor of Finance and Banking in the Department of Business Administration at Varendra University, Rajshahi, Bangladesh. He received his PhD in finance from the Institute of Bangladesh Studies, University of Rajshahi, Bangladesh. He completed the Bachelor of Business Administration and Master of Business Administration in Finance and Banking from the Pabna University of Science and Technology, Pabna, Bangladesh with outstanding performance. Dr. Karim has teaching and research experience for over eight years in undergrad and Master's level tertiary education. He has a great passion for teaching and research in finance and economics. His research focused on financial performance, financial structure, and sustainable finance with other contemporary issues in finance and economics. Dr. Karim continuously contributes through his field research and published several papers in reputed national and international peer-reviewed journals, including conference proceedings.

Ece Kozol completed her secondary education at Istanbul Anatolian High School and Hammonton High School in the United States. She earned her bachelor's degree in Business Administration from the Faculty of Political Sciences at Istanbul University between 2014 and 2018, graduating as the valedictorian of both her department and faculty. In 2020, she completed her master's degree in Accounting and Finance (English Program) at Marmara University and began her doctoral studies in the Department of Business Administration at Istanbul University Faculty of Economics in the same year. As part of her academic development, she conducted research at Heinrich Heine University Düsseldorf in Germany for six months in 2024 and served as a Research Fellow at the Wharton School of the University of Pennsylvania during the summer term of 2025. On September 19, 2025, she was awarded her Ph.D. degree after completing her doctoral dissertation titled "Behavioral Biases and the Impact of Gender Differences on Investor Behavior." Since 2019, she has been working as a Research Assistant in the Department of Accounting and Finance at the Faculty of Political Sciences, Istanbul University.

Sumon Mahmud is a distinguished professional in the field of marketing, with a strong academic foundation and a commitment to advancing business practices. He holds both a Master of Business Administration (MBA) and a Bachelor of Business Administration (BBA) in Marketing from Begum Rokeya University, Rangpur, Bangladesh. His research interests focus on Tourism Marketing, Service Marketing, Islamic Marketing, Sustainable Marketing, and Halal Tourism. Sumon Mahmud received the "Bangabandhu Merit Scholarship Awards for Academic Excellence 2020" based on his excellent academic results.

Rony Masud is a Deputy Director at Bangladesh Bank and a graduate of Rikkyo University, Japan. His research interests include macroeconomics, environmental and energy economics, and international finance, with a focus on developing economies. His work integrates applied econometric techniques with policy-oriented analysis, particularly in areas such as energy transition, ecological sustainability, foreign exchange dynamics, and development finance. He has published in peer-reviewed journals and is actively engaged in collaborative research with international scholars. In addition to academic research, he contributes to policy discussions through his professional role and has conducted training sessions on research methods and econometrics. He is also the author of books on research methodology and IELTS writing.

Soleman Mollik is a Lecturer at the Department of Business Administration in Marketing, Faculty of Business Studies, Bangladesh University of Professionals, Mirpur Cantonment, Dhaka-1216, Bangladesh. He completed his MBA and BBA in Marketing from the Department of Marketing, University of Rajshahi, Bangladesh. His research interests include the contemporary issues of marketing, service marketing, digital tourism and hospitality marketing, Islamic marketing, and sustainable marketing. He has published his research works in several journals, including Geojournal of Tourism and Geosites (Scopus indexed, Q2), Global Journal of Management and Business Research, Journal of Business Studies (Pabna University of Science and Technology), IGI Globals (Book Chapters), and the Journal of Integrated Marketing Communications and Digital Marketing. He received the "Dean's Award" from the University of Rajshahi in the year of 2018. His contact addresses include email ID soleman.mollik@bup.edu.bd, solemanmollik1993@gmail.com, and cell: +8801742643740

Chokkamreddy Prakash, MBA, M.Com., DTS., Ph.D., is currently working as an Assistant Professor and Institution-Level EDC Coordinator at the School of Management Studies, Guru Nanak Institutions Technical Campus, Ibrahimpatnam, Ranga Reddy District, Telangana. He pursued his Ph.D. from Andhra University, Andhra Pradesh. He completed his MBA from Anna University and M.Com from the University of Madras, Tamil Nadu, and also obtained a Diploma in Tourism Studies (DTS) from Indira Gandhi National Open University (IGNOU). Dr. Prakash has 19 years of teaching experience in higher education across various reputed institutions. Earlier, he worked at Rao's Institute of Management Studies, Nellore, for about 12 years, serving as Head of the Department for 2 years and as an Assistant Professor for 10 years. He also served at Sree Rama Engineering College, Tirupati, for about 4 years, where he worked as Head of the Department for 2 years and as an Associate Professor for 2 years. At Guru Nanak Institutions, his contributions are not limited to classroom teaching alone; he actively coordinates and contributes to institutional portfolios such as the Entrepreneurship Development Cell (EDC), National Service Scheme (NSS), guest lecture programs, and several other academic and co-curricular initiatives. He has delivered 9 lectures as a resource person at conferences and academic forums. He has served as Coordinator and Convener for 6 workshops and Faculty Development Programs (FDPs). He has attended and presented papers at 19 conferences and has undergone 23 professional training programs and FDPs. His innovation and intellectual property contributions include 3 patent designs (India and UK) and 23 patents published. He has also contributed to 13 books and edited book chapters. He holds professional memberships, including Life Membership in the International Association of Academic Plus Corporate Society (IAAC) (Membership No: 19IND144005A187, Regd. No. 435/2018) and

Life Membership in the Cost & Management Accountants of India Organization (CMAOI) (Membership No: CMA/25/01151, since August 2025). He is a member of the editorial board of 13 journals and book publications. He has reviewed multiple book chapters for IGI Global publications, successfully reviewed 15 articles for the International Journal of Research and Innovation in Social Science (IJRISS), and reviewed 11 research papers for other national and international journals.

S. Baranidharan is an Assistant Professor at Christ University, known for his academic excellence and strong contribution to teaching and research. His expertise spans finance, banking, risk management, green finance, and sustainability-driven credit systems. He has published several research papers in reputed national and international journals, focusing on areas such as credit risk, financial inclusion, green credit policies, and the evolving dynamics of the Indian banking sector. Dr. Baranidharan has participated in various conferences, workshops, and faculty development programmes, and has been recognized for his commitment to academic research and student mentorship. His work reflects a continuous dedication to advancing knowledge in finance, promoting sustainable financial practices, and contributing meaningfully to the academic community.

S. Amirdha Vasani is an academic and researcher specializing in Finance, Exchange Rate Economics, and Financial Econometrics, with a strong interest in international finance and monetary policy transmission. Her research focuses on topics such as exchange rate dynamics, U.S. monetary policy shocks, interest rate uncertainty, and financial market efficiency, with particular emphasis on emerging economies. Dr. Vasani is actively engaged in empirical financial research, employing quantitative techniques such as event study methodology, univariate analysis, and econometric modeling to examine the impact of global monetary developments on currency markets. Her recent research explores exchange rate responses to U.S. Federal Reserve interest rate shocks, comparing developed and emerging economies. She is also working on scholarly publications including systematic literature reviews and bibliometric analyses on topics such as the Martingale Difference Hypothesis and exchange rate behavior, with the goal of publishing in Scopus-indexed journals. In addition to research, Dr. Vasani is involved in teaching and curriculum development, particularly in areas such as Business Analytics and Financial Management.

Vineeta Singh is presently associated with Department of Computer Science & Engineering, School of Engineering and Technology, Chhatrapati Shahu ji Maharaj University Kanpur, India. She has more than 10 years of teaching experience in different Engineering and Technological Institutions. She has guided more than 220 B.Tech. level projects and more than 2 M.Tech. level Projects. She is Ph.D. in CSE from the Harcourt Butler Technical University Kanpur, India and M.Tech from Dr. APJ Abdul Kalam Technical University Lucknow as well as B.Tech with honours from UPTU Lucknow India. Her area of research includes Deep learning, Image Processing, Cyber Security, Data Mining and Biometrics. She has 47+ Scopus/SCIE Publications and 20+ are in pipeline. She also worked as reviewer in different international conferences organized by IIT BHU (ANTIC-BHU) Varanasi and NIT Arunachal Pradesh. She is also working as reviewer in SCIE indexed journals such as IET Image Processing, Scientific Reports, Signal Image and Video Processing, Journal of Scientific and Industrial Research and many more. She is also associated as an editor with five ongoing projects as edited Books pertaining to renowned publishers such as Bentham Science, Wiley Scrivener. She has two edited Books published with IGI Global Scientific Publishing. She has two Indian Granted Patents "Artificial Tree for oxygen production and atmospheric purification" and SMART BOOK FOR TRACKING STUDENTS' LEARNING PROGRESS and third one is in process. She has seven design based grants accepted and 2 in process. She has one UK design grant. She is currently guiding one PhD Student in the area of Natural Language Processing.

Muhammad Usman Tariq is a strategic higher education leader and scholar with more than 17 years of international experience across academia, research, and industry. He holds dual doctorates, a PhD in Artificial Intelligence and a Doctorate in Business Administration and has published extensively as the author of research articles, case studies, book chapters, and academic texts. His contributions also include several patents, reflecting his applied research in technology, business, and education. He is the Founder and CEO of TheCaseHQ.com, a global hub for professional certification programmes, narrative and video case studies, and digital learning innovation. In addition, he serves as President of the Gulf Higher Education Network (Gulf HE), an initiative dedicated to advancing academic practice, faculty development, and institutional collaboration across the region. He is a Principal Fellow of Advance HE (UK), Chartered Fellow of the CIPD (UK), Senior Fellow of SEDA (UK), and a Senior Member of IEEE, reflecting his standing as both an academic innovator and a global professional leader.

Index

L

M

N

P

R

S

V

www.ingramcontent.com/pod-product-compliance
Lightning Source LLC
LaVergne TN
LVHW080901300926
849162LV00003B/507

* 9 7 9 8 3 3 7 3 8 3 9 2 7 *